lonely planet

Bangkok

"All you've got to do is decide to go
and the hardest part is over.

So go!"

TONY WHEELER, COFOUNDER – LONELY PLANET

THIS EDITION WRITTEN AND RESEARCHED BY
Austin Bush

Contents

RICHARD I'ANSON / LONELY PLANET IMAGES ©

PETER STUCKINGS / LONELY PLANET IMAGES ©

AUSTIN BUSH / LONELY PLANET IMAGES ©

(left) Wat Arun (p63) and the Chao Phraya River

....

(above) Thai dancers at Sala Rim Nam dance show (p124)

....

(right) Dish of *kuaytiaw* (noodle soup)

....

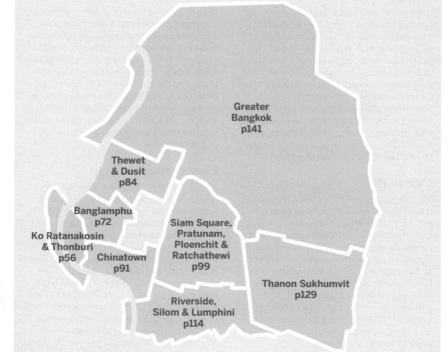

Welcome to Bangkok

Same same, but different. This Thailish T-shirt philosophy sums up Bangkok, where many tastes make an often-spicy dish.

Full-On Food

Until you've eaten on a Bangkok street, your noodles mingling with your sweat, and your senses dulled by chilli, exhaust and noise, you haven't actually eaten real Thai food. It can be an overwhelming mix: the underlying flavours – spicy, sour, sweet and salty – aren't exactly meat and potatoes. But for those who love full-on cuisine and don't need white tablecloths, there's probably no better dining destination in the world. And with immigration bringing every regional Thai and international cuisine to the capital, it's also a truly diverse experience.

Fun Folks

The language barrier may seem huge, but it has never prevented anybody from loving the Thai people. The capital's cultural underpinnings are evident in virtually all facets of everyday life, and most enjoyably through its residents' sense of *sà·nùk* (fun). In Bangkok, anything worth doing should have an element of *sà·nùk*. Ordering food, changing money and haggling at markets will usually involve a sense of playfulness – a dash of flirtation, perhaps, and a smile. It's a language that doesn't require words, and one that's easy to learn.

Urban Exploration

With so much of life conducted on the street, there are few cities in the world that reward exploration as handsomely as Bangkok. Cap off an extended boat trip with a visit to a hidden market. A stroll off Banglamphu's beaten track can end in conversation with a monk. Get lost in the tiny lanes of Chinatown and come face to face with a live Chinese opera performance. After dark, let the BTS (Skytrain) escort you to Th Sukhumvit, where the local nightlife scene reveals a sophisticated and dynamic city.

Contrasts

It's the contradictions that give the City of Angels its rich, multifaceted personality. Scratch the surface and you'll find a city of climate-controlled megamalls and international brand names just minutes from 200-year-old village homes; gold-spired Buddhist temples sharing space with neon-lit strips of sleaze; slow-moving rivers of traffic bypassed by long-tail boats plying the royal river; and streets lined with food carts, overlooked by restaurants at the top of skyscrapers. As Bangkok races toward the future, rest assured that these contrasts will continue to supply the city with its never-ending Thai-ness.

Why I Love Bangkok

By Austin Bush, Author

Admittedly, there are some things – the hot weather, the pollution, the political instability – that make Bangkok a less-than-ideal city. But there's so much more that makes it amazing. I love the food. What other city has such a full-flavoured, no-holds-barred, insatiable, fanatical approach to eating? I love old Bangkok. Districts such as Banglamphu and Chinatown still carry the grit and character of the city that used to be. And I'd be lying if I didn't also say that I love new Bangkok – don't we all have a soft spot for megamalls and air-con?

For more about our authors, see p272.

Above: Traditional Thai dancers at Wat Arun (p63)

Bangkok's
Top 10

Open-Air Dining *(p24)*

1 Bangkok's reputation as a polluted city belies its forte as an outdoor-dining capital. Despite the modern conveniences of air-conditioning and fashion cafes, some of the most memorable meals in the city also called the 'Big Mango' are had at the open-air markets and food stalls that make it possible to nibble the day away. Forget about three square meals: in Bangkok, locals snack throughout the day, packing away at least four meals before sunset – and so should you.

✕ *Eating*

Jim Thompson's House *(p101)*

2 American entrepreneur Jim Thompson used his traditional Thai-style home as a repository for ageing Thai traditions and artwork. Thompson mysteriously disappeared in 1967, but today his former home is a museum – one that visitors secretly wishes to live in for a day or more. Why? The rooms are adorned with his exquisite art collection and personal possessions, including rare Chinese porcelain pieces and Burmese, Cambodian and Thai artefacts, and the garden is a miniature jungle of tropical plants and lotus ponds, converging in the epitome of the Thai house.

◉ *Siam Square, Pratunam, Ploenchit & Ratchathewi*

KIMBERLEY COOLE / LONELY PLANET IMAGES ©

Chatuchak Weekend Market

(p143)

3 In a city obsessed with commerce, Chatuchak Weekend Market takes the prize as Bangkok's biggest and baddest market. Silks, sneakers, fighting cocks and fighting fish, fluffy puppies and souvenirs for the insatiable *fa·ràng* (Westerner) – if it can be sold in Thailand, you'll find it here. From everyday to clubby, clothes dominate much of the market, but this being Thailand, food and drink also have a strong and refreshing presence, making Chatuchak as much about entertainment as it is about shopping. PORTRAITS OF ROYALTY AT CHATUCHAK WEEKEND MARKET

◉ *Greater Bangkok*

Banglamphu *(p72)*

4 Easily Bangkok's most charming neighbourhood, Banglamphu is the city's former aristocratic heart, once filled with minor royalty and riverside mansions. Today the old quarter is dominated by antique shophouses, backpackers seeking R&R on famous Th Khao San, civil servants sauntering between offices and lunch spots, and Bangkok's only enclave of bohemian artists and students. Vendor carts and classic restaurants make a patchwork quilt of Banglamphu, allowing ample sightseeing for a roving stomach, and the area is also home to some of the city's best bars. TÚK-TÚKS ON TH KHAO SAN

◉ *Banglamphu*

Wat Pho *(p61)*

5 The grounds of Wat Pho date from the 16th century, predating Bangkok itself. In addition to being the country's biggest temple, Wat Pho is home to a school for traditional Thai medicine, where on-site massage pavilions facilitate that elusive convergence of sightseeing and relaxation. Still not impressed? Let us not forget Wat Pho's primary Buddha – a reclining figure that nearly dwarfs its sizeable shelter. Symbolic of Buddha's death and passage into nirvana, the reclining Buddha measures 46m and is gilded with gold leaf, making it truly larger than life. RECLINING BUDDHA AT WAT PHO

◉ *Ko Ratanakosin & Thonburi*

Mae Nam Chao Phraya *(p64)*

6 Mae Nam Chao Phraya (Chao Phraya River) is always teeming with activity: hulking freighter boats trail behind dedicated tugs, river-crossing ferries skip across the wake, and children practise cannonballs into the muddy water. You can witness this from the shore (ideally from Ko Ratanakosin or Thonburi), from a chartered long-tail boat, or while on the deck of a river taxi. Regardless of your vantage point, as evening sets in and the blinding sun slips into serene streaks of reds and golds, sooty Bangkok suddenly looks beautiful. WAT ARUN, SEEN FROM MAE NAM CHAO PHRAYA

👁 *Ko Ratanakosin & Thonburi*

Shopping *(p43)*

7 Even avowed anticonsumerists weaken in Bangkok. One minute they're touting the virtues of a life without material possessions, the next they're admiring the fake Rolex watches and mapping out the route to MBK. Bangkok's malls, however, are just a warm-up for the markets, the cardio workout of shopping. In this city, footpaths are for additional retail space, not for pedestrians. In addition to Chatuchak Weekend Market – one of the world's largest markets – Bangkok is home to an emerging fashion scene and, thanks to the diplomatic corps, a long-running sartorial tradition. GAYSORN PLAZA SHOPPING MALL (P109)

🔒 *Shopping*

6

Chinatown *(p91)*

8 Forgive us for positing that Bangkok's Chinatown is something of an Asian El Dorado. The main artery, Th Yaowarat, is crowded with gold shops – sealed glass-front buildings that look more like Chinese altars than downtown jewellers. Likewise, the Buddha statue at Wat Traimit has more gold than you've ever seen in one place, and the pencil-thin lanes that branch off Talat Mai are decked with gold-leaf-coated goods. Add to this the pure energy bundled into blazing neon signs and belching buses and you have the urban explorer's fantasy. WAT TRAIMIT (P93)

👁 *Chinatown*

Thai Cookery Schools *(p50)*

9 Why let a plump tummy be the only sign of your visit to Thailand? Instead, learn to create the kingdom's zesty dishes in your own kitchen to counter a ho-hum menu or spice up a dinner party. Cooking schools in Bangkok range from formal affairs for amateur chefs to home cooking for the recipe-phobic. Everyone always has a grand time, visiting a wet market, fumbling with ingredients, tasting the fruits of their labour and trotting home with new cooking techniques.

🏃 *Sports & Activities*

Songkran *(p20)*

10 With origins in an ancient religious practice of Buddha images being 'bathed', in recent decades the celebration of the Thai lunar new year has devolved into a citywide water fight. If the idea of no-holds-barred water-based warfare appeals to you, make a point of being in Bangkok during April. Festivities include open-air concerts, visits to Buddhist temples and, yes, water-throwing. Foreigners, especially well-dressed ones, are obvious targets for the latter, and the majority of the mayhem occurs on Th Khao San.

✨ *Month by Month*

What's New

White Guys Cooking Thai Food

The last few years have seen a handful of foreigners open Thai restaurants in Bangkok. Thais can be very protective about their cuisine, and the chefs involved generated a huge amount of local and international press – not all of it favourable. The storm has since passed, and in its wake we reap the benefit of several excellent Thai restaurants including nahm (p122), Bo.lan (p131), Sra Bua (p104) and Soul Food Mahanakorn (p132).

Talat Rot Fai

Watch out Chatuchak: despite the distinct emphasis on the retro, Talat Rot Fai is Bangkok's newest and hottest open-air market.

NapPark Hostel

Flashpacker hostels have been around for a while now, but few can top the hi-tech dorm beds that come equipped with a mini-TV, wi-fi and a reading lamp at his new place.

Helping Hands

Unlike most Thai cookery courses, which are held in upscale hotels, this new outfit is located in a Bangkok slum and 10% of the profits go back to the community.

Praya Palazzo

Making the old new, this long forgotten 19th-century riverside mansion was turned into one of Bangkok's classiest boutique hotels in 2011.

Club Culture

Bangkok's quirkiest club has relocated to new digs in an almost NYC-style warehouse-like building a short distance from Th Khao San.

Wat Traimit

The home of the Golden Buddha has seen a significant renovation, the results of which include a new structure to house the statue as well as two worthwhile museums.

Hyde & Seek

This classy bar's take on homey dishes and clever cocktails singlehandedly introduced Bangkok to the concept of the gastropub.

ZudRangMa Records

Thai DJ Maft Sai has opened his record collection to the public. Come here to flip through vintage Thai vinyl or to pick up a copy of the eponymous label's compilations.

Iron Fairies

In recent years Bangkok bars have moved away from tired themes and towards more sophisticated concepts. Case in point is this sexy new bar, which emulates an antique fairy factory.

ThaiCraft Fair

This organisation, which supports rural industry, has been around for more than 20 years, but its recently initiated craft fairs are a fresh alternative to the standard souvenir shop.

For more recommendations and reviews, see **lonelyplanet.com/ bangkok**

Need to Know

Currency
Thai baht (B)

Language
Thai

Visas
International air arrivals receive a 30-day visa; 60-day visas available from a Thai consulate before leaving home. For more information see Directory (p231).

Money
ATMs widespread; 150B foreign-account fee. Upmarket places accept Visa and MasterCard.

Mobile Phones
GSM and 3G network through inexpensive pre-paid SIM cards.

Time
Asia/Bangkok (GMT/UTC plus seven hours)

Tourist Information
Tourism Authority of Thailand (TAT; ☎1672; www.tourismthai land.org) National tourism department.

Bangkok Information Center (☎0 2225 7612-5; www.bang koktourist.com) City-specific tourism office; staffed booths throughout city.

Your Daily Budget
The following are average costs per day.

Budget
less than 1500B
➡ Dorm bed/basic guesthouse room 160B to 800B

➡ Street-stall meals

➡ A couple of the big-hitter sights, supplemented with free temples and parks

➡ Get around town using public transport

Midrange
1500B to 3000B
➡ Flashpacker guesthouse or midrange hotel room 800B to 1500B

➡ Restaurant meals

➡ Most, if not all, of the big sights

➡ Get around town using public transport and occasional taxis

Top end
more than 3000B
➡ Boutique hotel room 3000B

➡ Fine dining

➡ Private tours

➡ Get around town using taxis

Advance Planning
Three months before Book a room at a smaller boutique hotel, especially if visiting during December/January.

One month before If you plan to stay longer than 30 days, apply for a visa at the Thai embassy or consulate in your home country; make reservations at nahm (p122).

One week before Buy clothes appropriate for hot weather; book lessons at a Thai cooking school.

Websites
➡ **Lonely Planet** (www.lonely planet.com/bangkok) Destination information, hotel bookings, traveller forum and more.

➡ **BK** (www.bk.asia-city.com) Online version of Bangkok's best listings magazine.

➡ **CNNGo** (www.cnngo.com/bangkok) Quirky city-related news.

➡ **Bangkok 101** (www.bangkok101.com) Tourist-friendly listings mag.

➡ **Bangkok Post** (www.bangkokpost.com) English-language daily.

WHEN TO GO

Winter (late Dec/early Jan) is the coolest time of year in Bangkok and also peak tourist season. November or February offers cool weather and fewer people.

°C/°F Temp — Rainfall inches/mm

J F M A M J J A S O N D

Arriving in Bangkok

Suvarnabhumi International Airport The vast majority of visitors to Bangkok arrive via air. The new Airport Rail Link runs a local service (45B, 30 minutes) to Phaya Thai station and an express service (150B, 17 minutes) to Makkasan or Phaya Thai stations; both run from 6am to midnight. Meter taxis cost approximately 200B to 300B plus 50B airport surcharge and tolls. It takes about an hour to the city, depending on traffic, and taxis run 24 hours.

For much more on **arrival** see p220

Getting Around

➡ **BTS** The elevated Skytrain runs from 6am to midnight. Tickets 15B to 40B.

➡ **MRT** The metro runs from 6am to midnight. Tickets 15B to 40B.

➡ **Taxi** Outside of rush hours, Bangkok taxis are a great bargain. Flag fall 35B.

➡ **Chao Phraya Express** River boats run from 6am to 8pm, charging 10B to 32B.

➡ **Klorng boat** Bangkok's canal boats run from 6.15am to 7.30pm. Tickets 9B to 21B.

➡ **Bus** Cheap (7B to 23B) but slow and confusing way to get around Bangkok.

For much more on **getting around** see p221

Sleeping

Travellers are spoilt for accommodation options in Bangkok, with the added benefit that much of what's available is excellent value.

If you're on a budget, dorm beds can be had for as little as 160B, while cheapo rooms start at about 500B. There's a wide choice of midrange hotels and an astonishing number of top-end places.

Be sure to book ahead if you're arriving during peak tourist season (approximately November to February) and are keen on the smaller, boutique-type hotel.

Websites

➡ **Travelfish** (www.travelfish.org) Independent reviews of low end and midrange places with lots of reader feedback.

➡ **Trip Advisor** (www.tripadvisor.com) Yes, Bangkok is covered here.

➡ **Agoda** (www.agoda.org) Great advance deals.

➡ **Lonely Planet's Hotels & Hostels** (www.hotels.lonelyplanet.com) Find reviews and make bookings.

For much more on **sleeping** see p173

ENGLISH IN BANGKOK

Don't know a lick of Thai? Don't worry: Bangkok is well stocked with English speakers. Street-stall vendors, shop owners and taxi drivers generally speak enough English to conduct a basic transaction. If there is a communication problem, though, Thais will find someone to sort things out. Thais are patient with (and are honoured by) attempts to speak their language; with just a few phrases, you'll be rewarded with big grins and heaps of praise.

Top Itineraries

Day One

Ko Ratanakosin & Thonburi (p56)

 Get up as early as you can and take the Chao Phraya Express boat north to Tha Chang to explore one of Ko Ratanakoson's museums such as the **Museum of Siam**, as well as one of its must-see temples, such as **Wat Pho**.

> ✖️ **Lunch** Plunge into authentic Bangkok-style street food at Pa Aew (p69).

Riverside, Silom & Lumphini (p114)

☀️ Refresh with a spa treatment at **Health Land** or soothe those overworked legs with a traditional Thai massage at **Ruen-Nuad Massage Studio**. After freshening up, get a new perspective on Bangkok with rooftop cocktails at **Moon Bar**.

> ✖️ **Dinner** nahm (p122) serves what is arguably the best Thai food in Bangkok.

Riverside, Silom & Lumphini (p114)

🌙 If you've still got it in you, get dancing at **Tapas Room** or head over to **Telephone Pub** or any of the other bars in Bangkok's lushy gaybourhood. For a night that doesn't end until the sun comes up, bang on the door at **Wong's Place**.

Day Two

Siam Square, Pratunam, Ploenchit & Ratchathewi (p99)

☀️ Take the BTS (Skytrain) to National Stadium and start your day with a visit to the popular but worthwhile museum that is **Jim Thompson's House**. Follow this by exploring nearby **Baan Krua** or making a wish at the **Erawan Shrine**.

> **Lunch** The MBK Food Court (p105) is an ideal introduction to Thai food.

Siam Square, Pratunam, Ploenchit & Ratchathewi (p99)

☀️ Walk, or let the BTS escort you, through Bangkok's ultramodern commercial district, stopping off at linked shopping centres including **MBK Center**, **Gaysorn Plaza** and **Siam Square**. Make time for a sweet snack at **ka-nom** or an afternoon cuppa at the **Erawan Tea Room**.

>  **Dinner** Try Thai food with a modern twist at Sra Bua (p104).

Greater Bangkok (p141)

🌙 If it's a Friday or Saturday night, make a point of schlepping over to eastern Bangkok's RCA (Royal City Avenue) and the fun clubs there such as **Cosmic Café** or **Slim/Flix**. Otherwise, consider the stage shows at **Mambo Cabaret** or **Tawandang German Brewery**.

Day Three

Banglamphu (p72)

 Take the *klorng* (canal, also spelt *khlong*) boat to Banglamphu, where you'll spend the first half of your day learning the secrets of making Thai food at **Khao** on Th Khao San. If cooking isn't your thing, enrol in a *moo·ay tai* (Thai boxing, also spelt *muay thai*) lesson at **Sor Vorapin Gym**.

> **Lunch** Have a post-lesson dessert at Ann's Sweet (p78).

Banglamphu (p72)

Spend the afternoon shopping at the **Th Khao San Market** and visiting the surrounding sights such as the **Golden Mount** and **Wat Suthat**. Or, if you've got energy to spare, book an afternoon or night bike tour of the area with **Velo Thailand** or **Grasshopper Adventures**.

> **Dinner** Take a temporary break from Thai food at Nasir Al-Masri (p131).

Thanon Sukhumvit (p129)

End the night with a Thai-themed cocktail at a cosy local such as **WTF** or **Soul Food Mahanakorn**, or a streetside Singha at **Cheap Charlie's**. If it's still too early to head in, extend the night with a visit to **Bed Supperclub** or **Nest**.

Day Four

Greater Bangkok (p141)

 If it's a weekend, take the BTS north for a half-day of shopping at the **Chatuchak Weekend Market**. Otherwise, consider a half-day excursion outside the city to the provincial-feeling **Nonthaburi Market**, the man-made island of **Ko Kret** or the recreated ruins at **Ancient City** (Muang Boran).

> **Lunch** Chatuchak Weekend Market (p143) has cheap and tasty food stalls.

Chinatown (p91)

Take time to recover from the market (or your excursion), and in the relative cool of the late afternoon take the MRT (metro) to Chinatown and visit the home of the Golden Buddha, **Wat Traimit**, and the Chinese-style **Wat Mangkon Kamalawat**. Consider popping over to Phahurat to sample that neighbourhood's South Asian feel or, if you're there after dark, **Pak Khlong** flower market.

> **Dinner** Follow our walking tour of Chinatown's best street eats (p95).

Banglamphu (p72)

Make the brief taxi ride to Banglamphu and begin the evening with drinks at **Hippie de Bar**, followed by a rowdy live music show at **Brick Bar** or dancing at **Club Culture**. If bedtime is irrelevant, head up to upstairs to the *sheeshas* (water pipes) and dance floor of **Gazebo**.

If You Like...

Temples

Wat Phra Kaew The granddaddy of Thai temples, not to mention the home of a certain Emerald Buddha. (p58)

Wat Pho If you haven't seen the ginormous reclining Buddha here, you haven't seen Bangkok. (p61)

Wat Suthat One of Thailand's biggest Buddhas and equally impressive floor-to-ceiling temple murals await visitors here. (p77)

Wat Arun The predecessor of Bangkok is also one of the few Thai temples you're allowed to climb on. (p63)

Wat Mangkon Kamalawat The epitome of the busy, smoky, noisy Chinese-style Buddhist temple. (p94)

Sri Mariamman Temple Bangkok's main Hindu temple practically leaps from the street, taking people of all faiths. (p116)

Museums

National Museum An occasionally dusty but wholly worthwhile survey of Thai history. (p65)

Museum of Siam A fun explanation of the Thai people and their culture. (p68)

Bangkokian Museum Preserved house that's a time warp to the Bangkok of the early to middle 20th century. (p120)

Songkran Niyomsane Forensic Medicine Museum & Parasite Museum Not for the faint of

Row of sculptures at the National Museum (p65)

MICK ELMORE / LONELY PLANET IMAGES ©

heart; a queasy look at the more graphic side of death. (p65)

Architecture

Riverside Architecture Ramble Follow our walking tour and take in some of Bangkok's most notable secular structures. (p117)

Jim Thompson's House Beautiful former home that brings together Thailand's past and present. (p101)

Ban Kamthieng A perfectly preserved northern-style Thai home – right in the middle of modern Bangkok. (p132)

Ancient City (Muang Boran) A scan of Thailand's greatest structures without having to leave the greater Bangkok area. (p146)

Eating Like a Local

Poj Spa Kar Taste a piece of history at what is allegedly the city's oldest restaurant. (p77)

MBK Food Court Do the local thing by forgetting about ambience and focusing on the food at this mall-based food court. (p105)

A Taste of Chinatown Take our food-based walking tour and you'll see why Thais are willing to cross town for a bowl of noodles. (p95)

Pa Aew An open-air curry stall that excels in the flavours of Bangkok and Central Thailand. (p69)

Boats

Chao Phraya Express boat The slow but steady, not to mention scenic, way to get around Bangkok. (p222)

Long-tail boat tour of Thonburi canals Race through the narrow, wooden-house-lined canals of Thonburi, James Bond style. (p69)

Chaophraya Cruise Dinner on the deck of a cruise ship is a true Bangkok experience. (p121)

Royal Barges National Museum Riverside museum home to some of the most ornate boats in the world. (p66)

Hipster Haunts

Siam Paragon Window shopping or otherwise, this is the mall to be seen in. (p109)

Soi Ekamai 5 Home to some of the city's best dance clubs for the young and pretty crowd. (p136)

Central World Plaza It takes more than a torching by red-shirted protesters to set back Bangkok's hippest mall. (p111)

Soul Food Mahanakorn This cosy bar/restaurant is quite possibly the in-est place to eat Thai food in Bangkok. (p132)

Iron Fairies Burgers, live jazz and a fairy factory... an odd but successful combination embraced by Bangkok's in crowd. (p136)

For more top Bangkok spots, see the following:
➡ Eating (p24)
➡ Drinking & Nightlife (p33)
➡ Entertainment (p39)
➡ Shopping (p43)
➡ Sports & Activities (p48)

PLAN YOUR TRIP IF YOU LIKE...

Urban Exploration

Talat Mai Good luck finding your way out of this web-like riverside neighbourhood. (p94)

Sampeng Lane Explore the narrow lanes that spread from this market alley in the heart of Bangkok's Chinatown. (p96)

Amulet Market One of Bangkok's most bizarre markets is a great destination for aimless wandering. (p66)

Church of Santa Cruz Get lost in the winding, elevated lanes surrounding this Thonburi church. (p97)

Art

Jim Thompson's House Antique Thai-style house crammed with beautiful works of art from across Southeast Asia. (p101)

100 Tonson Gallery Housed in a villa, 101 Tonson is regarded as one of Bangkok's top commercial galleries. (p103)

Bangkok Art & Culture Centre Contemporary art meets commerce in the centre of Bangkok. (p102)

Tang Gallery Private gallery featuring the work of contemporary Thai and Chinese artists. (p116)

Month by Month

January

The weather is still relatively cool in Bangkok, and the number of foreign tourists remains quite high.

☆ Bangkok World Film Festival

More than 80 films are shown at this increasingly popular film festival (www.worldfilmbkk.com), which has an emphasis on Asian cinema. For popular films, book ahead.

✸ Chinese New Year

Sometime from late January to late February, Bangkok's large Thai-Chinese population celebrate their lunar new year, called ɗrùt jeen in Thai, with a week full of house cleaning, lion dances and fireworks. The most impressive festivities, not surprisingly, take place in Chinatown.

February

With relatively comfortable (although increasingly warm) temperatures and few tourists, February is a clever time to visit Bangkok.

☆ Kite Flying Season

During the windy season, from the middle of February to early April, colourful kites battle it out over the skies of Sanam Luang and Lumphini Park.

✸ Makha Bucha

Makha Bucha is held on the full moon of the third lunar month (late February to early March) to commemorate the Buddha preaching to 1250 monks who came to hear him 'without prior summons'. It culminates with a candlelit walk around the main chapel at every wát.

April

It's the height of Bangkok's hot season, so it should come as no surprise that the Thais have devised a festival that revolves around splashing water on each other.

✸ Songkran

Songkran is the Thai New Year, and although it has origins in a religious practice of 'bathing' Buddha images, today's celebrations resemble a city-wide water-fight. The most intense battles are fought on Th Khao San; don't carry anything you don't want to get wet.

May

May and June mean the beginning of the rainy season in most parts of Thailand, and some of the festivals during these months have origins in this significant occasion.

✸ Royal Ploughing Ceremony

To kick off the official rice-planting season in early May, the crown prince presides over this ancient Brahman ritual held at Sanam Luang. It culminates in sacred white oxen ploughing the earth and priests declaring it a good or bad year for farmers.

✹ Visakha Bucha

Visakha Bucha, on the full moon of the sixth lunar month (May or June), is considered the date of the Buddha's birth, enlightenment and *parinibbana* (passing away). Activities are centred on the local wát, with candlelit processions, chanting and sermonising.

July

Thailand's rainy season is well under way during this time, and tourist numbers are correspondingly low. The most significant event is a Buddhist holiday ushering in the rains.

✹ Asanha Bucha & Khao Phansa

Held on the full moon of the eighth lunar month (July or August), Asanha Bucha commemorates the Buddha's first post-enlightenment sermon. The following day, young men traditionally enter the monkhood and monks sequester themselves in a monastery for three months.

September

September is the wettest month in and around Bangkok and, as a result, most festivals alternate between being held indoors or taking place directly on water.

☆ Thailand International Swan Boat Races

More than 20 international teams race traditional Thai-style long boats in various classes (the largest has 55 paddlers) along Mae Nam Chao Phraya in Ayuthaya.

✗ Vegetarian Festival

During the first nine days of the ninth lunar month (September or October), this Chinese-Buddhist festival, *têt-sà-gahn gin jair*, sees street-side vendors serving meatless meals to help cleanse the body. Most of the action is in Chinatown: look for the yellow banners and white clothes.

November

The rain's (mostly) stopped, the weather's (relatively) cool, the crowds are low, and the festivals are plentiful; November is one of the best months to visit Bangkok.

✹ Bangkok Pride Week

Usually in mid-November, this week-long festival (www.bangkokpride.org) of parades, parties, awards, sequins and feather boas is organised by city businesses and organisations for Bangkok's gay, lesbian, bisexual and transgender community.

✹ Loi Krathong

On the night of the full moon of the 12th lunar month, *grà-tong* (boats made of a section of banana trunk) are floated on Mae Nam Chao Phraya. The ceremony is both an offering to the water spirits and a symbolic cleansing of bad luck.

◉ Wat Saket Fair

The grandest of Bangkok's temple fairs *(ngahn wát)* is held at Wat Saket and the Golden Mount around Loi Krathong. The temple grounds are taken over by a colourful, noisy fair selling flowers, incense, bells and saffron cloth and tonnes of Thai food.

December

The coolest month of the year sees a handful of outdoor-oriented festivals and events. Tourist numbers are at their peak, but this is arguably the most pleasant month to visit Bangkok.

✹ King's Birthday/ Father's Day

Celebrating King Bhumibol's birthday (5 December), the city is festooned with lights and large portraits of the king. In the afternoon, Sanam Luang is packed for a fireworks display that segues appropriately into a noisy concert with popular Thai musicians.

☆ Phra Nakhon Si Ayuthaya World Heritage Fair

A series of cultural performances and evening sound-and-light shows among the ruins of the World Heritage Site in the former Thai capital, Ayuthaya. Late December.

☆ Concert in the Park

Free concerts from the Bangkok Symphony Orchestra are performed Sunday evenings (from 5.30pm to 7.30pm) between mid-December and mid-February at Lumphini Park.

With Kids

There aren't a whole lot of attractions in Bangkok meant to appeal directly to the little ones, but there's no lack of locals willing to provide attention. This means kids are welcome almost anywhere and you'll rarely experience the sort of eye-rolling annoyance often seen in the West.

Kids having fun with a wax figure of Japanese cartoon character Doraemon at Madame Tussaud's

NARONG SANGNAK / EPA / CORBIS ©

Parks & Playgrounds

Lumphini Park

Central Bangkok's biggest park (p118) is a trusty ally in the cool hours of the morning and afternoon for kite flying (in season – February to April), boat rentals and fish feeding, as well as stretching of the legs and lungs. Nearby, kids can view lethal snakes become reluctant altruists at the antivenin-producing Snake Farm (p118).

Animals

In addition to the animals, Dusit Zoo (p88) has shady grounds plus a lake in the centre with paddle boats for hire and a small children's playground.

It's not exactly a zoo, but kids can join the novice monks and Thai children at **Tha Thewet** (Map p257; Th Samsen; ⊙7am-7pm; ⚓Tha Thewet) as they throw food (bought on the pier) to thousands of flapping fish.

Play Centres & Amusement Parks

For kid-specific play centres, consider Funarium (p140), central Bangkok's largest, or Siam Park City (p150), Safari World (p150) or Dream World (p150), all vast amusement parks found north of the city.

Rainy-Day Fun

If you're visiting during the rainy season (approximately June to October), the brief-but-daily downpours will inevitably complicate things, so you'll need a few indoor options in your back pocket.

Megamalls

MBK Center (p109) and Siam Paragon (p108) both have bowling alleys to keep the older ones occupied. The latter also has an IMAX theatre and Siam Ocean World (p103), a basement-level aquarium. All of these malls and most others in Bangkok have amusement centres with video games, small rides and playgrounds – they're often located near the food courts.

Bangkok Doll Factory & Museum

This somewhat hard-to-find museum (p104) houses a colourful selection of traditional Thai dolls, both new and antique.

Kid Friendly Museums

Museum of Siam

Although not specifically targeted towards children, the Museum of Siam (p68) has lots of interactive exhibits that will appeal to kids.

Madame Tussaud's

Siam Discovery Center (p111) has a branch of the famous wax museum.

Ancient City (Muang Boran)

Outside of town, this open-air museum (p146) recreates Thailand's most famous monuments. They're linked by bicycle paths and were practically built for being climbed on.

Practicalities

At a practical level, there are a few things worth knowing before you depart. Many hotels offer family deals, adjoining rooms and – in the midrange and above – cots, so enquire specifically. Car seats, on the other hand, are almost impossible to find, and even if you bring your own, most taxis have no seatbelt in the back. Taxi drivers generally won't temper their speed because you're travelling with a child, so if need be don't hesitate to tell them to *cháh cháh* (slow down).

For moving by foot, slings are often more useful than prams as Bangkok's sidewalks are infamously uneven.

Infants

Nappies (diapers), international brands of milk formula and other infant requirements are widely available, and for something more specific you'll find the Central Chidlom (p112) as well stocked as anywhere on earth (there's an entire floor devoted to kids). In general, Thai women don't breastfeed in public, though in department stores they'll often find a change room.

Eating

Dining with children in Thailand, particularly with infants, is a liberating experience as Thai people are so fond of kids. Take it for granted that your babies will be fawned over, played with, and more often than not, carried around, by restaurant wait staff. Regard this as a much-deserved break, not to mention a bit of free cultural exposure.

For the widest choice of food, child-friendly surroundings and noise levels that will drown out even the loudest child, you may find the food courts of Bangkok's many megamalls to be the most comfortable family dining options.

Because much of Thai food is so spicy, there is an entire art devoted to ordering 'safe' dishes for children, and the vast majority of Thai kitchens are more than willing to oblige. Many a child in Thailand has grown up on a diet of little more than *gaang jèut*, a bland, Chinese-influenced soup containing ground pork, soft tofu and a handful of noodles, or variations on *kôw pàt*, fried rice. Other mild options include *kôw man gài*, Hainanese chicken rice, and *jóhk*, rice gruel. For something bland, big hotels usually sell their baked goods for half price after 6pm. Highchairs are rare outside expensive restaurants.

Above: A dish of *gŏo·ay đĕe·o* (noodle soup).

 # Eating

Nowhere else is the Thai reverence for food more evident than in Bangkok. To the outsider, the life of a Bangkokian appears to be a string of meals and snacks punctuated by the odd stab at work, not the other way around. If you can adjust your mental clock to this schedule, your stay will be a delicious one indeed.

Above: Dining at street stalls in Bangkok's Chinatown (p91)

NEED TO KNOW

Price Ranges

Prices are for the cost of a main dish, as indicated in eating reviews.

$	less than 300B
$$	300B to 600B
$$$	more than 600B

Opening Hours

Restaurants serving Thai food are generally open from 10am to 8pm or 9pm. Foreign-cuisine restaurants tend to keep only lunch and dinner hours (ie 11am to 2pm and 6pm to 10pm).

Bangkok has passed a citywide ordinance banning street vendors from setting up shop on Mondays.

Reservations

If you have a lot of friends in tow or will be attending a formal restaurant (including hotel restaurants), reservations are recommended. Bookings are also recommended for Sunday brunches and dinner cruises. Otherwise, you shouldn't have a problem scoring a table at the vast majority of restaurants in Bangkok.

Tipping

You shouldn't be surprised to learn that tipping in Thailand isn't as exact as it is in Europe (tip no one) or the USA (tip everyone). Thailand falls somewhere in between, and some areas are left open to interpretation. Some people leave roughly 10% behind at any sit-down restaurant where someone fills their glass every time they take a sip. Others don't. Most upmarket restaurants will apply a 10% service charge to the bill. Some patrons leave extra on top of the service charge; others don't. The choice is yours.

Bangkok's Dining Scene

In the last couple of decades, Thai food has become internationally famous, and Bangkok is, not surprisingly, the best place in the world to eat it. From roadside stalls to restaurants with Michelin stars in their eyes, the whole spectrum of Thai food is available here. Bangkok is home to its own unique cuisine, and because of its position as a cultural and literal crossroads, just about every regional Thai cuisine is available in the city as well. More recent immigration to the city has resulted in a dining scene whose options range from Korean to French, touching on just about everything in between.

If you're new to Thai cuisine, check out our crash course on Thai food (p208) before digging in.

Where to Eat & Drink

Prepared food is available just about everywhere in Bangkok, and it shouldn't come as a surprise that the locals do much of their eating outside the home. In this regard, as a visitor, you'll fit right in.

Open-air markets and food stalls are among the most popular dining spots for Thais. In the mornings, stalls selling coffee and Chinese-style doughnuts spring up along busy commuter corridors. At lunchtime, diners might grab a plastic chair at yet another stall for a simple stir-fry, or pick up a foam box of noodles to scarf down at the office. In Bangkok's suburbs, night markets often set up in the middle of town with a cluster of food vendors, metal tables and chairs, and some shopping as an after-dinner mint.

For impromptu drinking and snacking, Bangkok also has an overabundance of modern cafes – including branches of several international chains. Most serve passable, if not amazing takes on Western-style coffee drinks and equally inauthentic cakes and sweets.

Above: Traders buy, sell and prepare food on the water at Damnoen Saduak Floating Market (p167) outside Bangkok

Left: Chilli peppers

Eating by Neighbourhood

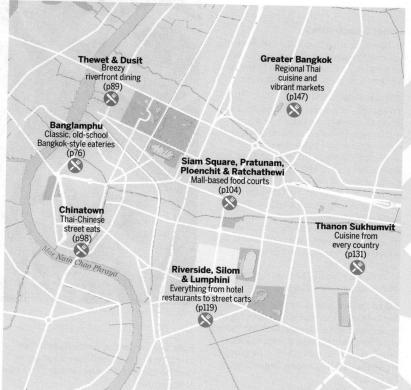

Thewet & Dusit
Breezy
riverfront dining
(p89)

Greater Bangkok
Regional Thai
cuisine and
vibrant markets
(p147)

Banglamphu
Classic, old-school
Bangkok-style eateries
(p76)

**Siam Square, Pratunam,
Ploenchit & Ratchathewi**
Mall-based food courts
(p104)

Chinatown
Thai-Chinese
street eats
(p98)

Thanon Sukhumvit
Cuisine from
every country
(p131)

Mae Nam Chao Phraya

**Riverside, Silom
& Lumphini**
Everything from hotel
restaurants to street carts
(p119)

There are, of course, restaurants (*ráhn ah·hǎhn*) in Bangkok. Lunchtime is the right time to point and eat at the *ráhn kôw gaang* (rice and curry shops), which sell a selection of pre-made dishes. The more generic *ráhn ah·hǎhn đahm sàng* (made-to-order restaurant) can often be recognised by a display of raw ingredients – including Chinese kale, tomatoes, chopped pork, fresh or dried fish, noodles, eggplant, spring onions – offering a standard repertoire of Thai and Chinese-Thai dishes. As the name implies, the cooks will attempt to prepare any dish you can name – a potentially difficult operation if you can't speak Thai.

The most common type of restaurant – and arguably the most delicious – is the shophouse restaurant. The cooks at these places have most likely been serving the same dish, or a limited repertoire of dishes, for several decades, and really

know what they're doing. The food may cost slightly more than on the street, but the setting is usually more comfortable and hygienic, not to mention the fact that you're eating a piece of history. While such restaurants rarely have English-language menus, you can usually point to a picture or dish. If that fails, turn to the language chapter and practise your Thai (p233).

Bangkok is, of course, also home to dozens of upscale restaurants, many of which are attached to hotels. For the most part, those serving Thai cuisine have adjusted their recipes to suit foreign palates – for more authentic food you're much better off eating at the cheaper shophouse-style restaurants. On the other hand, upscale and hotel restaurants are probably the best place in Bangkok to get authentic Western-style food. If this is outside your price range, you'll be happy to know that there's also a huge spread of midrange foreign restaurants in today's Bangkok, many of them quite good.

Local Specialities

In Bangkok, geography, the influence of the royal palace and the country's main minorities – Chinese and Muslims – have all served to shape the local cuisine.

CENTRAL THAI CUISINE

The people of central Thailand are fond of sweet/savoury flavours, and many dishes here include freshwater fish, pork, coconut milk and palm sugar – common ingredients in the central Thai plains. Because of the region's proximity to the waters of the Gulf of Thailand, central Thai eateries, particularly those in Bangkok, also serve a wide variety of seafood. Chinese labourers and vendors contributed to this rich culinary heritage, introducing a huge variety of noodle and wok-fried dishes to central Thailand up to 200 years ago.

Must-eat central Thai and Bangkok dishes include the following:

Pàt tai Thin rice noodles stir-fried with dried and/or fresh shrimp, bean sprouts, tofu, egg and seasonings, traditionally served with lime halves and a few stalks of Chinese chives and a sliced banana flower. Thip Samai (p77), in Banglamphu, is probably Bangkok's most lauded destination for the dish.

Yam ƀlah dùk foo Fried shredded catfish, chilli and peanuts served with a sweet/tart mango dressing. Try it at Kimleng (p78), in Bangkok's Banglamphu district.

Đôm yam Lemon grass, kaffir lime leaf and lime juice give this soup its characteristic tang; fresh chillies or an oily chilli paste provide its legendary sting. Available just about everywhere, but it's hard to beat the version at Krua Apsorn (p76).

Yen đah foh Combining a slightly sweet crimson-coloured broth with a variety of meat balls, cubes of blood and crispy greens, *yen đah foh* is probably both the most intimidating and popular noodle dish in Bangkok. It's can be found at Soi 10 Food Centres (p122) at Silom and many street stalls.

Gaang sôm Central Thailand's famous 'sour soup' often includes freshwater fish, vegetables and/or herbs, and a thick, tart broth. Available at Poj Spa Kar (p77).

Gǒo•ay đěe•o reua Known as boat noodles because they were previously served from small

Above: Southern Thai dishes

boats along the canals of central Thailand, these intense pork- or beef-based bowls are among the most full-flavoured of Thai noodle dishes. Try a bowl at Bharani (p134).

ROYAL THAI CUISINE

Another significant influence on the city's kitchens has come from the Bangkok-based royal court, which has been producing sophisticated and refined takes on central Thai dishes for nearly 300 years. Although originally only available within the palace walls, these so-called 'royal' Thai dishes and are now available across the city.

Máh hór With origins in the palace, this is a Thai appetiser that combines chunks of mandarin orange or pineapple and a sweet/savoury/peppery topping that includes pork, chicken, peanuts, sugar, peppercorns and coriander root. Available as part of the set meal at nahm (p122).

Ƀlah hâang Dried fish combined with sugar and crispy deep-fried shallots, served on top of slices of watermelon – this ancient and refreshing palace recipe is available at Mangkud Cafe (p69).

Kà·nŏm bêuang The old-school version of these refined taco-like snacks comes in two varieties: sweet and savoury.

Mèe gròrp Crispy noodles made the traditional way, with a sweet/sour flavour (a former palace recipe), are a dying breed. Banglamphu restaurant Chote Chitr (p78) serves an excellent version of the dish.

THAI-CHINESE CUISINE

Immigrants from southern China have been influencing Thai cuisine for centuries, and it was most likely Chinese labourers and vendors who introduced the wok and several varieties of noodle dishes to Thailand. They also influenced Bangkok's cuisine in other ways: beef is not widely eaten in Bangkok due to a Chinese-Buddhist teaching that forbids eating 'large' animals.

Thai-Chinese dishes you're likely to run across in Bangkok include the following:

Kôw kăh mŏo Braised pork leg served over rice, often with sides of greens and a hard-boiled egg, is the epitome of the Thai-Chinese one-dish meal. Available at the Soi 10 Food Centres (p122) and other street markets.

Kôw man gài Chicken rice, originally from the Chinese island of Hainan, is now found in just about every corner of Bangkok. We particularly like the version served at Boon Tong Kiat Singapore Hainanese Chicken Rice (p131).

Bà·mèe Chinese-style wheat and egg noodles typically served with slices of barbecued pork, a handful of greens and/or wontons. **Mangkorn Khǎo** (มังกรขาว; Map p258; cnr Th Yawarat & Th Yaowaphanit), a street stall in Chinatown, does one of Bangkok's better bowls.

Săh·lah ɓow Chinese-style steamed buns, served with sweet or savoury fillings, are a favourite snack in Bangkok.

Gŏo·ay đĕe·o kôoa gài Wide rice noodles fried with little more than egg, chicken, salted squid and garlic oil is a popular dish in Bangkok's Chinatown.

Or sòo·an Another Bangkok Chinatown staple, this dish combines a sticky, eggy batter topped with mussels or oysters. Nay Mŏng (p95) does what is arguably Bangkok's best take on this dish.

Gŏoay jáp This dish consists of an intensely peppery broth and pork offal; look for it on our food-based walking tour of Chinatown (p95).

Above: A plate of *mèe gròrp*, a crispy noodle dish

THAI-MUSLIM CUISINE

Muslims are thought to have first visited Thailand during the late 14th century. Along with the Quran, they brought with them a meat- and dried-spice-based cuisine from their homelands in India and the Middle East. Nearly 700 years later, the impact of this culinary commerce can still be felt in Bangkok.

While some Muslim dishes such as *roh·đee*, a fried bread similar to the Indian paratha, have changed little, if at all, others such as *gaang mát·sà·màn* are a unique blend of Thai and Indian/Middle Eastern cooking styles and ingredients.

Common Thai-Muslim dishes include the following:

Kôw mòk Biryani, a dish found across the Muslim world, also has a foothold in Bangkok. Here the dish is typically made with chicken and is served with a sweet and sour dipping sauce and a bowl of chicken broth. We love the version served at Naaz (p119).

Sà·đé (satay) These grilled skewers of meat probably came to Thailand via Malaysia. The savoury peanut-based dipping sauce is often mistakenly associated with Thai cooking. Typically available at street markets such as Soi 38 Night Market (p135).

Má·đà·bà Known as murtabak in Malaysia and Indonesia, these are *roh·đee* that have been stuffed with a savoury or sometimes sweet filling and fried until crispy. Available at Roti-Mataba (p78).

Súp hăhng woo·a Oxtail soup, possibly another Malay contribution, is even richer and often more sour than the 'Buddhist' Thai *đôm yam*. Try the dish at Muslim Restaurant (p119).

Sà·làt kàak Literally 'Muslim salad' (*kàak* is a somewhat derogatory word used to describe people or things of Indian and/or Muslim origin), this dish combines iceberg lettuce, chunks of firm tofu, cucumber, hard-boiled egg and tomato, all topped with a sweet peanut sauce.

Gaang mát·sà·màn 'Muslim curry' is a rich coconut-milk-based dish, which, unlike most Thai curries, gets much of its flavour from dried spices. As with many Thai-Muslim dishes, there is an emphasis on the sweet. Longstanding Muslim Restaurant (p119) does a good take on the dish.

Roh·đee This crispy fried pancake, drizzled with condensed milk and sugar, is the perfect street dessert. Get yours on the street or at Roti-Mataba (p78).

Top: *Hor mok,* a steamed fish curry
Middle: Bangkok's food stalls come alive at night
Bottom: Condiments for noodle dishes at a stall

BANGKOK'S BEST BITES

David Thompson is a Michelin-starred chef and a best-selling author; he's also Head Chef at Bangkok restaurant nahm (p122).

Classic Bangkok-Style Dishes

I like some of the dishes in Chinatown, whether it be the oyster place I adore (Nay Mŏng (p95), or whether it be noodles with fish dumplings or with roast duck. *Þoo pat pong gàrìì* [crab fried with curry powder], when done well, is easy, but is bloody delicious and accessible. And *pàt tai* – well, you can't really escape from the cliché, however delicious it might be.

Best Food 'Hood

It depends on what I'm looking for. Chinatown, for smoked duck or noodles. But if you want to eat Thai food, you need to go to the markets. Bangkok still has some remnants of the city or villages that it was. For Muslim food you can go down near the Oriental Hotel (Haroon village; p117), or for Portuguese cakes, you can go to Santa Cruz.

Favourite Restaurant

It changes all the time. I like Krua Apsorn (p76). It's local. It's good. It's unreformed. It's not too precious. They cook for Thais, they feed Thais and it is Thai.

Best Market

Of course, Or Tor Kor Market (p147). Even though it's sanitised, its soul has not been expunged from it as it's modernised. There's some great stuff there.

Best Eating Advice for a First-Time Visitor

Just bloody well eat it – don't think about it – just eat it. It's so unlikely you'll get sick, but you will kick yourself for not actually just diving in. Go to places that look busiest, because they're busy for a reason. And a bit of food poisoning, well that adds local colour, doesn't it?

Cooking Courses

Bangkok has a number of great cooking courses (p50) that are geared towards visitors wanting to recreate the cuisine at home.

Food Markets

If you take pleasure in seeing food in its raw form, Bangkok is home to dozens of traditional-style wet markets (p32), ranging from the grungy to the flashy.

Lonely Planet's Top Choices

nahm (p122) Upscale Thai that's worth every baht.

Krua Apsorn (p76) Rich central Thai fare in a homey setting.

Bo.Lan (p131) Ancient Thai recipes served with a modern twist.

MBK Food Court (p105) Cheap, cheerful and tasty: the city's best food court.

D'sens (p119) Flawless upscale French with a view.

Best by Budget

$

Boon Tong Kiat Singapore Hainanese Chicken Rice (p131)

Pa Aew (p69)

Nay Mŏng (p95)

Naaz (p119)

Kai Thort Jay Kee (p123)

Imoya (p133)

$$

Crystal Jade La Mian Xiao Long Bao (p104)

Th Phadungdao Seafood Stalls (p98)

Kalapapruek (p120)

Taling Pling (p121)

Hemlock (p77)

Ngwanlee Lung Suan (p123)

$$$

Jay Fai (p76)

Le Normandie (p119)

Four Seasons Sunday Brunch (p104)

Zanotti (p122)

Sra Bua (p104)

Best for Old-School Thai Dining

Muslim Restaurant (p119)

Ngwanlee Lung Suan (p123)

Sanguan Sri (p106)

Roti-Mataba (p78)

Chote Chitr (p78)

Best Foreign Cuisine Restaurants

Zanotti (p122)

Boon Tong Kiat Singapore Hainanese Chicken Rice (p131)

Nasir Al-Masri (p131)

Myeong Ga (p133)

Nadimos (p120)

Best for Vegetarian

Baan Suan Pai (p148)

Saras (p133)

Arawy Vegetarian Food (p79)

Chennai Kitchen (p121)

Best for Regional Thai Cuisine

Khua Kling + Pak Sod (p132)

Mallika Restaurant (p106)

Likhit Kai Yang (p90)

Jay So (p121)

Best for Bangkok-Style Food

Pa Aew (p69)

Poj Spa Kar (p77)

Thip Samai (p77)

Kimleng (p78)

Nang Loeng Market (p147)

Best for Dessert

Ann's Sweet (p78)

Duc de Praslin (p135)

Old Siam Plaza (p98)

Ka-nom (p106)

Nang Loeng Market (p147)

Best Riverside Views

Le Normandie (p119)

Mangkud Cafe (p69)

Kaloang Home Kitchen (p89)

Khinlom Chom Sa-Phan (p90)

Lord Jim's (p119)

Best Buffets

Four Seasons Sunday Brunch (p104)

Rang Mahal (p135)

Marriott Café (p135)

Sunday Jazzy Brunch (p135)

Lord Jim's (p119)

Chocolate Buffet (p123)

Best Markets

Or Tor Kor Market (p147)

Nonthaburi Market (p146)

Talat Mai (p94)

Nang Loeng Market (p147)

Above: View from Sirocco Sky Bar (p123)

Drinking & Nightlife

Despite what your dodgy uncle might have told you, having a good time in Bangkok does not necessarily have to involve ping-pong balls or the word 'go-go'. As in any big international city, the drinking and partying scene in Bangkok ranges from classy to trashy, touching on just about everything in between.

The Scene

Bangkok is a party animal – even when on a tight leash. Back in 2001, the Thaksin administration started enforcing closing times and curtailing other excesses that made the city's nightlife famous. Since the 2006 ousting of Thaksin, the laws have been conveniently circumvented or inconsistently enforced, and several years on, the post-coup party scene has shown signs of restoring Bangkok to its old position as Southeast Asia's fun master – a role uptight Singapore

almost usurped. But it is still common for the men in brown to switch on the lights in clubs and bars way before most folks' bedtime, or at least before dawn.

Bars

Bangkok's watering holes cover the spectrum from English-style pubs where you can comfortably sit with a pint and the paper to chic dens where the fair and beautiful go to be seen, not to imbibe. Its bar scene is also unique in that Bangkok is one of the few big

NEED TO KNOW

Opening Hours
Since 2004, authorities have ordered most of Bangkok's bars and clubs to close by 1am. A complicated zoning system sees venues in designated 'entertainment areas', including RCA, Th Silom, and parts of Th Sukhumvit, open until 2am, but even these 'later' licences are subject to police whimsy.

Smoking
Smoking has been outlawed at all indoor (and some quasi-outdoor) entertainment places since 2008.

Dress Code
Most rooftop bars enforce a dress code – no shorts or sandals. This is also the case with many of Bangkok's dance clubs.

ID
The drinking age in Thailand is 20, although it's only usually dance clubs that ask for ID.

Wine Whinge
Imported wine is subject to a litany of taxes, making Thailand among the most expensive places in the world to drink wine. A bottle typically costs 400% of its price back home, up to 600% in upmarket restaurants. Even domestic wines are subject to many of the same taxes, making them only marginally cheaper.

Other Resources
To keep crowds interested, clubs host weekly theme parties and visiting DJs that ebb and flow in popularity. To find out what's on, check out **Dude Sweet** (www.dudesweet.org), **Club Soma** (www. clubsoma.tumblr.com) or **Paradise Bangkok** (www.zudrangmarecords.com), all organisers of hugely popular monthly parties, or local listings rags such as CNNGo, BK and the Bangkok Post's Friday supplement, Guru.

cities in the world where nobody seems to mind if you slap a bar at the top of a skyscraper (although it's worth noting that most rooftop bars enforce a dress code – no shorts or sandals).

But many visitors associate Bangkok with the kind of bars that don't have an address – found just about everywhere in the city. Think streetside seating, plastic chairs, auto exhaust, and tasty dishes that are absent-mindedly nibbled between toasts.

Bangkok bars don't have cover charges, but they do generally enforce closing time at 1am, and sometimes earlier if they suspect trouble from the cops.

If you want to drink your way through Bangkok's best nightlife zone, follow our Banglamphu pub crawl (p81).

Dance Clubs
Fickleness is the reigning characteristic of the Bangkok club scene, and venues that were pulling in thousands a night just last year are often only vague memories today. Also, Bangkok clubs tend to burn strong and bright on certain nights – a visit from a foreign DJ or the music flavour of the month – then hibernate every other night.

What used to be a rotating cast of hot spots has slowed to a few standards on the sois off Sukhumvit, Silom, Ratchadapisek and RCA (Royal City Ave), the city's 'entertainment zones', which qualify for the 2am closing time. Most places don't begin filling up until midnight. Cover charges run as high as 600B and usually include a drink or two. You'll need ID to prove you're legal (20 years old); they'll card even the grey-haired.

If you find 2am too early to call it a night, don't worry – Thais have found curiously creative methods of flouting closing times. Speakeasies have sprung up all over the city, so follow the crowds – no one is heading home. Some places just remove the tables and let people drink on the floor (somehow this is an exemption), while other places serve beer in teapots. If it seems strange...welcome to Bangkok.

For live music, traditional performances and Bangkok's infamous 'adult' shows, see the Entertainment chapter (p39).

Drinks
Bangkok is justifiably renowned for its food and nightlife, but markedly less so for its beverages. Yet drinks are the glue that fuse these elements, and without them, that cabaret show would be markedly less entertaining.

BEER
Advertised with such slogans as 'ʽbrà·têht row, bee-a row' ('our land, our beer'), the Singha label is considered the quintessential Thai beer by fa·ràng (Westerners) and

locals alike. Pronounced *sĭng*, this pilsner claims about half the domestic market. The alcohol content for Singha beer is a heady 6%. It is sold in brown glass bottles (330mL and 660mL) with a shiny gold lion on the label, as well as in cans (330mL). It's also available on tap as *bee·a sòt* (draught beer) – much tastier than either bottled or canned brew – in many Bangkok pubs and restaurants.

Singha's biggest rival, Beer Chang, pumps the alcohol content up to 7%. Beer Chang has managed to gain an impressive following mainly because it retails at a significantly lower price than Singha and thus offers more bang per baht.

Boon Rawd (the maker of Singha) responded with its own cheaper brand, Leo. Sporting a black-and-red leopard label, Leo costs only slightly more than Beer Chang but is similarly high in alcohol.

Dutch-licensed but Thailand-brewed Heineken comes third after Singha and Chang in sales rankings. Similar 'domestic imports' include Asahi and San Miguel. Other Thai-brewed beers, all at the lower end of the price spectrum, include Cheers and Beer Thai. More variation in Thai beer brands is likely in the coming years as manufacturers scramble to command market share by offering a variety of flavours and prices.

To the surprise of many foreigners, most Thais drink their beer with ice. Before you rule this supposed blasphemy out completely, there are a few reasons why we and the Thais actually prefer our beer on the rocks. Thai beer does not possess the most sophisticated bouquet in the world and is best drunk as cold as possible. The weather in Thailand is often extremely hot, so it makes sense to maintain your beer at maximum chill. And lastly, domestic brews are generally quite high in alcohol and the ice helps to dilute this, preventing dehydration and an infamous Beer Chang hangover the next day. Taking these theories to the extreme, some places serve *bee·a wún*, 'jelly beer', beer that has

been semi-frozen until it reaches a deliciously slushy and refreshing consistency.

RICE WHISKY, WHISKY & RUM

Thai rice whisky has a sharp, sweet taste not unlike rum, with an alcohol content of 35%. The most famous brand for many years was Mekong (pronounced *'mâa kŏng'*), but currently the most popular brand is the slightly more expensive rum Sang Som. Both come in 750mL bottles called *glom* or in 375mL flask-shaped bottles called *baan*.

There are also the more-expensive barley-based whiskies produced in Thailand, which appeal to the can't-afford-Johnnie-Walker-yet set. Such whiskies include Blue Eagle, 100 Pipers and Spey Royal, each with a 40% alcohol content. Thais normally buy whisky by the bottle and drink it with ice, plenty of soda water and a splash of Coke. If you don't finish your bottle, simply tell your waiter, who will write your name and the date on the bottle and keep it for your next visit.

Drinking & Nightlife by Neighbourhood

➡ **Ko Ratanakosin & Thonburi** (p70) Home to the city's most romantic riverside bar.

➡ **Banglamphu** (p79) Rowdy Th Khao San is one of the city's best areas for a night out.

➡ **Siam Square, Pratunam, Ploenchit & Ratchathewi** (p106) Bangkok's most central zone is home to a scant handful of bars.

➡ **Riverside, Silom & Lumphini** (p123) Bangkok's gaybourhood, as well as fun bars and dance clubs for all comers.

➡ **Thanon Sukhumvit** (p136) This long street is home to Bangkok's most sophisticated bars and clubs.

➡ **Greater Bangkok** (p148) Suburban RCA is the city's best clubbing strip; good live-music venues dot other regions.

Lonely Planet's Top Choices

WTF (p136) A sophisticated yet friendly local boozer.

Hippie de Bar (p79) Retro-themed bar in the middle of Th Khao San.

Moon Bar (p124) Bangkok's best rooftop bar.

Tapas Room (p124) Long-standing club with a fun vibe.

Slim/Flix (p148) The epitome of the club alley that is RCA.

Best Bars for Relaxed Chilling

Rolling Bar (p80)

Taksura (p79)

Tuba (p137)

Barbican (p123)

Best Bars for Thai-Style Drinking

Co-Co Walk (p106)

Bangkok Bar (p136)

Nung-Len (p137)

Ad Makers (p107)

To-Sit (p107)

Best Bars for Cocktails

Hyde & Seek (p107)

Soul Food Mahanakorn (p132)

Diplomat Bar (p107)

Long Table (p136)

Coyote On Convent (p124)

Best Rooftop Bars

Sirocco Sky Bar (p123)

Phranakorn Bar (p79)

RedSky (p107)

Roof (p107)

Barley (p123)

Sky Train Jazz Club (p108)

Best Bars with Views

Amorosa (p70)

Long Table (p136)

viva aviv (p123)

River Bar Café (p90)

Best Bars with Food

viva aviv (p123)

Wine Pub (p108)

Soul Food Mahanakorn (p132)

Phranakorn Bar (p79)

Nest (p137)

HOBS (p137)

Best Bars & Clubs for Late-Nwight Fun

Wong's Place (p124)

Gazebo (p80)

Narz (p137)

Scratch Dog (p138)

Best Bars & Clubs in Which to Be Seen

Soi Ekamai 5 (p136)

Iron Fairies (p136)

Bed Supperclub (p136)

LED (p149)

Bangkok's Best Dance Clubs

Bed Supperclub (p136)

Soi Ekamai 5 (p136)

Club (p80)

Club Culture (p79)

LED (p149)

Q Bar (p137)

Gay & Lesbian Bangkok

Bangkok has a notoriously pink vibe to it. From kinky male-underwear shops mushrooming at street corners to lesbian-only nightclubs, as a homosexual you could eat, shop and play here for weeks without ever leaving the comfort of gay-friendly venues. Unlike elsewhere in Southeast Asia, homosexuality is not criminalised in Thailand and the general attitude remains extremely laissez-faire.

The Scene

Gay people are out and ubiquitous in Bangkok. Professionals enjoy relative equality in the workplace and a pride parade is celebrated annually with great fanfare. Homosexual couples, like straight couples, do not show public affection, unless they are purposefully flouting social mores.

Lesbians

Although it would be a stretch to claim that Bangkok has a lesbian scene, lesbians have become more visible in recent years, and there are a couple of lesbian-oriented dance clubs and bars.

It's worth noting that, perhaps because Thailand is still a relatively conservative place, lesbians in Bangkok generally adhere to rather strict gender roles. Overtly 'butch' lesbians, called *tom* (from 'tomboy'), typically have short hair, bind their breasts and wear men's clothing. Femme lesbians refer to themselves as *dêe* (from 'lady'). Visiting lesbians who don't fit into one of these categories may find themselves met with confusion.

Transgender People

Bangkok is famous for its open and visible transgender population – known locally as *gà·teu·i* (ladyboys; also spelt *kàthoey*). Some are cross-dressers, while others have had sexual-reassignment surgery – Thailand is one of the leading countries for this procedure.) Foreigners seem to be especially fascinated by transgender people as they are often very convincing as women, and *gà·teu·i* cabarets aimed at tourists are popular venues for observing gender bending.

For more, see our interview with a transgender activist (p107).

Issues

Beneath the party vibe, serious issues remain for Bangkok's vast and visible population of LGBT people. After the government's initial success slowing the progression of HIV among the general population, there are new signs of an epidemic among young gay men. Transgender people are often treated as outcasts, same-sex couples enjoy no legal rights and lesbians have the added burden of negotiating a patriarchal society. In short, Bangkok's LGBT community may party as they please, sleep with whomever they want or even change sex, but they do so without the protection, respect and rights enjoyed by heterosexuals – particularly heterosexual men.

Festivals

The single biggest event of the year is the Bangkok Pride Festival (www.bangkokpride. org), usually held in mid-November.

Gay & Lesbian by Neighbourhood

➡ **Riverside, Silom & Lumphini** (p125) Lower Th Silom is Bangkok's unofficial gaybourhood.

➡ **Greater Bangkok** (p141) Th Kamphaeng Phet, lower Th Ratchada and the Lamsalee Intersection on Th Ramkhamhaeng are suburban Bangkok's gay zones.

NEED TO KNOW

Websites

→ **Bangkok Lesbian** (www.bangkoklesbian. com) The city's premier website for ladies who love ladies.

→ **Utopia** (www.utopia -asia.com) Publisher of the *Utopia Guide to Thailand,* covering gay-friendly businesses in 18 Thai cities, including Bangkok. Its website is also a good, if slightly outdated source of information.

Other Resources

Look for gay-themed entertainment tips in local listings rags such as *CNNGo* (www.cnngo. com/bangkok), *BK* (www. bk.asia-city.com) and the *Bangkok Post* Friday supplement, Guru (www. bangkokpost.com/guru).

Bed Supperclub (p136) hosts the hugely popular 'Confidential Sundays', and other posh locales often play host to weekend-long 'circuit parties'. Visit G Circuit (www.gcircuit. com) to find out when and where the next one is.

Lonely Planet's Top Choices

DJ Station (p125) Quite possibly one of the most legendary gay bars in Asia.

Zeta (p149) Bangkok's only lesbian dance club.

Telephone Pub (p125) Long-standing pub right in the middle of Bangkok's pinkest zone.

Ratchada Soi 8 (p149) Escape the main drag for Thai-style gay fun.

Best Gay & Lesbian Dance Clubs

G.O.D. (p125)

Confidential Sundays (Bed Supperclub (p136))

70's Bar (p125)

Best Gay & Lesbian Bars

Balcony (p125)

Fake Club (p150)

ICK (p150)

Duangthawee Plaza (p125)

Best Camp & Drag

Calypso Cabaret (p108)

Mambo Cabaret (p150)

Balcony (p125)

Nana Entertainment Plaza (p138)

Best Gay- & Lesbian-Friendly Hotels

Babylon (p125)

LUXX XL (p180)

Baan Saladaeng (p182)

Siam Heritage (p181)

Heritage Baan Silom (p182)

Rose Hotel (p182)

Traditional dancers performing at Sala Rim Nam (p124) dance show at the Mandarin Oriental Hotel

⭐ Entertainment

Although Bangkok's hyperurban environment caters to the inner philistine in all of us, the city is home to a significant but low-key art scene. Add to this dance performances, live music, some of the world's best-value cinemas and, yes, the infamous go-go bars, and you have a city whose entertainment scene spans from, in local parlance, lo-so (low society) to hi-so (high society).

Live Music

Music is a part of almost every Thai social gathering and, as Thailand's media capital, Bangkok is the centre of the Thai music industry, packaging and selling pop, crooners, *lôok tûng* (Thai-style country music) and the recent phenomenon of indie bands. The matriarchs and patriarchs like dinner with an easy-listening soundtrack: typically a Filipino band and a synthesiser. Patrons pass their request (on a napkin) up to the stage. An indigenous rock style, *pleng*

pêu·a chee·wít (songs for life), makes appearances at a dying breed of country-and-western bars decorated with buffalo horns and pictures of Native Americans. Several dedicated bars throughout the city feature blues and rock bands, but are quite scant on live indie-scene performances. Up-and-coming garage bands occasionally pop up at free concerts where the kids hang out: Santichaiprakan Park (Th Phra Athit), Th Khao San and Siam Square. Music festivals like Noise Pop and Fat Festival also feature the new breed. For more subdued tastes,

NEED TO KNOW

Opening Hours

Live music venues generally close by 1am. A complicated zoning system sees venues in designated 'entertainment areas', including RCA (Royal City Ave), Th Silom and parts of Th Sukhumvit, open until 2am, but even these 'later' licenses are subject to police whimsy.

Bars in the red-light district are open until 2am.

Reservations

Reservations are recommended for prominent theatre events, and tickets can often be purchased through **Thai Ticket Major** (www.thaiticketmajor.com).

Bangkok also attracts grade-A jazz musicians to several hotel bars.

See the music section of the People & Culture (p204) chapter for more on the ins and outs of the Thai music scene.

Most bars and clubs close at 1am, but this is subject to police discretion. The drinking age is 20 years old.

Traditional Theatre & Dance

The stage in Thailand typically hosts a *kŏhn* performance, one of the six traditional dramatic forms. Acted only by men, *kŏhn* drama is based upon stories of the *Ramakian*, Thailand's version of India's epic *Ramayana*, and was traditionally only for royal audiences. Places to watch *kŏhn* include the National Theatre (p70) and Sala Chalermkrung (p98).

The less formal *lá·kon* dances, of which there are many dying subgenres, usually involve costumed dancers (of both sexes) performing elements of the *Ramakian* and traditional folk tales. If you hear the din of drums and percussion from a temple or shrine, follow the sound to see traditional *lá·kon gâa bon* (shrine dancing). At Lak Meuang (p68) and the Erawan Shrine (p103), worshippers commission costumed troupes to perform dance movements that are similar to classical *lá·kon*, but not as refined.

Another option for viewing Thai classical dance is through dinner theatre. Most dinner theatres in Bangkok are heavily promoted through hotels to an ever-changing clientele, so standards are poor to fair. The performances at Sala Rim Nam (p124) and Silom Village (p125) come recommended.

Royal marionettes *(lá·kon lék)*, once on the brink of extinction, have been revived by Aksra Theatre (p108). The metre-high creations are elaborately costumed and perform all the subtle manipulations required of their human *kŏhn* counterparts.

See the traditional dance and theatre section of the People & Culture (p207) chapter for more on Thai dance.

Gà·teu·i Cabaret

Watching men dressed as women perform tacky show tunes has, not surprisingly, become the latest 'must-do' fixture on the Bangkok tourist circuit. Both Calypso Cabaret (p108) and Mambo Cabaret (p150) host choreographed stage shows featuring Broadway high kicks and lip-synched pop tunes by the most well-endowed dudes you'll find anywhere.

Cinemas

Hollywood movies are released in Bangkok's theatres in a timely fashion. But as home-grown cinema grows bigger, more and more Thai films, often subtitled in English, fill the roster. Foreign films are sometimes altered by Thailand's film censors before distribution; this usually involves obscuring nude sequences.

The shopping-centre cinemas have plush VIP options (p108). Despite the heat and humidity on the streets, keep in mind that Bangkok's movie theatres pump the air-conditioning with such vigour that a jumper is an absolute necessity. Ticket prices range from 120B to 220B for regular seats, and up to 500B for VIP seats. For movie listings and reviews, check the *Nation, Bangkok Post* and Movie Seer (www. movieseer.com).

Bangkok also hosts a handful of annual film festivals, including the Bangkok World Film Festival (www.worldfilmbkk.com) in January.

See the cinema section in People & Culture (p205) for more on Thai film.

Moo·ay tai (Thai Boxing)

Quintessentially Thai, almost anything goes in *moo·ay tai* (also spelt *muay thai*), the martial art more commonly known elsewhere as Thai boxing or kickboxing. If you don't mind the violence, a Thai boxing match is well worth attending for the pure spectacle – the wild musical accompaniment, the ceremonial beginning of each match and the frenzied betting.

The best of the best fight at Bangkok's two boxing stadiums. Built on royal land at the end of WWII, the art-deco-style Ratchadamnoen Stadium (p90) is the original and has a relatively formal atmosphere. Lumphini Boxing Stadium (p124) was constructed by the Thai army in 1956 and has a looser and more populist atmosphere than at Ratchadamnoen. Lumphini is also more encouraging of non-Thai boxers.

Admission fees are the same at both stadiums and vary according to seating. Ringside seats (2000B) are the most expensive and will be filled with subdued VIPs; tourists usually opt for the 2nd-class seats (1500B); and diehard *moo·ay tai* fans bet and cheer from 3rd class (1000B). If you're thinking these prices sound a bit steep for your average fight fan (taxi drivers are big fans and they make about 600B a day), then you're right. Foreigners pay more than double what Thais do.

We recommend the 2nd- or 3rd-class seats. Second class is filled with numbers-runners who take bets from fans in rowdy 3rd class, which is fenced off from the rest of the stadium. Akin to a stock-exchange pit, hand signals communicate bets and odds fly between the areas. Most fans in 3rd class follow the match (or their bets) too closely to sit down, and we've seen stress levels rise near to boiling point. It's all very entertaining.

Most programs have eight to 10 fights of five rounds each. English-speaking 'staff' outside the stadium, who will practically tackle you upon arrival, hand you a fight roster and steer you to the foreigners' ticket windows; they can also be helpful in telling you which fights are the best match-ups (some say that welterweights, between 61.2kg and 66.7kg, are the best). To keep everyone honest, however, remember to purchase tickets from the ticket window, not from a person outside the stadium.

See the boxed text Kicking & Screaming (p89) for more on the history of *moo·ay tai*; for the inside scoop on the fighters and upcoming programs, see www.muaythai2000.com.

Go-Go Bars

Although technically illegal, prostitution is fully 'out' in Bangkok, and the influence of organised crime and healthy kickbacks mean that it will be a long while before the existing laws are ever enforced. Yet, despite the image presented by much of the Western media, the underlying atmosphere of Bangkok's red-light districts is not one of illicitness and exploitation (although these do inevitably exist), but rather an aura of tackiness and boredom.

Patpong (p124) earned notoriety during the 1980s for its wild sex shows, involving everything from ping-pong balls to razors to midgets on motorbikes. Today it is more of a circus for curious spectators than sexual deviants. Soi Cowboy (p138) and Nana Entertainment Plaza (p138) are the real scenes of sex for hire. Not all of the love-you-long-time business is geared towards Westerners: Th Thaniya, off Th Silom, is filled with massage parlours for Japanese expats and visitors, while the immense massage parlours outside of central Bangkok attract Thai customers.

See the Sex Industry chapter (p215) for background on Thailand's sex industry.

Entertainment by Neighbourhood

→ **Ko Ratanakosin & Thonburi** (p70) This area is home to both state-sponsored and privately run galleries, studios and performance spaces.

→ **Banglamphu** (p80) Home to some of the city's best live music venues.

→ **Thewet & Dusit** (p90) This is where you'll find the city's oldest Thai boxing stadium.

→ **Siam Square, Pratunam, Ploenchit & Ratchathewi** (p108) *Gà·teu·i* (ladyboy) cabaret and live music.

→ **Thanon Sukhumvit** (p138) Live music is a great entertainment option here.

→ **Greater Bangkok** (p150) Bangkok's 'burbs are where you'll find some of the city's best live music clubs.

Lonely Planet's Top Choices

Brick Bar (p80) Tabletop dancing to live Thai pop – right on Th Khao San.

Ratchadamnoen Stadium (p90) The country's premier venue for Thai boxing.

Living Room (p138) Bangkok's best and classiest locale for live jazz.

Aksra Theatre (p108) Life-like traditional Thai puppet performances.

Best for Thai-Style Live Music

Raintree (p108)

Tawandang German Brewery (p150)

Parking Toys (p150)

Hollywood (p150)

Best for Western-Style Live Music

Ad Here the 13th (p80)

Titanium (p138)

Saxophone Pub & Restaurant (p108)

Fat Gut'z (p138)

Rock Pub (p108)

Cotton (p98)

Best for a Quirky Night Out

Tawandang German Brewery (p150)

Rock Pub (p108)

Hollywood (p150)

Best for Traditional Performance

National Theatre (p70)

Sala Chalermkrung (p98)

Sala Rim Nam (p124)

Siam Niramit (p151)

Best for Contemporary Performance

Mambo Cabaret (p150)

Patravadi Theatre (p70)

Calypso Cabaret (p108)

Best Cinemas

Paragon Cineplex (p108)

House (p150)

Scala (p108)

Lido (p108)

Best for Moo·ay Tai (Thai Boxing)

Ratchadamnoen Stadium (p90)

Lumphini Boxing Stadium (p124)

Traditional hats for sale at one of Bangkok's vibrant markets

IGNACIO PALACIOS / LONELY PLANET IMAGES ©

Shopping

Prime your credit card and shine your baht, as shopping is serious business in Bangkok. Hardly a street corner in the city is free from a vendor, hawker or impromptu stall, and it doesn't stop there: Bangkok is also home to one of the world's largest outdoor markets, not to mention Southeast Asia's second-largest mall.

Markets & Malls

Although the tourist brochures tend to tout the upmarket malls, Bangkok still lags slightly behind Singapore and Hong Kong in this area, and the open-air markets are where the best deals and most original items are found.

Antiques

Real Thai antiques are rare and costly and reserved primarily for serious collectors. Everything else is designed to look old and most shopkeepers are happy to admit it.

Reputable antique dealers will issue an authentication certificate. Contact the **Department of Fine Arts** (Map p257; ✆0 2221 4443; www.finearts.go.th; 81/1 Th Si Ayuthaya) to obtain the required licence for exporting religious images and fragments, either antique or reproductions.

It's worth noting that trading in bona fide antiquities might not be either ethical or, in your country, legal. For more on this issue and the campaign to preserve Southeast Asia's cultural heritage, see **Heritage Watch** (www.heritagewatchinternational.org).

NEED TO KNOW

Opening Hours

Most family-run shops are open from 10am to 7pm daily. Street markets are either daytime (from 9am to 5pm) or night-time (from 7pm to midnight). Note that city ordinance forbids street-side vendors from cluttering the pavements on Mondays but are present every other day. Shopping centres are usually open from 10am to 10pm.

Scams

Thais are generally so friendly and laid back that some visitors are lulled into a false sense of security, forgetting that Bangkok is a big city with the usual untrustworthy characters. While your personal safety is rarely at risk in Thailand, you may be unwittingly charmed out of the contents of your wallet or fall prey to a scam (p229).

Bargaining

At Bangkok's markets and at a handful of its malls, you'll have to bargain for most, if not all, items. In general, if you see a price tag, it means that the price is fixed and bargaining isn't an option.

Counterfeits

Bangkok is ground-zero for the production and sale of counterfeit goods. Although they may seem cheap, keep in mind that counterfeit goods are almost always shoddy.

Shopping Guide

Bangkok's intense urban tangle sometimes makes orientation a challenge, and it can be difficult to find smaller, more intimate shops and markets. Like having your own personal guide, Nancy Chandler's Map of Bangkok (p46) tracks all sorts of small, out-of-the-way shopping venues and markets, as well as dissecting the innards of the Chatuchak Weekend Market (p143). The colourful map is sold in bookstores throughout the city.

Gems & Jewellery

Countless tourists are sucked into the prolific and well-rehearsed gem scam in which they are taken to a store by a helpful stranger and tricked into buying bulk gems that can supposedly be resold in their home country for 100% profit. The expert con artists (part of a well-organised cartel) seem trustworthy and convince tourists that they need a citizen of the country to circumvent tricky customs regulations. Unsurprisingly, the gem world doesn't work like that, and what most tourists end up with are worthless pieces of glass. By the time you sort all this out, the store has closed and changed names, and the police can do little to help.

Tailor-Made Clothes

Many tourists arrive in Bangkok with the notion of getting clothes custom-tailored at a bargain price. While this is entirely possible, there are a few things to be aware of. Prices are almost always lower than what you'd pay at home, but common scams ranging from commission-hungry túk-túk (pronounced đúk đúk; a type of motorised rickshaw) drivers to shoddy workmanship and inferior fabrics make bespoke tailoring in Bangkok a potentially disappointing investment.

The golden rule of custom tailoring is that you get what you pay for. If you sign up for a suit, two pants, two shirts and a tie, with a silk sarong thrown in, for US$199 (a very popular offer in Bangkok), the chances are it will look and fit like a sub-US$200 wardrobe. Although an offer may seem great on the surface, the price may fluctuate significantly depending on the fabric you choose. Supplying your own fabric won't necessarily reduce the price by much, but it should ensure you get exactly the look you're after.

Have a good idea of what you want before walking into a shop. If it's a suit you're after, should it be single- or double-breasted? How many buttons? What style of trousers? Of course, if you have no idea, the tailor will be more than happy to advise. Alternatively, bring a favourite garment from home and have it copied.

Set aside a week to get clothes tailored. Shirts and trousers can often be turned around in 48 hours or less with only one fitting, but no matter what a tailor may tell you, it takes more than one and often more than two fittings to create a good suit. Most reliable tailors will ask for two to five sittings. Any tailor that can sew your order in less than 24 hours should be treated with caution.

Counterfeits

One of the most ubiquitous aspects of shopping in Bangkok, and a drawcard for many visitors, is fake merchandise. Counterfeit clothes, watches and bags line sections of Th Sukhumvit and Th Silom, while there are entire malls dedicated to copied DVDs, music CDs and software. Fake IDs are available up and down Th Khao San, and there are even fake Lonely Planet guides, old editions of which are made over with a new cover and 'publication date' to be resold (often before the new editions have even been written!). Fakes are so prominent in Bangkok that there's even a **Museum of Counterfeit Goods** (0 2653 5555; www.tillekeandgibbins. com/museum/museum.htm; Tilleke & Gibbins, Supalai Grand Tower, 1011 Th Phra Ram III, access by taxi; admission free; 8am-5pm Mon-Fri by appointment only; Khlong Toei) where all the counterfeit booty that has been collected by the law firm Tilleke and Gibbins over the years is on display.

The brashness with which fake goods are peddled in Bangkok gives the impression that black-market goods are fair game, which is and isn't true. Technically, knock-offs are illegal, and periodic crackdowns by the Thai police have led to the frequent closure of shops and the arrest of vendors. The shops typically open again after a few months, however, and the purchasers of fake merchandise are rarely the target of such crackdowns.

The tenacity of Bangkok's counterfeit goods trade is largely due to the fact that tourists aren't the only ones buying the stuff. A poll conducted by Bangkok University's research centre found that 79.9% of the 1104 people polled in Bangkok admitted to having purchased counterfeit goods (only 48% admitted they felt guilty for having bought fakes).

It's worth pointing out that some companies, including even a few luxury brands, argue that counterfeit goods can be regarded as a net positive. They claim that a preponderance of fake items inspires brand awareness and fosters a demand for 'real' luxury items while also acting as a useful gauge of what's hot. But the arguments against fake goods claim that the industry supports organised crime and potentially exploitative and abusive labour conditions, circumvents taxes and takes jobs away from legitimate companies.

If the legal or moral repercussions aren't enough to convince you, keep in mind that in general, with fake stuff, you're getting exactly what you pay for. Consider yourself lucky if, after arriving home, you can actually watch all of season four of the *Simpsons* DVD you bought, if the Von Dutch badge on your new hat hasn't peeled off within a week, and if your 'Rolex' is still ticking after the first rain.

Bargaining

Many of your purchases in Bangkok will involve an ancient skill that has long been abandoned in the West: bargaining. Contrary to what you'll see on a daily basis on Th Khao San, bargaining (in Thai, *gahn dòr rah·kah*) is not a terse exchange of numbers and animosity. Rather, bargaining Thai style is a generally friendly transaction where two people try to agree on a price that is fair to both of them.

The first rule to bargaining is to have a general idea of the price. Ask around at a few vendors to get a rough notion. When you're ready to buy, it's generally a good strategy to start at 50% of the asking price and work up from there. If you're buying several of an item, you have much more leverage to request and receive a lower price. If the seller immediately agrees to your first price, you're probably paying too much, but it's bad form to bargain further at this point. In general, keeping a friendly, flexible demeanour throughout the transaction will almost always work in your favour. And remember: only begin bargaining if you're really planning on buying the item. Most importantly, there's simply no point in getting angry or upset over a few baht. The locals, who inevitably have less money than you, never do this.

Tax Refunds

A 7% Value Added Tax (VAT) applies to most purchases in Thailand, but if you spend enough and get the paperwork, the kindly Revenue Department will refund it at the airport when you leave. To qualify to receive a refund, you must not be a Thai citizen, part of an airline air crew or have spent more than 180 days in Thailand during the previous year. Your purchase must have been made at an approved store; look for the blue and white VAT Refund sticker. Minimum purchases must add up to 2000B per store in a single day and to at least 5000B total

AN INSIDER'S TIPS ON SHOPPING IN BANGKOK

Nima Chandler, of **Nancy Chandler Graphics** (www.nancychandler.net), whose colourful maps are some of the best guides to local shopping, shares her Bangkok secrets.

Your favourite Bangkok market? For visitors, Chatuchak Weekend Market (p143), but personally I prefer quirky smaller markets catering to locals, such as the Flashlight Market (p96) on Friday and Saturday nights, where collectibles of all kinds are on sale. My most bizarre find there: an antique popcorn machine.

Your favourite Bangkok mall? MBK Center (p109), the market in a mall. It's one of the few that has retained a distinctly Thai atmosphere, unlike the gleaming malls nearby. MBK's vendors also carry 'fa·ràng (foreigner) size' clothing. Highlights for visitors: silly shirts and beachwear on the 3rd floor, food court and crafts on the 6th floor.

Where's a good place to go for Thai handicrafts? Chatuchak Weekend Market (p143) is the most popular for arts and crafts, but I find it easier and more fulfilling to shop for crafts at ThaiCraft Fair (p138). ThaiCraft is a self-financed social enterprise dedicated to helping promote traditional arts and crafts direct from the villages under fair-trade practices. Favourite finds: yoga mat carry bags with tribal motifs, necklaces made of recycled materials, wonderful woven baskets and silver jewellery.

A good place for quirky souvenirs? Propaganda (Map p270; ☑info 2664 8574; 2nd fl, Siam Discovery Center; ☉10am-8pm; ☐National Stadium or Siam), a Thai brand gone international with cheeky modern design products, such as a 'Help' wine stopper (with a drowning swimmer's hand raised) and an emergency wedding ring, which comes on a credit-card-sized plastic card and can be popped out when needed.

What are some high-quality Thai brands visitors should seek out? The 3rd floor of Siam Center (p111) houses several top Thai fashion designer boutiques. For high-quality Thai antiques and crafts, the 3rd floor of Gaysorn Plaza (p109) is worth a visit.

Where's a good place for antiques? River City (p126) is home to several antique galleries, selling real and reproduction antiques. We recommend serious antique buyers do some research before visiting, as several top dealers only offer private appointments.

Any insider tips for approaching Chatuchak Weekend Market? If you see something you know you'll love, buy it, as it can be difficult to retrace your steps back to a shop.

Plan to use the restrooms in advance. Lines can be long.

Stop to rest and drink water every hour. Chatuchak can be a draining experience.

Try to stay until closing, then enjoy an early evening drink at Viva's (p144) while watching the market transform into something else after dark.

for the whole trip. Before you leave the store get a VAT Refund form and tax invoice. Most major malls in Bangkok will direct you to a dedicated VAT Refund desk, which will organise the appropriate paperwork (it takes about five minutes). Note that you won't get a refund on VAT paid in hotels or restaurants.

Your purchases must be declared and stamped at the customs desk in the airport departure hall. Smaller items (such as watches and jewellery) should be hand-carried as they will need to be reinspected once you've passed immigration. You actually get your money at a **VAT Refund Tourist Office** (☑0 2272 8198); at Suvarnabhumi Airport these are located on Level 4 in both the east and west wings. For a how-to brochure see www.rd.go.th/vrt.

Shopping by Neighbourhood

➡ **Ko Ratanakosin & Thonburi** (p56) Amulet vendors and traditional medicine on Th Maha Rat.

➡ **Banglamphu** (p80) A couple of souvenir shops, and the street-side wares of Th Khao San.

➡ **Chinatown** (p97) Flea-market feel.

➡ **Siam Square, Pratunam, Ploenchit & Ratchathewi** (p109) Malls, malls, malls.

➡ **Riverside, Silom & Lumphini** (p126) The place to go for antiques and art.

➡ **Thanon Sukhumvit** (p138) Upscale malls and tourist street markets.

➡ **Greater Bangkok** (p151) Bangkok's best open-air markets.

PLAN YOUR TRIP SHOPPING

Lonely Planet's Top Choices

Chatuchak Weekend Market (p143) One of the world's largest markets and a must-do Bangkok experience.

MBK Center (p109) The Thai market in a mall.

Th Khao San Market (p80) Handicrafts, souvenirs and backpacker essentials.

Siam Square (p109) Ground zero for Thai teen fashion in Bangkok.

Best Markets

Talat Rot Fai (p146)

Pak Khlong Market (p96)

Talat Mai (p94)

Nonthaburi Market (p146)

Best Malls

Siam Paragon (p109)

Siam Center (p111)

Siam Discovery Center (p111)

Central World Plaza (p111)

Emporium (p139)

Best Housewares & Handicrafts

ThaiCraft Fair (p138)

Nandakwang (p138)

Gaysorn Plaza (p109)

Taekee Taekon (p82)

Tamnan Mingmuang (p127)

Narai Phand (p111)

Best for One-of-a-Kind Souvenirs

Ban Baat (p75)

Old Maps & Prints (p127)

Flashlight Market (p96)

Thai Nakon (p83)

House Of Chao (p127)

Talat Rot Fai (p146)

Best Thai Fashion Labels

It's Happened To Be A Closet (p111)

Flynow (p111)

Tango (p112)

Senada Theory (p111)

Best Tailors

Raja's Fashions (p139)

Rajawongse (p139)

Marco Tailors (p112)

Nickermann's (p139)

Pinky Tailors (p111)

Ricky's Fashion House (p139)

Best for Books

Kinokuniya (p109)

Shaman Bookshop (p83)

Dasa Book Café (p139)

Asia Books (p109)

Best Food & Drink

Nittaya Curry Shop (p82)

Chiang Heng (p127)

Or Tor Kor Market (p147)

Maison Des Arts (p127)

Best for Music

ZudRangMa Records (p138)

DJ Siam (p109)

Kitcharoen Dountri (p143)

Best for Cheap Stuff

Sampeng Lane (p96)

Pratunam Market (p111)

Phahurat (p96)

Soi Lalai Sap (p127)

Best for Gadgets

Digital Gateway (p109)

Fortune Town (p151)

Pantip Plaza (p111)

Siam Paragon (p109)

Best for Antiques

River City (p126)

House Of Chao (p127)

Ámantee (p151)

Talat Rot Fai (p146)

Flashlight Market (p96)

ZudRangMa Records (p138)

Thai boxer at Ratchadamnoen Stadium (p90), Bangkok's oldest and most venerable venue

Sports & Activities

Seen all the big sights? Eaten enough pàt tai for a lifetime? When you're done soaking it all in, consider some of Bangkok's more active pursuits. Massage and spa visits are justifiably a huge draw, but the city is also home to some great guided tours and courses, the latter in subjects ranging from Thai cookery to meditation.

Spas & Massage

According to the teachings of traditional Thai healing, the use of herbs and massage should be part of a regular health-and-beauty regimen, not just an excuse for pampering. You need no excuse to get a massage and it's just as well, because Bangkok could mount a strong claim to being the massage capital of the world. Exactly what type of massage you're after is another question. Variations range from store-front traditional Thai massage to an indulgent spa

'experience' with service and style. And even within the enormous spa category there are choices; there is plenty of pampering going around but some spas focus more on the medical than the sensory, while plush resort-style spas offer a laundry list of appealing treatments.

The most common variety is a traditional Thai massage (*nôo·at păan boh·rahn*). Although it sounds relaxing, at times it can seem more closely related to *moo·ay tai* (Thai boxing, also spelt *muay thai*) than to shiatsu. Thai massage is based on yogic techniques for general health involving pulling, stretching, bending and manipulating pressure points. If done well, a traditional massage will leave you sore but revitalised.

Full-body massages usually include camphor-scented balms or herbal compresses, or oil in cheaper establishments. Note that 'oil massage' is sometimes taken as code for 'sexy massage'. A foot massage is arguably (and it's a strong argument) the best way to treat the legweariness of sightseeing.

Depending on the neighbourhood, prices for massages in small parlours are 200B to 350B for a foot massage and 300B to 500B for a full-body massage. Spa experiences start at about 800B and climb like a Bangkok skyscraper.

Jogging & Cycling

Lumphini Park (p118) and Benjakiti Park (p131) host early-morning and late-evening runners.

For something more social, one of Bangkok's longest-running sports groups is the Hash House Harriers (www.bangkokhhh.com), which puts on weekly runs. Cyclists also have their own hash, with the Bangkok Hash House Bikers (www.bangkokbikehash.org) meeting one Sunday a month for a 40km to 50km mountain-bike ride and post-ride refreshments.

Gyms

Bangkok is well stocked with gyms, ranging in style from long-running open-air affairs in spaces such as Lumphini Park to ultramodern megagyms complete with hi-tech equipment. Most large hotels have gyms and swimming pools, as do a growing number of small hotels.

Yoga & Pilates

Yoga studios – and enormous accompanying billboards of smiling gurus – have popped up faster than mushrooms at a full-moon party. Expect to pay about 650B for a one-off class.

Golf

Bangkok's outer suburbs are well stocked with golf courses with green fees ranging from 250B to 5000B, plus the customary 200B tip for caddies. The website Thai Golfer (www.thaigolfer.com) rates

NEED TO KNOW

Bookings

Long-term courses like language or meditation should ideally be booked a month or so in advance to ensure vacancies. Shorter courses, including cookery courses, and most guided tours can be arranged a week or a few days in advance. Massage and spa treatments can often be booked on the same day.

every course in Thailand; click through to 'Course Review'.

Tours

GUIDED TOURS

If you're not travelling with a group but would like a guide, recommended outfits include **Tour with Tong** (☎ 0 81835 0240; www.tourwithtong.com; day tour from 1000B), whose team of guides conduct tours in and around Bangkok, and **Thai Private Tour Guide** (☎ 0 81860 9159; www.thaitourguide.com; day tour from 2000B), where Chob and Mee get good reviews.

WALKING/SPECIALITY TOURS

Although the pollution and heat are significant obstacles, Bangkok is a fascinating city to explore on foot. If you'd rather do it with an expert guide, **Bangkok Private Tours** (www.bangkokprivatetours.com; full-day walking tour 3400B) and Co van Kessel Bangkok Tours (p98) conduct customised walking tours of the city. Foodies will appreciate the offerings at **Bangkok Food Tours** (☎ 08 9126 3657; www.bangkokfoodtours.com; tours from 950B), which offers half-day culinary tours of Bangkok's older neighbourhoods.

BICYCLE & SEGWAY TOURS

You might be wondering who the hell would want to get on a bike and subject themselves to the notorious traffic jams and sauna-like conditions of Bangkok's streets. But the fact that they sound so unlikely is part of what makes these trips so cool. The other part is that you discover a whole side of the city that's virtually off-limits to four-wheeled transport. Routes include unusual ways around Chinatown and Ko Ratanakosin, but the pick are journeys across the river to Thonburi and, in particular, to the Phra Pradaeng Peninsula. Better known as Bang Kachao, this exquisite expanse of mangrove, banana and coconut plantations lies just a stone's throw from the frantic city centre, on the opposite side of Chao Phraya. You cycle to the river, take a boat to Bang Kachao and then follow elevated concrete paths that zigzag through the growth to a local village for lunch.

Several companies run regular, well-received tours starting at about 1000B for a half-day.

RIVER & CANAL TRIPS

The cheapest and most obvious way to commute between riverside attractions is on the commuter boats run by Chao Phraya Express (p222). The terminus for most northbound boats is Tha Nonthaburi and for most southbound boats it's Tha Sathon (also called Central Pier), near the Saphan Taksin BTS station, although some boats run as far south as Wat Ratchasingkhon.

For a more personal view, you might consider chartering a long-tail boat (p69) along the city's canals. Another option is the dinner cruises (p121) that ply Mae Nam Chao Phraya at night.

BANG PA-IN & AYUTHAYA CRUISES

A little faster than the days of sailing ships, river cruises from Bangkok north to the ruins of the former royal capital of Ayuthaya take in all the romance of the river. Normally only one leg of the journey between Bangkok and Ayuthaya is aboard a boat, while the return or departing trip is by bus. Outfits include Asian Oasis (p112) and Manohra Cruises (p151).

Courses

MEDITATION

Although at times Bangkok may seem like the most un-Buddhist place on earth, there are a few places where foreigners can practise Theravada Buddhist meditation. Some courses allow drop-ins on a daily basis, while others require a relatively long-term commitment.

See the Theravada Buddhism section of the People & Culture chapter (p201) for background information on Buddhism. Additional sources of information include Dharma Thai (www.dharmathai.com), which has a rundown on several prominent wát and meditation centres.

THAI BOXING

Training in *moo·ay tai* for foreigners has increased in popularity in the past five years and many camps all over the country are tailoring their programs for English-speaking fighters of both sexes. Food and accommodation can often be provided for an extra charge. The website www.muaythai.com contains loads of information on training camps.

THAI COOKERY

Having consumed everything Bangkok has to offer is one thing, but imagine the points you'll rack up if you can make the same dishes for your friends back at home. A visit to a Thai cooking school has become a must-do for many Bangkok itineraries, and for some visitors it is a highlight of their trip.

Courses range in price and value, but a typical half-day course should include at least a basic introduction to Thai ingredients and flavours and a hands-on chance to both prepare and cook several dishes. Nearly all lessons include a set of printed recipes and end with a communal lunch consisting of your handiwork.

THAI LANGUAGE

Although it generally involves a pretty serious time commitment, Bangkok is home to several schools that specialise in teaching Thai to foreigners.

THAI MASSAGE

There are few places in Bangkok that offer instruction in Thai-style massage; Wat Pho Thai Traditional Medical and Massage School (p71) and Pussapa Thai Massage School (p139) both have English-language curricula.

Sports & Activities by Neighbourhood

➡ **Ko Ratanakosin & Thonburi** (p70) Canal- and river-based boat tours, and Thai massage.

➡ **Banglamphu** (p83) Bike tours and cooking schools.

➡ **Siam Square, Pratunam, Ploenchit & Ratchathewi** (p112) Spas and language courses.

➡ **Riverside, Silom & Lumphini** (p128) Several of Bangkok's best cooking schools and spas are here.

➡ **Thanon Sukhumvit** (p139) This street is home to Bangkok's greatest variety of quality massages and spas.

➡ **Greater Bangkok** (p151) The suburbs are where you'll find Bangkok's most lauded Thai boxing schools.

Lonely Planet's Top Choices

Khao (p83) Learn how to cook Thai food with the pros.

Blue Elephant Thai Cooking School (p128) The city's largest and most well-equipped cooking school.

Oriental Spa (p128) Riverside spa that sets the standard for luxury and pampering.

Health Land (p140) Quite possibly one of the best-value massage studios in the world.

Ruen-Nuad Massage Studio (p128) Cosy, reputable massage studio.

Best Spas

1930 Spa (p112)

Thann Sanctuary (p112)

Divana Massage & Spa (p140)

Rakuten (p140)

Best for Thai-Style Massage

Asia Herb Association (p140)

Coran (p140)

Lavana (p140)

Wat Pho Thai Traditional Medical and Massage School (p140)

Baan Dalah (p140)

Best Thai Cookery Schools

Helping Hands (p139)

Baipai Thai Cooking School (p151)

Silom Thai Cooking School (p128)

Oriental Hotel Thai Cooking School (p128)

Best Bicycle & Segway Tours

Bangkok Bike Rides (p140)

Velo Thailand (p83)

Co van Kessel Bangkok Tours (p98)

Grasshopper Adventures (p83)

Segway Tour Thailand (p71)

Best for Kids

Safari World (p150)

Fun-arium (p140)

Siam Park City (p150)

Dream World (p150)

SF Strike Bowl (p113)

Best for Moo·ay Tai (Thai Boxing)

Sor Vorapin Gym (p83)

Muaythai Institute (p151)

Fairtex Muay Thai (p151)

Best for Meditation

International Buddhist Meditation Center (p70)

House of Dhamma (p151)

Meditation Study and Retreat Center (p70)

World Fellowship of Buddhists (p140)

Best for Learning Thai Massage

Pussapa Thai Massage School (p139)

Wat Pho Thai Traditional Medical and Massage School (p71)

Explore Bangkok

◉ BANGKOK
TOP SIGHTS

Neighbourhoods at a Glance

1 Ko Ratanakosin & Thonburi (p56)

The artificial island of Ko Ratanakosin is Bangkok's birthplace, and the Buddhist temples and royal palaces here comprise some of the city's most important and most-visited sights. By contrast, Thonburi, located across Mae Nam Chao Phraya (Chao Phraya River), is a seemingly forgotten yet visit-worthy zone

of sleepy residential districts connected by *klorng* (canals, also spelt *khlong*).

2 Banglamphu (p72)

Leafy lanes, antique shophouses, buzzing wet markets and golden temples convene in Bang lamphu – easily the city's most quintessentially 'Bangkok' neighbourhood. It's a quaint postcard picture of the city that used to be, that is until you stumble upon Th Khao San,

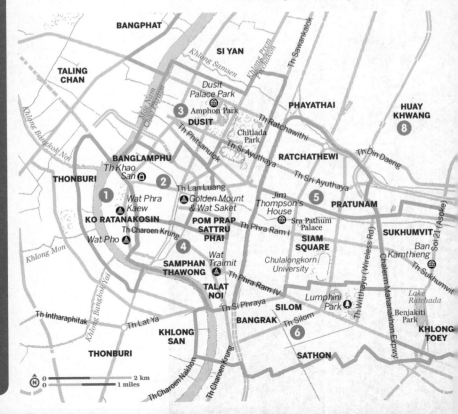

the intergalactic backpacker melting pot that's anything but traditional.

③ Thewet & Dusit (p84)

Dusit has a knack for making you second-guess what city you're in with its wide boulevards, manicured parks, imposing palaces and statues dedicated to former kings. The reality check comes in neighbouring Thewet, where its soggy riverside setting, busy wet market and relentless traffic are classic Bangkok.

④ Chinatown (p93)

)Although many generations removed from the mainland, Bangkok's Chinatown could be a bosom brother of any Chinese city. The streets are crammed with shark-fin restaurants, gaudy yellow-gold and jade shops and flashing neon signs in Chinese characters. It's Bangkok's most hectic neighbourhood,

and correspondingly, is a great place in which to get lost.

⑤ Siam Square, Pratunam, Ploenchit & Ratchathewi (p99)

Multi-storey malls, outdoor shopping precincts and never-ending markets leave no doubt that Siam Square, Pratunam and Ploenchit combine to form Bangkok's commercial district. The BTS (Skytrain) interchange at Siam has also made this area the centre of modern Bangkok, while only a few blocks away, scruffy Ratchathewi has a lot more in common with provincial Thai cities.

⑥ Riverside, Silom & Lumphini (p114)

Although you may not see it behind the office blocks, hi-rise condos and hotels, Mae Nam Chao Phraya forms a watery backdrop to these linked neighbourhoods. History is still palpable in the riverside area's crumbling architecture, while heading inland, Silom, Bangkok's de facto financial district, is frenetic and modern, and Th Sathon is the much more subdued embassy zone.

⑦ Thanon Sukhumvit (p129)

Japanese enclaves, French restaurants, Middle Eastern nightlife zones, tacky 'sex-pat' haunts: it's all here along Th Sukhumvit, Bangkok's unofficial international zone. Where temples and suburban rice fields used to be, today you'll also find shopping centres, nightlife and a host of other tidy amenities that cater to middle-class Thais and resident foreigners.

⑧ Greater Bangkok (p143)

Once ringed by rice fields, modern Bangkok has since expanded in every possible direction with few concessions to agriculture or charm. The sights may be relatively few and far between, but the upside to this is it means that Bangkok's 'burbs are a good place to get a taste of provincial Thailand if you don't have the time to go upcountry.

Historical Centre: Ko Ratanakosin & Thonburi

Neighbourhood Top Five

1 Trying to stop your jaw from dropping to the floor upon encountering the enormous reclining Buddha at **Wat Pho** (p61) for the first time.

2 Basking in the glow of the Emerald Buddha at **Wat Phra Kaew** (p58).

3 Getting lost in the weirdness of commerce that is the **Amulet Market** (p66).

4 Enjoying sunset views of Wat Arun and cocktails at **Amorosa** (p70).

5 Learning about the origins of Thai culture at the **Museum of Siam** (p68).

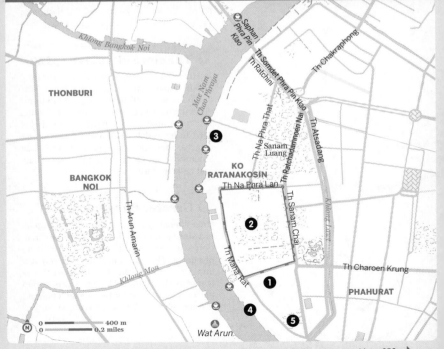

For more detail of this area, see Map p252 ➡

Explore: Ko Ratanakosin & Thonburi

Birthplace of Bangkok, the artificial island of Ko Ratanakosin is where it all began more than 200 years ago. The remnants of this history – which today are Bangkok's biggest sights – draw just about every visitor to the city. The big-hitters, Wat Phra Kaew & Grand Palace and Wat Pho, are a short walk from the Chao Phraya Express boat piers at Tha Chang and Tha Tien, and, although within walking distance of each other, the hot sun may make doing this a more demanding task than it appears. Túk-túks (pronounced *dúk dúk*) are a dime a dozen around here. If you're planning on doing our walking tour or visiting several sights, it's best to arrive early in the morning, both to avoid the crowds and to take advantage of the cooler weather. Evening is best for photography, particularly if you're hoping for the classic sunset shot of Wat Arun.

Located across the river, neighbouring Thonburi has significantly less to offer in terms of sights, but is great for those who fancy urban exploration. The cool morning is a wise time to visit the area, which is accessible via the 3B river-crossing ferries at Tha Chang and Tha Tien.

Local Life

➡ **Local Life** Ko Ratanakosin is probably Bangkok's most touristy neighbourhood, but hop on any of the 3B river-crossing ferries and you'll be whisked across Mae Nam Chao Phraya to Thonburi, where regular Thai life carries on uninterrupted.

➡ **Dance Floor** Lak Meuang receives daily supplications from Thai worshippers, some of whom commission classical Thai dancers to perform *lákon gâa bon* (shrine dancing) as thanks for granted wishes.

➡ **Life Aquatic** Thonburi is home to several *klorng* (canals, also spelt *khlong*) that once were responsible for Bangkok's former nickname, 'Venice of the East'.

➡ **Traditional Healing** Along Th Maha Rat are dozens of shophouses overflowing with family-run herbal-medicine and traditional-massage shops, and street vendors selling used books and, oddly enough, dentures.

Getting There & Away

➡ **River boat** To Ko Ratanakosin: Tha Rajinee, Tha Tien and Tha Chang. To Thonburi: Tha Wang Lang (Siriraj), Thonburi Railway and Tha Saphan Phra Pin Klao.

➡ **BTS** To Thonburi: Krung Thonburi and Wong Wian Yai. To Ko Ratanakosin: National Stadium or Phaya Thai.

➡ **Bus** To Ko Ratanakosin: air-con 503, 508 and 511; ordinary 3, 25, 39, 47 and 53. To Thonburi: air-con 507 and 509; ordinary 21, 42 and 82.

Lonely Planet's Top Tip

Anyone standing outside of any of the big sights in Ko Ratanakosin who claims tthe sight is closed is either a gem tout or con artist; ignore them and proceed inside.

✕ Best Places to Eat

➡ Pa Aew (p69)

➡ Mangkud Cafe (p69)

➡ Coconut Palm (p69)

➡ Khunkung (p69)

For reviews, see 69 ➡

◉ Best Temples

➡ Wat Phra Kaew (p58)

➡ Wat Pho (p61)

➡ Wat Arun (p63)

For reviews, see p64 ➡

◉ Best Museums

➡ Museum of Siam (p68)

➡ National Museum (p65)

➡ Songkran Niyomsane Forensic Medicine Museum & Parasite Museum (p65)

For reviews, see 64 ➡

TOP SIGHTS
WAT PHRA KAEW & GRAND PALACE

Wat Phra Kaew (Map p252; The Temple of the Emerald Buddha) gleams and glitters with so much colour and glory that its earthly foundations seem barely able to resist the celestial pull. Architecturally fantastic, the temple complex is also the spiritual core of Thai Buddhism and the monarchy, symbolically united in what is the country's most holy image, the Emerald Buddha. Attached to the temple complex is the former royal residence, once a sealed city of intricate ritual and social stratification.

The ground was consecrated in 1782, the first year of Bangkok rule, and is today Bangkok's biggest tourist attraction and a pilgrimage destination for devout Buddhists and nationalists. The 94.5-hectare grounds encompass more than 100 buildings that represent 200 years of royal history and architectural experimentation. Most of the architecture, royal or sacred, can be classified as Ratanakosin (old-Bangkok style).

Guides can be hired at the ticket kiosk; ignore anyone outside. An audio guide can be rented for 200B for two hours. Wat Phra Kaew and the **Grand Palace** (Map p252) are best reached either by a short walk south from Banglamphu, via Sanam Luang, or by Chao Phraya Express boat to Tha Chang. From the Siam Sq area (in front of the MBK Center, Th Phra Ram I), take bus 47.

DON'T MISS...

➡ Emerald Buddha
➡ *Ramakian* murals
➡ Grand Palace structures

PRACTICALITIES

➡ วัดพระแก้ว/พระบรมมหาราชวัง
➡ Th Na Phra Lan
➡ admission 400B
➡ ⊘8.30am-3.30pm
➡ 🚤Tha Chang

Wat Phra Kaew

Ramakian Murals

Outside the main *bòht* (chapel) is a stone statue of the Chinese goddess of mercy, Kuan Im, and nearby are two cow figures, representing the year of Rama I's birth. In the 2km-long cloister that defines the perimeter of the complex are 178 murals depicting the *Ramakian* (the Thai version of the Indian Ramayana epic) in its entirety, beginning at the north gate and moving clockwise around the compound.

The story begins with the hero, Rama (the green-faced character), and his bride, Sita (the beautiful topless maiden). The young couple are banished to the forest, along with Rama's brother. In this pastoral setting, the evil king Ravana (the character with many arms and faces) disguises himself as a hermit in order to kidnap Sita.

Rama joins forces with Hanuman, the monkey king (logically depicted as the white monkey), to attack Ravana and rescue Sita. Although Rama has the pedigree, Hanuman is the unsung hero. He is loyal, fierce and clever. En route to the final fairytale ending, great battles and schemes of trickery ensue until Ravana is finally killed. After withstanding a loyalty test of fire, Sita and Rama are triumphantly reunited.

If the temple grounds seem overrun by tourists, the mural area is usually mercifully quiet and shady.

Emerald Buddha

Upon entering Wat Phra Kaew you'll meet the *yaksha,* brawny guardian giants from the *Ramakian.* Beyond them is a courtyard where the central *bòht* houses the Emerald Buddha. The spectacular ornamentation inside and out does an excellent job of distracting first-time visitors from paying their respects to the image. Here's why: the Emerald Buddha is only 66cm tall and sits so high above worshippers in the main temple building that the gilded shrine is more striking than the small figure it cradles. No one knows exactly where it comes from or who sculpted it, but it first appeared on record in 15th-century Chiang Rai in northern Thailand. Stylistically it seems to belong to Thai artistic periods of the 13th to 14th centuries.

Because of its royal status, the Emerald Buddha is ceremoniously draped in monastic robes. There are now three royal robes: for the hot, rainy and cool seasons. The three robes are still solemnly changed at the beginning of each season. This duty has traditionally been performed by the king, though in recent years the crown prince has presided over the ceremony.

Grand Palace

Adjoining Wat Phra Kaew is the Grand Palace (Phra Borom Maharatchawang), a former royal residence that is today only used on ceremonial occasions. Visitors are allowed to survey the Grand Palace grounds and four of the remaining palace buildings, which are interesting for their royal bombast.

DRESS CODE

At Wat Phra Kaew and the Grand Palace grounds, dress rules are strictly enforced. If you're wearing shorts or a sleeveless shirt you will not be allowed into the temple grounds – this applies to men and women. If you're flashing a bit too much calf or ankle, expect to be shown into a dressing room and issued with a sarong (rental is free, but you must provide a 200B deposit). Officially, sandals and flip-flops are not permitted, though the guards are less zealous in their enforcement of this rule.

Despite the name, the Emerald Buddha is actually carved from a single piece of nephrite, a type of jade.

TICKETS

Enter Wat Phra Kaew and the Grand Palace complex through the clearly marked third gate from the river pier. Tickets are purchased inside the complex; anyone telling you it's closed is a gem tout or con artist. Remember to hang on to your ticket as it also allows entry to Dusit Palace Park (p86).

THE TRAVELS OF THE EMERALD BUDDHA

Some time in the 15th century, the Emerald Buddha is said to have been covered with plaster and gold leaf and placed in Chiang Rai's own Wat Phra Kaew. Many valuable Buddha images were masked in this way to deter potential thieves and marauders during unstable times. Often the true identity of the image was forgotten over the years until a 'divine accident' exposed its precious core. The Emerald Buddha experienced such a divine revelation while it was being transported to a new location. In a fall, the plaster covering broke off, revealing the brilliant green inside. But while his was seen as a divine revelation, the return of the Phra Kaew would prove anything but peaceful for the people of Siam and Laos.

During territorial clashes with Laos, the Emerald Buddha was seized and taken to Vientiane in the mid-16th century. Some 200 years later, after the fall of Ayuthaya and the ascension of the Bangkok-based kingdom, the Thai army marched up to Vientiane, razed the city and hauled off the Emerald Buddha. The Buddha was enshrined in the then capital, Thonburi, before the general who led the sacking of Vientiane assumed the throne and had it moved to this location.

At the eastern end, **Borombhiman Hall** is a French-inspired structure that served as a residence for Rama VI (King Vajiravudh; r 1910–25). Today it can only be viewed through its iron gates. But in April 1981 General San Chitpatima used it as the headquarters for an attempted coup. **Amarindra Hall**, to the west, was originally a hall of justice but is used (very rarely indeed) for coronation ceremonies; the golden, boat-shaped throne looks considerably more ornate than comfortable.

The largest of the palace buildings is the triple-winged **Chakri Mahaprasat** (Grand Palace Hall). Completed in 1882 following a plan by British architects, the exterior shows a peculiar blend of Italian Renaissance and traditional Thai architecture, a style often referred to as *fa·ràng sài chá-dah* (Westerner wearing a Thai classical dancer's headdress), because each wing is topped by a *mon dòp* (a layered, heavily ornamented spire). It is believed the original plan called for the palace to be topped with a dome, but Rama V (King Chulalongkorn; r 1868–1910) was persuaded to go for a Thai-style roof instead. The tallest of the *mon dòp,* in the centre, contains the ashes of Chakri kings; the flanking *mon dòp* enshrine the ashes of the many Chakri princes who failed to inherit the throne.

The last building to the west is the Ratanakosin-style **Dusit Hall**, which initially served as a venue for royal audiences and later as a royal funerary hall.

Until Rama VI decided one wife was enough for any man, even a king, Thai kings housed their huge harems in the inner palace area (not open to the public), which was guarded by combat-trained female sentries. The intrigue and rituals that occurred within the walls of this cloistered community live on in the fictionalised epic *Four Reigns,* by Kukrit Pramoj, which follows a young girl named Phloi growing up within the Royal City.

DIANA MAYFIELD / LONELY PLANET IMAGES ©

Of all Bangkok's temples, Wat Pho is arguably the one most worth visiting for both its remarkable Reclining Buddha image and its sprawling, stupa-studded grounds. The temple boasts a long list of credits: the oldest and largest *wát* in Bangkok; the longest Reclining Buddha and the largest collection of Buddha images in Thailand; and the country's first public education institution. For all that, it sees fewer visitors than neighbouring Wat Phra Kaew and feels less commercial.

Narrow Th Chetuphon divides the grounds in two, and it's well worth entering Wat Pho from either this quiet lane or Th Sanam Chai to avoid the touts and tour groups of the main entrance on Th Thai Wang. You'll come into the northern compound (the southern part is closed to the public), where the main *bòht* is constructed in Ayuthaya style and is strikingly more subdued than Wat Phra Kaew. A temple has stood on this site since the 16th century, but in 1781 Rama I (King Phraphutthayotfa; r 1782–1809) ordered the original Wat Photharam to be completely rebuilt as part of his new capital. Rama I's remains are interred in the base of the presiding Buddha figure in the *bòht*.

The images on display in the four *wíhǎhn* (sanctuaries) surrounding the main *bòht* are worth investigation. Particularly beautiful are the Phra Jinnarat and Phra Jinachi Buddhas in the western and southern chapels, both rescued from Sukhothai by relatives of Rama I. The galleries extending between the four chapels feature no fewer than 394 gilded Buddha images.

Encircling the main *bòht* is a low marble wall with 152 bas-reliefs depicting scenes from the *Ramakian*. You'll recognise some of these figures when you exit the temple past the hawkers with mass-produced rubbings for sale; these are made from cement casts based on Wat Pho's reliefs.

DON'T MISS...

➡ Reclining Buddha
➡ Granite statues
➡ Massage pavilions

PRACTICALITIES

➡ วัดโพธิ์ (วัดพระเชตุพน) | Wat Phra Chetuphon
➡ Map p252
➡ Th Sanam Chai
➡ admission 100B
➡ ⊙8am-6pm
➡ 🚤Tha Tien

WAT PHO'S GRANITE STATUES

Aside from monks and sightseers, Wat Pho is filled with an altogether stiffer crowd: dozens of giants and figurines carved from granite. The rock giants first arrived in Thailand as ballast aboard Chinese junks and were put to work in Wat Pho (and other wát, including Wat Suthat), guarding the entrances of temple gates and courtyards. Look closely and you'll see an array of Chinese characters. The giants with bulging eyes and Chinese opera costumes were inspired by warrior noblemen and are called *Lan Than*. The figure in a straw hat is a farmer, forever interrupted during his day's work cultivating the fields. And can you recognise the guy in the fedora-like hat with a trimmed beard and moustache? Marco Polo, of course, who introduced such European styles to the Chinese court.

If you're hot and foot sore, the air-conditioned massage pavilions near Wat Pho's east gate could be a welcome way to cool down while experiencing high-quality and relatively inexpensive Thai massage.

On the western side of the grounds a collection of four towering tiled stupas commemorates the first four Chakri kings. The surrounding wall was built on the orders of Rama IV (King Mongkut; r 1851–68), who for reasons we can only speculate about decided he didn't want any future kings joining the memorial. Note the square bell shape with distinct corners, a signature of Ratanakosin style. Wat Pho's 91 smaller stupas include *chedi* (stupa) clusters containing the ashes of lesser royal descendants.

Small Chinese-style rock gardens and hill islands interrupt the tiled courtyards providing shade, greenery and quirky decorations depicting daily life. Keep an eye out for the distinctive rockery festooned with figures of the hermit Khao Mor, who is credited with inventing yoga, in various healing positions. According to the tradition, a few good arm stretches should cure idleness.

Massage Pavilions

A small pavilion west of the main *bòht* has Unesco-awarded inscriptions detailing the tenets of traditional Thai massage. These and other similar inscriptions led Wat Pho to be regarded as Thailand's first university. Today it maintains that tradition as the national headquarters for the teaching and preservation of traditional Thai medicine, including Thai massage. The famous traditional Thai medicine school has two **massage pavilions** (Map p252; Thai massage per hour 420B; ⊗8am-6pm) located within the temple area and additional rooms within the training facility (p71) outside the temple.

Reclining Buddha, Stupas & Gardens

In the northwest corner of the site you'll find Wat Pho's main attraction, the enormous Reclining Buddha. The 46m-long and 15m-high supine figure was commissioned by Rama III (King Phranangklao; r 1824–51), and illustrates the passing of the Buddha into nirvana. It is made of plaster around a brick core and finished in gold leaf, which gives it a serene luminescence that keeps you looking, and looking again, from different angles. The 3m-high feet are a highlight, with mother-of-pearl inlay depicting 108 different auspicious *láksànà* (characteristics of a Buddha).

TOP SIGHTS
WAT ARUN

The missile-shaped temple that rises from the banks of Mae Nam Chao Phraya is known as Temple of Dawn and was named after the Indian god of dawn, Aruna. It was here that, in the wake of the destruction of Ayuthaya, King Taksin stumbled upon a small local shrine and interpreted the discovery as such an auspicious sign that this should be the site of the new capital of Siam.

King Taksin built a palace beside the shrine, which is now part of Navy Headquarters, and a royal temple that housed the Emerald Buddha for 15 years before Taksin was assassinated and the capital moved across the royal river to Bangkok.

Climbing the Spire

Today, the central feature of Wat Arun is the 82m-high Khmer-style *bˈrahng* (spire), constructed during the first half of the 19th century by Rama II (King Phraphuttha-loetla Naphalai; r 1809–24), now immortalised in a riverfront statue with three elephants, and Rama III. From the river it is not apparent that this corn-cob-shaped steeple is adorned with colourful floral murals made of glazed porcelain, a common temple ornamentation in the early Ratanakosin period, when Chinese ships calling at Bangkok used porcelain as ballast.

You must wear appropriate clothing two climb on Wat Arun. If you are flashing too much flesh you'll have to rent a sarong for 20B.

Buddhist Murals

Also worth a look is the interior of the *bòht*. The main Buddha image is said to have been designed by Rama II, whose ashes are interred beneath. The murals date to the reign of Rama V. Particularly impressive is one depicting Prince Siddhartha (the Buddha) encountering examples of birth, old age, sickness and death outside his palace walls, an experience that led him to abandon the worldly life.

Exploring the Neighbourhood

Wat Arun is directly across from Wat Pho, on the Thonburi side of the river. A lot of people visit the wát on long-tail boat tours, but it's dead easy and more rewarding to just jump on the 3B cross-river ferry from Tha Tien. For our money, visiting Wat Arun in the late afternoon is best, with the sun shining from the west lighting up the *bˈrahng* and the river behind it. If you come earlier, consider taking a stroll away from the river on Th Wang Doem, a quiet tiled street of wooden shophouses.

Sunset Cocktails

Sunset views of the temple compound can be caught from across the river at the riverfront warehouses that line Th Maha Rat – although be forewarned that locals may ask for a 20B 'fee'. Another great viewpoint is from Amorosa (p70), the rooftop bar at the Arun Residence.

DON'T MISS...

➡ Climbing on the Khmer-style *bˈrahng* (spire)

➡ Buddhist murals inside the main the *bòht*

➡ Exploring the surrounding neighbourhood

➡ A sunset cocktail and photo op at Amorosa

PRACTICALITIES

➡ วัดอรุณฯ

➡ Map p252

➡ www.watarun.org

➡ Th Arun Amarin

➡ admission 50B

➡ ⏰7am-6pm

➡ 🚢Tha Tien

◉ SIGHTS

WAT PHRA KAEW & GRAND PALACE   BUDDHIST TEMPLE, PALACE
See p58.

WAT PHO   BUDDHIST TEMPLE
See p61.

WAT ARUN   BUDDHIST TEMPLE
See p63.

SILPAKORN UNIVERSITY   UNIVERSITY
Map p252 (มหาวิทยาลัยศิลปากร; www.su.ac.th; 31 Th Na Phra Lan; ⊠Tha Chang) Thailand's universities aren't usually repositories for interesting architecture, but Silpakorn (pronounced *sĭn lá ʼbà gorn*), the country's premier art school, breaks the mould. The classical buildings form the charming nucleus of what was an early Thai aristocratic enclave, and the traditional artistic temperament still survives. The building immediately facing the Th Na Phra Lan gate was once part of a palace and now houses the Silpakorn University Art Centre. To the right of the building is a shady sculpture garden displaying the work of Corrado Feroci (also known as Silpa Bhirasri), the Italian art professor and sculptor who came to Thailand at royal request in the 1920s and later established the university (which is named after him), sculpted parts of the Democracy Monument and, much to his own annoyance, the Victory Monument.

FREE **SILPAKORN UNIVERSITY ART CENTRE**   ART GALLERY
Map p252 (www.su.ac.th; 31 Th Na Phra Lan; ⊗9am-7pm Mon-Fri, to 4pm Sat; ⊠Tha Chang) This gallery, located inside Thailand's most prestigious arts school, showcases faculty and student exhibitions. There's also an accompanying courtyard cafe and art shop.

THAMMASAT UNIVERSITY   UNIVERSITY
Map p252 (มหาวิทยาลัยธรรมศาสตร์; www.tu.ac.th; 2 Th Phra Chan; ⊠Tha Chang) Much of the drama that followed Thailand's transition from monarchy to democracy has unfolded on this quiet riverside campus. Thammasat University was established in 1934, two years after the bloodless coup that deposed the monarchy. Its remit was to instruct students in law and political economy, considered to be the intellectual necessities for an educated democracy.

The university was founded by Dr Pridi Phanomyong, whose statue stands in Pridi Court at the centre of the campus. Pridi was the leader of the civilian People's Party that successfully advocated a constitutional monarchy during the 1920s and '30s. He went on to serve in various ministries, organised the Seri Thai movement (a Thai resistance campaign against the Japanese during WWII) and was ultimately forced into exile when the postwar government was seized by a military dictatorship in 1947.

Pridi was unable to counter the dismantling of democratic reforms, but the university he established continued his crusade. Thammasat was the hotbed of pro-democracy activism during the student uprising era of the 1970s. On 14 October 1973 (*sìp-sèe đù·lah*), an estimated 10,000 protesters convened on the parade grounds beside the university's Memorial Building demanding the government reinstate the constitution. From the university, the protest grew and moved to the Democracy Monument, where the military and police opened fire on the crowd, killing 77 and wounding 857. The massacre prompted the

---

king to revoke his support of the military rulers and for a brief period a civilian government was reinstated. On 6 October 1976 (*hòk dù·lah*), Thammasat itself was the scene of a bloody massacre, when at least 46 students were shot dead while rallying against the return from exile of former dictator Field Marshal Thanom Kittikachorn. Near the southern entrance to the university is the Bodhi Court, where a sign beneath the Bodhi tree explains more about the democracy movement that germinated at Thammasat.

Walk north from Tha Phra Chan pier to go straight through Thammasat, emerging near Th Phra Athit in Banglamphu.

NATIONAL MUSEUM   MUSEUM

Map p252 (พิพิธภัณฑสถานแห่งชาติ; 4 Th Na Phra That; admission 200B; ◷9am-3.30pm Wed-Sun; ☀Tha Chang) Thailand's National Museum is the largest museum in Southeast Asia and covers a broad range of subjects, from historical surveys to religious sculpture displays. The buildings were originally constructed in 1782 as the palace of Rama I's viceroy, Prince Wang Na. Rama V turned it into a museum in 1884.

The **history wing** presents a succinct chronology of events and figures from the prehistoric, Sukhothai, Ayuthaya and Bangkok eras. Despite the corny dioramas, there are some real treasures here: look for King Ramkamhaeng's inscribed stone pillar (allegedly the oldest record of Thai writing, although this has recently been contested), King Taksin's throne and the Rama V section.

The other parts of the museum aren't as well presented, but this might be part of the charm. Dimly lit rooms, ranging in temperature from lukewarm to boiling, offer an articlike collection of Thai art and handicrafts. In the **decorative arts and ethnology exhibit**, there are collections of traditional musical instruments from Thailand, Laos, Cambodia and Indonesia, as well as ceramics, clothing and textiles, woodcarving, royal regalia, and Chinese art and weaponry. The **archaeology and art history wing** covers every Southeast Asian art period and style, from Dvaravati to Ratanakosin. The collection is impressive but hard to digest due to poor signage and sheer volume.

The museum grounds also contain the restored **Phra Thi Nang Phutthaisawan (Bhuddhaisawan Chapel)**. Inside the chapel (built in 1795) are well-preserved original murals and one of the country's

most revered Buddha images, Phra Phuttha Sihing. Legend claims the image came from Ceylon (legend claims a lot of Buddha images came from Ceylon), but art historians attribute it to the 13th-century Sukhothai period.

While the museum isn't nearly as dynamic as the more recent Museum of Siam, it does run (highly recommended) free tours on Wednesday and Thursday. All tours start from the ticket pavilion at 9.30am.

NATIONAL GALLERY   ART GALLERY

Map p254 (4 Th Chao Fa; admission 200B; ◷9am-4pm Wed-Sun; ☀Tha Phra Athit) Housed in a weathered colonial building that was the Royal Mint during the reign of Rama V, the National Gallery's permanent exhibition is a rather dusty and dated affair. Secular art is a relatively new concept in Thailand and most of the country's best examples of fine art reside in the temples for which they were created – much as historic Western art is often found in cathedrals. Most of the permanent collection here documents Thailand's homage to modern styles. More interesting are the rotating exhibits held in the spacious rear galleries; check the posters out front to see what's on.

SONGKRAN NIYOMSANE FORENSIC MEDICINE MUSEUM & PARASITE MUSEUM   MUSEUM

Map p252 (พิพิธภัณฑ์นิติเวชศาสตร์สงกรานต์นิยมแสน; 2nd fl, Adulyadejvikrom Bldg, Siriraj Hospital; admission 40B; ◷9am-4pm Mon-Sat; ☀Tha Wang Lang (Siriraj)) While it's not exactly CSI, pickled body parts, ingenious murder weapons and other crime-scene evidence are on display at this medical museum, the intent of which is ostensibly to educate rather than nauseate. Among the grisly displays is a bloodied T-shirt from a victim stabbed to death with a dildo, and the preserved but rather withered cadaver of Si Ouey, one of Thailand's most prolific and notorious serial killers who murdered – and then ate – more than 30 children in the 1950s. Despite being well and truly dead (he was executed), today his name is still used to scare misbehaving children into submission: 'Behave yourself or Si Ouey will come for you'. Next door, the Parasite Museum continues the queasy theme.

The best way to get here is by express ferry or cross-river ferry to Tha Wang Lang (Siriraj) in Thonburi; turn right (north) into the hospital and follow the green 'Museum' signs.

ROYAL BARGES NATIONAL MUSEUM
MUSEUM

Map p252 (เรือพระที่นั่ง; Khlong Bangkok Noi or 80/1 Th Arun Amarin; admission 100B, camera/video 100/200B; ⊙9am-5pm; from Tha Saphan Phra Pin Klao) Every foreign country has its famous religious monuments and museums, but how many have their own fleet of royal boats on display? The royal barges were once used daily by the royal family to get about their realm, but are now used only for grand ceremonies. They are not barges like the wide, lumbering vessels you'll see hauling sand and produce up and down Mae Nam Chao Phraya. These barges are slender like their mainstream cousins, the long-tail boats, and fantastically ornamented with religious symbolism. The largest is more than 45m long and requires a rowing crew of 50 men, plus seven umbrella bearers, two helmsmen and two navigators, as well as a flag bearer, rhythm keeper and chanter.

Suphannahong (Golden Swan) is the king's personal barge. Built on the orders of Rama I after an earlier version had been destroyed in the sacking of Ayuthaya, *Suphannahong* is made from a single piece of timber, making it the largest dugout in the world. Appropriately, a huge swan's head is carved into the prow. More recent barges feature bows carved into other Hindu-Buddhist mythological shapes, such as the seven-headed naga (sea dragon) and Garuda (Vishnu's bird mount).

To mark auspicious Buddhist calendar years, the royal barges, in all their finery, set sail during the royal *gà·tĭn,* the ceremony that marks the end of the Buddhist retreat (*pan săh*) in October or November. During this ceremony, a barge procession travels to the temples to offer new robes to the monastic contingent, and countless Bangkokians descend on the river to watch.

The museum consists of sheds near the mouth of Khlong Bangkok Noi. To get here take the 3B ferry across the river to Tha Saphan Phra Pin Klao and follow the signs. Most long-tail boat tours will stop here unless you ask them not to.

AMULET MARKET
MARKET

Map p252 (ตลาดพระเครื่องวัดมหาธาตุ; Th Maha Rat; ⊙7am-5pm; ⛴Tha Chang) This arcane and fascinating market claims both the footpaths along Th Maha Rat and Th Phra Chan, as well as a dense network of covered market stalls near Tha Phra Chan.

The trade is based around small talismans carefully prized by collectors, monks, taxi drivers and people in dangerous professions. Potential buyers, often already sporting many amulets, can be seen bargaining and flipping through magazines dedicated to the amulets, some of which command astronomical prices. While money changes hands between vendor and customer, both use the euphemism of 'renting' to get around the prohibition of selling Buddhas.

This is a great place to just wander and watch men (because it's rarely women) looking through magnifying glasses at the tiny amulets, seeking hidden meaning and, if they're lucky, hidden value. The market stretches all the way to the riverside, where a narrow alley leads north to wooden kitchens overhanging the water. Each humble kitchen garners a view of the river; students from nearby Thammasat University congregate here for cheap eats before heading off to class. It's an ideal stop for a lunch of classic Thai comforts and Western adaptations popular with students.

Also along this strip are handsome shophouses overflowing with family-run herbal-medicine and traditional-massage shops.

FREE SANAM LUANG
PARK

Map p252 (สนามหลวง; bounded by Th Na Phra That, Th Ratchadamnoen Nai & Th Na Phra Lan; admission free; ⊙24hr; ⛴Tha Chang) On a hot day, Sanam Luang (Royal Field) is far from charming – a shadeless expanse of dying grass and concrete pavement ringed by flocks of pigeons and homeless people. Despite its shabby appearance, it has been at the centre of both royal ceremony and political upheaval since Bangkok was founded. Indeed, many of the colour-coded protests you've probably seen on TV in recent years have been held here.

Less dramatic events staged here include the annual Royal Ploughing Ceremony, in which the king (or more recently, the crown prince) officially initiates the rice-growing season; an appropriate location given Sanam Luang was used to grow rice for almost 100 years after the royals moved into Ko Ratanakosin. After the rains, the kite-flying season (mid-February to April) sees the air above filled with butterfly-shaped Thai kites. Matches are held between teams flying either a 'male' or 'female' kite in a particular territory; points are won if they can force a competitor into their zone.

START **THA CHANG**
END **WAT ARUN**
DISTANCE **APPROXIMATELY 4KM**
DURATION **THREE TO FIVE HOURS**

Neighbourhood Walk
Ko Ratanakosin Stroll

The bulk of Bangkok's 'must-see' destinations are found in the former royal district, Ko Ratanakosin. It's best to start early to beat the heat and get in before the hordes have descended. Remember to dress modestly in order to gain entry to the temples and ignore any strangers who approach you offering advice on sightseeing or shopping.

Start at Tha Chang and follow Th Na Phra Lan east with a quick diversion to
1 Silpakorn University, Thailand's premier fine-arts university. If you haven't already been, continue east to the main gate into **2 Wat Phra Kaew & Grand Palace**, two of Bangkok's most famous attractions.

Return to Th Maha Rat and proceed north, through a gauntlet of herbal apothecaries and sidewalk amulet sellers. Immediately after passing the cat-laden newsstand (you'll know it when you smell it), turn left into **3 Trok Tha Wang**, a narrow alleyway holding a seemingly hidden classic Bangkok neighbourhood. Returning to Th Maha Rat, continue moving north. On your right is
4 Wat Mahathat, one of Thailand's most respected Buddhist universities.

Across the street, turn left into crowded Trok Mahathat to discover the cramped
5 Amulet Market. As you continue north along the river, amulets soon turn to food vendors. The emergence of white-and-black uniforms is a clue that you are approaching
6 Thammasat University, known for its law and political science departments.

Exiting at Tha Phra Chan, cross Th Maha Rat and continue east until you reach
7 Sanam Luang, the 'Royal Field'. Cross the field and continue south along Th Ratchadamnoen Nai until you reach the home of Bangkok's city spirit, **8 Lak Meuang**.

After paying your respects, head south along Th Sanam Chai and turn Th Thai Wang, leading to the entrance of **9 Wat Pho**, home of the giant reclining Buddha.

If you've still got the energy, head to adjacent Tha Tien to catch the cross-river ferry to **10 Wat Arun**, one of the few Buddhist temples you're actually encouraged to climb on.

Large funeral pyres are constructed here during elaborate, but infrequent, royal cremations, and explain the field's alternate name, Thung Phra Men (Cremation Ground). The most recent cremation was a six-day, 300-million baht ceremony for King Bhumibol Adulyadej's sister, Princess Galyani Vadhana, in November 2009; it took 11 months to prepare.

In a way the park is suffering a career crisis, having lost most of its full-time employment to other locales or the whims of fashion. Until 1982 Bangkok's famous Weekend Market was regularly held here (it's now at Chatuchak Park; p143). Previously, the wealthy came here for imported leisure sports; these days they head for the country club. Today the cool mornings and evenings still attract a health-conscious crowd of joggers, walkers and groups playing *dà·grôr* (sepak takraw; kick volleyball). If you fancy a big-crowd experience, Sanam Luang draws the masses in December for the King's Birthday (5 December), Constitution Day (10 December) and New Year.

Across Th Ratchadamnoen Nai to the east is the **statue of Mae Thorani,** the earth goddess (borrowed from Hindu mythology's Dharani), which stands in a white pavilion. Erected in the late 19th century by Rama V, the statue was originally attached to a well that provided drinking water to the public.

FREE LAK MEUANG ANIMIST SHRINE

Map p252 (ศาลหลักเมือง; cnr Th Sanam Chai & Th Lak Meuang; ◎6.30am-6.30pm; ⓢTha Chang) What would otherwise be an uninteresting mileage marker, this shrine has both religious and historical significance in Thailand. Lak Meuang is the city shrine, a wooden pillar erected by Rama I in 1782 to represent the founding of the new Bangkok capital. From this point, distances are measured to all other city shrines in the country. But its importance doesn't stop there. The pillar is endowed with a spirit, Phra Sayam Thewathirat (Venerable Siam Deity of the State), and is considered the city's guardian. To the east of the main shrine are several other idols added during the reign of Rama V.

Like the sacred banyan trees and the holy temples, Lak Meuang receives daily invocations from Thai worshippers in the form of commissioned *lákon gâa bon* as thanks for granted wishes. Offerings also include those cute yet macabre pigs' head with sticks of incense sprouting from their foreheads.

SARANROM ROYAL GARDEN PARK

Map p252 (สวนสราญรมย์; bounded by Th Ratchini, Th Charoen Krung & Th Sanam Chai; ◎5am-9pm; ⓢTha Tien) Easily mistaken for a European public garden, this Victorian-era green space was originally designed as a royal residence in the time of Rama IV. After Rama VII (King Prajadhipok; r 1925–35) abdicated in 1935, the palace served as the headquarters of the People's Party, the political organisation that orchestrated the handover of the government. The open space remained and in 1960 was opened to the public.

Today, a wander through the garden reveals a Victorian gazebo, paths lined with frangipani and a moat around a marble monument built in honour of one of Rama V's favourite wives, Queen Sunantha, who died in a boating accident in 1880. The queen was on her way to Bang Pa-In Summer Palace in Ayuthaya when her boat began to sink. The custom at the time was that commoners were forbidden to touch royalty, which prevented her attendants from saving her from drowning.

MUSEUM OF SIAM MUSEUM

Map p252 (สถาบันพิพิธภัณฑ์การเรียนรู้แห่งชาติ; www.museumsiam.com; Th Maha Rat; admission 300B; ◎10am-6pm Tue-Sun; ⓢTha Tien) This fun museum employs a variety of media to explore the origins of the Thai people and their culture. Housed in a European-style 19th-century building that was once the Ministry of Commerce, the exhibits are presented in an engaging, interactive fashion not often found in Thailand. They are also refreshingly balanced and entertaining, with galleries dealing with a range of questions about the origins of the nation and its people. Each room has an informative narrated video started by a sensory detector, keeping waiting to a minimum. An Ayuthaya-era battle game, a room full of traditional Thai toys and a street vending cart where you can be photographed pretending to whip up a pan of *pàt tai* (fried noodles) will help keep kids interested for at least an hour, adults for longer. Check out the shop and cafe in the grounds for some innovative gift ideas.

EATING

In stark contrast to the rest of Bangkok, there aren't many restaurants in the Ko Ratanakosin area, and those that do exist serve only Thai food. For something more international, consider heading to Banglamphu, a short taxi ride away.

PA AEW
CENTRAL THAI $

Map p252 (Th Maha Rat; mains 20-60B; ⊘9am-3pm; ⚓Tha Tien) Yes, it's a bare-bones open-air curry stall, but if we're talking taste, Pa Aew is hands-down our favourite place to eat in this part of town. Pull up a plastic stool for rich, seafood-heavy Bangkok-style dishes such as *pàt chàh lôok chín 'blah* (freshwater fish dumplings fried with fresh herbs) or a fragrant *gaang mát·sà·màn* (a dried spice-heavy 'Muslim' curry). Pa Aew is located near the corner with Soi Pratu Nok-yung; look for the exposed trays of dishes.

MANGKUD CAFE
CENTRAL THAI $$

Map p252 (www.clubartsgallery.com; Soi Wat Ra-khang; mains 125-300B; ⊘11am-10pm Tue-Thu, to 11pm Sat; from Tha Chang) Combining a minimalist restaurant, warehouse-style art gallery, and an enviable riverfront location, Mangkud is probably the most sophisticated place to eat on this side of Mae Nam Chao Phraya. The herb-heavy Thai dishes are clever and tasty; try the watermelon with dried fish, a traditional sweet-savoury snack. Look for the sign that says Club Arts.

COCONUT PALM
CENTRAL THAI $$

Map p252 (392/1-2 Th Maha Rat; mains 75-720B; ⊘11am-6pm; ⚓Tha Tien) Coconut Palm serves a generous spread of Thai dishes, but most locals come for the Sukhothai-style noodles – thin rice noodles served with pork, ground peanuts and dried chili. Even if you're not hungry, you might want to stop by for the reinvigorating blast of air-con and the refreshing drinks.

KHUNKUNG
CENTRAL THAI $$

Map p252 (Khun Kung Kitchen; 77 Th Maha Rat; mains 75-720B; ⊘11am-10pm; ⚓Tha Chang) The restaurant of the Royal Navy Association has one of the few coveted riverfront locations along this stretch of the Chao Phraya. Locals come for the combination of riverfront views and cheap and tasty seafood-based eats – ostensibly not for the cafeteria-like atmosphere. The entrance to the restaurant is near the ATM machines at Tha Chang.

RUB AROON
CENTRAL THAI $

Map p252 (Th Maha Rat; mains 75-120B; ⊘8am-6pm; ⚓Tha Tien) This traveller-friendly cafe is a pleasant escape from sightseeing in Ko Ratanakosin. The restored shopfront opens directly out to the street with cosy seating and patient service. The dishes are basic and satisfying, served alongside fruit drinks and coffees for sipping away tropical fatigue.

LOCAL KNOWLEDGE

ROLLIN' ON THE... CANAL

For an up-close view of Thonburi's famed canals, long-tail boats are available for charter at Ko Ratanakosin piers Tha Chang and Tha Tien. Prices at these piers are slightly higher than elsewhere and allow little room for negotiation, but you stand the least chance of being taken for a ride or being hit up for tips and other unexpected fees.

Trips explore the canals **Khlong Bangkok Noi** and **Khlong Bangkok Yai**, taking in the Royal Barges National Museum, Wat Arun and a riverside temple with fish feeding. Longer trips diverge into **Khlong Mon**, between Bangkok Noi and Bangkok Yai, which offers more typical canal scenery, including orchid farms. On weekends, you have the option of visiting the Taling Chan Floating Market (p167). However, it's worth pointing out that to actually disembark and explore any of these sights, the most common tour of one hour (1000B, up to six people) is simply not enough time and you'll most likely need 1½ (1300B) or two hours (1600B). Most operators have set tour routes, but if you have a specific destination in mind, you can request it.

A cheaper alternative is to take the **commuter long-tail boat** (per hr 50B; ⊘4-7pm) that also departs from Tha Chang, although it's one way only and you'll have to find your own way back from Bang Yai, located at the distant northern end of Khlong Bangkok Noi.

🍷 DRINKING & NIGHTLIFE

As with restaurants, bars are a rare sight in Ko Ratanakosin, with Amorosa being the only option. Luckily, the bars of Banglamphu are only a short taxi ride away.

AMOROSA   BAR
Map p252 (www.arunresidence.com; rooftop, Arun Residence, 36-38 Soi Pratu Nokyung; ⊘5.30pm-midnight Mon-Thu, to 1am Fri-Sun; 🛳Tha Tien) Perched above the Arun Residence, Amorosa takes advantage of a location directly above the river and opposite Wat Arun to make it one of the best places for a sundowner in Bangkok. The cocktails aren't going to blow you away, but watching boats ply their way along the royal river as Wat Arun is lit up behind is richly evocative of traditional images of the East. A memorable end to a day or start to an evening.

☆ ENTERTAINMENT

NATIONAL THEATRE   THEATRE
Map p252 (⌛0 2224 1352; 2 Th Ratchini; tickets 60-100B; 🛳Tha Chang) After a lengthy renovation, the National Theatre is again open for business. Performances of *kŏhn*, masked dance-drama often depicting scenes from the *Ramayana*, are held on the first and second Sundays of the month; *lá kon*, Thai dance-dramas, are held on the first Friday of the month; and Thai musical performances are held on the third Friday of the month.

PATRAVADI THEATRE   THEATRE
Map p252 (www.facebook.com/patravaditheatre; 69/1 Soi Sala Ton Chan; tickets from 500B; ⊘show times vary; 🛳Tha Chang) Patravadi is Bangkok's sole modern-dance venue. The dance-troupe performance is a blend of traditional Thai dance and modern choreography, music and costume. The theatre is also ground zero for the Bangkok International Fringe Festival, held in January and February.

🏃 SPORTS & ACTIVITIES

WAT MAHATHAT   MEDITATION
Map p252 (3 Th Maha Rat; 🛳Tha Chang) This temple is home to two independently operating meditation centres. The **International Buddhist Meditation Center** (Map p252; ⌛0 2222 6011; www.centermeditation.org; Section 5, Wat Mahathat; donations accepted) offers informal daily meditation classes at 7am, 1pm and 6pm. Taught by English-speaking Prasuputh Chainikom (Kosalo), classes last three hours. The **Meditation Study and Retreat Center** (Map p252; ⌛0 223 6878; www.meditation-watmahadhat.com; Wat Mahathat; donations accepted) offers a regimented daily program of meditation. Longer stays, including accommodation and food, can be arranged at both, but students are expected to follow a strict regimen of conduct.

WHAT'S IN A NAME?

Upon completion of the royal district in 1785, at a three-day consecration ceremony attended by tens of thousands of Siamese, the capital of Siam was given a new name: 'Krungthep mahanakhon amonratanakosin mahintara ayuthaya mahadilok popnopparat ratchathani burirom udomratchaniwet mahasathan amonpiman avatansathit sakkathattiya witsanukamprasit'. This lexical gymnastic feat translates roughly as: 'Great City of Angels, the Repository of Divine Gems, the Great Land Unconquerable, the Grand and Prominent Realm, the Royal and Delightful Capital City full of Nine Noble Gems, the Highest Royal Dwelling and Grand Palace, the Divine Shelter and Living Place of Reincarnated Spirits'.

Understandably, foreign traders continued to call the capital Bang Makok, which eventually truncated itself to 'Bangkok', the name most commonly known to the outside world. These days all Thais understand 'Bangkok' but use a shortened version of the official name, Krung Thep (City of Angels). When referring to greater Bangkok, they talk about Krung Thep Mahanakhon (Metropolis of the City of Angels). Expats living in Bangkok have numerous nicknames for their adopted home, with the Big Mango being the most common.

MEDITATIONS ON MEDITATION

Prasuputh Chainikom (Kosalo) is a meditation master at Wat Mahathat.

Why did you become a monk? I can develop my own life and help other people.

Why teach foreigners? I have English skills and experience with meditation – most Thai monks don't have these skills.

Why are so many foreigners interested in meditation? We're all stressed. Meditation teaches us how to relax our minds. If we know how to relax, we can find peace.

Can one study meditation if one is not Buddhist or has no experience? Yes. When we practice meditation, we're not thinking of the Buddha, we're just trying to make our minds empty.

What benefits does meditation provide? 1. It purifies your mind. 2. It gets rid of sorrow and lamentation. 3. It gets rid of physical and mental suffering. 4. It helps us understand the truth of life. 5. You can extinguish suffering and attain Nirvana. Five is difficult, but if you try, you can attain one to four.

WAT PHO THAI TRADITIONAL MEDICAL AND MASSAGE SCHOOL   MASSAGE

Map p252 (☑0 2622 3550; www.watpomassage. com; 392/25-28 Soi Phen Phat; tuition from 9500B; ☺8am-6pm; ☒Tha Tien) Associated with the nearby temple of the same name, this pint-sized institute offers basic and advanced courses in traditional massage; basic courses offer 30 hours spread out over five days and cover either general massage or foot massage. The advanced level spans 60 hours, requires the basic course as a prerequisite, and covers therapeutic and healing massage. Other advanced courses include oil massage and aromatherapy, and infant and child massage. The school is outside the temple compound in a restored Bangkok shophouse at the end of unmarked Soi Phen Phat; look for Coconut Palm restaurant.

SEGWAY TOUR THAILAND   TOUR

Map p252 (☑0 2221 4525; www.segwaytourthai land.com; Maharaj Pier Building, Tha Maharaj, off Th Maha Rat; half-day tours from 3500B; ☺9.30am-6.30pm Tue-Sun; ☒Tha Chang) Bicycles are so 20th-century – explore Bangkok from the, er, platform of an electronic Segway. This outfit runs half-day and full-day Segway tours in and around Bangkok, including excursions among the ruins in Ayuthaya.

Old Bangkok: Banglamphu

Neighbourhood Top Five

1 Visiting Th Khao San: more than just freaks in dreadlocks and fisherman pants, it's a unique cultural melting pot with something for (almost) everyone (p82).

2 Taking in the panoramic views of old Bangkok from **Golden Mount** (p78).

3 Tasting classic Bangkok-style nosh at old-school restaurants such as **Krua Apsorn** (p76) and **Jay Fai** (p76).

4 Dancing on the tables with Thai hipsters at **Brick Bar** (p80).

5 Sitting and gazing at the huge Buddha and sky-high murals in **Wat Suthat** (p77).

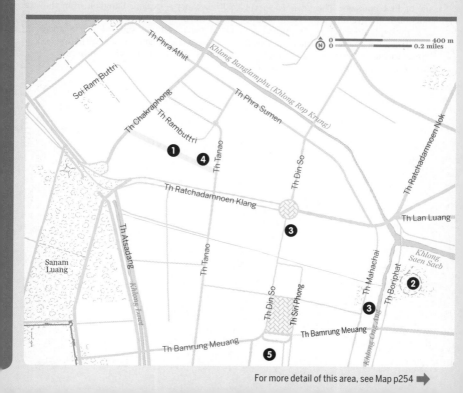

For more detail of this area, see Map p254 ➡

Explore: Banglamphu

Antique shophouses, classic restaurants, ancient temples...Banglamphu is old Bangkok encapsulated in one leafy, breezy district. If you've come for the sights, arrive early while the heat is still tolerable and the touts few. It's worth sticking around Banglamphu for lunch, as this is when the majority of the area's street stalls and shophouse restaurants are operating. Come evening, young locals flood the area in search of a cheap meal and a beer, giving the area an entirely different vibe, but there are enough restaurants and bars here that there's no need to consider another destination for the night.

Despite being one of the city's best areas for accommodation, sights, eating and nightlife, Banglamphu is also among Bangkok's most impenetrable 'hoods. During the day, a good strategy is to approach the area from the river ferry pier at Tha Phra Athit (Banglamphu) – most of the sights are within walking distance. At night, most of the action is centered around Th Khao San, which can be accessed via taxi from the BTS stop at National Stadium or the MRT stop at Hua Lamphong.

Local Life

➡ **Local Cuisine** Bangkok's most traditional district is not surprisingly one of the best places to try authentic central Thai and Bangkok-style food.

➡ **Street-side Shopping** The spectrum of goods available in this district ranges from backpacker staples along Th Khao San to Thai curry pastes and quality handicrafts in the more traditional areas nearby.

➡ **Pop & Lock** Most evenings the wide expanse in front of Bangkok's City Hall becomes a gathering place for kids who meet to practice their break-dancing.

➡ **Bangkok's Champs Élysées** The royal boulevard of Th Ratchadamnoen Klang serves to link the Grand Palace in Ko Ratanakosin with newer palaces in Dusit, and is suitably adorned with billboard-sized pictures of the king, queen and other royal family members.

➡ **Lucky Number** Because the national lottery office has its office nearby, both sides of Th Ratchadamnoen Klang east of the Democracy Monument are often clogged with vendors selling lottery tickets.

Getting There & Away

➡ **River boat** Tha Phra Athit (Banglamphu).

➡ **Taxi** From the BTS stops at National Stadium or Phaya Thai.

➡ **Klorng boat** Tha Phan Fah.

➡ **Bus** Air-con 44, 79, 503 and 511; ordinary 2, 15, 49, 59, 60, 69 and 70.

Lonely Planet's Top Tip

Boats – both the Chao Phraya River Express and the *klorng* (canal, also spelt *khlong*) boats – are a steady, if slow, way to reach Banglamphu, but remember that they only run until about 8pm on weekdays, 7pm on weekends.

✖ Best Places to Eat

➡ Krua Apsorn (p76)
➡ Jay Fai (p76)
➡ Shoshana (p77)
➡ Hemlock (p77)

For reviews, see p76 ➡

☕ Best Places to Drink

➡ Hippie de Bar (p79)
➡ Phranakorn Bar (p79)
➡ Club Culture (p79)
➡ Madame Musur (p79)

For reviews, see p79 ➡

🔒 Best Places to Shop

➡ Th Khao San Market (p80)
➡ Nittaya Curry Shop (p82)
➡ Taekee Taekon (p82)

For reviews, see p80 ➡

⊙ SIGHTS

PHRA SUMEN FORT & SANTICHAIPRAKAN PARK
FORT, PARK

Map p254 (ป้อมพระสุเมรุ/สวนสันติชัยปราการ; Th Phra Athit; admission free; ⊙5am-10pm; ⬚Tha Phra Athit (Banglamphu)) Beside Mae Nam Chao Phraya in Banglamphu stands one of Bangkok's original 18th-century forts. Built in 1783 to defend against potential naval invasions and named for the mythical Phra Sumen (Mt Meru) of Hindu-Buddhist cosmology, the octagonal brick-and-stucco bunker was one of 14 city watchtowers that punctuated the old city wall alongside Khlong Rop Krung (now Khlong Banglamphu but still called Khlong Rop Krung on most signs). Apart from Mahakan Fort, this is the only one still standing.

Alongside the fort and fronting the river is a small, grassy park with an open-air pavilion, river views, cool breezes and a bohemian mix of alternative young Thais and fisherman-pants-wearing, fire-stick-twirling backpackers. It's an interesting place to sit, people-watch and see what are said to be the last two *lam·poo* trees in Banglamphu.

WAT BOWONNIWET
BUDDHIST TEMPLE

Map p254 (วัดบวรนิเวศวิหาร; www.watbowon.org; Th Phra Sumen; admission free; ⊙8.30am-5pm; ⬚Tha Phra Athit (Banglamphu)) Founded in 1826, Wat Bowonniwet (Wat Bowon) is the national headquarters for the Thammayut monastic sect, a reformed version of Thai Buddhism. Rama IV (King Mongkut; r 1851–68), who set out to be a scholar, not a king, founded the Thammayuts and began the royal tradition of ordination at this temple. In fact, Mongkut was the abbot of Wat Bowon for several years. Rama IX (King Bhumibol Adulyadej; r 1946–present) and Crown Prince Vajiralongkorn, as well as several other males in the royal family, have been ordained as monks here. Because of its royal status, visitors should be particularly careful to dress properly for admittance to this *wát* – shorts and sleeveless clothing are not allowed.

The murals in the panels of the *ubosot* (chapel) of this temple are noteworthy, and include Thai depictions of Western life (possibly copied from magazine illustrations) during the early 19th century.

TOOT YUNG
ART GALLERY

Map p254 (www.tootyunggallery.com; ⊙6pm-1am Thur-Sat; ⬚Tha Phan Fah) This funky shophouse gallery features the work of young Thai artists, and also doubles as an artsy bar.

DEMOCRACY MONUMENT
MONUMENT

Map p254 (อนุสาวรีย์ประชาธิปไตย; Th Ratchadamnoen Klang; admission free; ⊙24hr; ⬚Tha Phan Fah) The Democracy Monument is the focal point of the grand, European-style boulevard that is Th Ratchadamnoen Klang. As the name suggests, it was erected to commemorate Thailand's momentous transformation from absolute to constitutional monarchy. It was designed by Thai architect Mew Aphaiwong and the relief sculptures were created by Italian Corrado Feroci who, as Silpa Bhirasri, gives his name to Silpakorn University. Feroci combined the square-jawed 'heroes of socialism' style popular at the time with Mew Aphaiwong's art deco influences and keen sense of relevant revolutionary dates.

There are 75 cannonballs around the base, to signify the year BE (Buddhist Era) 2475 (AD 1932); the four wings of the monument stand 24m tall, representing 24 June, the day the constitution was signed; and the central plinth stands 3m high (June was then the third month in the Thai calendar) and supports a chiselled constitution. Each wing has bas-reliefs depicting soldiers, police and civilians who helped usher in the modern Thai state.

During the era of military dictatorships, demonstrators often assembled here to call for a return to democracy, most notably in 1973 and 1992.

OCTOBER 14 MEMORIAL
MONUMENT

Map p254 (อนุสรณ์สถาน ๑๔ ตุลา; cnr Th Ratchadamnoen Klang & Th Tanao; admission free; ⊙24hr; ⬚Tha Phan Fah) A peaceful amphitheatre commemorates the civilian demonstrators who were killed by the military during a pro-democracy rally on 14 October 1973. Over 200,000 people had assembled at the Democracy Monument and along the length of Th Ratchadamnoen to protest against the arrest of political campaigners and continuing military dictatorship. Although some in Thailand continue to deny it, photographs confirm that more than 70 demonstrators were killed when the tanks met the crowd. The complex is an interesting adaptation of Thai temple architecture for a secular and political purpose. A central *chedi* (stupa) is dedicated to the fallen and a gallery of historic photographs lines the interior wall.

SAO CHING-CHA   MONUMENT

Map p254 (เสาชิงช้า | Giant Swing; Th Bamrung Meuang; ☺24hr; ⊠Tha Phan Fah) It is easy to forget the powers of the Brahmans in Thai Buddhism, unless you happen upon the giant red poles of Sao Ching-Cha (the Giant Swing). During the second lunar month (usually in January), Brahman beliefs dictate that Shiva comes down to earth for a 10-day residence and should be welcomed by great ceremonies and, in the past, great degrees of daring. Each year, the acrobatic and desperate braved the Giant Swing. The ceremony saw these men swing in ever-higher arcs in an effort to reach a bag of gold suspended from a 15m bamboo pole. Whoever grabbed the gold could keep it. But that was no mean feat, and deaths were as common as successes. A black-and-white photo illustrating the risky rite can be seen at the ticket counter at adjacent Wat Suthat.

The Brahmans enjoyed a mystical position within the royal court, primarily in the coronation rituals. But after the 1932 revolution, the Brahmans' waning power was effectively terminated and the festival, including the swinging, was discontinued during the reign of Rama VII (King Prajadhipok; r 1925–35). In 2007 the Giant Swing was replaced with a newer model, made from six giant teak logs from Phrae, in northern Thailand. The previous version is kept at the National Museum.

TH BAMRUNG MEUANG
RELIGIOUS SHOPS   SHOPPING DISTRICT

Map p254 (ถนนบำรุงเมือง; Th Bamrung Meuang; ☺9am-6pm; ⊠Tha Phan Fah) The stretch of Th Bamrung Meuang (one of Bangkok's oldest streets and originally an elephant path leading to the Grand Palace) from Th Mahachai to Th Tanao is lined with shops selling all manner of Buddhist religious paraphernalia. You probably don't need a Buddha statue or an eerily lifelike model of a famous monk, but looking is fun and who knows when you might need to do a great deal of merit making. Behind the storefronts, back-room workshops produce gigantic bronze Buddha images for wát all over Thailand.

BAN BAAT   ARTISANS VILLAGE

Map p254 (บ้านบาตร | Monk's Bowl Village; Soi Ban Baat; ☺8am-5pm; ⊠Tha Phan Fah) Ban Baat is the only remaining village of three established in Bangkok by Rama I (King Phraphutthayotfa; r 1782–1809) for the purpose of handcrafting *bàht* (monk's bowls), the ceremonial bowls used to collect alms from the faithful each morning. As cheaper factory-made bowls are now the norm, the artisanal tradition has shrunk to about half a dozen families. You can observe the process of hammering the bowls together from eight separate pieces of steel, said to represent Buddhism's Eightfold Path. The joints are then fused with melted copper wire, and the bowl is beaten, polished and coated with several layers of black lacquer. A typical *bàht*-smith's output is one large bowl per day; more if they are smaller bowls.

The alms bowls are sold for between 600B and 2000B and make great souvenirs. To find the village, walk south on Th Boriphat, south of Th Bamrung Meuang, then follow the signs into narrow Soi Ban Baat.

WAT RATCHANATDA   BUDDHIST TEMPLE

Map p254 (วัดราชนัดดาราม; cnr Th Ratchadamnoen Klang & Th Mahachai; admission free; ☺8am-5pm; ⊠Tha Phan Fah) Across Th Mahachai from the Golden Mount, this temple is most stunning at night when the 37 spires of the all-metal **Loha Prasat** (Metal Palace) are lit up like a medieval birthday cake. It was built for Rama III (King Phranangklao; r 1824–51) in the 1840s in honour of his granddaughter. The design is said to derive from metal temples built in India and Sri Lanka more than 2000 years ago. The 37 spires represent the 37 virtues that lead to enlightenment. Recently restored, the interior is relatively unadorned by Thai temple standards, but the hallways and square edges contribute to a symmetry reminiscent of the much earlier temples at Angkor, in Cambodia.

At the back of the compound, behind the formal gardens, is a well-known market selling Buddhist *prá krêu·ang* in all sizes, shapes and styles. These amulets feature images not only of Buddha, but also famous Thai monks and Indian deities. Full Buddha images are also for sale.

MAHAKAN FORT   FORT

Map p254 (ป้อมมหากาฬ; Th Ratchadamnoen Klang; ☺24hr; ⊠Tha Phan Fah) The area around white-washed Mahakan Fort, one of two surviving citadels that defended the old walled city, has recently been converted into a small park overlooking Khlong Ong Ang. The octagonal fort is a picturesque, if brief and hot, stop en route to Golden Mount, but the neighbouring village is more interesting. This small community of wooden houses has been here for more than 100 years. But since the mid-1990s it has fought the Bangkok municipal government's plan to demolish it and create a 'tourist' park. The community blocked progress and even proposed the development of another tourist attraction: a *li-gair* museum honouring the dance tradition that traces its creation to a school located here in 1897. Some of the homes were eventually demolished, resulting in the park you see today. Behind the fort many others remain (for now). Visitors are welcome. Climb the ramparts (not for children) running away from the fort and walk to the far end, where stairs lead down and into the village.

QUEEN'S GALLERY
ART GALLERY

Map p254 (www.queengallery.org; 101 Th Ratchadamnoen Klang; admission 30B; ☺10am-7pm Thu-Tue; ☒Tha Phan Fah) This royal-funded museum presents five floors of rotating exhibitions of modern and traditionally influenced art. The building is contemporary and the artists hail from the upper echelons of the conservative Thai art world. The attached shop is filled with books and gifts.

KING PRAJADHIPOK MUSEUM
MUSEUM

Map p254 (พิพิธภัณฑ์พระบาทสมเด็จพระปกเกล้าเจ้าอยู่หัว; 2 Th Lan Luang; admission 40B; ☺9am-4pm Tue-Sun; ☒Tha Phan Fah) This collection uses modern techniques to relate the rather dramatic life of Rama VII, while neatly documenting Thailand's transition from absolute to constitutional monarchy. The museum occupies a grand neocolonial-style building constructed on the orders of Rama V for his favourite firm of Bond St merchants; it was the only foreign business allowed on the royal road linking Bangkok's two palace districts.

The exhibitions reveal that Prajadhipok did not expect to become king, but once on the throne showed considerable diplomacy in dealing with what was, in effect, a revolution fomented by a new intellectual class of Thais. The 1st floor deals with the life of Queen Rambhai Barni, while the upper two floors cover the king's own life. It reveals, for example, that the army officer–turned-king spent many of his formative years in Europe where he became fond of British democracy. Ironically, those plotting his downfall had themselves learned of democracy during years of European education. A coup, carried out while the king and queen were playing golf, ended Thailand's absolute monarchy in 1932. Prajadhipok's reign eventually ended when he abdicated while in England in 1935; he died there in 1941.

✖ EATING

Banglamphu is famous for its old-school Thai food – the dominant cuisine in this part of town. For something more international, head to Th Khao San, where you'll find a few international fast-food franchises as well as foreign and vegetarian restaurants.

⧉TOP CHOICE KRUA APSORN
THAI $$

Map p254 (www.kruaapsorn.com; Th Din So; mains 65-350B; ☺10.30am-8pm Mon-Sat; ☒Tha Phan Fah) This homey dining room is a favourite of members of the Thai royal family and, back in 2006, was recognised as Bangkok's Best Restaurant by the *Bangkok Post*. Must-eat dishes include mussels fried with fresh herbs, the decadent crab fried in yellow chilli oil and the *tortilla Española*–like crab omelette. There's another branch on Th Samsen.

JAY FAI
THAI $$

Map p254 (327 Th Mahachai; mains from 400B; ☺3pm-2am; ☒Tha Phan Fah) You wouldn't think so by looking at her bare-bones dining room, but Jay Fai is known far and wide for serving Bangkok's most expensive *pàt kêe mow* (drunkard's noodles – wide rice noodles fried with seafood and Thai herbs). The price is justified by the copious fresh seafood, as well as Jay Fai's distinct frying style that results in a virtually oil-free finished product. Jay Fai is located in a virtually unmarked shophouse on Th Mahachai, directly across from a 7-Eleven.

LOCAL KNOWLEDGE

WHAT'S YOUR NAME?

Banglamphu means 'Place of Lamphu', a reference to the *lam-poo* tree (*Duabanga grandiflora*) that was once prevalent in the area.

TOP SIGHTS
WAT SUTHAT

The main attraction at Wat Suthat is Thailand's biggest *wí·hăhn* (main chapel) and the imperious yet serene 8m-high **Phra Si Sakayamuni** that resides within. The Buddha image is Thailand's largest surviving Sukhothai-period bronze, cast in the former capital in the 14th century. Today the ashes of Rama VIII (King Ananda Mahidol; r 1935–46) are contained in the base of the image.

Colourful, if now somewhat faded, *Jataka* (murals depicting scenes from the Buddha's life) cover every wall and pillar. The deep-relief wooden doors are also impressive and were carved by artisans including Rama II (King Phraphutthaloetla Naphalai; r 1809–24) himself.

Behind the *wí·hăhn*, the ordination hall is the largest in the country. To add to its list of 'largests', Wat Suthat holds the rank of Rachavoramahavihan, the highest royal temple grade. It maintains a special place in the national religion because of its association with the Brahman priests who perform important ceremonies, such as the Royal Ploughing Ceremony in May. These priests also perform religious rites at two Hindu shrines near the *wát* – **Dhevasathan** (Map p254) on Th Din So, and the smaller **Saan Jao Phitsanu** on Th Siri Phong.

DON'T MISS...

➡ Phra Si Sakayamuni
➡ Temple murals

PRACTICALITIES

➡ วัดสุทัศน์
➡ Map p254
➡ Th Bamrung Meuang
➡ admission 20B
➡ ⏱8am-9pm
➡ 🚌10, 12, 🚤Tha Phan Fah

SHOSHANA
ISRAELI **$**

Map p254 (88 Th Chakraphong; mains 60-220B; ⏱lunch & dinner; 🌱; 🚤Tha Phra Athit (Banglamphu)) One of Th Khao San's longest-running Israeli restaurants, Shoshana resembles your grandparents' living room, right down to the tacky wall art and plastic placemats. The 'I heart Shoshana' T-shirts worn by the wait staff may be a hopelessly optimistic description of employee morale, but the gut-filling chips-felafel-and-hummus plates leave nothing to be desired.

HEMLOCK
THAI **$**

Map p254 (56 Th Phra Athit; mains 60-220B; ⏱4pm-midnight; 🌱; 🚤Tha Phra Athit/Banglamphu) Taking full advantage of its cosy shophouse location, this perennial favourite has enough style to feel like a special night out but doesn't skimp on flavour or preparation. The eclectic menu reads like an ancient literary work, reviving old dishes from aristocratic kitchens across the country. Try the flavourful *mêe·ang kam* (wild tea leaves wrapped around ginger, shallots, peanuts, lime and shredded coconut) or *yam kà·moy* (thieves' salad).

THIP SAMAI
THAI **$**

Map p254 (www.thipsamai.com; 313 Th Mahachai; mains 25-120B; ⏱5.30pm-1.30am; 🚤Tha Phan Fah) Brace yourself, but you should be aware that the fried noodles sold from carts along Th Khao San have nothing to do with the dish known as *pàt tai*. Luckily, less than a five-minute túk-túk ride away lies Thip Samai, also known by locals as *pàt tai ฝà·doo pěe,* and home to the most legendary *pàt tai* in town. For something a bit different, try the delicate egg-wrapped version, or the *pàt tai* fried with *man gûng,* decadent shrimp fat. Closed on alternate Wednesdays.

POJ SPA KAR
THAI **$**

Map p254 (443 Th Tanao; mains 100-200B; ⏱lunch & dinner; 🚤Tha Phan Fah) Pronounced *pôht sà·pah kahn,* this is allegedly the oldest restaurant in Bangkok, continuing to maintain recipes handed down from a former palace cook. Be sure to order the simple but tasty lemon grass omelette or the deliciously sour-sweet *gaang sôm,* a traditional central Thai soup.

TOP SIGHTS
GOLDEN MOUNT & WAT SAKET

Before glass and steel towers began growing out of Bangkok's riverine plain, the massive **Golden Mount** (ภูเขาทอง, Phu Khao Thong; Map p254) was the only structure to make any significant impression on the horizon. The mount was commissioned by Rama III (King Phranangklao; r 1824–51), who ordered that the earth dug out to create Bangkok's expanding *klorng* (canal) network be piled up to build a 100m-high, 500m-wide *chedi* (stupa). As the hill grew, the weight became too much for the soft soil beneath and the project was abandoned until his successor built a small gilded *chedi* on its crest and added trees to stave off erosion. Rama V (King Chulalongkorn; r 1886–1910) later added to the structure and interred a Buddha relic from India in the *chedi*. The walls were added during WWII. At the peak is a 360-degree view of Bangkok's most photogenic side.

Next door, seemingly peaceful **Wat Saket** (วัดสระเกศ; Map p254) contains murals that are among both the most beautiful and the goriest in the country; proceed directly to the pillar behind the Buddha statue for explicit depictions of Buddhist hell. In November there's a festival in the grounds that includes an enchanting candlelight procession up the Golden Mount.

DON'T MISS...

➡ View from summit of Golden Mount

➡ Temple paintings at Wat Saket

PRACTICALITIES

➡ ภูเขาทอง & วัดสระเกศ

➡ Th Boriphat

➡ admission to summit of Golden Mount 10B

➡ ⏱7.30am-5.30pm

➡ 🚤Tha Phan Fah

ROTI-MATABA
MUSLIM-THAI $

Map p254 (136 Th Phra Athit; mains 50-90B; ⏱9am-10pm Tue-Sun; 🚤Tha Phra Athit/Banglamphu) This classic Bangkok eatery may have become a bit too big for its britches in recent years, but it still serves tasty Thai-Muslim dishes such as roti, *gaang mát·sà·màn* (Muslim curry), a brilliantly sour fish curry, and *má·tà·bà* (a sort of stuffed Muslim-style pancake). An upstairs air-con dining area and outdoor tables provide barely enough seating for its loyal fans.

CHOTE CHITR
THAI $

Map p254 (146 Th Phraeng Phuton; mains 30-200B; ⏱11am-10pm; 🚤Tha Phan Fah) This third-generation shophouse restaurant boasting just six tables is a Bangkok foodie landmark. The kitchen can be inconsistent and the service consistently grumpy, but when they're on, dishes like *mèe gròrp* (crispy fried noodles) and *yam tòoa ploo* (wing-bean salad) are in a class of their own.

BAAN PHRA ARTHIT
CAFE $

Map p254 (Coffee & More; 102/1 Th Phra Athit; mains 50-120B; ⏱10am-9pm Sun-Thu, to 10pm Fri-Sat; 🚤Tha Phra Athit/Banglamphu) When

only air-conditioning will do, why not do it in style? This classy cafe features a few basic Western-Thai fusion dishes, decent coffee, and even better cakes and sweets. And all of this for less than the price of a latte back at home.

ANN'S SWEET
CAFE $

Map p254 (138 Th Phra Athit; mains 75-150B; ⏱10am-10pm; 🚤Tha Phra Athit/Banglamphu) Anshada, a native of Bangkok and a graduate of the Cordon Bleu cooking program, makes some of the most authentic Western-style desserts in Bangkok. Come to her cozy cafe for coffee and her mouth-watering sweets.

KIMLENG
THAI $

Map p254 (158-160 Th Tanao; mains 20-60B; ⏱10am-10pm Mon-Sat; 🚤Tha Phan Fah) This tiny family-run restaurant specialises in the dishes and flavours of central Thailand. It's a good place to whet your appetite with an authentic *yam* (Thai-style salad) such as *yam ƀlah dùk foo,* a mixture of crispy catfish and mango. Located on Th Tanao across from the October 14 Memorial.

PHEN THAI FOOD THAI $

Map p254 (Th Rambutri; mains 50-90B; ⊙11.30am-10pm; 🚤Tha Phra Athit/Banglamphu) If you're looking for authentic Thai but don't want to stray far from the comforts of Th Khao San, this street-side eatery is your best bet. Simply look for the overflowing tray of prepared dishes, point to what you want and Phen will plate it up for you. The clientele is decidedly international, but the flavours wholly domestic.

🍷 DRINKING & NIGHTLIFE

⌑TOP CHOICE⌐ HIPPIE DE BAR BAR

Map p254 (46 Th Khao San; ⊙6pm-2am; 🚤Tha Phra Athit/Banglamphu) Our vote for Banglamphu's best bar, Hippie boasts a funky retro vibe, indoor and outdoor seating, and a soundtrack you're unlikely to hear elsewhere in town. Despite being located smack-dab in the middle of Th Khao San, there are surprisingly few foreign faces, and it's a great place to make some new Thai friends.

PHRANAKORN BAR BAR

Map p254 (58/2 Soi Damnoen Klang Tai; 🚤Tha Phan Fah) It must have taken a true visionary to transform this characterless multilevel building into a warm, fun destination for a night out. Located an arm's length from the hype of Th Khao San, Phranakorn Bar is a home away from hovel for students and arty types, with eclectic decor and changing gallery exhibits. Our tip: head directly for the breezy rooftop and order some of the bar's cheap 'n tasty Thai food.

Although Th Khao San remains associated with foreign tourists, in recent years it's also become a popular nightlife destination for young locals. Check out the live-music pubs along Th Phra Athit or the low-key bars south of Th Ratchadamnoen Klang for a more local drinking scene.

CLUB CULTURE NIGHTCLUB

Map p254 (www.club-culture-bkk.com; Th Ratchadamnoen Klang; admission from 250B; 🚤Tha Phan Fah) Housed in a seemingly abandoned four-storey building, Club Culture is the quirkiest member of Bangkok's club scene. Opening dates and times depend on events, so check the website first to see what's going on.

MADAME MUSUR BAR

Map p254 (41 Soi Ram Buttri; ⊙noon-1am; 🚤Tha Phra Athit (Banglamphu)) Saving you the trip north to Pai, Madame Musur pulls off that elusive combination of northern Thailand-meets-*The Beach*-meets-Th Khao San. It's an inviting place to chat, drink and people-watch. Serving a short menu of northern Thai dishes (including what some consider to be one of the city's better bowls of *kâo soy* – a northern-style curry noodle soup), it's also not a bad place to eat.

TAKSURA BAR

Map p254 (156/1 Th Tanao; 🚤Tha Phan Fah) There's little English-language signage to lead you to this 90-year-old mansion in the heart of old Bangkok, which is all the better, according to the overwhelmingly Thai, uni/artsy crowd that frequents the place. Take a seat outside to soak up the breezes

---

VEG OUT IN BANGLAMPHU

Due to the strong foreign influence, there's an abundance of vegetarian restaurants in the Banglamphu area. In addition to Hemlock (p77) and Shoshana (p77), which have hefty meat-free sections, the meat-free dining destinations include:

Arawy Vegetarian Food (Map p254; 152 Th Din So; mains 20-40B; ⊙7am-8pm; 🖉; 🚤Tha Phan Fah) Housed in a narrow shophouse, Arawy ('Delicious') has heaps of prepared meat-free curries, dips and stir-fries.

Ranee Guesthouse (Map p254; 77 Trok Mayom; mains 70-320B; ⊙8am-10pm; 🖉; 🚤Tha Phra Athit/Banglamphu) A guesthouse-bound restaurant with an extensive vegie menu.

May Kaidee's (Map p254; www.maykaidee.com; 33 Th Samsen; mains 50-100B; ⊙9am-10pm; 🖉; 🚤Tha Phra Athit/Banglamphu) A longstanding restaurant that also houses a vegie Thai cooking school.

STREET TROUBADOURS

Banglamphu is home to Bangkok's greatest concentration of live-music bars. The western stretch of Th Phra Athit in particular boasts almost a dozen back-to-back pint-sized music pubs that offer lots of loud Thai pop, but not a lot of breathing room.

For something a bit more approachable, head to Th Khao San's chilled-out next door neighbour, Th Rambuttri, where there's an abundance of open-air live-music pubs including the bluesy **Barlamphu** (Map p254; Th Rambuttri; ⏰11am-2am; 🚢Tha Phra Athit), the poppier **Suksabai** (Map p254; 96 Th Rambuttri; ⏰24hr; 🚢Tha Phra Athit) and **Molly Bar** (Map p254; 108 Th Rambuttri; ⏰8pm-1am; 🚢Tha Phra Athit), and reggae-influenced **Orchid Bar** (Map p254; Th Rambuttri; ⏰8pm-1am; 🚢Tha Phra Athit).

Elsewhere, Th Khao San is home to one of our favourite places in Bangkok for live music, Brick Bar (p80). And just around the corner is Gazebo (p80), which occasionally hosts indie Thai rock bands, while Ad Here the 13th (p80), a Bangkok blues legend, is only a couple of blocks away.

and go domestic by ordering some spicy nibbles with your drinks.

CAFÉ DEMOC — NIGHTCLUB

Map p254 (www.cafe-democ.com; 78 Th Ratchadamnoen Klang; admission free; 🚢Tha Phan Fah) Up-and-coming DJs present their turntable dexterity and occasional live-music acts perform at this narrow unpretentious club in old Bangkok. Hip hop, break beat, drum and bass and tribal fill the night roster, but only special events actually fill the floor.

ROLLING BAR — BAR

Map p254 (Th Prachathipatai; 🚢Tha Phan Fah) An escape from hectic Th Khao San is a good-enough excuse to schlep to this quiet canal-side boozer. Live music and capable bar snacks are good reasons to stay.

CLUB — NIGHTCLUB

Map p254 (www.theclubkhaosan.com; 123 Th Khao San; admission free; 🚢Tha Phra Athit (Banglamphu)) Located right in the middle of Th Khao San, this cavernlike dance hall hosts a fun mix of locals and backpackers.

★ ENTERTAINMENT

TOP CHOICE BRICK BAR — LIVE MUSIC

Map p254 (basement, Buddy Lodge, 265 Th Khao San; ⏰8pm-1am; 🚢Tha Phra Athit (Banglamphu)) This basement pub, one of our fave destinations in Bangkok for live music, hosts a nightly revolving cast of bands for an almost exclusively Thai crowd – most of whom will end the night dancing on the tables. Brick Bar can get infamously packed,

so be sure to get there early if you want a table to rest your bottle of whiskey on.

GAZEBO — LIVE MUSIC

Map p254 (www.gazebobkk.com; 3rd fl, 44 Th Chakraphong; ⏰6pm-late; 🚢Tha Phra Athit (Banglamphu)) This vaguely Middle Eastern–themed bar represents the posh alter ego of Th Khao San. There's live music, lounges for sucking down a sheesha, and a dark club. The bar's elevated setting appears to lend it some leniency with the city's strict closing times, but guys are advised to arrive before 11pm to avoid the 300B admission fee.

AD HERE THE 13TH — LIVE MUSIC

Map p254 (13 Th Samsen; ⏰6pm-midnight; 🚢Tha Phra Athit (Banglamphu)) Located beside Khlong Banglamphu, Ad Here is everything a neighbourhood joint should be: lots of regulars, cold beer and heart-warming tunes delivered by a masterful house band starting at 10pm. Everyone knows each other, so don't be shy about mingling.

🛍 SHOPPING

TOP CHOICE TH KHAO SAN MARKET — MARKET

Map p254 (Th Khao San; ⏰10am-midnight Tue-Sun; 🚢Tha Phra Athit (Banglamphu)) The main guesthouse strip in Banglamphu is a day-and-night shopping bazaar, selling all but the baby and the bathwater. Cheap T-shirts, trendy purses, wooden frogs, fuzzy puppets, bootleg CDs, hemp clothing, fake student ID cards, knock-off designer wear, souvenirs, corn on the cob, orange juice... You name it, they've got it.

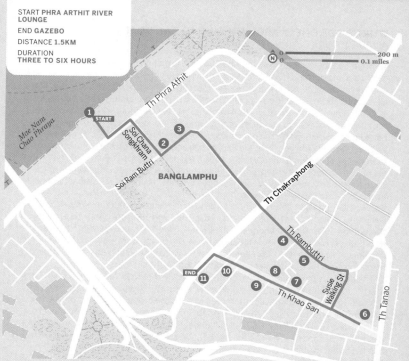

Neighbourhood Walk
Banglamphu Pub Crawl

You don't need to go too far to find a decent bar in Banglamphu, but why limit yourself to one? With this in mind, we've assembled a pub crawl that spans river views, people-watching, live music and late-night shenanigans.

Start your crawl with dinner and/or sunset drinks along Th Phra Athit. For intermittent Chao Phraya views try **1 Phra Arthit River Lounge**, an attractive wooden lounge-like bar with an open-air deck and comfy bean-bag seating.

From Th Phra Athit, enter Soi Chana Songkhram and take a left at Soi Ram Buttri, where you begin Phase Two of your crawl: people-watching. **2 Gecko Bar** is a frugal and fun place to gawk at other patrons and passers by, while a few doors down, **3 Madame Musur** offers the same perks, but with a bit more sophistication and tasty northern-style eats.

It's time to add some music to the mix, so for Phase Three, cross Th Chakraphong and head down Th Rambuttri towards one of the open-air live-music bars such as **4 Barlamphu** or **5 Molly Bar**.

At this point, you should be lubricated enough for the main event, so, crossing via Susie Walking St, proceed to Th Khao San. If you need a bathroom or a blast of air-con, make a pit stop at **6 Mulligans**, a tidy Irish-themed bar in Buddy Boutique Hotel. Otherwise, get a front-row view of the human parade from elevated **7 Roof Bar**, the ground-level **8 draught Singha stall** in front of 7-Eleven or from the noisy and buzzy **9 Center Khao San**.

End the night on a good note by planting yourself at **10 Hippie de Bar**, one of Banglamphu's best pubs. Or if 1am is too early to call it a night, crawl over to **11 Gazebo**, a rooftop lounge and disco that stays open until morning.

WHAT'S SO LONELY ABOUT THE KHAO SAN ROAD?
ANDREW BURKE

Th Khao San, better known as the Khao San Rd, is genuinely unlike anywhere else on earth. It's an international clearing house of people either entering the liberated state of travelling in Southeast Asia or returning to the coddling bonds of first-world life, all together in a neon-lit melting pot in Banglamphu. Its uniqueness is probably best illustrated by a question: apart from airports, where else could you share space with the citizens of dozens of countries at the same time, people ranging from first-time backpackers scoffing banana pancakes to 75-year-old grandparents ordering G&Ts, and everyone in between, including hippies, trendies, squares, style queens, package tourists, global nomads, people on a week's holiday and those taking a gap year, people of every colour and creed looking at you looking at them looking at everyone else?

Th Khao San (cow-sarn), meaning 'uncooked rice', is perhaps the most high-profile bastard child of the age of independent travel. Of course, it hasn't always been this way. For its first two centuries or so it was just another unremarkable road in old Bangkok. The first guesthouses appeared in 1982 and, as more backpackers arrived through the '80s, the old wooden homes were converted one by one into low-rent dosshouses. By the time Alex Garland's novel *The Beach* was published in 1997, with its opening scenes set in the seedier side of Khao San, staying here had become a rite of passage for backpackers coming to Southeast Asia.

The publicity from Garland's book and the movie that followed pushed Khao San into the mainstream, romanticising the seedy, and stereotyping the backpackers it attracted as unwashed and counterculturalist. It also brought the long-simmering debate about the relative merits of Th Khao San to the top of backpacker conversations. Was it cool to stay on KSR? Was it uncool? Was this 'real travel' or just an international anywhere surviving on the few baht Western backpackers spent before they headed home to start their high-earning careers? Was it really Thailand at all?

Perhaps one of Garland's characters summed it up most memorably when he said: 'You know, Richard, one of these days I'm going to find one of those Lonely Planet writers and I'm going to ask him, what's so fucking lonely about the Khao San Road?'

Today more than ever the answer would have to be: not that much. With the help of all that publicity, Khao San continued to evolve, with bedbug-infested guesthouses replaced by boutique hotels, and downmarket TV bars showing pirated movies transformed into hip design bars peopled by flashpackers in designer threads. But the most interesting change has been in the way Thais see Khao San.

Once written off as home to cheap, dirty *fa·ràng kêe ngók* (stingy foreigners), Banglamphu has become just about the coolest district in Bangkok. Attracted in part by the long-derided independent traveller and their modern ideas, the city's own counterculture kids have moved in and brought with them a tasty selection of small bars, organic cafes and shops. Indeed, Bangkok's indie crowd has proved to be the Thai spice this melting pot always lacked.

Not that Khao San has moved completely away from its backpacker roots. The strip still anticipates every traveller need: meals to soothe homesickness, cafes and bars for swapping travel tales about getting to the Cambodian border, tailors, travel agents, teeth whitening, secondhand books, hair braiding and the perennial Akha women trying to harass everyone they see into buying wooden frogs. No, it's not very lonely at all....

NITTAYA CURRY SHOP FOOD & DRINK
Map p254 (136-40 Th Chakhraphong; ⊘9am-7pm Mon-Sat; ⊡Tha Phra Athit (Banglamphu)) Follow your nose: Nittaya is famous throughout Thailand for her pungent but high-quality curry pastes. Pick up a couple of takeaway canisters for prospective dinner parties or peruse the snack and gift sections, where visitors to Bangkok load up on local specialities for friends back in the provinces.

TAEKEE TAEKON HANDICRAFTS
Map p254 (118 Th Phra Athit; ⊘9am-6pm Mon-Sat; ⊡Tha Phra Athit (Banglamphu)) This atmospheric shop has a decent selection of Thai textiles from the country's main silk-

producing areas, especially northern Thailand, as well as the type of assorted local knick-knackery and interesting postcards not widely available elsewhere.

SHAMAN BOOKSHOP BOOKSTORE
Map p254 (Th Khao San; ⊙9am-9pm; ⬟Tha Phra Athit/Banglamphu) With locations on Th Khao San and **Susie Walking St** (Map p254; Susie Walking St; ⊙9am-11pm; ⬟Tha Phra Athit/ Banglamphu), Shaman has the area's largest selection of used books. Titles can conveniently be searched on computer.

THAI NAKON HANDICRAFTS
Map p254 (79 Th Prachathipatai; ⊙10am-6pm Mon-Sat; ⬟Tha Phan Fah) This family-owned enterprise has been in business for 70 years and often fills commissions from the royal family for niolloware and silver ornaments. Silver-moulded cases and clutches, ceremonial bowls and tea sets are also among the offerings. If you can navigate the language barrier, ask to go behind the showroom to witness the aged artisans at work.

RIMKHOBFAH BOOKSTORE BOOKSTORE
Map p254 (78/1 Th Ratchadamnoen Klang; ⊙10am-7pm; ⬟Tha Phan Fah) Without having to commit loads of your suitcase space, you can sample an array of slim scholarly publications from the Fine Arts Department on Thai art and architecture.

SARABAN BOOKSTORE
Map p254 (106/1 Th Rambutri; ⊙9.30am-10.30pm; ⬟Tha Phan Fah) Stocking the largest selection of international newspapers and travel guides, this claustrophobic shop also has a good selection of used yarns.

🏃 SPORTS & ACTIVITIES

TOP CHOICE KHAO COOKING COURSE
Map p254 (☎08 9111 0947; www.khaocooking school.com; D&D Inn, 68-70 Th Khao San; lessons 1500B; ⊙9.30am-12.30pm & 1.30-4.30pm; ⬟Tha Phra Athit/Banglamphu) Although it's located smack dab in the middle of foreigner-dominated Khao San, this new cooking school was started up by an authority on Thai food and features instruction on a

LOOK, MA – NO HANDS!

Wandering around Bangkok, it's likely you'll encounter a group of men playing a volleyball-like game with a small plastic ball. Characterised by gravity-defying flips and spikes, the sport is known as *đà·grôr* (also spelt takraw, or known as sepak takraw).

Traditionally *đà·grôr* is played by men standing in a circle (the size of which depends on the number of players) and trying to keep the ball airborne by kicking it soccer-style. Points are scored for style, difficulty and variety of kicking manoeuvres. A modern variation of the game incorporates a net and the rules of volleyball, while only allowing contact with the ball using feet, knees and the head. *Đà·grôr* is also popular in several neighbouring countries and is a hotly contested sport in the Southeast Asian Games; at the 2011 games, Thailand won gold in four of the six categories.

wide variety of authentic dishes. Located in the courtyard directly behind D&D Inn.

VELO THAILAND BICYCLE TOURS
Map p254 (☎08 9201 7782; www.velothailand. com; 29 Soi 4, Th Samsen; tours from 1000B; ⊙10am-9pm; ⬟Tha Phra Athit/Banglamphu) Velo is a small and personal outfit based out of Banglamphu. Day and night tours to Thonburi and further afield are on offer.

SOR VORAPIN GYM THAI BOXING
Map p254 (☎0 2282 3551; www.thaiboxings.com; 13 Th Kasab; tuition per day/month 500/9000B; ⊙lessons 7.30-9.30am & 3-5pm; ⬟Tha Phra Athit/Banglamphu) Specialising in training foreign students of both genders, this gym is sweating distance from Th Khao San. Serious training is held at a gym outside the city.

GRASSHOPPER ADVENTURES BICYCLE TOURS
Map p254 (☎0 2280 0832; www.grasshopperadven tures.com; 57 Th Ratchadamnoen Klang; tours US$35-105; ⊙8.30am-6.30pm Mon-Fri; ⬟Tha Phan Fah) This lauded outfit runs a variety of unique bicycle tours in and around Bangkok, including a night tour and a tour of the city's green zones.

Dusit Palace Park & Around: Thewet & Dusit

Neighbourhood Top Five

1 Witnessing Victorian sense and Thai sensibilities merge in the former royal enclave of **Dusit Palace Park** (p86).

2 Cheering on Thai boxing – the sport that makes Steven Seagal look as soft as a pillow – at **Ratchadamnoen Stadium** (p90).

3 Sampling homestyle Thai food good enough for royalty at **Krua Apsorn** (p89).

4 Wondering what country you're in while among the Carrara marble, European-style frescoes and red carpet of **Wat Benchamabophit** (p88).

5 Enjoying the breezy, tasty riverside dining at **Kaloang Home Kitchen** (p89) or **Khinlom Chom Sa-Phan** (p90).

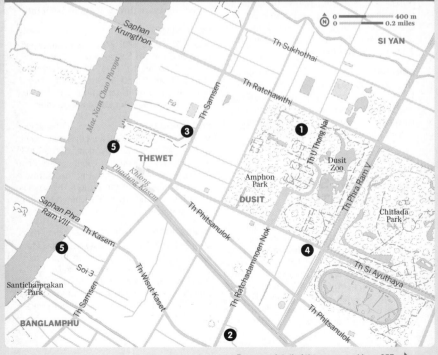

For more detail of this area, see Map p257 ➡

Explore: Thewet & Dusit

Thewet, particularly the area near Th Samsen, has the hectic, buzzy feel often associated with Bangkok: relentless traffic, throngs of civil servants and schoolkids, and a soggy market. The adjacent river is the only respite from the action, and most sights and restaurants are a short walk from the river ferry pier. Plan to visit at lunch or dinner time to take advantage of the riverside restaurants.

Dusit, on the other hand, is possibly Bangkok's most orderly district, home to the kind of tree-lined avenues and regal monuments you'd expect to find in Paris. Set aside a few hours – ideally in the morning – for the area's gems: Dusit Palace Park and Wat Benchamabophit.

The two districts are a brief walk apart, one made more difficult by the Bangkok sun. Dusit's sights are relatively far apart and are best reached by taxi or túk-túk.

Local Life

➡ **Riverside Eats** The primary culinary draw to Thewet is the almost rural-feeling riverside setting, with restaurants that drink in the cool river breeze and grill whole fish for communal picking.

➡ **Local Hero** Visit the Rama V (King Chulalongkorn; r 1868–1910) Memorial (p88) on any Tuesday (the day of the monarch's birth) to witness worshippers make offerings of candles, flowers, incense and bottles of whisky. A larger celebration is held on 23 October, the former monarch's birthday.

➡ **Boxing Day Dinner** If you're heading to a Thai boxing match at Ratchadamnoen Stadium (p90), follow the example of the locals: as a pre-match warm-up, grab a plate of *gài yâhng* (grilled chicken) from the restaurants surrounding the stadium, such as Likhit Kai Yang (p90).

➡ **Royal Digs** Dusit is home to Chitlada Palace (p88), the official residence of the royal family. The compound is generally closed to the public – at the time of writing the king was living at Sirirat Hospital in Thonburi – but it's worth taking a peek through one of the gates.

Getting There & Away

➡ **River boat** The easiest way to approach the Thewet and Dusit areas is via the river ferry stop at Tha Thewet. From here it's a brief walk to the riverside restaurants or a short túk-túk or taxi ride to Dusit Palace Park.

➡ **Bus** Air-con 505, 510 and 510; ordinary 3, 16, 18, 32, 53, 70 and 72.

➡ **Skytrain** An option best attempted outside of rush hours is to take the BTS to the stop at Phaya Thai before continuing by taxi.

Lonely Planet's Top Tip

If you're keen to see a Thai boxing match at Ratchadamnoen Stadium, aficionados say the best-matched bouts are reserved for Thursday nights.

✕ Best Places to Eat

➡ Krua Apsorn (p89)
➡ Kaloang Home Kitchen (p89)
➡ Khinlom Chom Sa-Phan (p90)

For reviews, see p89 ➡

Best Drinking & Entertainment

➡ River Bar Café (p90)
➡ Post Bar (p90)
➡ Ratchadamnoen Stadium (p90)

For reviews, see p90 ➡

◉ Best Historical Structures

➡ Vimanmek Teak Mansion (p86)
➡ Wat Benchamabophit (p88)
➡ Abhisek Dusit Throne Hall (p87)
➡ Ananta Samakhom Throne Hall (p88)

For reviews, see p88 ➡

DUSIT PALACE PARK & AROUND: THEWET & DUSIT

TOP SIGHTS
DUSIT PALACE PARK

Following Rama V's first European tour in 1897 (he was the first Thai monarch to visit the continent), he returned home with visions of European castles swimming in his head and set about transforming those styles into a uniquely Thai expression, today's Dusit Palace Park. The royal palace, throne hall and minor palaces for extended family were all moved here from Ko Ratanakosin, and were supplemented with beaux-arts institutions and Victorian manor houses. All of this and the expansive gardens make the compound a worthwhile escape from the chaos of modern Bangkok.

Vimanmek Teak Mansion

The highlight of the park is this structure, said to be the world's largest golden-teak mansion, built with nary a single nail. The mansion was originally constructed on Ko Si Chang in 1868 as a retreat for Rama V; the king had it moved to its present site in 1901. For the following few years it served as Rama V's primary residence, with the 81 rooms accommodating his enormous extended family. The interior of the mansion contains various personal effects of the king and a treasure-trove of early Ratanakosin and European art objects and antiques. Compulsory English-language tours of the building start every 30 minutes and last an hour, though it's up to luck as to whether your guide will actually speak decent English or not.

DON'T MISS...

➡ Vimanmek Teak Mansion
➡ Abhisek Dusit Throne Hall
➡ Royal Thai Elephant Museum
➡ Ancient Cloth Museum

PRACTICALITIES

➡ วังสวนดุสิต
➡ Map p257
➡ bounded by Th Ratchawithi, Th U Thong Nai & Th Ratchasima
➡ adult/child 100/50B or free with Grand Palace ticket
➡ ⊙9.30am-4pm
➡ ⓜPhaya Thai exit 3 & taxi

Abhisek Dusit Throne Hall

Visions of Moorish palaces and Victorian mansions must have still been spinning around in King Rama V's head when he commissioned this intricate building of porticoes and fretwork fused with a distinctive Thai character. Built as the throne hall for the palace in 1904, it opens onto a big stretch of lawn and flowerbeds, just like any important European building. Inside, the heavy ornamentation of the white main room is quite extraordinary, especially if you've been visiting a lot of overwhelmingly gold temples or traditional wooden buildings. Look up to just below the ceiling to see the line of brightly coloured stained-glass panels in Moorish patterns. The hall displays regional handiwork crafted by members of the Promotion of Supplementary Occupations & Related Techniques (Support), a charity foundation sponsored by Queen Sirikit.

Other Exhibits

Beside the Th U Thong Nai gate, the **Royal Elephant Museum** (Map p257; ☑2628 6300; Th Ratchawithi, Dusit Palace Park; full 250B, ticket for all Dusit Palace Park sights (free with Grand Palace ticket); ☻9:30am-4pm; ▣510, 72) showcases two large stables that once housed three white elephants; it's more interesting than it sounds. Near the Th Ratchawithi entrance, two residence halls display the **HM King Bhumibol Photography Exhibitions**, a collection of photographs and paintings by the present monarch. The **Ancient Cloth Museum** (Map p257; ☑2628 6300; Th Ratchawithi, Dusit Palace Park; ticket for all Dusit Palace Park sights 250B (free with Grand Palace ticket); ☻9:30am-4pm; ▣510, 72) presents a beautiful collection of traditional silks and cottons that make up the royal cloth collection.

VERSAILLES OF BANGKOK

In 1897, Rama V became the first Thai monarch to visit Europe, a trip that seemingly had a profound impact on the king in more ways than one. Upon returning to Siam, Rama V soon set about building a new royal district comprised of relocated Thai structures and spacious, grand western-style buildings surrounded by expansive gardens (Suan Dusit means 'Celestial Gardens') – a significant contrast with the increasingly crowded walled district of Ko Ratanakosin. Having chosen a rural-feeling spot within walking distance of the Grand Palace – the king was allegedly a fan of the new-fangled trend of bicycling – Rama V hired a team of German and Italian architects and imported materials such as marble from Carrara, Italy, for the construction of his new European-style home.

COVER UP!

Because Dusit Palace Park is royal property, visitors should wear long pants (no capri pants) or long skirts and sleeved shirts.

◉ SIGHTS

DUSIT PALACE PARK   MUSEUM, ROYAL PALACE
See p86.

**ANANTA SAMAKHOM
THRONE HALL**   MUSEUM
Map p257 (พระที่นั่งอนันตสมาคม; www.artsofthek
ingdom.com; Th U Thong Nai; admission 150B;
☉10am-6pm Tue-Sun; 🚇Phaya Thai exit 3 & taxi)
The domed neoclassical building behind
the Rama V Memorial was originally built
as a royal reception hall during the reign
of Rama V, but wasn't completed until 1915,
five years after his death. It was designed as
a place to host – and impress – foreign dig-
nitaries, and on occasion it still serves this
purpose, most notably during celebrations
of King Bhumibol Adulyadej's 60th year on
the throne, when royals from around the
world converged here in full regalia (you
may encounter a much-published picture
of this meeting while in Bangkok). The first
meeting of the Thai parliament was held in
the building before being moved to a facility nearby. Today the building houses an
exhibit called *Arts of the Kingdom*, which,
like the nearby Abhisek Dusit Throne Hall,
displays the products of Queen Sirikit's
Support foundation.

RAMA V MEMORIAL   MONUMENT
Map p257 (พระบรมรูปทรงม้า; Th U Thong Nai; 🚇Phaya
Thai exit 3 & taxi) A bronze figure of a military-
garbed leader may seem like an unlikely
shrine, but Bangkokians are flexible in their
expression of religious devotion. Most importantly, the figure is no forgotten general
– this is Rama V, who is widely credited for
steering the country into the modern age
and for preserving Thailand's independence from European colonialism. He is
also considered a champion of the common
people for his abolition of slavery and cor-
vée (the requirement that every citizen be
available for state labour when called). The
statue is also the site of a huge celebration
on 23 October, the anniversary of the monarch's death.

DUSIT ZOO   ZOO
Map p257 (สวนสัตว์ดุสิต (เขาดิน); Th Ratchawithi; admission adult/child 100/50B; ☉8am-6pm; 🚇Phaya
Thai exit 3 & taxi) Originally a private botanic
garden for Rama V, Dusit Zoo (Suan Sat
Dusit or *kŏw din*) was opened in 1938 and is
now one of the premier zoological facilities
in Southeast Asia. That, however, doesn't

mean that all the animal enclosures are up
to modern zoological standards, with one
endlessly pacing tiger being particularly
heart-rending. Squeezed into the 19 hectares are more than 300 mammals, 200
reptiles and 800 birds, including relatively
rare indigenous species. The shady grounds
feature trees labelled in English, plus a lake
in the centre with paddle boats for rent.

CHITLADA PALACE   ROYAL PALACE
Map p257 (พระราชวังจิตรลดา; cnr Th Ratchawithi & Th
Phra Ram V; ☉closed to the public; 🚇Phaya Thai
exit 3 & taxi) The current royal family's official residence, Chitlada Palace is also a
royally funded agriculture centre demon-
strating the reigning king's commitment to
the progress of the country's major industry. The palace is not open to the general
public and it's pretty difficult to see from
the outside, but you can spot rice paddies
and animal pastures – smack in the middle
of Bangkok – through the perimeter fence.

WAT BENCHAMABOPHIT   BUDDHIST TEMPLE
Map p257 (วัดเบญจมบพิตร (วัดเบญฯ); cnr Th Si Ayuthaya & Th Phra Ram V; admission 20B; ☉8am-
6pm; 🚇Phaya Thai exit 3 & taxi) Inside and out,
this temple is one of the most unusual and
most extravagant in the kingdom. Built at
the turn of the century on the orders of
Rama V, the *bòht* (chapel) is made of white
Carrara marble (hence its alternative name,
'Marble Temple') imported from Italy especially for the job. This structure is a prime
example of modern Thai temple architecture, as is the interior design, which melds
Thai motifs with European influences: the
red carpets, the gold-on-white motifs painted repetitively on the walls, the walls painted like stained-glass windows and the royal
blue wall behind the central Buddha image
are strongly reminiscent of a European palace. It's not all that surprising when you
consider how enamoured Rama V (whose
ashes are in the base of said Buddha image) was with Europe – just walk across the
street to Dusit Park for further evidence.

The courtyard behind the *bòht* has 53
Buddha images (33 originals and 20 copies)
representing every *mudra* (gesture) and
style from Thai history, making this the
ideal place to compare Buddhist iconogra-
phy. If religious details aren't for you, this
temple still offers a pleasant stroll beside
landscaped canals filled with blooming lotus and Chinese-style footbridges.

FREE NATIONAL LIBRARY   LIBRARY

Map p257 (Th Samsen; ◷9am-6.30pm Mon-Fri, to 5pm Sat & Sun; ⛴Tha Thewet) The country's largest repository of books has few foreign-language resources, but its strength is in its astrological books and star charts; the collection also holds recordings by the king, sacred palm-leaf writings and ancient maps.

EATING

Thewet's workaday vibe and Dusit's nearly restaurant-free avenues mean that Thai is virtually the only option in this part of town. For a bit more culinary diversity, head to adjacent Banglamphu.

TOP CHOICE KRUA APSORN   THAI $

Map p257 (www.kruaapsorn.com; 503-505 Th Samsen; mains 40-250B; ◷10.30am-7.30pm Mon-Fri, to 6pm Sat; ⛴Tha Thewet) This is the original branch of this homey, award-winning and royally patronised restaurant. Expect a clientele made up of fussy families and big-haired, middle-aged ladies, and a cuisine revolving around full-flavoured, largely seafood- and vegetable-heavy central Thai dishes. If you have dinner in mind, be sure to note the early closing times.

KALOANG HOME KITCHEN   THAI $

Map p257 (Th Si Ayutthaya; mains 60-170B; ◷11am-11pm; ⛴Tha Thewet) Don't be alarmed by the peeling paint and dilapidated deck – the owners at Kaloang Home Kitchen certainly aren't. The laid-back atmosphere and seafood-heavy menu will quickly dispel any

DUSIT PALACE PARK & AROUND: THEWET & DUSIT EATING

KICKING & SCREAMING

More formally known as Phahuyut (from the Pali-Sanskrit *bhahu* or 'arm' and *yodha* or 'combat'), Thailand's ancient martial art of *moo·ay tai* (Thai boxing; also spelt *muay thai*) is one of the kingdom's most striking national icons. Overflowing with colour and ceremony as well as exhilarating moments of clenched-teeth action, the best matches serve up a blend of such skill and tenacity that one is tempted to view the spectacle as emblematic of Thailand's centuries-old devotion to independence in a region where most other countries fell under the European colonial yoke.

Many martial-arts aficionados agree that *moo·ay tai* is the most efficient, effective and generally unbeatable form of ring-centred, hand-to-hand combat practised today. According to legend, it has been for a while. After the Siamese were defeated at Ayuthaya in 1767, several expert *moo·ay boh·rahn* (from which *moo·ay tai* is derived) fighters were among the prisoners hauled off to Burma. A few years later a festival was held; one of the Thai fighters, Nai Khanom Tom, was ordered to fight prominent Burmese boxers for the entertainment of the king and to determine which martial art was most effective. He promptly dispatched nine opponents in a row and, as legend has it, was offered money or beautiful women as a reward; he promptly took two new wives. Today a *moo·ay tai* festival in Ayuthaya is named after Nai Khanom Tom.

Unlike some martial disciplines, such as kung fu or *qi gong*, *moo·ay tai* doesn't entertain the idea that martial-arts techniques can be passed only from master to disciple in secret. Thus the *moo·ay tai* knowledge base hasn't fossilised – in fact it remains ever open to innovation, refinement and revision. Thai champion Dieselnoi, for example, created a new approach to knee strikes that was so difficult to defend that he retired at 23 because no one dared to fight him anymore.

Another famous *moo·ay tai* champion is Parinya Kiatbusaba, aka Nong Thoom, a *kàthoey* (transgendered person) from Chiang Mai who arrived for weigh-ins wearing lipstick and rouge. After a 1998 triumph at Lumphini, Parinya used the prize money to pay for sex-change surgery; in 2003 the movie *Beautiful Boxer* was made about her life.

While Bangkok has long attracted foreign fighters, it wasn't until 1999 that French fighter Mourad Sari became the first non-Thai fighter to take home a weight-class championship belt from a Bangkok stadium. Several Thai *nák moo·ay* (fighters) have gone on to triumph in world championships in international-style boxing. Khaosai Galaxy, the greatest Asian boxer of all time, successfully defended his World Boxing Association super-flyweight world title 19 times before retiring in 1991.

concerns about sinking into Chao Phraya, and a beer and the breeze will temporarily erase any scarring memories of Bangkok traffic. To reach the restaurant, follow the final windy stretch of Th Si Ayuthaya all the way to the river.

LIKHIT KAI YANG NORTHEASTERN THAI **$**

Map p257 (74/1 Th Ratchadamnoen Nok; mains 30-150B; ☺lunch & dinner; ☻Tha Phan Fah) Located virtually next door to Ratchadamoen Stadium, this decades-old restaurant is where locals come for a quick meal of papaya salad and grilled chicken before a Thai boxing match. The flavours are uncompromisingly authentic and so is the state of the kitchen (we don't suggest investigating the latter).

KHINLOM CHOM SA-PHAN THAI **$**

Map p257 (☏0 2628 8382; www.khinlom chomsaphan.com; 11/6 Soi 3, Th Samsen; mains 75-280B; ☺11am-2am; ☻Tha Thewet) Locals come here for the combination of riverfront views and tasty seafood-based eats. It's popular, so be sure to call ahead to book a riverfront table.

🍷 DRINKING & NIGHTLIFE

There's very little — almost nothing, really — in terms of nightlife in this part of town. Luckily, Banglamphu and Th Khao San are a brief taxi ride away. Alternatively, the riverside restaurants also function as open-air bars.

RIVER BAR CAFÉ BAR, RESTAURANT

Map p257 (405/1 Soi Chao Phraya; ☺5pm-midnight; ☻Tha Saphan Krung Thon) Sporting a picture-perfect riverside location, good food and live music, River Bar Café combines all the essentials of a perfect Bangkok night out. Grab a table closest to the river to fully take advantage of the breeze, as well as to avoid noise fallout from the sometimes overly enthusiastic bands.

POST BAR BAR

Map p257 (Th Samsen; ☺5pm-1am; ☻Tha Thewet) If 'Chinese pawn shop' can be considered a legitimate design theme, Post Bar has nailed it. The walls of this narrow, shophouse-bound bar are decked with retro Thai kitsch; the soundtrack is appropriately classic rock; and the clientele overwhelmingly Thai.

☆ ENTERTAINMENT

TOP CHOICE RATCHADAMNOEN STADIUM THAI BOXING

Map p257 (off Th Ratchadamnoen Nok; tickets 3rd-/2nd-class/ringside 1000/1500/2000B; ☻Tha Phan Fah) Ratchadamnoen Stadium, Bangkok's oldest and most venerable venue for *moo·ay tai*, hosts matches on Monday, Wednesday, Thursday and Sunday starting at 6.30pm. Be sure to buy tickets from the official ticket counter, not from the touts who hang around outside the entrance.

Chinatown

Neighbourhood Top Five

1 Dining al fresco at Chinatown's decades-old street food stalls such as **Nay Mŏng** (p95) and **Nay Lék Ûan** (p95).

2 Witnessing 5.5 tonnes of solid gold Buddha at **Wat Traimit** (p93).

3 Checking out the oil-stained machine shops, hidden Chinese temples and twisting lanes of **Talat Noi** (p94)

4 Watching chaos and commerce battle it out in hectic **Talat Mai** (p94),

Chinatown's photogenic fresh-food market.

5 Enjoying Bollywood-style markets and the city's cheapest and best Indian food in **Phahurat** (p96).

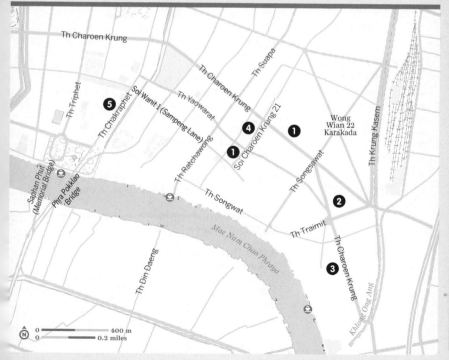

For more detail of this area, see Map p258 ➡

Lonely Planet's Top Tip

Most of Bangkok's street-food vendors close up shop on Monday, so don't plan on eating in Chinatown on this day.

✕ Best Places to Eat

➡ Th Phadungdao Seafood Stalls (p98)

➡ Royal India (p98)

➡ Nay Mŏng (p95)

➡ Nay Lék Ûan (p95)

For reviews, see p98 ➡

🔒 Best Markets

➡ Talat Mai (p94)

➡ Pak Khlong Market (Flower Market) (p96)

➡ Phahurat (p96)

➡ Sampeng Lane (p96)

For reviews, see p94 ➡

⊙ Best Temples & Churches

➡ Wat Traimit (p93)

➡ Wat Mangkon Kamalawat (p94)

➡ Church of Santa Cruz (p97)

➡ Holy Rosary Church (p94)

For reviews, see p94 ➡

Explore: Chinatown

Chinatown embodies everything that's hectic, noisy and polluted about Bangkok, but that's what makes it such a fascinating area to explore. Be sure to set aside enough time to do some map-free wandering among the neon-lit gold shops, hidden temples, crumbling shopfronts and pencil-thin alleys, especially the tiny winding lanes that extend from Soi Wanit 1 (aka Sampeng Lane).

For ages, Chinatown was home to Bangkok's most infamous traffic jams, but the arrival of the MRT (Metro) in 2005 finally made the area a sane place to visit. Still, the station is about a kilometre from many sights, so you'll have to take a longish walk or a short taxi ride. An alternative is to take the Chao Phraya Express boat to the stop at Tha Ratchawong, from where it's a brief walk to most restaurants and a bit further to most sights.

The whole district is buzzing from dawn until after dusk, but Chinatown is at its best during these two times. The best time to eat is from 7pm to 9pm but forget Mondays: that's when most of the city's vendors stay home.

Local Life

➡ **Street Food** Although Chinatown seems to be dominated by restaurants serving shark fin and bird's nest soup, the true Chinatown meal is prepared by the street vendors that line Th Yaowarat after dark. Locals come from all over Bangkok to eat at Chinatown's stalls.

➡ **Markets** The Phahurat (p96) and Chinatown districts have interconnected markets selling fabrics, clothes and household wares, as well as wholesale shops and a few places selling gems and jewellery.

➡ **Living on a Prayer** In many of Chinatown's temples, you'll see locals shaking cans of thin sticks called *seeam see*. When a stick falls to the floor, look at its number and find the corresponding paper that gives a no-nonsense appraisal of your future in Thai, Chinese and English.

➡ **Nightlife** Or should we say, lack thereof... Other than Cotton (p98), there's zilch in the realm of non-dodgy nightlife here. Instead, fuel up on street eats first, then head to nearby Banglamphu or Silom for drinks.

Getting There & Away

➡ **MRT** Hua Lamphong.

➡ **River boat** Tha Marine Department, Tha Ratchawong, Tha Saphan Phut (Memorial Bridge).

➡ **Bus** Air-con 507 and 508; ordinary 1, 4, 25, 33, 37, 49 and 53.

TOP SIGHTS
WAT TRAIMIT (GOLDEN BUDDHA)

Wat Traimit, also known as the Temple of the Golden Buddha, is home to the world's largest gold statue, a gleaming, 3m-tall, 5.5-tonne Buddha image with a mysterious past and a current value of more than US$40 million in gold alone. Sculpted in the graceful Sukhothai style, the image is thought to date from the late Sukhothai period. But if it is possible for a Buddha image to lead a double life, then this priceless piece has most certainly done so.

At what is thought to have been a time of great danger to the Siamese kingdom – presumably prior to an invasion from Burma – the Buddha image was rendered with a plaster exterior in an attempt to disguise it from the looting hordes. And it worked. After various assaults, the Burmese hauled off vast quantities of Thai treasure, but this most valuable of all Buddha images – indeed the most valuable image in all of Buddhism – remained as shabby-looking and anonymous as intended. It was moved first to Bangkok and later to Wat Traimit, the only temple in the Chinatown area modest enough to take such a world-weary Buddha. And thus it remained, beneath a tin roof, until the mid-1950s when the temple had collected enough money to build a proper shelter for the image. During the move the Buddha was dropped from a crane, an act of such ill fortune that the workers are said to have downed tools and run. When the abbot inspected the Buddha the following day he found the plaster had cracked and, wouldn't you know it, the golden Buddha's true identity was finally revealed.

The image remained seated in its modest pavilion until 2009, smiling benevolently down upon an underwhelming and seemingly endless procession of tour groups, which seem to have scared off most of the genuine worshippers. But Wat Traimit's days of poverty are long gone. A new marble hall has been built with a combination of Chinese-style balustrades and a steep, golden Thai-style roof. Surrounding it is a narrow strip of grass watered via mist fountains.

The 2nd floor of the structure is home to the **Phra Buddha Maha Suwanna Patimakorn Exhibition** (Map p258; admission 100B; ☉8am-5pm Tues-Sun), which has exhibits on how the statue was made, discovered and came to arrive at its current home, while the 3rd floor is home to the **Yaowarat Chinatown Heritage Center** (Map p258; admission 100B; ☉8am-5pm Tues-Sun), a small but engaging museum with multimedia exhibits on the history of Bangkok's Chinatown and its residents.

DON'T MISS...

➡ Wat Traimit (Golden Buddha)

➡ Phra Buddha Maha Suwanna Patimakorn Exhibition

➡ Yaowarat Chinatown Heritage Center

PRACTICALITIES

➡ วัดไตรมิตร | Temple of the Golden Buddha

➡ Map p258

➡ cnr Th Yaowarat & Th Charoen Krung

➡ admission 40B

➡ ☉8am-5pm Tue-Sun

➡ Ⓜ Hua Lamphong, Tha Ratchawong

◉ SIGHTS

WAT TRAIMIT (GOLDEN BUDDHA)
BUDDHIST TEMPLE

See p93.

FREE HOLY ROSARY CHURCH
CHURCH

Map p258 (วัดแม่พระลูกประคำ กาลหว่าร์; Th Yotha; ⊘Mass 7.30pm Mon-Sat, 8am, 10am & 7.30pm Sun; 🚢Marine Department) Portuguese seafarers were among the first Europeans to establish diplomatic ties with Siam, and their influence in the kingdom was rewarded with prime riverside real estate. When a Portuguese contingent moved across the river to the present-day Talat Noi (p94) area of Chinatown in 1787, they were given this piece of land and built the Holy Rosary Church, known in Thai as Wat Kalawan, from the Portuguese 'Calvario'. Over the years the Portuguese community dispersed and the church fell into disrepair. However, Vietnamese and Cambodian Catholics displaced by the Indochina wars adopted it and together with Chinese speakers now constitute much of the parish. Of particular note are the splendid Romanesque stained-glass windows, gilded ceilings and a Christ statue that is carried through the streets during Easter celebrations.

TALAT NOI
NEIGHBOURHOOD

Map p258 (ตลาดน้อย; Soi Phanurangsi; 🚢Marine Department) This microcosm of soi life is named after a *nóy* (small) market that sets up between Soi 22 and Soi 20, off Th Charoen Krung. Here you'll find convoluted, streamlike soi, weaving through people's living rooms, noodle shops and grease-stained machine shops. Opposite the River View Guesthouse, **San Jao Sien Khong** (Map p258; admission free; ⊘6am-6pm) is one of the city's oldest Chinese shrines, and is guarded by a playful rooftop terracotta dragon; it's one of the best places to come during the yearly Vegetarian Festival.

HUALAMPHONG TRAIN STATION
HISTORICAL BUILDING

Map p258 (สถานีรถไฟหัวลำโพง; Th Phra Ram IV; Ⓜ Hua Lamphong exit 2) At the southeastern edge of Chinatown, Bangkok's main train station was built by Dutch architects and engineers between 1910 and 1916. Above the 14 platforms it was designed in a neoclassical style by Italian architect and engineer combination Mario Tamagno and Annibale Rigotti, who were working at the same time on the grand Ananta Samakhom Throne Hall (p88) at Dusit. It also embraces other influences, such as the patterned, two-toned skylights that exemplify nascent De Stijl Dutch modernism – it is through these that is known as an early example of the shift towards Thai art deco. If you can zone out of the chaos for a moment, look for the vaulted iron roof and neoclassical portico that were a state-of-the-art engineering feat.

TALAT MAI
MARKET

Map p258 (ตลาดใหม่; Soi 6 (Trok Itsaranuphap), Th Yaowarat; ⊘6am-6pm; 🚢Tha Ratchawong, Ⓜ Hua Lamphong exit 1 & taxi,) With nearly two centuries of commerce under its belt, 'New Market' is no longer an entirely accurate name for this strip of commerce. Regardless, this is Bangkok's, if not Thailand's, most Chinese market, and the dried goods, seasonings, spices and sauces will be familiar to anyone who's ever lived on the mainland. Even if you're not interested in food, the hectic atmosphere (be on guard for the motorcycles that squeeze between shoppers) and exotic sights and smells culminate in something of a surreal sensory experience.

While much of the market centres on cooking ingredients, the section north of Th Charoen Krung (equivalent to Soi 21, Th Charoen Krung) is known for its incense, paper effigies and ceremonial sweets – the essential elements of a traditional Chinese funeral.

FREE WAT MANGKON KAMALAWAT
CHINESE TEMPLE

Map p258 (วัดมังกรกมลาวาส; Th Charoen Krung; ⊘9am-6pm; 🚢Tha Ratchawong, Ⓜ Hua Lamphong exit 1 & taxi) Explore the cryptlike sermon halls of this busy Chinese temple (also known as Leng Noi Yee) to find Buddhist, Taoist and Confucian shrines. During the annual Vegetarian Festival, religious and culinary activities are centred here. But almost any time of day or night this temple is busy with worshippers lighting incense, filling the ever-burning altar lamps with oil and making offerings to their ancestors. Offering oil is believed to provide a smooth journey into the afterlife and to fuel the fire of the present life. Mangkon Kamalawat means 'Dragon Lotus Temple'. Surrounding the temple are vendors selling food for the gods – steamed lotus-shaped dumplings and oranges – which are used for merit making.

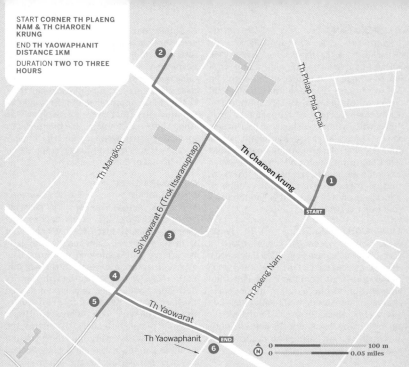

START **CORNER TH PLAENG NAM & TH CHAROEN KRUNG**

END **TH YAOWAPHANIT**
DISTANCE **1KM**

DURATION **TWO TO THREE HOURS**

Neighbourhood Walk
A Taste of Chinatown

Street food rules in Chinatown, making the area ideal for a culinary adventure. Although many vendors stay open late, the more popular stalls tend to sell out quickly, and the best time to feast in this area is from 7pm to 9pm. Don't try this walk on a Monday when most of the city's street vendors stay at home. Bringing a friend or three and sharing is a good way to ensure that you can try as many dishes as possible.

Start your walk at the intersection of Th Plaeng Nam and Th Charoen Krung. Head north along Th Phlap Phla Chai, staying on the right-hand side for about 50m, until you reach ❶ **Nay Mŏng**, a shophouse restaurant renowned for its delicious *or sòo·an* (mussels or oysters fried with egg and a sticky batter).

Backtrack to Th Charoen Krung and turn right. Upon reaching Th Mangkon make a right and immediately on your left-hand side you'll see ❷ **Jék Pûi**, a table-less stall known for its Chinese-style Thai curries.

Cross Th Charoen Krung again, turn left, and continue east until you reach Soi 16, also known as ❸ **Talat Mai**, the area's most famous strip of commerce. At the end of the alley you'll see a gentleman making ❹ **gŏo·ay dĕe·o kôo·a gài**, rice noodles fried with chicken, egg and garlic oil.

Upon emerging at Th Yaowarat, cross over to the busy market area directly across the street. The first vendor on the right, ❺ **Nay Lék Ûan**, sells *gŏo·ay jáp nám săi*, an intensely peppery broth containing noodles and pork offal.

Returning back to Th Yaowarat, turn right and continue until the next intersection. On the corner of Th Yaowaphanit and Th Yaowarat you'll see ❻ **Mangkorn Khăo**, a stall selling *bà·mèe* (Chinese-style wheat noodles) and barbecued pork.

SAMPENG LANE
MARKET

Map p258 (สำเพ็ง; Soi Wanit 1, Th Ratchawong; ⊙8am-6pm; 🚤Tha Ratchawong, Ⓜ️Hua Lamphong exit 1 & taxi) Sampeng Lane is a narrow artery running parallel to Th Yaowarat and bisecting the commercial areas of Chinatown and Phahurat. The Chinatown portion of Sampeng Lane is lined with wholesale shops of hair accessories, pens, stickers, household wares and beeping, flashing knick-knacks. Near Th Chakrawat, gem and jewellery shops abound. Weekends are horribly crowded, and it takes a gymnast's flexibility to squeeze past the pushcarts, motorcycles and other roadblocks.

FLASHLIGHT MARKET
MARKET

Map p258 (ตลาดไฟฉาย; cnr Th Phlap Phla Chai & Th Luang; ⊙5am Sat-5pm Sun; 🚤Tha Ratchawong, Ⓜ️Hua Lamphong exit 1 & taxi) This street market extends west from the Phlap Phla Chai intersection, forging a trail of antiques, secondhand items and, well, sometimes just plain junk, along the area's footpaths. It's open 24 hours, but is at its busiest on Saturday night, when a flashlight is needed to see many of the goods for sale.

PHAHURAT
NEIGHBOURHOOD

Map p258 (พาหุรัด; cnr Th Phahurat & Th Chakrawat; 🚌82, 169, 🚤Tha Saphan Phut (Memorial Bridge)) Heaps of South Asian traders set up shop in this small but bustling Little India, where everything from Bollywood movies to bindis are sold by enthusiastic small-time traders. The emphasis is on cloth, and Phahurat proffers boisterous Bollywood-coloured textiles, traditional Thai dance costumes, tiaras, sequins, wigs and other accessories to make you look like a cross-dresser, a *mŏr lam* (Thai country music) performer, or both. Amid the colour spectacle there are also good deals on machine-made Thai textiles and children's clothes.

Behind the more obvious storefronts are winding alleys that criss-cross Khlong Ong Ang, where merchants grab a bite to eat or make travel arrangements for trips home – it's a great area to just wander, stopping for masala chai or lassi as you go.

GURDWARA SIRI GURU SINGH SABHA
SIKH TEMPLE

Map p258 (พระศาสนสถานคุรุดวารา; Th Phahurat; ⊙9am-5pm; 🚌82, 169, 🚤Tha Saphan Phut (Memorial Bridge)) Just off Th Chakraphet is this gold-domed Sikh temple. Basically it's a large hall, somewhat reminiscent of a mosque interior, devoted to the worship of the *Guru Granth Sahib*, the 17th-century Sikh holy book, which is itself considered the last of the religion's 10 great gurus. Prasada (blessed food offered to Hindu or Sikh temple attendees) is distributed among devotees every morning around 9am, and if you arrive on a Sikh festival day you can partake in the *langar* (communal Sikh meal) served in the temple. If you do visit this shrine, be sure to climb to the top for panoramic views of Chinatown. Stores surrounding the temple sell assorted religious paraphernalia.

PAK KHLONG MARKET (FLOWER MARKET)
MARKET

Map p258 (ปากคลองตลาด; cnr Th Chakkaphet & Th Atsadang; ⊙24hr; 🚤Tha Saphan Phut/Memo-

---

WAVING THE YELLOW FLAG

During the annual Vegetarian Festival in September/October, Bangkok's Chinatown becomes a virtual orgy of nonmeat cuisine. The festivities centre on Chinatown's main street, Th Yaowarat, and the Talat Noi (p94) area, but food shops and stalls all over the city post yellow flags to announce their meat-free status.

Celebrating alongside the ethnic Chinese are Thais who look forward to the special dishes that appear during the festival period. Most restaurants put their normal menus on hold and instead prepare soy-based substitutes for standard Thai dishes like *dôm yam* and *gaang kĕe·o wăhn* (green curry). Even Thai regional cuisines are sold, without the meat, of course. Yellow Hokkien-style noodles often make an appearance in the special festival dishes, usually in stir-fried dishes along with meaty mushrooms and big hunks of vegetables.

Along with abstinence from meat, the 10-day festival is celebrated with special visits to the temple, often requiring worshippers to dress in white.

CHINATOWN'S SHOPPING STREETS

Chinatown is the neighbourhood version of a big-box store divided up into categories of consumerables.

→ **Th Charoen Krung** Chinatown's primary thoroughfare is a prestigious address. Starting on the western end of the street, near the intersection of Th Mahachai, there's a collection of old record stores. **Talat Khlong Ong Ang** (Map p258) consumes the next block, selling all sorts of used and new electronic gadgets. **Nakhon Kasem** (Map p258; ⊘8am-8pm; ⓢTha Saphan Phut) is the reformed thieves' market where vendors now stock up on nifty gadgets for portable food prep. Further east, near Th Mahachak, is **Talat Khlong Thom** (Map p258), a hardware centre. West of Th Ratchawong, everything is geared towards the afterlife and the passing of life.

→ **Th Yaowarat** A hundred years ago this was a poultry farm; now it is gold street, the biggest trading centre of the precious metal in the country. Along Th Yaowarat, gold is sold by the *bàht* (a unit of weight equivalent to 15g) from neon-lit storefronts that look more like shrines than shops. Near the intersection of Th Ratchawong, stores shift to Chinese and Singaporean tourists' tastes: dried fruit and nuts, chintzy talismans and accoutrements for Chinese festivals. The multistorey buildings around here were some of Bangkok's first skyscrapers and a source of wonder for the local people. Bangkok's skyline has grown and grown, but this area retains a few Chinese apothecaries, smelling of wood bark and ancient secrets.

→ **Th Mittraphan** (Map p258) Sign-makers branch off Wong Wian 22 Karakada, near Wat Traimit and the Golden Buddha; Thai and Roman letters are typically cut out by a hand-guided lathe placed prominently beside the pavement.

→ **Th Santiphap** (Map p258) Car parts and other automotive gear make this the place for kicking tyres.

→ **Sampeng Lane** (p96) Plastic cuteness in bulk, from pencil cases to pens, stuffed animals, hair flotsam and enough bling to kit out a rap video – it all hang outs near the eastern end of the alley.

→ **Talat Mai** (p94) This ancient fresh market splays along the cramped alley between Th Yaowarat and Th Charoen Krung.

rial Bridge) This sprawling wholesale flower market has become a tourist attraction in its own right. The endless piles of delicate orchids, rows of roses and stacks of button carnations are a sight to be seen, and the shirtless porters wheeling blazing piles of colour set the place in motion. The best time to come is late at night, when the goods arrive from upcountry.

During the morning Pak Khlong Market is also one of the city's largest wholesale vegetable markets.

SAPHAN PHUT NIGHT BAZAAR MARKET
Map p258 (ตลาดนัดสะพานพุทธ; Th Saphan Phut; ⊘8pm-midnight Tue-Sun; ⓢTha Saphan Phut (Memorial Bridge)) On the Bangkok side of Tha Saphan Phut, this night market has bucketloads of cheap clothes, late-night snacking and a lot of people-watching. As Chatuchak Weekend Market (p143) becomes more design oriented, Saphan Phut has filled the closets of fashion-forward, baht-challenged teenagers.

FREE **CHURCH OF SANTA CRUZ** CHURCH
Map p258; (โบสถ์ซางตาครู้ส; Soi Kuti Jiin; ⊘7am-noon Sat & Sun; ⓢfrom Tha Pak Talat (Atsadang)) Centuries before Sukhumvit became the international district, the Portuguese claimed *fa·rang* (Western) supremacy and built the Church of Santa Cruz in the 1700s. The land was offered as a gift from King Taksin in appreciation for the loyalty the Portuguese community had displayed after the fall of Ayuthaya. The surviving church dates to 1913. Very little activity occurs on the grounds itself, but small and fascinating village streets break off from the main courtyard into the area known as Kuti Jiin, the local name for the church. On Soi Kuti Jiin 3, several houses sell Portuguese-inspired cakes and sweets.

EATING

TH PHADUNGDAO
SEAFOOD STALLS
THAI $

Map p258 (cnr Th Phadungdao & Th Yaowarat; mains 180-300B; ⊙dinner Tue-Sun; ⛴Tha Ratchawong, ⓂHua Lamphong exit 1 & taxi) After sunset, these two opposing open-air restaurants – each of which claims to be the original – become a culinary train wreck of outdoor barbecues, screaming staff, iced seafood trays and messy sidewalk seating. True, the vast majority of diners are foreign tourists, but this has little impact on the cheerful setting, the fun experience and the cheap bill.

ROYAL INDIA
INDIAN $

Map p258 (392/1 Th Chakraphet; mains 65-250B; ⊙lunch & dinner; ⛴Tha Saphan Phut/Memorial Bridge) A windowless dining room of 10 tables in a dark alley may not be everybody's ideal lunch destination, but this legendary north Indian place continues to draw foodies despite the lack of aesthetics. Try any of the delicious breads or saucy curries, and finish with a sugary homemade Punjabi sweet.

HUA SENG HONG
CHINESE $$$

Map p258 (371-373 Th Yaowarat; mains 100-1050B; ⊙9am-1am; ⛴Tha Ratchawong, ⓂHua Lamphong exit 1 & taxi) Shark-fin soup may draw heaps of Asian tourists into this place, but Hua Seng Hong's varied menu, which includes dim sum, braised goose feet and noodles, makes it a handy destination for anybody craving Chinese.

OLD SIAM PLAZA
THAI SWEETS $

Map p258 (cnr Th Phahurat & Th Triphet; mains 30-90B; ⊙6am-6.30pm; ⛴Tha Saphan Phut (Memorial Bridge)) Sugar junkies, be sure to include this stop on your Bangkok eating itinerary. The ground floor of this shopping centre is a candy land of traditional Thai sweets and snacks, most made right before your eyes.

SHANGARILA RESTAURANT
CHINESE $$

Map p258 (306 Th Yaowarat; mains 220-500B; ⊙11am-10pm; ⛴Tha Ratchawong, ⓂHua Lam-

phong exit 1 & taxi) This massive, banquet-style restaurant prepares a variety of banquet-sized Cantonese dishes for ravenous families. The dim sum lunches are worth the effort of muscling your way past the outdoor steam tables.

☆ ENTERTAINMENT

FREE COTTON
LIVE MUSIC

Map p258 (3rd fl, Shanghai Mansion, 479-481 Th Yaowarat; ⊙live music 9-11.30pm; ⛴Tha Ratchawong, ⓂHua Lamphong exit 1 & taxi) Walk through a bland restaurant to this cosy Chinatown-themed lounge in the Shanghai Mansion hotel. Virtually the only non-karaoke-based place of entertainment in Chinatown, Cotton features smooth acoustic jazz and affordable cocktails.

SALA CHALERMKRUNG
THEATRE

Map p258 (☏0 2222 0434; www.salachalermkrung.com; 66 Th Charoen Krung; tickets 800-1200B; ⊙shows 7.30pm Thu & Fri; ⛴Tha Saphan Phut (Memorial Bridge)) This art deco Bangkok landmark, a former cinema dating to 1933, is one of the few remaining places *kŏhn* can be witnessed. The traditional Thai dance-drama is enhanced here by laser graphics, hi-tech audio and English subtitles. Concerts and other events are also held; check the website for details.

🏃 SPORTS & ACTIVITIES

CO VAN KESSEL
BANGKOK TOURS
BICYCLE TOURS

Map p258 (☏0 2688 9933; www.covankessel.com; 3rd fl, Grand China Princess Hotel, 215 Th Yaowarat; tours 750-1950B; ⊙6am-7pm) This Dutch company, very popular with Dutch travellers, offers Thonburi bicycle tours at a variety of times, plus some unusual Chinatown walking tours.

Shopping District: Siam Square, Pratunam, Ploenchit & Ratchathewi

Neighbourhood Top Five

1 Visiting **Jim Thompson's House** (p101) – the teak mansion that put Thai style on the map...before its ex-spy owner disappeared off that map.

2 Shopping at the malls, department stores and shops that surround Siam Square, such as **MBK Center** (p109).

3 Exploring **Baan Krua** (p102), the canal-side Muslim village where Jim Thompson first encountered Thai silk.

4 Making a wish at the crossroads of commerce and faith that is the **Erawan Shrine** (p103).

5 Enjoying the luxury of what must be one of the world's best-value cinemas, **Paragon Cineplex** (p108).

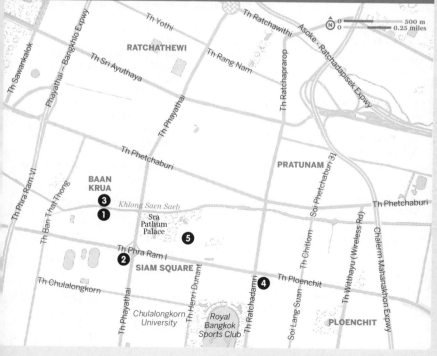

For more detail of this area, see Map p260 & p263 ➡

Lonely Planet's Top Tip

Admittedly, they tend to have all the ambience of a hospital cafeteria, but the mall-based food courts that abound in this part of town are among the most user-friendly introductions to Thai food in Bangkok. They're generally clean and convenient, and also have the benefit of having English-language menus, so ordering is a snap.

✕ Best Places to Eat

➡ MBK Food Court (p105)
➡ Crystal Jade La Mian Xiao Long Bao (p104)
➡ Mallika Restaurant (p106)
➡ Sra Bua (p104)

For reviews, see p104 ➡

☕ Best Places to Drink

➡ Co-Co Walk (p106)
➡ Hyde & Seek (p107)
➡ Wine Pub (p108)

For reviews, see p106 ➡

🔒 Best Places to Shop

➡ MBK Center (p109)
➡ Gaysorn Plaza (p109)
➡ Siam Square (p109)
➡ Siam Paragon (p109)
➡ Pratunam Market (p111)

For reviews, see p109 ➡

Explore: Siam Square, Pratunam, Ploenchit & Ratchathewi

Siam Square, Pratunam and Ploenchit combine to form the de facto geographical and commercial centre of modern Bangkok. Huge air-conditioned malls, towering hotels, fast-food chains and open-air shopping centres dominate, and if you're serious about shopping, set aside the better part of a day to burn your baht here. Try to arrive around 11am, when the crowds are minimal, and avoid Sundays when much of Bangkok seems to flock to the air-con malls. Siam Square is most easily accessed via the BTS (Skytrain); National Stadium is a good start.

Ratchathewi has a lot less to offer – unless of course you have a specific sight in mind or want to check out a more workaday side of Bangkok. The attractions in this area can be covered in a few hours, and most are within walking distance of the BTS stop at Victory Monument.

Local Life

➡ **Mall-hopping** Although there often appears to be more snacking than shopping, on Sundays a significant part of Bangkok's population is drawn to this area's malls to socialise in air-conditioned style and comfort.

➡ **Air-Conditioned Dining** A mall-based food court may not seem like the most authentic place to eat *pàt tai* (fried noodles), but several of Bangkok's most famous restaurants and stalls maintain branches at the various Siam Square area malls.

➡ **Wholesale Retail** For penny-pinchers and visiting wholesalers the ultimate destination is Pratunam district, where a seemingly never-ending clothing bazaar stocks locally made and cheap import togs.

➡ **Keeping It Real** For a view of Bangkok without the malls, bakeries, fashionistas and tourists, take the BTS north to the Victory Monument in Ratchathewi district, where ordinary Thais are doing ordinary Thai things.

Getting There & Away

➡ **BTS** To Siam Square, Pratunam and Ploenchit: Siam, National Stadium, Chit Lom, Phloen Chit and Ratchadamri. To Ratchathewi: Ratchathewi, Phaya Thai and Victory Monument.

➡ **Klorng boat** To Siam Square, Pratunam and Ploenchit: Tha Hua Chang, Tha Pratunam and Tha Withayu. To Ratchathewi: Tha Pratunam.

➡ **Bus** To Siam Square, Pratunam and Ploenchit: air-con 141, 183, 204, 501, 508 and 547; ordinary 15, 16, 25, 47 and 73. To Ratchathewi: air-con 503, 513 and 536; ordinary 29, 36, 54, 59 and 112

TOP SIGHTS
JIM THOMPSON'S HOUSE

In 1959, 12 years after he single-handedly turned Thai silk into a hugely successful export business, American Jim Thompson bought a piece of land next to Khlong Saen Saeb and built himself a house. It wasn't, however, any old house. Thompson's love of all things Thai saw him buy six traditional wooden homes and reconstruct them in his garden. Although he met a mysterious end in 1967, today Thompson's house remains, both as a museum to these unique structures and as a tribute to the man.

The Man
Born in Delaware in 1906, Jim Thompson served in a forerunner of the CIA in Thailand during WWII. When in 1947 he spotted some silk in a market and was told it was woven in Baan Krua, he found the only place in Bangkok where silk was still woven by hand.

Thompson's Thai silk eventually attracted the interest of fashion houses in New York, Milan, London and Paris, and he gradually built a worldwide clientele for a craft that had, just a few years before, been in danger of dying out.

By 1967 Thai silk had annual sales of almost US$1.5 million. In March that year Thompson went missing while out for an afternoon walk in the Cameron Highlands of western Malaysia; his success as a businessman and background as a spy made it an international mystery. Thompson has never been heard from since, but the conspiracy theories have never stopped. Was it communist spies? Business rivals? A man-eating tiger? Although the mystery has never been solved, evidence revealed by American journalist Joshua Kurlantzick in his profile of Thompson, *The Ideal Man*, suggests that the vocal anti-American stance Thompson took later in his life may have made him a potential target of suppression by the CIA.

The House
Traditional Thai homes were multipurpose affairs, with little space for luxuries like separate living and sleeping rooms. Thompson adapted his six buildings, joining some, to create a larger home in which each room had a more familiar Western function. One room became an air-conditioned study, another a bedroom and the one nearest the *klorng* (canal; also spelt *khlong*) his dining room. Another departure from tradition is the way Thompson arranged each wall with its exterior side facing the house's interior, thus exposing the wall's bracing system.

Thompson's small but splendid Asian art collection is also on display in the main house; photography is not allowed inside any of the buildings. After the tour, be sure to poke around the house's jungle-like gardens, which include ponds filled with exotic fish. Recent additions to the compound include the excellent **Jim Thompson Art Center** (Map p260; www.jimthompsonhouse.com; Jim Thompson's House, 6 Soi Kasem San 2, Th Phra Ram I; ◎9am-5pm; 🛥Tha Hua Chang, 🚇National Stadium exit 1), a cafe and a shop flogging Jim Thompson–branded goods.

Beware of well-dressed touts in soi near the Thompson house who will tell you it is closed and then try to haul you off on a dodgy buying spree.

DON'T MISS...
➡ Thompson's art and antique collection
➡ A walk in the jungle-like garden
➡ Jim Thompson Art Center

PRACTICALITIES
➡ Map p260
➡ www.jimthompson house.com
➡ 6 Soi Kasem San 2
➡ adult/child 100/50B
➡ ◎9am-5pm, compulsory tours in English & French every 20min
➡ 🚇National Stadium exit 1

👁 SIGHTS

👁 Siam Square, Pratunam & Ploenchit

JIM THOMPSON'S HOUSE   HISTORICAL BUILDING
See p101.

BAAN KRUA   NEIGHBOURHOOD
Map p260 (บ้านครัว; Th Phayathai & Th Phra Ram VI; 🚤Tha Hua Chang, 🚇National Stadium exit 1) This canal-side neighbourhood is one of Bangkok's oldest communities. It dates back to the turbulent years at the end of the 18th century, when Cham Muslims from Cambodia and Vietnam fought on the side of the new Thai king and were rewarded with this plot of land east of the new capital. The immigrants brought their silk-weaving traditions with them, and the community grew when the residents built Khlong Saen Saeb to better connect them to the river.

The 1950s and '60s were boom years for Baan Krua after Jim Thompson hired the weavers and began exporting their silks across the globe. The last 40 years, however, haven't been so good. Silk production was moved elsewhere following Thompson's disappearance and the community spent 15 years successfully fighting to stop a freeway being built right through it. Through all this many Muslims moved out of the area; today it is estimated that only about 30% of the population is Muslim, the rest primarily immigrants from northeast Thailand. However, Baan Krua retains its Muslim character, and one of the original families is still weaving silk on old teak looms. The village, which is great for self-guided exploration, consists of old, tightly packed homes threaded by tiny paths barely wide enough for two people to pass. It has been described as a slum, but the house-proud residents are keen to point out that they might not live in high-rise condos, but that doesn't make their old community a slum.

BANGKOK ART & CULTURE CENTRE   ART GALLERY
Map p260 (BACC; www.bacc.or.th; cnr Th Phayathai & Th Phra Ram 1; ⊙10am-9pm Tue-Sat; 🚇National Stadium exit 3) This large, modern building in the centre of Bangkok is the

👁 TOP SIGHTS
SUAN PHAKKAD PALACE MUSEUM

Everyone loves Jim Thompson's House, but few have even heard of Suan Phakkad Palace Museum (Lettuce Farm Palace), another noteworthy traditional Thai house-museum. Once the residence of Princess Chumbon of Nakhon Sawan (and before that a lettuce farm – hence the name), the museum is a collection of five traditional wooden Thai houses linked by elevated walkways containing varied displays of art, antiques and furnishings. The landscaped grounds are a peaceful oasis complete with ducks, swans and a semi-enclosed, Japanese-style garden.

The diminutive **Lacquer Pavilion** at the back of the complex dates from the Ayuthaya period (the building originally sat in a monastery compound on the banks of Mae Nam Chao Phraya, just south of Ayuthaya) and features gold-leaf *Jataka* and *Ramayana* murals as well as scenes from daily Ayuthaya life. Larger residential structures at the front of the complex contain displays of Khmer, Hindu and Buddhist art, Ban Chiang ceramics and a collection of historic **Buddhas**, including a beautiful late U Thong–style image. In the noise and confusion of Bangkok, the gardens offer a tranquil retreat.

DON'T MISS...

➡ Lacquer Pavilion
➡ Buddha statue collection

PRACTICALITIES

➡ วังสวนผักกาด
➡ Map p263
➡ Th Sri Ayuthaya
➡ admission 100B
➡ ⊙9am-4pm
➡ 🚇Phaya Thai exit 4

most recent and promising addition to the city's arts scene. In addition to three floors and 3000 sq metres of gallery space, the centre also contains a handful of shops, private galleries and cafes.

SIAM OCEAN WORLD AQUARIUM
Map p260 (สยามโอเชี่ยนเวิร์ล; www.siamoceanworld. com; basement, Siam Paragon, Th Phra Ram I; adult/child 900/700B; ◎10am-9pm; ⬛Siam exit 5) Southeast Asia's largest oceanarium is also one of its most impressive. More than 400 species of fish, crustaceans and even penguins populate this vast underground facility. The main tank is the highlight, with an acrylic tunnel allowing you to walk beneath sharks, rays and all manner of fish. Diving with sharks (for a fee) is also an option if you have your diving licence, though you'll have almost as much fun timing your trip to coincide with the shark and penguin feedings; the former are usually at 1pm and 4pm, the latter at 12.30pm and 4.30pm; check the website for details.

JAMJUREE ART GALLERY ART GALLERY
Map p260 (Jamjuree Bldg, Chulalongkorn University, Th Phayathai; ◎10am-7pm Mon-Fri, noon-6pm Sat & Sun; ⬛Siam exit 2 & taxi) This gallery, part of Chulalongkorn University's Faculty of Arts, emphasises modern spiritual themes and brilliantly coloured abstracts from emerging student artists.

WHITESPACE ART GALLERY
Map p260 (www.whitespacegallery.com; 2nd fl, Lido Bldg, Soi 3, Siam Sq; ◎1-7pm Tue-Fri, 11.30am-8pm Sat & Sun; ⬛Siam exit 2) An active design studio, Whitespace also includes a small non-commercial gallery that features a diverse array of exhibitions by emerging artists.

FREE ERAWAN SHRINE HINDU SHRINE
Map p260 (ศาลพระพรหม; cnr Th Ratchadamri & Th Ploenchit; ◎6am-11pm; ⬛Chit Lom exit 8) The Erawan Shrine was originally built in 1956 as something of a last-ditch effort to end a string of misfortunes that occurred during the construction of a hotel, at that time known as the Erawan Hotel. After several incidents ranging from injured construction workers to the sinking of a ship carrying marble for the hotel, a Brahmin priest was consulted. Since the hotel was to be named after the elephant escort of Indra in Hindu mythology, the priest determined that Erawan required a passenger, and suggested it be that of Lord Brahma. A statue

was built and, lo and behold, the misfortunes miraculously ended.

Although the original Erawan Hotel was demolished in 1987, the shrine still exists, and today remains an important place of pilgrimage for Thais, particularly those in need of some material assistance. Those making a wish from the statue should ideally come between 7am and 8am, or 7pm and 8pm, and should offer a specific list of items that includes candles, incense, sugar cane or bananas, all of which are almost exclusively given in multiples of seven. Particularly popular are teak elephants, the money gained through the purchase of which is donated to a charity run by the current hotel, the Grand Hyatt Erawan. And as the tourist brochures depict, it is also possible to charter a classical Thai dance, often done as a way of giving thanks if a wish was granted.

FREE LINGAM SHRINE ANIMIST SHRINE
Map p260 (ศาลเจ้าแม่ทับทิม; Swissôtel Nai Lert Park, Th Witthayu/Wireless Rd; ◎24hr; ⬛Tha Withayu, ⬛Phloen Chit exit 1) Every village and neighbourhood has a local shrine, either a sacred banyan tree tied up with coloured scarves or a spirit house. But it isn't every day you see a phallus garden like this lingam shrine, tucked back behind the staff quarters of the Swissôtel Nai Lert Park. Clusters of carved stone and wooden shafts surround a spirit house and shrine built by millionaire businessman Nai Loet to honour Jao Mae Thap Thim, a female deity thought to reside in the old banyan tree on the site. Someone who made an offering shortly after the shrine was built had a baby, and the shrine has received a steady stream of worshippers – mostly young women seeking fertility – ever since.

If facing the entrance of the hotel, follow the small concrete pathway to the right, which winds down into the building beside the car park. The shrine is at the end of the building next to the *klorng*.

100 TONSON GALLERY ART GALLERY
Map p260 (www.100tonsongallery.com; 100 Soi Tonson; ◎11am-7pm Thu-Sun; ⬛Chit Lom exit 4) Housed in a spacious residential villa, and generally regarded as one of the city's top commercial galleries, 100 Tonson hosts a variety of contemporary exhibitions of all genres by local and international artists.

⊙ Ratchathewi

BANGKOK DOLL FACTORY & MUSEUM   MUSEUM

Map p263 (พิพิธภัณฑ์ตุ๊กตาบางกอกดอลล์; ☑0 2245 3008; www.bangkokdolls.com; 85 Soi Ratchataphan/ Mo Leng; ◷8am-5pm Mon-Sat; ᥅Phaya Thai exit 3 & taxi) This quirky museum and workshop was founded by Khunying Tongkorn Chandevimol in 1956 after she completed a doll-making course while living in Japan. Upon her return to Thailand, she began researching and making dolls, drawing from Thai mythology and historical periods. Today her personal collection includes 400 dolls from around the world, plus important pieces from her own workshop, where you can watch the figures being crafted by hand.

The museum is rather tricky to find; the easiest option is to take a taxi from BTS Phaya Thai and get the driver to call the museum for directions.

BAIYOKE II TOWER   NOTABLE BUILDING

Map p263 (ตึกใบหยก ๒; 22 Th Ratchaprarop; admission 250B; ◷9am-11pm; ᥅Tha Pratunam) Thailand's tallest tower soars to 88 storeys (85 of them above ground), the upper of which are often clad with some truly huge advertising signs. Naturally the main attraction here is the 84th-floor revolving observation deck. The views are as impressive as you'd expect from this height (unless it's too smoggy) but only just compensate for the tacky decor, uninspiring restaurant and inconvenient location.

VICTORY MONUMENT   MONUMENT

Map p263 (อนุสาวรีย์ชัย; cnr Th Ratchawithi & Th Phayathai; ᥅ordinary 12 & 62, ᥅Victory Monument) This obelisk monument was built by the then military government in 1941 to commemorate a 1940 campaign against the French in Laos. Today the monument is primarily a landmark for observing the social universe of local university students and countless commuters. It's worth exploring the neighbourhood around Victory Monument, which is reminiscent of provincial Thai towns, if not exactly hicksville. It's also something of a transport hub with minivans to Ko Samet, Kanchanaburi and Ayuthaya stopping here, and there's a useful BTS stop.

✖ EATING

✖ Siam Square, Pratunam & Ploenchit

CRYSTAL JADE LA MIAN XIAO LONG BAO   CHINESE $

Map p260 (Urban Kitchen; basement, Erawan Bangkok, 494 Th Ploenchit; mains 115-420B; ◷lunch & dinner; ᥅Chit Lom exit 8) The tongue-twistingly long name of this excellent Singaporean chain refers to the restaurant's signature *la mian* (wheat noodles) and the famous Shanghainese *xiao long pao* ('soup' dumplings). If you order the hand-pulled noodles (which you should do), allow the staff to cut them with kitchen shears, otherwise you'll end up with ample evidence of your meal on your shirt.

SRA BUA   THAI $$$

Map p260 (☑0 2162 9000; www.kempinskibangkok.com; ground fl, Siam Kempinski Hotel, 991/9 Th Rama I; set meal 1500-2400B; ◷noon-3pm & 6-11pm Mon-Fri, 6-11pm Sat & Sun; ᥅Siam exit 3 & 5) Helmed by a Thai and a Dane whose Copenhagen restaurant, Kiin Kiin, has snagged a Michelin star, Sra Bua takes a correspondingly international approach to Thai food. Putting Thai dishes and ingredients through the wringer of molecular gastronomy, the couple have created dishes such as frozen red curry with lobster salad, and pomelo salad with grilled fish and warm yam sauce. Reservations recommended.

FOUR SEASONS SUNDAY BRUNCH   INTERNATIONAL $$$

Map p260 (☑0 2250 1000; Four Seasons Hotel, 155 Th Ratchadamri; 2350B; ◷11.30am-3pm Sun; ᥅Ratchadamri exit 4) All of the Four Seasons' highly regarded restaurants – Spice Market, Shintaro, Biscotti and Madison – set up steam tables for this decadent Sunday brunch buffet. Numerous cooking stations and champagne options take this light years beyond your normal Sunday brunch. It's popular, so be sure to reserve your table a couple of weeks in advance.

GIANNI RISTORANTE   ITALIAN $$$

Map p260 (☑0 2252 1619; www.giannibkk.com; 34/1 Soi Tonson; mains 290-1290B; ◷lunch & dinner; ᥅Chit Lom exit 4) Widely considered among Bangkok's finest Italian restaurants, Gianni also offers more than 250 wines and

FOOD COURT FRENZY

The Siam Square area is home to the majority of Bangkok's malls, which means that it's also home to several mall-based food courts. The following are some choices:

MBK Food Court (Map p260; 6th fl, MBK Center, cnr Th Phra Ram I & Th Phayathai; mains 35-150B; ☺10am-9pm; ☒National Stadium exit 4) The granddaddy of the genre, MBK's expansive food court offers vendors selling dishes from virtually every corner of Thailand and beyond. Exchange cash for tickets and burn them at the tasty vegetarian food stall (stall C8) or the decent northeastern Thai food vendor (C22). Any tickets you don't use can be refunded at another desk.

Gourmet Paradise (Map p260; ground fl, Siam Paragon, 991/1 Th Phra Ram I; mains 35-500B; ☺10am-10pm; ☒Siam exits 3 & 5) The perpetually busy Gourmet Paradise unites international fast-food chains, domestic restaurants and food court—style stalls, with a particular emphasis on the sweet stuff. Purchasing at the food court is done by a temporary credit card that you must top up in advance at one of two counters. The Gourmet Market is one of the city's best-stocked supermarkets.

Food Loft (Map p260; 6th fl, Central Chidlom, 1027 Th Ploenchit; mains 65-950B; ☺10am-9pm) This department store pioneered the concept of the upscale food court, and mock-ups of the various Indian, Italian, Greek and other international dishes aid in the decision-making process. Upon entering, you'll be given a temporary credit card. Paying is done on your way out.

FoodPark (Map p260; 4th fl, Big C, 97/11 Th Ratchadamri; mains 30-90B; ☺9am-9pm) The food selections here are not going to inspire you to move east, but they are abundant and cheap, and representative of the kind of 'fast food' Thais enjoy eating. To pay you must first exchange your cash for a temporary credit card at one of several counters; your change is refunded at the same desk.

one of the more generous lunch specials in town. The eponymous and ebullient owner is always on site, and more than willing to recommend a dish or the right bottle to accompany it.

GAGGAN INDIAN $$$
Map p260 (☎0 2652 1700; www.eatatgaggan.com; 68/1 Soi Langsuan; set menu 1600B; ☺dinner; ☒Ratchadamri exit 2) The white, refurbished villa that houses Gaggan seems more appropriate for an English-themed tea house than a restaurant serving self-proclaimed 'progressive Indian', but Gaggan is all about incongruity. The set menu here spans 10 courses, ranging from the daring (a ball of raita) to the traditional (some excellent tandoori), with bright flavours and unexpected but satisfying twists as a unifying element.

FOOD PLUS THAI $
Map p260 (alleyway btwn Soi 5 & Soi 6, Siam Sq; mains 30-70B; ☺7am-6pm; ☒Siam exit 2) This claustrophobic alleyway is bursting with the wares of several *ráhn kôw gaang* (rice and curry stalls). Everything is made ahead of time, so simply point to what looks tasty.

You'll be hard-pressed to spend more than 100B, and the flavours are unanimously authentic and delicious. Try to avoid the heart of the lunch rush (approximately 12.15pm to 12.45pm) when virtually every shopkeeper in the area (and believe us, there are many) seems to descend on the place.

COCA SUKI CHINESE-THAI $
Map p260 (416/3-8 Th Henri Dunant; mains 60-200B; ☺lunch & dinner; ☒Siam exit 6) Immensely popular with Thai families, *sù·gêe* takes the form of a bubbling hotpot of broth and the raw ingredients to dip therein. Coca is one of the oldest purveyors of the dish, and this branch reflects the brand's efforts to appear more modern. Fans of spice be sure to request the tangy 'tom yam' broth.

SOM TAM NUA NORTHEASTERN THAI $
Map p260 (392/14 Soi 5, Siam Sq; mains 59-130B; ☺10.45am-9.30pm; ☒Siam exit 4) It can't compete with the street stalls for flavour and authenticity, but if you need to be seen, particularly while in air-con and trendy surroundings, this is a good place to sample northeastern Thai specialities. Expect a lengthy line at dinner.

ERAWAN TEA ROOM THAI $$

Map p260 (2nd fl, Erawan Bangkok, 494 Th Ploenchit; mains 180-480B; ⊘lunch & dinner; ⎘Chit Lom exit 8) The oversized chairs, panoramic windows and variety of hot drinks make this one of Bangkok's best places to catch up with the paper. The lengthy menu will likely encourage you to linger longer, and the selection of jams and teas to take away allows you to re-create the experience at home.

SANGUAN SRI THAI $

Map p260 (59/1 Th Witthayu/Wireless Rd; mains 40-150B; ⊘10am-3pm Mon-Sat; ⎘Phloen Chit exit 5) This restaurant, essentially a concrete bunker filled with furniture circa 1973, can afford to remain decidedly *chev-i* (old fashioned) simply because of its reputation. Mimic the area's hungry office staff and try the excellent *gaang pèt ъèt yâhng*, red curry with grilled duck breast served over snowy white *kà·nŏm jeen* noodles.

NEW LIGHT COFFEE HOUSE THAI $

Map p260 (426/1-4 Soi Chulalongkorn 64; mains 60-200B; ⊘lunch & dinner; ⎘Siam exit 2) Travel back in time to 1960s-era Bangkok at this vintage diner popular with students from nearby Chulalongkorn University. Try old-school Western dishes, all of which come accompanied by a soft roll and green salad, or choose from the extensive Thai menu.

KOKO THAI $

Map p260 (262/2 Soi 3, Siam Sq; mains 70-220B; ⊘11am-9pm; ⌕; ⎘Siam exit 2) This casual cafelike restaurant offers a lengthy vegie menu, not to mention a brief but solid repertoire of meat-based Thai dishes, such as a Penang curry served with tender pork, or fish deep-fried and served with Thai herbs. Perfect for a mixed crowd.

KA-NOM BAKERY $

Map p260 (266/8 Soi 3, Siam Sq; mains 20-80B; ⊘10am-8pm; ⎘Siam exit 2) Self-proclaimed 'fashion bakery', ka-nom serves delicious *kà·nŏm kài,* a baked sweet similar to Portuguese egg tarts. Great excuse to break up your Siam Square shopping spree. There's also a branch in Siam Paragon (p106).

✗ Ratchathewi

MALLIKA RESTAURANT SOUTHERN THAI $$

Map p263 (21/36 Th Rang Nam; mains 70-480B; ⊘lunch & dinner Mon-Sat; ⎘Victory Monument exit 2) Visit this corner of northern Bangkok for a taste of Thailand's southern provinces. The menu spans the region with spicy hits such as *kôo·a glîng* (minced meat fried with curry paste) or *gaang sôm* (a turmeric-laden seafood soup). Prices are slightly higher than elsewhere, but you're paying for quality.

TIDA ESARN NORTHEASTERN THAI $

Map p263 (1/2-5 Th Rang Nam; mains 50-150B; ⊘10.30am-10.30pm; ⎘Victory Monument exit 2) Tida Esarn sells country-style Thai food in a decidedly urban setting. Appropriately, foreigners provide the bulk of the restaurant's customers, but the kitchen still insists on serving full-flavoured Isan-style dishes such as *súp nòr mái,* a tart salad of shredded bamboo.

PATHÉ INTERNATIONAL-THAI $

Map p263 (507 Th Ratchawithi; mains 75-160B; ⊘2pm-1am; ⎘Victory Monument exit 4) The modern Thai equivalent of a 1950s-era American diner, this popular place combines solid Thai food, a fun atmosphere and a jukebox playing scratched records. The menu is equally eclectic, and combines Thai and Western dishes and ingredients; be sure to save room for the deep-fried ice cream.

VICTORY POINT THAI $

Map p263 (cnr Th Phayathai & Th Ratchawithi; mains 30-60B; ⊘6pm-midnight; ⎘Victory Monument exit 4) In Bangkok, the best meals are always in unlikely places. Far from the foreign forces of inner Bangkok, Victory Point can be as provincial as it wants, with a squat village of supercasual and delicious street stalls.

🍷 DRINKING & NIGHTLIFE

🍸 Siam Square, Pratunam & Ploenchit

CO-CO WALK BAR

Map p260 (87/70 Th Phayathai; ⎘Ratchathewi exit 2) This covered compound is a smorgasbord of pubs, bars and live music popular with Thai university students. The Tube left its heart in London, and is heavy on Brit pop, Chilling House Café features a few pool tables and Thai hits played on live acoustic guitar, and 69 sets the pace with cover bands playing Western rock staples and current hits.

HYDE & SEEK   BAR

Map p260 (ground fl, Athenee Residence, 65/1 Soi Ruam Rudi; ☺11am-1am; ⊠Phloen Chit exit 4) The tasty and comforting English-inspired bar snacks and meals have earned Hyde & Seek the right to call itself a 'gastro bar', but we reckon the real reasons to come are arguably Bangkok's most well-stocked bar and some of the city's tastiest and most sophisticated cocktails.

AD MAKERS   BAR

Map p260 (ground fl, Athenee Residence, 65/1 Soi Ruam Rudi; ☺11am-2pm & 5pm-1am Mon-Fri, 5pm-1am Sat & Sun; ⊠Phloen Chit exit 4) The most recent incarnation of this long-standing bar-restaurant – originally started up in 1985 by a group of ad executive buddies – draws in diners and partiers with tasty regional Thai eats, live tunes (from Tuesday to Saturday) and draught beer.

DIPLOMAT BAR   BAR

Map p260 (ground fl, Conrad Hotel, 87 Th Witthayu/Wireless Rd; ☺5pm-1am; ⊠Phloen Chit exit 5) Named for its location in the middle of the embassy district, this is one of the few hotel lounges that locals make a point of visiting. Choose from an expansive list of innovative martinis and sip to live jazz, played gracefully at conversation level.

TO-SIT   BAR

Map p260 (www.tosit.com; Soi 3, Siam Sq; ⊠Siam exit 2) Live, loud and sappy music; cheap and spicy food; good friends and cold beer: To-Sit epitomises everything a Thai university student could wish for on a night out. There are branches all over town (check the website), but the Siam Sq location has the advantage of being virtually the only option in an area that's buzzing during the day but dead at night.

ROOF   BAR

(25th fl, Siam@Siam, 865 Th Phra Ram I; ⊠National Stadium exit 1) In addition to superb views of central Bangkok from 25 floors up, Roof offers a dedicated personal martini sommelier and an extensive wine and champagne list. Party House One, on the ground floor of the same hotel, offers live music most nights.

REDSKY   BAR

Map p260 (55th fl, Centara Grand, Central World Plaza; ☺5pm-1am; ⊠Chit Lom exit 9 to Sky Walk, Siam exit 6 to Sky Walk) Perched on the 55th floor of a striking new skyscraper, Bangkok's most recent rooftop dining venture is formal and boasts an extensive martini menu.

FOREIGN CORRESPONDENTS' CLUB OF THAILAND   BAR-RESTAURANT

Map p260 (FCCT; www.fccthai.com; Penthouse, Maneeya Center, 518/5 Th Ploenchit; ☺noon-2.30pm & 6pm-midnight; ⊠Chit Lom exit 2) A bar-restaurant, not to mention a bona-fide gathering place for the city's hacks and photogs, FCCT also hosts art exhibitions ranging in genre from photojournalism to contemporary painting. Check the website to see what's on.

DON'T CALL ME LADYBOY

Prempreeda Pramoj Na Ayutthaya is a transwoman researcher and activist.

Why does Thailand appear to have so many transgender people? It's a cultural heritage based in a very old concept of gender that can even be found in ancient palm leaf manuscripts.

The Thai word ladyboy is sometimes used in English to refer to transgender people. How do you prefer to be called? I prefer [the Thai word] *gà·teu·i* [also spelt *kàthoey*] because it goes back to an indigenous Thai belief that sex isn't binary. The words ladyboy and shemale are often used to sell sex and can stigmatise transgender people.

To outsiders, Thailand appears very open to homosexuals and transgender people – is this really the case? In everyday life, transgender people can live freely, but on a policy level we still face many difficulties.

What do you hope to achieve as an activist? I'm working to change the laws and policies so that homosexuals and transgender people can feel more comfortable in Thailand.

🍷 Ratchathewi

WINE PUB
BAR

Map p263 (www.pullmanbangkokkingpower; Pullman Bangkok King Power, 8/2 Th Rang Nam; ⏱6pm-2am; 🚇Victory Monument exit 2) If the upmarket but supremely chilled setting and spinning DJ aren't compelling enough reasons to venture from your Thanon Sukhumvit comfort zone, then consider that this is probably the least expensive place in town to drink wine. Check the website for revolving nibbles promotions that span everything from imported cheeses and cold cuts to tapas.

SKY TRAIN JAZZ CLUB
BAR

Map p263 (cnr Th Rang Nam & Th Phayathai; 🚇Victory Monument exit 2) A visit to this comically misnamed bar is more like chilling on the rooftop of your stoner buddy's flat than any jazz club we've ever been to. But there are indeed views of the BTS, jazz on occasion and a scrappy speakeasy atmosphere. To find it, look for the sign and proceed up the graffiti-strewn stairway until you reach the roof.

⭐ ENTERTAINMENT

TOP CHOICE AKSRA THEATRE
THEATRE

Map p263 (📞0 2677 8888, ext 5730; www.aksratheatre.com; 3rd fl, King Power Complex, 8/1 Th Rang Nam; tickets 400-600B; ⏱shows 7.30-8.30pm Mon-Wed, dinner shows 6.30-7pm Thu-Sun; 🚇Victory Monument exit 2) A variety of performances are now held at this modern theatre, but the highlight is performances of the *Ramakian* by using knee-high puppets that require three puppeteers to strike humanlike poses. Come early in the week for a performance in the Aksra Theatre, or later for a Thai buffet dinner coupled with a show.

SAXOPHONE PUB & RESTAURANT
LIVE MUSIC

Map p263 (www.saxophonepub.com; 3/8 Th Phayathai; ⏱6pm-2am; 🚇Victory Monument exit 2) Saxophone is still Bangkok's premier live-music venue - a dark, intimate space where you can pull up a chair just a few metres away from the band and see their every bead of sweat. If you like some mystique in your musicians, watch the blues, jazz, reggae or rock from the balcony.

CALYPSO CABARET
THEATRE

Map p260 (📞0 2653 3960; www.calypsocabaret.com; Asia Hotel, 296 Th Phayathai; tickets 1200B; ⏱show times 8.15pm & 9.45pm; 🚇Ratchathewi exit 1) Watching *kàthoey* (transgender people) perform tacky show tunes has, not surprisingly, become the latest 'must-do' fixture on the Bangkok tourist circuit. Calypso caters to the trend with choreographed stage shows featuring Broadway high kicks and lip-synched pop tunes.

RAINTREE
LIVE MUSIC

Map p263 (116/63-64 Th Rang Nam; 🚇Victory Monument exit 2) This rustic pub is one of the few remaining places in town to hear 'songs for life', Thai folk music with roots in the communist insurgency of the 1960s and '70s. Tasty bar snacks also make it a clever place to have a bite to eat.

ROCK PUB
LIVE MUSIC

Map p260 (www.therockpub-bangkok.com; 93/26-28 Th Phayathai; ⏱9.30pm-2am; 🚇Ratchathewi) With posters of Iron Maiden as interior design, and black jeans and long hair as the dress code, this cavelike live-music bar is Thailand's unofficial Embassy of Heavy Metal.

SIAM SQUARE'S SILVER SCREENS

The Siam Square area is home to Bangkok's ritziest cinemas. Each mall has its own theatre, but **Siam Paragon Cineplex** (Map p260; 📞0 2129 4635; www.paragoncineplex.com; 5th fl, Siam Paragon, 991/1 Th Phra Ram I; 🚇Siam exits 3 & 5), with its 16 screens (including an IMAX theatre), 5000 seats and Enigma, a members-only theatre, most likely comes out on top. If you're looking for something with a bit more character, consider the old-school stand-alone theatres just across the street such as **Scala** (Map p260; 📞0 2251 2861; Soi 1, Siam Sq; 🚇Siam exit 2) and **Lido** (Map p260; 📞0 2252 6498; www.apexsiam-square.com; btwn Soi 2 & Soi 3, Siam Sq; 🚇Siam exit 2).

LOCAL BRANDS WORTH BUYING

D&O Shop (Gaysorn Plaza) This government-sponsored shop is an effort to raise the profile of modern Thai design. The items, which range from furniture to knick-knacks, are modern and funky, and give a new breath of life to the concept of Thai design.

Doi Tung (Siam Discovery Center) This royally funded enterprise sells beautiful hand-woven carpets, ceramics and some of Thailand's best domestic coffee beans.

Thann Native (Gaysorn Plaza) Smell good enough to eat with these botanical-based spa products. Products are all natural, rooted in Thai traditional medicine, and stylish enough to share space with brand-name beauty.

A.V. Aranyik (Gaysorn Plaza) Born out of the ancient sword-making traditions of Ayuthaya Province, this family-owned business produces distinctively Thai stainless-steel cutlery.

Propaganda (Siam Discovery Center) Thai designer Chaiyut Plypetch dreamed up this brand's signature character, the devilish Mr P, who appears in anatomically correct cartoon lamps and other products.

🛍 SHOPPING

TOP CHOICE **MBK CENTER** SHOPPING CENTRE

Map p260 (www.mbk-center.com; cnr Th Phra Ram I & Th Phayathai; ⊙10am-9pm; ⊠National Stadium exit 4) This unbelievably immense shopping mall is quickly becoming one of Bangkok's top attractions. Swedish and other languages can be heard as much as Thai, and on any given weekend half of Bangkok can be found here combing through an inexhaustible range of small stalls and shops. You can buy everything you need here: mobile phones, accessories, shoes, name brands, wallets, handbags and T-shirts. The mall's 6th-floor food court is one of the city's most expansive.

And although you're not going to find many bargains, MBK is also one of the more convenient one-stop shopping destinations for photo equipment. Foto File, on the ground floor, has a good selection of used gear; the shop's sister venture, Photo Thailand, stocks all manner of new gear on the 3rd floor. There's well-stocked Sunny Camera, also on the 3rd floor, and Big Camera, on the 5th.

GAYSORN PLAZA SHOPPING CENTRE

Map p260 (www.gaysorn.com; cnr Th Ploenchit & Th Ratchadamri; ⊙10am-8pm; ⊠Chit Lom exit 9) A haute couture catwalk, Gaysorn has spiralling staircases, all-white halls and mouthfuls of top-name designers. The 2nd-floor 'Thai Fashion Chic' zone is a crash course in Bangkok's local fashion industry. Relatively well-established Thai labels including Kai, GGUB and Stretsis are rep-

resented, or you could head over to Myth, an umbrella store for emerging domestic brands.

Stores on the 3rd floor offer the same level of sophistication for your home. Thann Native sells locally inspired soaps and shampoos fragrant enough to eat. Lamont carries elegant ceramics, and Almeta, Thai silk. The open-air D&O Shop is the first retail venture of an organisation created to encourage awareness of Thai design abroad.

TOP CHOICE **SIAM SQUARE** SHOPPING CENTRE

Map p260 (Th Phra Ram I, near Th Phayathai, Siam Square; ⊙11am-9pm; ⊠Siam exits 2, 4 & 6) Siam Square is ground zero for teenage culture in Bangkok. Pop music blares out of tinny speakers, and gangs of hipsters in various costumes ricochet between fast-food restaurants and closet-sized boutiques. **Digital Gateway** (Map p260; cnr Th Phra Ram I & Soi 4; ⊙10am-9pm) stocks everything electronic, from computers to cameras. **DJ Siam** (Map p260; Soi 4) carries all the Thai indie and T-pop albums you'll need to speak 'teen'. Small shops peddle pop-hip styles along Soi 2 and Soi 3, but most outfits require a barely there waist.

SIAM PARAGON SHOPPING CENTRE

Map p260 (www.siamparagon.co.th; 991/1 Th Phra Ram I; ⊙10am-10pm; ⊠Siam exits 3 & 5) Paragon epitomises the city's fanaticism for the new, the excessive, and absurd slogans. In addition to the usual high-end brands, there's a Lamborghini dealer on the 2nd floor should you need a ride home, and one floor up the

START **JIM THOMPSON'S HOUSE**
END **HYDE & SEEK**
DISTANCE **ABOUT 3KM**
DURATION **TWO TO FOUR HOURS**

Neighbourhood Walk
Siam Square Shopping Spree

This walk cuts across the heart of Bangkok's most commercial district via elevated walkways, escalators and air-conditioned malls. Start no earlier than 11am, when most shopping centres open.

Begin at ❶ **MBK Center**, where you can pick up some new sneakers or fuel up for the rest of the walk at the mall's 6th-floor food court.

From MBK, it's possible to continue, more or less, without touching the ground again. Following the elevated walkway to ❷ **Siam Discovery Center**, continue to ❸ **Siam Center** and ❹ **Siam Paragon** via linking walkways. Have a sweet snack at the latter's basement-level food court, or if you're missing the heat and exhaust, make a detour across Th Phra Ram 1 to the teen-themed shops and restaurants of ❺ **Siam Square**.

From Siam BTS station, continue east along the elevated walkway known as Sky Walk. After a couple of minutes, on your left you'll see ❻ **Wat Pathum Wanaram**, an incongruously located Buddhist temple. Turn left on the bridge that connects to ❼ **Central World Plaza**, or continue forward until you reach busy ❽ **Ratchaprasong Intersection**, the area seized by Red Shirt protesters for three months in 2010. The intersection is also home to the busy ❾ **Erawan Shrine**.

Returning to the Sky Walk, ride the escalator to ❿ **Gaysorn Plaza**, where on the 3rd floor you'll find some of the city's classiest handicrafts, housewares and souvenirs. If you still need gifts, pop into the adjacent ⓫ **Narai Phand**, a government-sponsored handicraft emporium.

If there's anything you've forgotten, you can most likely pick it up at your last stop, ⓬ **Central Chidlom**, a seven-storey department store. Otherwise, end your walk, simultaneously balancing your chequebook and sipping one of Bangkok's best mixed drinks, at ⓭ **Hyde & Seek**.

SIAM SQUARE, PRATUNAM, PLOENCHIT & RATCHATHEWI

True Urban Park 'lifestyle centre' featuring a cafe, internet access and a shop selling books, music and camera equipment. Bookworms will fancy Kinokuniya (3rd floor), the largest English-language bookstore in Thailand, as well as the expansive branch of Asia Books (2nd floor).

Even more audacious than the retail sections are the spectacular aquarium Siam Ocean World, an IMAX theatre and Gourmet Paradise, an expansive basement level-food court. Whew.

PRATUNAM MARKET   MARKET
Map p260 (cnr Th Phetchaburi & Th Ratchaprarop; ◷9am-midnight; 🚤Tha Pratunam, 🚇Chit Lom exit 9) The emphasis here is on cheap clothes, and you could spend hours flipping through the T-shirts at the seemingly endless Baiyoke Garment Center.

The greater market area occupies the neighbourhood behind the shopfronts on the corner of Th Phetchaburi and Th Ratchaprarop, but it doesn't end here: across the street is the five-storey Platinum Fashion Mall, which sports the latest in no-brand couture.

SIAM CENTER   SHOPPING CENTRE
Map p260 (cnr Th Phra Ram I & Th Phayathai, Siam Sq; ◷10am-9pm; 🚇Siam exit 1) Siam Center, Thailand's first shopping centre, was built in 1976 but, since a recent nip and tuck, hardly shows its age. Its 3rd floor is one of the best locations to check out established local labels such as Flynow, Senada Theory and Tango.

SIAM DISCOVERY CENTER   SHOPPING CENTRE
Map p260 (cnr Th Phra Ram I & Th Phayathai, Siam Sq; ◷10am-9pm; 🚇Siam exit 1) This is, somewhat incongruously, one of the best places in town to stock up on camping gear, and within tent-pitching distance of each other on the 3rd floor are Procam-Fis, Equinox Shop and the North Face. There's also a branch of **Madam Tussaud's** (www.madametussauds.com/Bangkok/en/; 6th fl, Siam Discovery Center; admission 600-800B; ◷10am-9pm).

CENTRAL WORLD PLAZA   SHOPPING CENTRE
Map p260 (www.centralworld.co.th; cnr Th Ploenchit & Th Ratchadamri; ◷10am-10pm; 🚇Chit Lom exit 9 to Sky Walk, Siam exit 6 to Sky Walk) Spanning eight storeys of more than 500 shops and 100 restaurants, Central World is one of Southeast Asia's largest shopping cen-

tres. But it suffered a huge setback in May 2010 when its centrepiece Zen department store was torched by fleeing protesters. Other parts of the complex were largely unaffected, and in 2012, the Zen department store was finally reopened.

NARAI PHAND   SOUVENIRS
Map p260 (www.naraiphand.com; ground fl, President Tower, 973 Th Ploenchit; ◷10am-8pm; 🚇Chit Lom exit 7) Souvenir-quality handicrafts are given fixed prices and comfortable air-conditioning at this government-run facility. You won't find anything here that you haven't already seen at all of the tourist street markets, but it is a good stop if you're pressed for time or are spooked by haggling.

PINKY TAILORS   CLOTHING
Map p260 (www.pinkytailor.com; 888/40 Mahatun Plaza Arcade, Th Ploenchit; ◷10am-7.30pm Mon-Sat; 🚇Phloen Chit exits 2 & 4) Suit jackets have been Mr Pinky's speciality for 35 years. His custom-made dress shirts, for both men and women, also have dedicated fans. Located behind the Mahatun Building.

IT'S HAPPENED TO BE A CLOSET   CLOTHING
Map p260 (1st fl, Siam Paragon, 991/1 Th Phra Ram I; ◷10am-10pm; 🚇Siam exits 3 & 5) Garbled grammar aside, this domestic brand has gained a glowing reputation for its bright colours and bold patterns. The ever-expanding Closet empire now even features a bakery shop at the basement level of Siam Paragon (p109).

FLYNOW   CLOTHING
Map p260 (www.flynowbangkok.com; 2nd fl, Gaysorn Plaza, cnr Th Ploenchit & Th Ratchadamri; 🚇Chit Lom exit 9) A long-standing leader in Bangkok's home-grown fashion scene, Flynow creates feminine couture that has appeared in several international shows. Also available at Siam Center and Central World Plaza.

PANTIP PLAZA   COMPUTER EQUIPMENT
Map p260 (604 Th Phetchaburi; ◷10am-9pm; 🚇Ratchathewi exit 4) If you can tolerate the crowds and annoying pornography vendors ('DVD sex? DVD sex?'), Pantip, a multistorey computer and electronics warehouse, might just be your kinda paradise. Technorati will find pirated software and music, gear for hobbyists to enhance their machines, flea market–style peripherals and other odds

and ends. Up on the 5th floor is IT City, a reliable computer megastore that can provide VAT Refund forms for tourists.

TANGO
CLOTHING

Map p260 (www.tango.co.th; 2nd fl, Gaysorn Plaza, cnr Th Ploenchit & Th Ratchadamri; ⊠Chit Lom exit 9) This homegrown brand specialises in funky leather goods, but you may not even recognise the medium under the layers of bright embroidery and chunky jewels. Also available at Siam Center.

MARCO TAILORS
CLOTHING

Map p260 (430/33 Soi 7, Siam Sq; ⊙9am-7pm Mon-Fri; ⊠Siam exit 2) Dealing solely in men's suits, this long-standing and reliable tailor has a wide selection of banker-sensibility wools and cottons. If you're considering getting suited, be sure to set aside at least a week for the various fittings.

UTHAI'S GEMS
JEWELLERY

Map p260 (☎0 2253 8582; 28/7 Soi Ruam Rudi, Th Ploenchit; ⊙10am-6pm Mon-Sat; ⊠Phloen Chit exit 4) Uthai's Gems' showroom is in quiet Soi Ruam Rudi serving the discriminating embassy community. Nonhagglers appreciate his fixed prices and good service. Appointments recommended.

WHAT'S YOUR NUMBER?

The 4th floor of MBK Center resembles something of a digital produce market. A confusing maze of stalls sell all the components to send you into the land of cellular: a new phone, a new number and a SIM card. Even if you'd rather keep yourself out of reach, do a walk-through to observe the chaos and the mania over phone numbers. Computer print-outs displaying all the available numbers for sale turn the phone numbers game into a commodities market. The luckier the phone number, the higher the price; upwards of thousands of dollars have been paid for numbers composed entirely of nines, considered lucky in honour of the current king, Rama IX (King Bhumibol Adulyadej; r 1946–present), and because the Thai word for 'nine' is similar to the word for 'progress'.

CENTRAL CHIDLOM
SHOPPING CENTRE

Map p260 (www.central.co.th; 1027 Th Ploenchit; ⊙10am-10pm; ⊠Chit Lom exit 5) Central is a modern Western-style department store with locations throughout the city. This flagship store, Thailand's largest, is the snazziest of all the branches.

🏃 SPORTS & ACTIVITIES

1930 SPA
SPA

Map p260 (☎0 2254 8606; www.spa1930.com; 42 Soi Tonson; à la carte from 1000B, packages 2000-4500B; ⊙9.30am-9.30pm; ⊠Chit Lom exit 4) Discreet and sophisticated, Spa 1930 rescues relaxers from the contrived spa ambience of New Age music and ingredients you'd rather see at a dinner party. The menu is simple (face, body care and body massage) and the scrubs and massage oils are logical players.

THANN SANCTUARY
SPA

Map p260 (☎0 2658 0550; www.thann.info; 5th fl, Siam Discovery Center, cnr Th Phra Ram I & Th Phayathai; ⊙10am-9pm; ⊠Siam exit 1) This local brand of herbal-based cosmetics has launched a series of mall-based spas – perfect for post-shopping therapy. Also in Gaysorn Plaza.

ASIAN OASIS
CRUISE

Map p260 (☎0 2655 6246; www.asian-oasis.com; 7th floor, Nai Lert Tower, 2/4 Th Witthayu/Wireless Rd; 2-day trip 6450-10,450B ; ⊠Phloen Chit exit 1) Cruise the Chao Phraya River aboard a fleet of restored rice barges with old-world charm and modern conveniences. Trips include either an upstream or downstream journey to/from Ayuthaya with bus transfer in the opposite direction. Costs vary according to season and direction.

YOGA ELEMENTS STUDIO
YOGA

Map p260 (www.yogaelements.com; 23rd fl, Vanissa Bldg, 29 Soi Chitlom; sessions from 500B; ⊠Chit Lom exit 5) Run by American Adrian Cox, who trained at Om in New York and teaches primarily vinyasa and ashtanga, this is the most respected studio in town. The high-rise location helps you rise above it all, too.

UNION LANGUAGE SCHOOL LANGUAGE COURSE

Map p260 (☑0 2214 6033; www.unionlanguage
school.com; 7th fl, 328 CCT Office Bldg, Th Phayathai; tuition from 7000B; ☐Ratchathewi exit 1) This
school is recognised as having the best and
most rigorous courses (many missionaries
study here), employing a balance of struc-
ture- and communication-oriented method-
ologies in 80-hour, four-week modules.

SF STRIKE BOWL BOWLING

Map p260 (☑0 2611 4555; 7th fl, MBK Center, cnr
Th Phra Ram I & Th Phayathai; from 30B; ☺10am-
1am; ☐National Stadium exit 4) Thai teenagers
crowd this psychedelically decorated bowling alley at all hours of the day and night.
The cost varies, depending on what time
you play.

AMERICAN UNIVERSITY ALUMNI
LANGUAGE CENTER LANGUAGE COURSE

Map p260 (AUA; ☑0 2252 8398; www.auathai.
com; 179 Th Ratchadamri; tuition per hr 128B;
☐Ratchadamri exit 2) This long-standing institute features various levels of tuition that
can be completed within a sliding timescale.

AAA THAI LANGUAGE
CENTER LANGUAGE COURSE

Map p260 (☑0 2655 5629; www.aaathai.com;
6th fl, 29 Vanissa Bldg, Th Chitlom; ☐Chit Lom
exit 3) Opened by a group of experienced
Thai-language teachers from other schools,
good-value AAA Thai has a loyal following.

ABSOLUTE YOGA YOGA

Map p260 (☑0 2252 4400; www.absoluteyoga
bangkok.com; 4th fl, Amarin Plaza, Th Ploenchit;

LIVING LARGE

In your home town you may be considered average or even petite but,
based on the Thai measuring stick,
you're an extralarge, clearly marked
in the tag as 'LL' or, worse still, 'XL'.
If that batters the body image, then
skip the street markets, where you'll
bust the seams from the waist up – if
you can squirm that far into the open-
ings. If you're larger than a US size
10 or an Australian size 14, you strike
out altogether. Men will find that they
exceed Thai clothes in length and
shoulder width, as well as shoe sizes.
For formal wear, many expats turn to
custom orders through tailors. For
ready-to-wear, many of the vendors at
Pratunam Market and several stalls on
the 7th floor of MBK Center stock the
larger sizes.

---

membership per month from 2064B; ☐Chit Lom
exit 6) This is the largest of Bangkok's yoga
-studio businesses, teaching Bikram hot
yoga plus a host of other styles.

PILATES STUDIO YOGA

Map p260 (☑0 2650 7797; www.pilatesbang
kok.com; 888/58-9 Mahatun Plaza, Th Ploenchit;
☐Phloen Chit exit 2) The first choice for those
in Bangkok looking for Pilates instruction
and training.

Riverside, Silom & Lumphini

RIVERSIDE | THANON SILOM | LUMPHINI & AROUND

Neighbourhood Top Five

1 Dining at **nahm** (p122), quite possibly the best Thai restaurant in the city.

2 Soaking up the views at Bangkok's tower-top bars, **Moon Bar** (p124) and **Sirocco Sky Bar** (p123).

3 Relaxing Bangkok-style among the exercisers and exercise-observers in **Lumphini Park** (p118), the 'lungs of the city'.

4 Confronting your fear of snakes at **Queen Saovabha Memorial Institute** (p118).

5 Ending the day (or starting the night) with a **dinner cruise** (p121) on Mae Nam Chao Phraya.

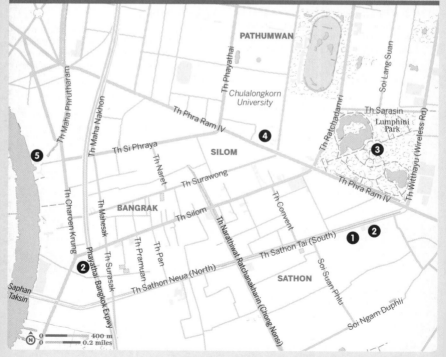

For more detail of this area, see Map p264, p266 & p268 ➡

Explore: Riverside, Silom & Lumphini

Th Silom, with its towering hotels and office buildings, is Bangkok's de facto financial district, while adjacent Th Sathon is home to many of the city's embassies. Incongruously, lower Silom functions as Bangkok's lush gaybourhood. There's a dearth of sights in this part of town, so unless you're heading to Lumphini Park – at its best in the early morning – take advantage of the area's street stalls and upscale restaurants and combine your visit with lunch or dinner. The BTS stop at Sala Daeng and the MRT stop at Si Lom put you at lower Silom, perfect jumping-off points for either Lumphini Park or the area's restaurants and sights.

The Riverside area is significantly less flashy, and is a great area for an aimless wander among old buildings. This stretch of Mae Nam Chao Phraya was formerly Bangkok's international zone, but today boasts a particularly Chinese and Muslim feel. Most of the sights in this area can be seen in a morning; the BTS stop at Saphan Taksin is a good starting point.

Local Life

⇒ **Halal 'hood** The intersection of Th Silom and Th Charoen Krung is home to several Muslim-Thai and Indian restaurants.

⇒ **Rainbow Flag** Lower Th Silom, particularly the strip from Soi 2 to Soi 4, is Bangkok's pinkest district and popular with both local and visiting gay men.

⇒ **Good Morning** Pretend you're Thai-Chinese by getting up at 5am and taking part in the early-morning stretching rituals at Lumphini Park. Or you can just show up at a slightly saner hour and watch.

⇒ **Art Attack** Those looking for a painting by a contemporary Burmese artist, or an Ayuthaya-era Buddhist manuscript cabinet, will undoubtedly find something interesting in one of Th Silom area's numerous art galleries and antique shops.

Getting There & Away

⇒ **BTS** To Riverside: Saphan Taksin. To Silom: Sala Daeng (interchange with MRT Si Lom). To Lumphini: Ratchadamri, Sala Daeng, Chong Nonsi, Surasak and Saphan Taksin.

⇒ **MRT** To Silom: Si Lom (interchange with BTS Sala Daeng). To Lumphini: Lumphini.

⇒ **River boat** To Riverside: Tha Si Phraya, Tha Oriental and Tha Sathon. To Lumphini: Tha Sathon.

⇒ **Bus** To Silom: air-con 76 and 77; ordinary 1, 15, 33 and 7.

Lonely Planet's Top Tip

Getting out on Mae Nam Chao Phraya is a great way to escape the Bangkok traffic and experience the city's maritime past. So it's fortunate that the city's riverside hotels also have some of the most attractive boats shuttling along the river (technically for hotel guests, but staff don't check). In most cases these free services run from Tha Sathon (also known as Central Pier) to their mother hotel, departing every 10 or 15 minutes. There's no squeeze, no charge and a uniformed crew to help you on and off.

Best Places to Eat

⇒ nahm (p119)
⇒ D'sens (p119)
⇒ Zanotti (p122)
⇒ Le Normandie (p119)
⇒ Muslim Restaurant (p119)
⇒ Kai Thort Jay Kee (p123)

For reviews, see p119 ⇒

Best Places to Drink

⇒ Moon Bar (p124)
⇒ Sirocco Sky Bar (p123)
⇒ viva aviv (p123)

For reviews, see p123 ⇒

Best Places to Shop

⇒ River City (p126)
⇒ Jim Thompson (p127)
⇒ House of Chao (p127)

For reviews, see p126 ⇒

 **SIGHTS**

◉ Riverside

OLD CUSTOMS HOUSE　HISTORICAL BUILDING

Map p266 (กรมศุลกากร; Soi 36, Th Charoen Krung; Tha Oriental) Old Customs House was once the gateway to Thailand, levying taxes on traders moving in and out of the kingdom. It was designed by an Italian architect and built in the 1890s; the front door opened onto its source of income (the river) and the grand facade was ceremoniously decorated in columns and transom windows. Today it's a crumbling yet hauntingly beautiful home to the fire brigade, with sagging shutters, peeling yellow paint and laundry flapping on the balconies. For years the building has been used as a base for the waterborne fire brigade and the firefighters' families.

ASSUMPTION CATHEDRAL　CHURCH

Map p266 (อาสนวิหารอัสสัมชัญ; Soi 40/Oriental, Th Charoen Krung; ⏰7am-7pm; Tha Oriental) Marking the ascendancy of the French missionary influence in Bangkok during the reign of Rama II (King Phraphutthaloetla Naphalai; r 1809–24), this Romanesque church with its rich golden interior dates from 1910 and hosted a Mass by Pope John Paul II in 1984; his statue now stands outside the main door. The schools associated with the cathedral are considered some of the best in Thailand.

◉ Thanon Silom

FREE **SRI MARIAMMAN TEMPLE**　HINDU TEMPLE

Map p264 (วัดพระศรีมหาอุมาเทวี (วัดแขก); Wat Phra Si Maha Umathewi; cnr Th Silom & Th Pan; ⏰6am-8pm; Surasak exit 3) Arrestingly flamboyant, Sri Mariamman is a Hindu temple that is a wild collision of colours, shapes and deities. The official Thai name of the temple is Wat Phra Si Maha Umathewi, but

> **LOCAL KNOWLEDGE**
>
> Hard-core movie buffs with a keen eye will recognise the Old Customs House from its cameo appearance in Wong Kar Wai's film *In the Mood for Love* (2000).

sometimes it is shortened to its colloquial name Wat Khaek – *kàak* being a common expression for people of Indian descent. The literal translation is 'guest', an obvious euphemism for any group of people not particularly wanted as permanent residents; hence most Indian Thais don't appreciate the term.

The temple was built in the 1860s by Tamil immigrants and features a 6m facade of intertwined, full-colour Hindu deities. While most of the people working in the temple hail from the Indian subcontinent, you will likely see plenty of Thai and Chinese devotees praying here as well. This is because the Hindu gods figure just as prominently in their individualistic approach to religion.

NEILSON HAYS LIBRARY　LIBRARY

Map p264 (www.neilsonhayslibrary.com; 195 Th Surawong; family membership 3300B; ⏰9.30am-5pm Tue-Sun; Surasak exit 3) The oldest English-language library in Thailand, the Neilson Hays dates back to 1922, and today remains the city's noblest place for a read – with the added benefit of air-con. It has a good selection of children's books and a decent selection of titles on Thailand. Non-members are expected to pay a 50B fee to use the facilities.

KATHMANDU PHOTO GALLERY　ART GALLERY

Map p264 (www.kathmandu-bkk.com; 87 Th Pan; ⏰11am-7pm Tue-Sun; Surasak exit 3) Bangkok's only gallery wholly dedicated to photography is housed in an attractively restored Sino-Portuguese shophouse. The owner, photographer Manit Sriwanichpoom, wanted Kathmandu to resemble photographers' shops of old, where customers could flip through photographs for sale. Manit's own work is on display on the ground floor, and the small but airy upstairs gallery plays host to changing exhibitions by local and international artists and photographers.

TANG GALLERY　ART GALLERY

Map p264 (basement, Silom Galleria, 919/1 Th Silom; ⏰11am-7pm Mon-Sat; Surasak exit 3) Bangkok's primary venue for modern artists from China has edged its way to become one of the city's top contemporary galleries. Check the posters in the lobby of its home, Silom Galleria, to see what's on.

START **BTS SAPHAN TAKSIN**
END **VIVA AVIV**
DISTANCE **APPROXIMATELY 3KM**
DURATION **TWO TO FOUR HOURS**

Neighbourhood Walk
Riverside Architecture Ramble

Bangkok isn't known for its architecture, but the area that runs along Mae Nam Chao Phraya is home to the bulk of the city's noteworthy secular structures.

Board the BTS, heading towards the river, and get off at Saphan Taksin. Walk north along Th Charoen Krung, passing ancient **❶ shophouses** between Th Charoen Wiang and Th Si Wiang, and the ugly neoclassical **❷ State Tower** at the corner with Th Silom. Turn left on Soi 40 (aka Soi Oriental), home to the **❸ Mandarin Oriental**, Bangkok's oldest and most storied hotel. Directly across from the entrance is the classical Venetian-style facade of the **❹ East Asiatic Company**, built in 1901. Proceed beneath the overhead walkway linking two buildings to the red-brick **❺ Assumption Cathedral**.

Return to Soi 40 and take the first left. On your right is **❻ O.P. Plaza**, built as a department store in 1905. Pass the walls of the French embassy and turn left. Head towards the river and the **❼ Old Customs House**.

Backtrack and turn left beneath the green sign that says Haroon Mosque. You're now in **❽ Haroon village**, a Muslim enclave full of sleeping cats, playing kids and gingerbread wooden houses. Wind through Haroon and you'll eventually come to Soi 34, which will lead you back to Th Charoen Krung. Turn left and cross the street opposite the art deco **❾ General Post Office**. Turn right onto Soi 43 and proceed to the **❿ Bangkokian Museum**, home to three antique wooden homes.

Head back to Th Charoen Krung, cross the street and turn right. Turn left on Soi 30. Follow this road past the walls of the **⓫ Portuguese Embassy**, Bangkok's oldest, to River City – not noteworthy in an architectural sense, but its riverside bar **⓬ viva aviv** is a good place to end the walk.

NUMBER1 GALLERY
ART GALLERY

Map p264 (www.number1gallery.com; basement, Silom Galleria, 919/1 Th Silom; ⊙10am-7pm Mon-Sat; 🚇Surasak exit 3) This relatively new gallery has featured the attention-grabbing contemporary work of Thai artists such as Vasan Sitthiket, Sutee Kunavichayanont and Thaweesak Srithongdee.

THAVIBU GALLERY
ART GALLERY

Map p264 (www.thavibu.com; 3rd fl, Silom Galleria, 919/1 Th Silom; ⊙11am-7pm Tue-Sat; 🚇Surasak exit 3) Thavibu is an amalgam of Thailand, Vietnam and Myanmar (Burma). The gallery specialises in contemporary paintings by younger and emerging artists from the three countries.

H GALLERY
ART GALLERY

Map p264 (www.hgallerybkk.com; 201 Soi 12, Th Sathon Neua; ⊙10am-6pm Wed-Sat, by appointment Tue; 🚇Chong Nonsi exit 1) Housed in a refurbished colonial-era wooden building, H is generally considered among the city's leading private galleries. It is also seen as a jumping-off point for Thai artists with international ambitions, such as Jakkai Siributr and Somboon Hormthienthong.

⊙ Lumphini & Around

QUEEN SAOVABHA
MEMORIAL INSTITUTE
WILDLIFE INSTITUTE

Map p268 (สถานเสาวภา; Snake Farm; cnr Th Phra Ram IV & Th Henri Dunant; adult/child 200/50B; ⊙9.30am-3.30pm Mon-Fri, to 1pm Sat & Sun; ⓂSi Lom exit 1, 🚇Sala Daeng exit 3) Venomous snakes such as the formidable cobra, banded krait and pit viper live a peaceful and – though they probably don't know it – altruistic existence at this unusual institute affiliated with the Thai Red Cross. Founded in 1923, it is only the second of its kind (the first one was in Brazil), and has gone on to become one of the world's leading centres in the study of snakes. You can watch the venom being collected during the weekday **milkings** (⊙11am Mon-Fri) – it's then used to make snake-bite antivenenes, which are distributed throughout the country. **Snake-handling performances** (⊙2.30pm Mon-Fri, 11am Sat & Sun) are held at the outdoor amphitheatre daily and are free with admission.

👁 TOP SIGHTS
LUMPHINI PARK

Named after Buddha's birthplace in Nepal, Lumphini Park is central Bangkok's largest and most popular park. Its 58 hectares are home to an artificial lake surrounded by broad, well-tended lawns, wooded areas, walking paths and the odd scurrying monitor lizard to complement the shuffling Bangkokians – it's the best outdoor escape from Bangkok without leaving town.

The park was originally a royal reserve but in 1925 Rama VI (King Vajiravudh; r 1910–25) declared it a public space. In the years since it has matured and, as the concrete has risen all around, become the city's premier exercise space. One of the best times to visit is early morning, when the air is (relatively) fresh and legions of Chinese are practising t'ai chi, doing their best to mimic the aerobics instructor or doing the half-run half-walk version of jogging that makes a lot of sense in oppressive humidity. A weight-lifting area in one section becomes a miniature 'muscle beach' on weekends, when the park takes on a festive atmosphere as the day cools down into evening. Cold drinks are available at the entrances and street-food vendors set up tables outside the park's northwest corner from about 5pm.

DON'T MISS...

➡ Enormous monitor lizards

➡ Early-morning t'ai chi and evening aerobics

PRACTICALITIES

➡ สวนลุมพินี

➡ Map p268

➡ bounded by Th Sarasin, Th Phra Ram IV, Th Witthayu/Wireless Rd & Th Ratchadamri

➡ admission free

➡ ⊙4.30am-9pm

➡ ⓂLumphini exit 3, Si Lom exit 1, 🚇Sala Daeng exit 3, Ratchadamri exit 2

MR KUKRIT PRAMOJ HOUSE — MUSEUM

Map p268 (บ้านหม่อมราชวงศ์คึกฤทธิ์ปราโมช; Soi 7 (Phra Phinij), Th Narathiwat Ratchankharin; adult/child 50/20B; ⏱10am-4pm; 🚈Chong Nonsi exit 2) Author and statesman Mom Ratchawong Kukrit Pramoj (1911–95) once resided in this charming complex now open to the public for tours. Surrounded by a manicured garden famed for its Thai bonsai trees, five teak buildings introduce visitors to traditional Thai architecture, arts and to the former resident, who wrote more than 150 books (including the highly respected *Four Reigns*), served as prime minister of Thailand in 1974 and '75, and spent 20 years decorating this house.

SURAPON GALLERY — ART GALLERY

Map p268 (www.rama9art.org/gallery/surapon/index.html; 1st fl, Tisco Tower, 48/3 Th Sathon Neua; ⏱11am-6pm Tue-Sat; Ⓜ Lumphini exit 2) Perhaps the most 'Thai' of the city's respected commercial art galleries, Surapon has featured work by some of the country's most renowned artists such as painters Chatchai Puipia and Muangthai Busamaro.

 EATING

✕ Riverside

LE NORMANDIE — FRENCH $$$

Map p266 (📞0 2236 0400; www.mandarinoriental.com; Mandarin Oriental Hotel, Soi 40/Oriental, Th Charoen Krung; mains 750-3900B; ⏱noon-2.30pm & 7-11pm Mon-Sat, 7-11pm Sun; 🚤Tha Oriental or hotel shuttle boat from Tha Sathon (Central Pier)) For decades Le Normandie was synonymous with fine dining in the city. And although today's Bangkok boasts a plethora of upmarket choices, Le Normandie has maintained its niche and is still the only place to go for a genuinely old-world 'continental' dining experience. A revolving cast of Michelin-starred guest chefs and some of the world's most decadent ingredients keep up the standard, and appropriately formal attire (including jacket) is required. Book ahead.

MUSLIM RESTAURANT — MUSLIM-THAI $

Map p266 (1354-6 Th Charoen Krung; mains 40-140B; 🚤Tha Oriental) Plant yourself in any random wooden booth of this ancient eatery for a glimpse into what restaurants in Bangkok used to be like. The menu, much like the interior design, doesn't appear to have changed much in the restaurant's 70-year history, and the birianis, curries and samosas are still more Indian-influenced than Thai.

LORD JIM'S — INTERNATIONAL $$$

Map p266 (📞0 2659 9000; Mandarin Oriental, Soi 40/Oriental, Th Charoen Krung; buffet 1500B; ⏱noon-2.30pm Mon-Fri, 11.30am-3pm Sat, 11am-3pm Sun; 🚤Tha Oriental or hotel shuttle boat from Tha Sathon (Central Pier)) Even if you can't afford to stay at the Oriental, you should save up for the hotel's decadent riverside buffet. Dishes such foie gras are standard, and weekends, when reservations are recommended, see additional seafood stations.

NAAZ — MUSLIM-THAI $

Map p266 (24/9 Soi 45, Th Charoen Krung; mains 35-90B; ⏱8.30am-10pm Mon-Sat; 🚤Tha Oriental) Hidden in a nondescript alleyway is Naaz (pronounced 'Nát'), a tiny shophouse restaurant serving some of the city's richest *kôw mòk gài* (chicken biriani). Various daily specials include chicken masala and mutton korma, but we're most curious to visit on Thursday when the restaurant serves something called Karai Ghost.

INDIAN HUT — INDIAN $$

Map p266 (www.indian-hut.com; 311/2-5 Th Surawong; mains 160-380B; ⏱11am-10.30pm; 🚤Tha Oriental) Despite the fast-food overtones in the name and logo, this long-standing restaurant is classy and popular with visiting businesspeople. The emphasis is on northern Indian cuisine, including excellent flatbreads, tandoor-baked meats and homemade paneer in a tomato and onion curry.

✕ Thanon Silom

TOP CHOICE D'SENS — FRENCH $$$

Map p264 (📞0 2200 9000; www.dusit.com; 22nd fl, Dusit Thani Hotel, 946 Th Phra Ram IV; set dinner 2200-3100B; ⏱11.30am-2pm & 6-10pm Mon-Fri, 6-10pm Sat; Ⓜ Si Lom exit 3, 🚈Sala Daeng exit 4) Perched atop the Dusit Thani Hotel, D'sens combines stunning views over Lumphini Park with some of the city's best upscale dining. The dishes, overseen

TOP SIGHTS
BANGKOKIAN MUSEUM

The Bangkokian Museum consists of a collection of three **antique structures** and illustrates an often-overlooked period of Bangkok's history. The main building was built in 1937 as a home for the Surawadee family and, as the signs inform us, was finished by Chinese carpenters on time and for less than the budgeted 2400B (which would barely buy a door handle today). It is filled with beautiful wooden furniture and the detritus of postwar family life, and offers a fascinating window into the period. An adjacent two-storey shophouse contains themed displays of similar items on the ground floor (don't miss the replicated traditional Thai kitchen), while the upper level is a surprisingly well done museum profiling Khet Bang Rak, the district in which the compound is located. The third building, at the back of the block, was built in 1929 as a surgery for an Indian doctor, though he died soon after arriving in Thailand. A visit takes the form of an informal guided tour in halting English, and photography is encouraged.

DON'T MISS...

➡ Antique wooden buildings

➡ Bang Rak Museum

PRACTICALITIES

➡ พิพิธภัณฑ์ชาวบางกอก

➡ Map p266

➡ 273 Soi 43, Th Charoen Krung

➡ admission free

➡ ⊙10am-4pm Wed-Sun

➡ 🚢Tha Si Phraya (N3)

---

by Michelin star-lauded brothers, Jacques and Laurent Pourcel, take their inspiration from the classic French repertoire, but are given a modern kick in the pants with bright accents and bold flavours. If dinner is too large a financial commitment, consider the business set lunch, which starts at 950B. Book ahead.

KALAPAPRUEK
THAI $

Map p264 (27 Th Pramuan; mains 80-120B; ⊙8am-6pm Mon-Sat, to 3pm Sun; 🚇Surasak exit 3) This venerable Thai eatery has numerous branches and mall spin-offs around town, but we still fancy the quasi-concealed original branch. The diverse menu spans Thai specialities from just about every region, daily specials and, occasionally, seasonal treats as well. Look for the high brown fence about halfway down Th Pramuan.

NADIMOS
LEBANESE $$

Map p264 (www.nadimos.com; Baan Silom, cnr Th Silom & Soi 19; mains 70-400B; ⊙lunch & dinner; 🥗; 🚇Surasak exit 3) This semiformal dining room does tasty versions of all the Lebanese standards, plus quite a few dishes you'd never expect to see this far from Beirut. Lots of vegetarian options as well.

SOMBOON SEAFOOD
THAI $$$

Map p264 (📞0 2233 3104; www.somboonseafood.com; cnr Th Surawong & Th Narathiwat Ratchanakharin; mains 120-900B; ⊙4pm-midnight; 🚇Chong Nonsi exit 3) Somboon, a busy seafood hall with a reputation far and wide, is known for doing the best curry-powder crab in town. Soy-steamed sea bass (*blah grà·pohng nêung see·ew*) is also a speciality and, like all good Thai seafood, should be enjoyed with an immense platter of *kôw pàt boo* (fried rice with crab) and as many friends as you can gather together.

SUSHI TSUKIJI
JAPANESE $$$

Map p264 (Th Thaniya; sushi per item 60-700B; ⊙lunch & dinner; Ⓜ️Si Lom exit 2, 🚇Sala Daeng exit 1) Th Thaniya is home to many hostess bars catering to visiting Japanese, so naturally the quality of the street's Japanese restaurants is high. Our pick is Tsukiji, named after Tokyo's famous seafood market. Dinner at this sleek sushi joint, specialising in raw fish, will leave a significant dent in the wallet, so come for lunch, when Tsukiji does several exceedingly good-value sushi sets for as little as 198B.

FOODIE
THAI $

Map p264 (Soi Phiphat 2; mains 80-150B; ⊙11am-11pm; 🚇Chong Nonsi exit 2) This airy, cafeteria-like restaurant boasts a lengthy menu of hard-to-find central- and southern-style Thai dishes. Highlights include the *yam som o*, a spicy-sour-sweet salad of pomelo, and the spicy *prik khing pla dook foo*, catfish fried in a curry paste until crispy.

SCOOZI
ITALIAN $$

Map p264 (www.scoozipizza.com; 174 Th Surawong; pizzas 100-425B; ⊙lunch & dinner; Ⓜ️Si Lom exit 2, 🚇Sala Daeng exit) At this chic pizzeria you can witness your pie being skilfully tossed and topped before it's blistered in a wood-burning oven from Italy. Go minimalist and order the salty Napoletana, a pizza topped with little more than mozzarella, anchovies and olives.

CHENNAI KITCHEN
INDIAN, VEGETARIAN $

Map p264 (10 Th Pan; mains 50-150B; ⊙10am-3pm & 6-9.30pm; 🖉; 🚇Surasak exit 3) This thimble-sized mom-and-pop restaurant near the Hindu temple puts out some of the most solid southern Indian vegetarian food around. Yard-long *dosai* (a crispy southern Indian pancake) is always a good choice, but if you're feeling indecisive (or exceptionally famished) go for the banana-leaf *thali* that seems to incorporate just about everything in the kitchen.

TALING PLING
THAI $

Map p264 (60 Th Pan; mains 120-330B; ⊙11am-10pm; 🚇Surasak exit 3) Locals and tourists feel equally at home at this cosy Thai restaurant. Flip through the thick photo-album-like menu of largely seafood- and vegetable-based Thai dishes, including a handful made with the eponymous tart vegetable. Tasty pies and cakes and refreshing drinks round out the choices, but slow service means you should go elsewhere if you're in a hurry.

RAN NAM TAO HU YONG HER
CHINESE $

Map p264 (68 Th Narathiwat Ratchanakharin; mains 40-205B; ⊙11am-10pm; 🚇Chong Nonsi exit 3) Although the name of this blink-and-you'll-miss-it shophouse eatery translates as 'soy milk restaurant', the emphasis here is on northern Chinese cuisine – a rarity in Bangkok. Try the Shanghainese speciality *xiao long bao,* described on the menu as 'small steamed bun', actually dumplings encasing a pork filling and rich hot broth that pours out when you bite into them.

JAY SO
NORTHEASTERN THAI $

Map p264 (146/1 Soi Phiphat 2; mains 20-50B; ⊙11am-4pm Mon-Sat; Ⓜ️Si Lom exit 2, 🚇Sala Daeng exit 2) This crumbling shack is living proof that, where authentic Thai food is concerned, ambience is often considered more a liability than an asset. Fittingly, Jay So has no menu as such, but a mortar and pestle and a huge grill are the telltale signs of ballistically spicy *sôm·đam* (green papaya salad), sublime herb-stuffed grilled catfish and other Isan specialities. Look for the white, Pepsi-decorated shack about halfway down Soi Phiphat 2.

DINNER CRUISES

Mae Nam Chao Phraya is lovely in the evenings, with the skyscrapers' lights twinkling in the distance and a cool breeze chasing the heat away. A dozen or more companies take advantage of this and run regular dinner cruises along the river. Some are mammoth boats so brightly lit inside that you'd never know you were on the water; others are more sedate and intimate, allowing patrons to see the surroundings. As a general rule, the food doesn't quite live up to the setting.

A good one-stop centre for all your dinner cruise needs is the **River City Information Desk** (🖉0 2639 4532; www.rivercity.co.th; ground fl, River City, 23 Th Yotha; ⊙10am-10pm; 🛳Tha Si Phraya, shuttle boat from Tha Sathon), where tickets (1200B) can be purchased for **Grand Pearl** (🖉0 2861 0255; www.grandpearlcruise.com; ⊙7.30pm), **Chaophraya Cruise** (🖉0 2541 5599; www.chaophrayacruise.com; ⊙7pm), **Wan Fah** (Map p266; 🖉0 2222 8679; www.wanfah.in.th; ⊙6.45pm), **Chao Phraya Princess** (🖉0 2860 3700; www.thaicruise.com; ⊙7.15pm & 7.45pm) and **White Orchid** (🖉0 2476 5207; www.thairivercruise.com; ⊙7.40pm). All cruises depart from River City Pier; take a look at the websites to see exactly what's on offer.

KRUA 'AROY-AROY' THAI $

Map p264 (Th Pan; mains 40-100B; ⊗8am-8.30pm; ⒭Surasak exit 3) Krua 'Aroy-Aroy' (Delicious Kitchen) is the kind of family-run Thai restaurant where nobody seems to mind a cat slumbering on the cash register. Stop by for some of the richest curries around, as well as the interesting daily specials including, on Thursdays, *kôw klúk gà·Ъì*, rice cooked in shrimp paste and served with sweet pork, shredded green mango and other toppings.

MIZU'S KITCHEN JAPANESE, INTERNATIONAL $

Map p264 (32 Soi Patpong 1; mains 65-200B; ⊗noon-midnight; Ⓜ Si Lom exit 2, ⒭Sala Daeng exit 1) This certifiable hole-in-the-wall place oozes character, not to mention the beefy essence of thousands of steaks served over the decades. Do order the house Sarika steak, and do take a hint from the regulars and use your chequered tablecloth to protect your clothes from the sizzle and spray of the hot plate when it arrives.

SOMTAM CONVENT ('HAI') NORTHEASTERN THAI $

Map p264 (2/4-5 Th Convent; mains 20-120B; ⊗10.30am-9pm Mon-Fri, to 5pm Sat & Sun; Ⓜ Si Lom exit 2, ⒭Sala Daeng exit 2) Northeastern-style Thai food is usually relegated to less-than-hygienic stalls perched by the side of the road with no menu or English-speaking staff in sight. A less intimidating introduction to the wonders of *lâhp* (a minced meat 'salad'), *sôm·dam* and other Isan delights can be had at this popular restaurant.

SOI 10 FOOD CENTRES THAI $

Map p264 (Soi 10, Th Silom; mains 20-60B; ⊗8am-2pm Mon-Fri; Ⓜ Si Lom exit 2, ⒭Sala Daeng exit 1) These two adjacent hangarlike buildings tucked behind Soi 10 are the main lunchtime fuelling stations for this area's office staff. Choices range from southern-style *kôw gaang* (point-and-choose curries ladled over rice) to virtually every form of Thai noodle.

CILI PADI MALAYSIAN $

Map p264 (160/9 Th Narathiwat Ratchanakharin; mains 70-130B; ⊗11am-10.30pm Sun-Thu; ⒭Chong Nonsi exit 4) This culinary outpost from south of the border exudes a casual cafelike atmosphere, and authentic *teh tarik* (Malaysian-style sweet tea) and *roti canai* (a crispy pancake served with a len-til dip) make it a clever locale for an air-conditioned break. Lunch specials and an expansive menu ranging from noodle dishes to hearty Malaysian-style curries provide even more excuses to linger.

SOI PRADIT MARKET THAI $

Map p264 (Soi 20/Pradit, Th Silom; mains 25-100B; ⊗11am-9pm; ⒭Surasak exit 3) This blue-collar street market is a virtual microcosm of Thai cuisine. Muslims deep-fry marinated chicken in front of the mosque, while across the way Chinese vendors chop up stewed pork leg and Isan women pound away at mortars of *sôm·dam*. Live on the edge a little and proceed past the stalls with English signs peddling the predictables.

✕ Lumphini & Around

⌖ NAHM THAI $$$

Map p268 (✆0 2625 3388; Metropolitan Hotel, 27 Th Sathon Tai; set lunch 800-1100B; set dinner 1700B; ⊗noon-2pm Mon-Fri & 7-10pm Mon-Sun; Ⓜ Lumphini exit 2) Australian chef-author David Thompson is behind what is quite possibly the best Thai restaurant in Bangkok. Using ancient cookbooks as his inspiration, Thompson has given new life to previously extinct dishes such as smoked fish curry with prawns, chicken livers, cockles and black pepper. Dinner takes the form of a multicourse set meal, while lunch means *kà·nŏm jeen*, thin rice noodles served with curries. If you're expecting bland, gentrified Thai food meant for foreigners, prepare to be disappointed. Reservations recommended.

ZANOTTI ITALIAN $$$

Map p268 (www.zanottigroup.com; 21/2 Th Sala Daeng; mains 200-880B; ⊗11.30am-2pm & 6-10.30pm; Ⓜ Si Lom exit 3, ⒭Sala Daeng exit 4) Zanotti has a well-deserved reputation as one of Bangkok's best destinations for Italian. Much of this is due to the menu, which is packed with satisfying meaty pasta and rice dishes. But we also fancy the dark woods and framed paintings of the gentlemen's club–like dining room, not to mention the professional and confident service – a rarity in Bangkok. Come midday for the amazing-value set lunch that starts at only 300B.

KAI THORT JAY KEE
THAI $

Map p268 (Soi Polo Fried Chicken; 137/1-3 Soi Sanam Khlii (Polo); mains 40-280B; ⊙11am-9pm; Ⓜ Lumphini exit 3) This Cinderella of a former street stall has become virtually synonymous with fried chicken. Although the *sôm·đam,* sticky rice and *lâhp* (spicy 'salad' of minced meat) give the impression of an Isan eatery, the restaurant's namesake deep-fried bird is more southern in origin. Regardless, smothered in a thick layer of crispy deep-fried garlic, it is none other than a truly Bangkok experience.

ISSAYA SIAMESE CLUB
THAI $$

Map p268 (www.issaya.com; 4 Soi Sri Aksorn; mains 150-580B; ⊙11.30am-2.30pm & 6-10.30pm; ☑; Ⓜ Khlong Toei exit 1 & access by taxi) Housed in a charming 1920s-era villa, Issaya is Thai celebrity chef Ian Kittichai's first effort at a domestic outpost serving the food of his homeland. Dishes are taken from the chef's 'Childhood Menu' and alternate between somewhat saucy, meaty dishes (chilli-glazed baby back ribs) and lighter dishes using produce from the restaurant's organic garden (including lots of vegie options). Loungelike rooms and garden chairs make up the Siamese Club half of the restaurant. The restaurant can be a bit tricky to find, and is best approached in a taxi via Soi Ngam Duphli.

NGWANLEE LUNG SUAN
CHINESE-THAI $$

Map p268 (cnr Soi Lang Suan & Th Sarasin; mains 50-900B; ⊙7am-3am; ☒ Ratchadamri exit 2) This open-air staple of copious consumption is still going strong after all these decades. If you can locate the entrance, squeeze in with the postclubbing crowd and try some of those Chinese-style street dishes you never dare to order elsewhere, such as *jàp chài* (Chinese-style stewed vegetables) or *hǒy lai pàt nám prík pǒw* (clams stir-fried with chilli sauce and Thai basil).

CAFÉ 1912
FRENCH-THAI $

Map p268 (Alliance Française, 29 Th Sathon Tai; dishes 50-185B; ⊙7am-7pm Mon-Sat, to 2pm Sun; Ⓜ Lumphini exit 2) Part of the French cultural centre, this cafeteria is a great place to fuel up while on an embassy run. Both French and Thai dishes are available, as well as coffee and delicious cakes and sweets provided by a local bakery.

CHOCOLATE BUFFET
DESSERT $$$

Map p268 (www.sukhothai.com; Sukhothai Hotel, 13/3 Th Sathon Tai; buffet 900-1350B; ⊙2-5.30pm Fri-Sun; Ⓜ Lumphini exit 2) For those who love the sweet stuff, the Sukhothai Hotel offers a unique, entirely cocoa-based high tea. The more expensive buffet option includes a glass of Lombard champagne.

🍷 DRINKING & NIGHTLIFE

🍺 Riverside

VIVA AVIV
BAR

Map p266; (Ground fl, River City, 23 Th Yotha; ⊙noon-midnight; ☒ Tha Si Phraya, Tha Sathon) An enviable riverside location, casual open-air seating and a funky atmosphere make this new restaurant-ish bar a contender for Bangkok's best sunset cocktail destination. Expect a pun-heavy menu (sample item: I 'foc'cat cia' name!) of pizzas, meaty snacks and salads that really is no joke.

SIROCCO SKY BAR
BAR

Map p266 (www.lebua.com/en/the-dome-dining/sky-bar-bangkok; 63rd fl, The Dome at State Tower, 1055 Th Silom; ☒ Saphan Taksin exit 3) Allegedly one of the highest alfresco bars in the world, Sky Bar, located high up on the 63rd floor of this upmarket restaurant compound, provides heart-stopping views over Chao Phraya River. Note that the dress code doesn't allow access to those wearing shorts and sandals.

🍺 Thanon Silom

BARLEY
BAR

Map p264 (www.barleybistro.com; Food Channel, Th Silom; ⊙8pm-late; Ⓜ Si Lom exit 2, ☒ Sala Daeng exit 2) The seemingly incongruous combo of Belgian beer and Thai-influenced snacks somehow works at this new bar. Seating is on the breezy rooftop or inside, occasionally in the company of live bands. Barley is located in the Food Channel building, between Soi 5 and Soi 7.

BARBICAN
BAR

Map p264 (www.greatbritishpub.com; 9/4-5 Soi Thaniya; ⊙11.30am-2am; Ⓜ Si Lom exit 2, ☒ Sala

Daeng exit 1) Decked out in slate grey and blonde wood, this upscale-ish pub is an oasis of subdued cool in a strip consisting mostly of Japanese-frequented massage parlours. Where else could you suck down a few cocktails with friends from Thailand, Singapore and Norway, and then stumble out to find a line of Thai women dressed like cheap prom dates reciting 'Hello, massage' in faulty Japanese?

COYOTE ON CONVENT BAR
Map p264 (www.coyoteonconvent.com; 1/2 Th Convent; ⏰11am-midnight; Mⓢi Lom exit 2, ⓢSala Daeng exit 2) Coyote on Convent serves decent but pricey Mexican nosh with a relatively light dose of kitsch. But what really keeps the people coming, in particular Bangkok's female population, are the 75-plus varieties of margaritas. Come on Wednesday evening, when from 6pm to 8pm the icy drinks are distributed free to all women who pass through the door. On weekdays the frosty drinks are 'buy one get one free' from 3pm to 7pm.

MOLLY MALONE'S PUB
Map p264 (www.mollymalonesbangkok.com; 1/5-6 Th Convent; ⏰11am-1am; Mⓢi Lom exit 2, ⓢSala Daeng exit 2) The third and, we hope, final reincarnation of this Bangkok Irish staple has retained much of the faux-shamrock charm of its predecessor. Like most of its countryfolk, Molly's is equal parts game for a quiet pint alone or a rowdy night out with friends.

Lumphini & Around

MOON BAR BAR
Map p268 (www.banyantree.com; 61st fl, Banyan Tree Hotel, 21/100 Th Sathon Tai; ⏰5.30pm-1am; MⓁumphini exit 2) The Banyan Tree Hotel's Moon Bar kick-started the rooftop trend and, as Bangkok continues to grow at a mad pace, the view from 61 floors up only gets better. Arrive well before sunset and grab a coveted seat to the right of the bar for the most impressive views. Save your shorts and sandals for another bar.

WONG'S PLACE BAR
Map p268 (27/3 Soi Si Bamphen; ⏰8pm-late; MⓁumphini exit 1) An odd choice for an institution if there ever was one, this dusty den is a time warp into the backpacker

world of the early 1980s. The namesake owner died several years ago, but a relative removed the padlock and picked up where Wong left off. Wong's works equally well as a destination or a last resort, but don't bother knocking until midnight, keeping in mind that it stays open until the last person crawls out.

☆ ENTERTAINMENT

TAPAS ROOM NIGHTCLUB
Map p264 (www.tapasroom.net; 114/17-18 Soi 4, Th Silom; admission 100B; ⏰9pm-2am; Mⓢi Lom exit 2, ⓢSala Daeng exit 1) Although it sits staunchly at the front of Bangkok's pinkest street, this long-standing two-level disco manages to bring in just about everybody. Come from Thursday to Saturday, when the combination of DJs and live percussion brings the body count to critical level.

LUMPHINI BOXING STADIUM THAI BOXING
Map p268 (Th Phra Ram IV; tickets 3rd/2nd class/ringside 1000/1500/2000B; MⓁumphini exit 3) The big-time *moo-ay tai* (Thai boxing, also spelt *muay thai*) fighters spar at Lumphini's coveted ring. Matches occur on Tuesday and Friday at 6.30pm and Saturday at 5pm and 8.30pm. The stadium doesn't usually fill up until the main event around 8pm.

PATPONG RED-LIGHT DISTRICT
Map p264 (Soi Patpong 1 & 2, Th Silom; Mⓢi Lom exit 2, ⓢSala Daeng exit 1) Possibly one of the most famous red-light districts in the world, today any 'charm' that the area used to possess has been eroded by modern tourism, and fake Rolexes and Diesel T-shirts are more ubiquitous than flesh. There is, of course, a considerable amount of naughtiness going on, although much of it takes place upstairs and behind closed doors. If you must, be sure to agree to the price of entry and drinks before taking a seat at one of Patpong's 'pussy shows', otherwise you're likely to receive an astronomical bill.

SALA RIM NAM DINNER THEATRE
Map p266 (☎0 2437 3080; www.mandarinoriental.com/bangkok; Mandarin Oriental, Soi 40, Th Charoen Krung; tickets 2650B; ⏰dinner & show 8.15-9.30pm; ⓣTha Oriental or shuttle boat from Tha Sathon) The historic Mandarin Oriental hosts dinner theatre in a sumptuous Thai

BANGKOK'S GAYBOURHOOD

The side streets off lower Th Silom are so gay that they make San Francisco look like rural Texas. In addition to heaps of gay locals and tourists, this area is home to massage parlours and boy bars with in-your-face sex shows in nearby Duangthawee Plaza, the chilled open-air bars along Soi 4 and the booming clubs near Soi 2; below are our picks.

Bars

Soi 4 is a tiny alleyway packed with gay bars, most with strategically positioned seats to best observe the nightly parade.

Telephone Pub (Map p264; www.telephonepub.com; 114/11-13 Soi 4, Th Silom; ⊙6pm-1am; Ⓜ️Si Lom exit 2, 🚉Sala Daeng exit 1) Telephone is famous for the phones that used to sit on every table, allowing you to ring up that hottie sitting across the room. Its popularity remains even if most of the phones are gone. The clientele is mostly 30-and-above white men with their Thai 'friends'.

Balcony (Map p264; www.balconypub.com; 86-88 Soi 4, Th Silom; ⊙5.30pm-1am; Ⓜ️Si Lom exit 2, 🚉Sala Daeng exit 1) Located directly across from Telephone, this is yet another long-standing cafelike pub that features the occasional drag-queen performance.

Duangthawee Plaza (Map p264; Soi Pratuchai; ⊙7pm-1am; Ⓜ️Si Lom exit 2, 🚉Sala Daeng exit 3) This strip of male-only go-go bars is the gay equivalent of nearby Th Patpong. Expect tacky sex shows by bored-looking boys.

Clubs

The area's clubs are located in dead-end Soi 2 and Soi 2/1; if the following are too packed, alternatives are just steps away.

DJ Station (Map p264; www.dj-station.com; 8/6-8 Soi 2, Th Silom; admission 100-200B; ⊙8pm-3am; Ⓜ️Si Lom exit 2, 🚉Sala Daeng exit 1) One of Bangkok's, and indeed Asia's, most legendary gay dance clubs, here the crowd is a mix of Thai guppies (gay professionals), money boys and a few Westerners.

G.O.D. (Map p264; Guys on Display; Soi 2/1, Th Silom; admission 300B; ⊙8pm-late; Ⓜ️Si Lom exit 2, 🚉Sala Daeng exit 1) As the name suggests, Guys on Display is not averse to a little shirtless dancing. Open late, this is where to go after DJ Station has closed.

70's Bar (Map p268; 231/16 Th Sarasin; admission free; ⊙6pm-1am; 🚉Ratchadamri exit 2) A tad too small to be a club proper, this retro-themed bar spins all the hits for Gen Y in the ultimate Me city. Like much of the tiny strip where it's found, the clientele is mixed, but often verges on the pink side of the fence.

Saunas

In Bangkok, there's a fine line – often no line at all – between male massage and prostitution. Saunas, on the other hand, don't involve any transaction past the entrance fee.

Babylon (Map p268; www.babylonbangkok.com; 34 Soi Nandha; admission 260B; ⊙10.30am-10.30pm; Ⓜ️Lumphini exit 2) Bangkok's first luxury sauna remains extremely popular with visitors, many from neighbouring Singapore and Hong Kong. B&B-style accommodation is also available.

pavilion across the river in Thonburi. Free shuttle boats transfer guests across the river. The price is well above average, reflecting the means of the hotel's client base, but the performance gets positive reviews.

SILOM VILLAGE DINNER THEATRE
Map p264 (📞0 2635 6313; www.silomvillage.co.th; 286 Th Silom; admission 600-900B; ⊙6-10pm; 🚉Surasak exit 3) More relaxed than most dinner-show venues, Silom Village delivers comfort, accessibility and decent dinners. Picky eaters swear by the crispy pork and cashew chicken, and witnessing the energetic demonstrations of traditional Thai dance and martial arts (8.20pm to 9.10pm nightly) will strike one 'to do' off many travellers' itinerary.

🛍 SHOPPING

TOP CHOICE RIVER CITY COMPLEX SHOPPING CENTRE
Map p266264; (www.rivercity.co.th; 23 Th Yotha; ⊙10am-10pm, many shops close Sun; ⛴Tha Si

Phraya or shuttle boat from Tha Sathon/Central Pier) This huge multistorey centre is an all-in-one stop for old-world Asiana, much of it too large to fit in the bags of most travellers. Several upscale art and antique shops

PUSSY GALORE *ANDREW BURKE*

Super Pussy! Pussy Collection! The neon signs leave little doubt about the dominant industry in Patpong, the world's most infamous strip of go-go bars and clubs running 'exotic' shows. There is enough skin on show in Patpong to make Hugh Hefner blush, and a trip to the upstairs clubs could mean you'll never look at a ping-pong ball or a dart the same way again.

For years opinion on Patpong has been polarised between those people who see it as an exploitative, immoral place that is the very definition of sleaze, and others for whom a trip to Bangkok is about little more than immersing themselves in planet Patpong. But Patpong has become such a caricature of itself that in recent times a third group has emerged: the curious tourist. Whatever your opinion, what you see in Patpong or in any of Bangkok's other high-profile 'adult entertainment' areas depends as much on your personal outlook on life as on the quality of your vision.

Prostitution is actually illegal in Thailand but there are as many as two million sex workers, the vast majority of whom – women and men – cater to Thai men. Many come from poorer regional areas, such as Isan in the northeast, while others might be students helping themselves through university. Sociologists suggest Thais often view sex through a less moralistic or romantic filter than Westerners. That doesn't mean Thai wives like their husbands using prostitutes, but it's only recently that the gradual empowerment of women through education and employment has led to a more vigorous questioning of this very widespread practice.

Patpong actually occupies two soi that run between Th Silom and Th Surawong in Bangkok's financial district. The two streets are privately owned by – and named for – the Thai-Chinese Patpongpanich family, who bought the land in the 1940s and initially built Patpong Soi 1 and its shophouses; Soi 2 was laid later. During the Vietnam War the first bars and clubs opened to cater to American soldiers on 'R&R'. The scene and its international reputation grew through the '70s and peaked in the '80s, when official Thai tourism campaigns made the sort of 'sights' available in Patpong a pillar of their marketing.

These days Patpong has mellowed considerably, if not matured. Thanks in part to the popular night market that fills the soi after 5pm, it draws so many tourists that it has become a sort of sex theme park. There are still plenty of the stereotypical middle-aged men ogling pole dancers, sitting in dark corners of the so-called 'blow-job bars' and paying 'bar fines' to take girls to hotels that charge by the hour. But you'll also be among other tourists and families who come to see what all the fuss is about.

Most tourists go no further than stolen glances into the ground-floor go-go bars, where women in bikinis drape themselves around stainless-steel poles. Others will be lured to the dimly lit upstairs clubs by men promising sex shows. But it should be said that the so-called 'erotic' shows usually feature bored-looking women performing acts that feel not so much erotic as demeaning to everyone involved. Several of these clubs are also infamous for their scams, usually involving the nonperforming (ie clothed, if just barely) staff descending on wide-eyed tourists like vultures on fresh meat. Before you know it you've bought a dozen drinks, racked up a bill for thousands of baht, and followed up with a loud, aggressive argument flanked by menacing-looking bouncers and threats of 'no money, no pussy!'.

Were we saying that Patpong had mellowed? Oh yes, there is a slightly softer side. Several bars have a little more, erm, class, and in restaurants such as Mizu's Kitchen in Patpong 1 you could forget where you are – almost.

occupy the 3rd and 4th floors, including **Verandah**, which deals in 'tribal' art from Borneo and abroad, and **Hong Antiques** (4th fl; ☺10am-7pm), with 50 years of experience in decorative pieces. **Acala** is a gallery of unusual Tibetan and Chinese artefacts. And **Old Maps & Prints** (Map p266; 4th fl; ☺11am-7pm Mon-Sat, 1-6pm Sun) proffers one of the best selections of one-of-a-kind, rare maps and illustrations you'll find. As with many antique stores in Bangkok, the vast majority of pieces at River City appear to come from neighbouring Myanmar and, to a lesser extent, Cambodia.

A free shuttle boat to River City departs from Tha Sathon (Central Pier) pier every half hour, from 10am to 8pm.

JIM THOMPSON TEXTILES

Map p264 (www.jimthompson.com; 9 Th Surawong; ☺9am-9pm; MSi Lom exit 2, ☐Sala Daeng exit 3) The surviving business of the renowned international promoter of Thai silk, the largest Jim Thompson shop sells colourful silk handkerchiefs, placemats, wraps, scarves and cushions. The styles and motifs will likely appeal to older, somewhat more conservative tastes. There's also a **factory outlet** (Map p264; 149/4-6 Th Surawong; ☺9am-6pm) just up the road, which sells discontinued patterns at a significant discount.

HOUSE OF CHAO ANTIQUES

Map p264 (9/1 Th Decho, Silom; ☺9.30am-7pm; ☐Chong Nonsi exit 3) This classic three-storey antique shop, appropriately located in an antique house, has everything necessary to deck out your fantasy colonial-era mansion. Particularly interesting are the various weatherworn doors, doorways, gateways and trellises that can be found in the covered area behind the showroom.

TAMNAN MINGMUANG HANDICRAFTS

Map p264 (2nd fl, Thaniya Plaza, Th Thaniya; ☺11am-8pm; MSi Lom exit 2, ☐Sala Daeng exit 1) As soon as you step through the doors of this museumlike shop, the earthy smell of dried grass and stained wood rushes to meet you. Rattan, *yahn lí-pow* (a fernlike vine), water hyacinth woven into silklike patterns, and coconut shells carved into delicate bowls are among the exquisite pieces that will outlast flashier souvenirs available on the streets.

THAI HOME INDUSTRIES HANDICRAFTS

Map p266 (35 Soi 40/Oriental, Th Charoen Krung; ☺9am-6.30pm Mon-Sat; ☐Tha Oriental) A visit to this templelike building and former monks' quarters is like discovering an abandoned attic of Asian booty. On our most recent visit, the display cases held an eclectic collection of cotton farmer shirts, handsome stainless-steel flatware and delicate mother-of-pearl spoons. Despite the odd assortment of items and lack of order (not to mention the dust), it's heaps more fun than the typically faceless Bangkok handicraft shop.

CHIANG HENG HOUSEWARES

Map p266 (1466 Th Charoen Krung; ☺10.30am-7pm; ☐Saphan Taksin exit 3) In need of a handmade stainless-steel wok, old-school enamel-coated crockery or a manually operated coconut-milk strainer? Then we suggest you stop by this third-generation family-run kitchen-supply store. Even if your cabinets are already stocked, a visit here is a glance into the type of specialised and cramped but atmospheric shops that have all but disappeared from Bangkok.

MAISON DES ARTS HANDICRAFTS

Map p266 (1334 Th Charoen Krung; ☺11am-6pm Mon-Sat; ☐Tha Oriental) Hand-hammered, stainless-steel tableware haphazardly occupies this warehouse retail shop. The bold style of the flatware dates back centuries and the staff applies no pressure to indecisive shoppers.

PATPONG NIGHT MARKET MARKET

Map p264 (Soi Patpong 1 & Soi Patpong 2, Th Silom; ☺6pm-midnight; MSi Lom exit 2, ☐Sala Daeng exit 1) You'll be faced with the competing distractions of strip-clubbing and shopping on this infamous street. And true to the area's illicit leanings, pirated goods (in particular watches) make a prominent appearance even amid a wholesome crowd of families and straight-laced couples. Bargain with determination, as first-quoted prices tend to be astronomically high.

SOI LALAI SAP MARKET

Map p264 (Soi 5, Th Silom; ☺9am-4pm Mon-Fri; MSi Lom exit 2, ☐Sala Daeng exit 2) The ideal place to buy an authentic Thai secretary's uniform, this 'money-dissolving soi' has mobs of vendors selling insanely cheap but frumpy clothing, as well as heaps of snacks and housewares.

LOCAL KNOWLEDGE

7-ELEVEN FOREVER

Be extremely wary of any appointment that involves the words 'meet me at 7-Eleven'. In Bangkok alone, there are 2700 branches of 7-Eleven (known as *sair·wên* in Thai) – nearly a third the number found in North America. In central Bangkok, 7-Elevens are so ubiquitous that it's not uncommon to see two branches staring at each other from across the street.

Although the company claims its stores carry more than 2000 items, the fresh flavours of Thai cuisine are not reflected in the wares of a typical Bangkok 7-Eleven, the food selections of which are even junkier than those of its counterpart in the West. Like all shops in Thailand, alcohol is only available from 11am to 2pm and 5pm to midnight, and branches of 7-Eleven located near hospitals, temples and schools do not sell alcohol or cigarettes at all (but do continue to sell unhealthy snack food).

7-Eleven stores carry a wide selection of drinks, a godsend in sweltering Bangkok. You can conveniently pay most of your bills at the Service Counter, and all manner of phonecards, prophylactics and 'literature' (although very few English-language newspapers) are also available. And sometimes the blast of air-conditioning alone is enough reason to stop by. But our single favourite item must be the dirt-cheap chilled scented towels for wiping away the accumulated grime and sweat before your next appointment.

SPORTS & ACTIVITIES

TOP CHOICE **ORIENTAL SPA** SPA

Map p266 (☑0 2659 9000; www.mandarin oriental.com/bangkok/spa; Mandarin Oriental, 48 Soi 40/Oriental, Th Charoen Krung; spa packages from 2900B; ◷9am-10pm; ☒Tha Oriental or hotel shuttle boat from Tha Sathon (Central Pier)) Regarded as among the premier spas in the world, the Oriental Spa also set the standard for Asian-style spa treatment. Depending on where you flew in from, the Jet Lag Massage might be a good option, but all treatments require advance booking.

TOP CHOICE **HEALTH LAND** SPA

Map p264 (☑0 2637 8883; www.healthlandspa.com; 120 Th Sathon Neua; Thai massage 2 hr 450B; ◷9am-midnight; ☒Surasak exit 3) This, the main branch of a long-standing Thai massage mini-empire, offers good-value, no-nonsense massage and spa treatments in a tidy environment.

TOP CHOICE **RUEN-NUAD MASSAGE STUDIO** MASSAGE

(☑0 2632 2662; 42 Th Convent; Thai massage per hr 350B; ◷10am-9pm; ⓜSi Lom exit 2, ☒Sala Daeng exit 2) Set in a refurbished wooden house, this charming place successfully avoids both the tackiness and New Aged-ness that characterise most Bangkok massage joints. Prices are approachable, too.

BLUE ELEPHANT THAI COOKING SCHOOL COOKING COURSE

Map p264 (☑0 2673 9353; www.blueelephant.com; 233 Th Sathon Tai; lessons 2945-3300B; ◷8.45am-1pm & 1.30-4.30pm Mon-Sat; ☒Surasak exit 2) Bangkok's most chi-chi Thai cooking school offers two lessons daily. The morning class squeezes in a visit to a local market, while the afternoon session includes a detailed introduction to Thai ingredients.

SILOM THAI COOKING SCHOOL COOKING COURSE

Map p264 (☑08 4726 5669; www.bangkokthai cooking.com; 68 Soi 13, Th Silom; lessons 1000B; ◷9am-1pm & 1.40-6pm; ☒Chong Nonsi exit 3) The facilities are basic but Silom crams a visit to a local market and instruction of six dishes into four hours, making it the best bang for your baht. Transportation is available.

ORIENTAL HOTEL THAI COOKING SCHOOL COOKING COURSE

Map p266 (☑0 2659 9000; www.mandarinorien tal.com; Mandarin Oriental, 48 Soi 40/Oriental, Th Charoen Krung; ◷9am-1pm Mon-Sat; ☒Tha Oriental or hotel shuttle boat from Tha Sathon (Central Pier)) Located across the river in an antique wooden house, the Oriental's cooking class spans a daily revolving menu of four dishes. Cooking is significantly less 'hands on' than elsewhere, and is done in teams, rather than individually.

New Bangkok: Thanon Sukhumvit

Neighbourhood Top Five

1 Spending a night out at **Soi Ekamai 5** (p136), **WTF** (p136) and other buzz-worthy clubs and bars the in-crowd would approve of.

2 Rejuvenating at one of Th Sukhumvit's excellent-value spas, such as **Health Land** (p140) or **Asia Herb Association** (p140).

3 Sampling Th Sukhumvit's spread of international restaurants, from **Nasir Al-Masri** (p131) to **Bei Otto** (p132).

4 Witnessing a corner of northern Thailand in modern Bangkok at **Ban Kamthieng** (p132).

5 Getting lost in **Khlong Toey Market** (p131), the city's largest.

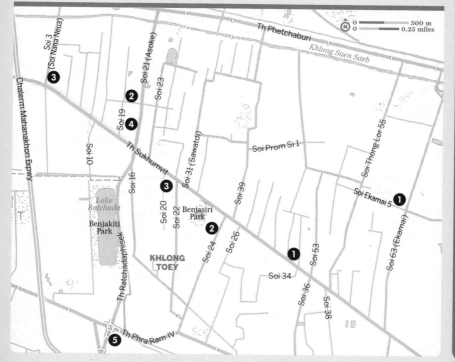

For more detail of this area, see Map p270 ➡

Lonely Planet's Top Tip

All odd-numbered soi branching off Th Sukhumvit head north, while even numbers run south. Unfortunately, they don't line up sequentially (eg Soi 11 lies directly opposite Soi 8; Soi 39 is opposite Soi 26). Also, some larger soi are better known by alternative names, such as Soi Nana (Soi 3), Soi Asoke (Soi 21), Soi Thong Lor (Soi 55) and Soi Ekamai (Soi 63).

✕ Best Places to Eat

➤ Bo.lan (p131)

➤ Boon Tong Kiat Singapore Hainanese Chicken Rice (p131)

➤ Nasir Al-Masri (p131)

➤ Rang Mahal (p135)

➤ Khua Kling + Pak Sod (p132)

🍷 Best Places to Drink

➤ WTF (p136)

➤ Soul Food Mahanakorn (p132)

➤ Cheap Charlie's (p136)

➤ Bar 23 (p136)

☆ Best Dance Clubs

➤ Soi Ekamai 5 (p136)

➤ Bed Supperclub (p133)

➤ Q Bar (p137)

Explore: Sukhumvit

You'll probably spend more time on Th Sukhumvit eating, drinking and perhaps sleeping (there's a high concentration of hotels here), rather than sightseeing. Thankfully the BTS (Skytrain) runs along the length of Th Sukhumvit. BTS stops are also a convenient way to define the street's various vibes. Lower Sukhumvit, particularly the area around Nana BTS station, is a discombobulating mix of sexpats and Middle Eastern tourists; street markets and touts make this a frustrating zone to navigate. Middle Sukhumvit, around BTS Asok/MRT Sukhumvit, is dominated by midrange hotels, upscale condos, international restaurants and businesses meant to appeal to both tourists and resident foreigners. Starting at BTS Phrom Phong is where you'll find the well-concealed compounds of wealthy Thai residents and tidy Japanese enclaves, while extending east from BTS Ekkamai, the feel becomes more provincial and more Thai.

Local Life

➤ **Hi-So Hangouts** Th Sukhumvit is Bangkok's ritziest zone, and is *the* area to observe hi-so (high society) Thais in their natural environment: chatting at a wine bar on Soi 55 (Thong Lor) or topping up on Fendi bags at Emporium (p139).

➤ **International Dining** Th Sukhumvit's various ethnic enclaves are a logical destination if you've grown tired of Thai food. Known colloquially as Little Arabia, Soi 3/1 is home to Middle Eastern restaurants, while a handful of Korean restaurants can be found at Soi 12 and several Japanese restaurants are located near BTS Phrom Phong.

➤ **Club Alley** The streets that extend from Th Sukhumvit are home to many of Bangkok's most popular clubs. Ravers of uni age tend to head to Soi 63 (Ekamai), while the pampered elite play at Soi 55 (Thong Lor) and expats head to the clubs around Soi 11.

Getting There & Away

➤ **BTS** Nana, Asok (interchange with MRT Sukhumvit), Phrom Phong, Thong Lo, Ekkamai, Phra Khanong, On Nut, Bang Chak, Punnawithi, Udom Suk, Bang Na and Bearing.

➤ **MRT** Queen Sirikit National Convention Centre, Sukhumvit (interchange with BTS Asok), Phetchaburi.

➤ **Klorng boat** Tha Asoke, Tha Nana Neua and Tha Nana Chard.

➤ **Bus** Air-con 501, 508, 511 and 513; ordinary 2, 25, 30, 48 and 72.

◉ SIGHTS

THAILAND CREATIVE & DESIGN CENTER
DESIGN CENTRE

Map p270 (ศูนย์สร้างสรรค์งานออกแบบ; TCDC; ☑️0 2664 8448; www.tcdc.or.th; cnr Th Sukhumvit & Soi 24, 6th fl, Emporium; ☺10.30am-9pm Tue-Sun; 🛜; 🚇Phrom Phong exit 3) The Thailand Creative & Design Center is a government-backed initiative that acts as both showroom and shop for Thai design. Rotating exhibitions feature profiles of international products and retrospectives of regional handicrafts and creativity. The centre includes a permanent library of design-related books and materials and is a good place to meet young Thai designers and students; the adjoining cafe has free wi-fi and good views.

FREE CHUVIT GARDEN
PARK

Map p270 (Th Sukhumvit; admission free; ☺6-10am & 4-8pm; 🚇Nana exit 4) The story behind this park is shadier than the plantings. Chuvit Kamolvisit, the benefactor of the park, was Bangkok's biggest massage-parlour owner. He was arrested in 2003 for illegally bulldozing, rather than legally evicting, tenants off the land where the park now stands (between Soi 8 and Soi 10). With all the media attention, he sang like a bird about the police bribes he handed out during his career and became an unlikely activist against police corruption. Chuvit later ran unsuccessfully for Bangkok governor in 2004 and successfully for the Thai parliament in 2005 and 2011. This park was one of his early campaign promises. It's a pretty green patch in a neighbourhood lean on trees.

BENJAKITI PARK
PARK

Map p270 (สวนเบญจกิติ; Th Ratchadaphisek; ☺5am-8pm; 🚇Queen Sirikit National Convention Centre exit 3) This 130-rai (20.8-hectare) park is built on what was once a part of the Tobacco Monopoly, a vast, Crown-owned expanse of low-rise factories and warehouses. There's an artificial lake that's good for jogging and cycling (bikes can be hired) around its 2km track.

KHLONG TOEY MARKET
MARKET

Map p270 (ตลาดคลองเตย; cnr Th Ratchadaphisek & Th Phra Ram IV; ☺5-10am; 🚇Khlong Toei exit 1) This wholesale market, one of the city's largest, is inevitably the origin of many of the meals you'll eat during your stay in Bangkok. Although some corners of the market can't exactly be described as photogenic, you'll want to bring a camera to capture the cheery fishmongers and stacks of durians. Get there early, ideally before 10am, when most vendors have packed up and left.

✖ EATING

TOP CHOICE BO.LAN
THAI $$$

Map p270 (☑️0 2260 2962; www.bolan.co.th; 42 Soi Rongnarong Phichai Songkhram, Soi 26, Th Sukhumvit; set meal 1680B; ☺6pm-midnight Tue-Sun; 🚇Phrom Phong exit 4) Upscale Thai is usually more garnish than flavour, but Bo.lan, started up by two former chefs of London's Michelin-starred nahm, is the exception. Bo and Dylan (Bo.lan, a play on words that also means 'ancient') take a scholarly approach to Thai cuisine; generous set meals featuring full-flavoured Thai dishes are the results of this tuition. Bo and Dylan also host a Thai cookery class (3900B) on the last Saturday of the month and a small farmers market on the first Saturday of the month. Reservations recommended.

BOON TONG KIAT SINGAPORE HAINANESE CHICKEN RICE
SINGAPOREAN $

Map p270 (440/5 Soi 55 (Thong Lor), Th Sukhumvit; mains 60-150B; ☺lunch & dinner; 🚇Thong Lo exit 3 & taxi) After taking in the exceedingly detailed and ambitious chicken rice manifesto written on the walls, order a plate of the restaurant's namesake and witness how a dish can be so simple, yet so delicious. And while you're there you'd be daft not to order *rojak,* the spicy/sour fruit 'salad', which is referred to here tongue-in-cheek as 'Singapore Som Tam'.

NASIR AL-MASRI
EGYPTIAN $

Map p270 (4/6 Soi 3/1, Th Sukhumvit; mains 80-350B; ☺24hr; 🍴; 🚇Nana exit 1) Part restaurant, part shrine to the glories of stainless-steel furnishings, this popular Egyptian joint simply can't be missed. This is Muslim food, with the emphasis on meat, meat and more meat, but the kitchen also pulls off some brilliant vegie meze as well. Enhance your postprandial digestion and catch up on the Arabic-language TV news with a puff on the hookah in the street-side patio area.

TOP SIGHTS
SIAM SOCIETY & BAN KAMTHIENG

Stepping off cacophonous Soi Asoke and into the Siam Society's **Ban Kamthieng** is as close to visiting a northern Thai village as you'll come in Bangkok. Ban Kamthieng is a traditional 19th-century home that was located on the banks of Mae Nam Ping in Chiang Mai. Now relocated to Bangkok, the house presents the daily customs and spiritual beliefs of the Lanna tradition. Communicating all the hard facts as well as any sterile museum (with detailed English signage and engaging video installations), Ban Kamthieng instils in the visitor a palpable sense of place, from the attached rice granary and handmade tools to the wooden loom and woven silks. You can't escape the noise of Bangkok completely, but the houses are refreshingly free of concrete and reflecting glass and make a pleasant, interesting break.

Next door are the headquarters of the prestigious **Siam Society** (admission free), publisher of the renowned *Journal of the Siam Society* and a valiant preserver of traditional Thai culture. Those with a serious interest can use the **reference library**, which has the answers to almost any question you might have about Thailand (outside the political sphere, since the society is sponsored by the royal family).

DON'T MISS...

➡ Ban Kamthieng
➡ Siam Society's reference library

PRACTICALITIES

➡ สยามสมาคม & บ้านคำเที่ยง
➡ Map p270
➡ ✆0 2661 6470
➡ www.siam-society.com
➡ 131 Soi Asoke (Soi 21), Th Sukhumvit
➡ admission adult/child 100B/free
➡ ⊙9am-5pm Tue-Sat
➡ Ⓜ Sukhumvit exit 1, ⊟Asok exit 3 or 6

KHUA KLING + PAK SOD   SOUTHERN THAI $

Map p270 (98/1 Soi Thong Lor 5; mains 120-350B; ⊙11am-2pm & 5.30-10pm; ⊟Thong Lo exit 3 & taxi) One of the classiest family-run places in town, as well as one of the only semi-formal dining rooms serving regional Thai, this restaurant serves up the high-intensity specialities of Thailand's south. Try the namesake dish of minced meat fried in a curry paste, or the incendiary yellow curry (actually a seafood-based soup) – if you can't tolerate the heat, this is not the kitchen for you. There's no English-language sign here, but the restaurant is just north of Soi Thong Lor 5, on the west side of the street.

BEI OTTO   GERMAN $$

Map p270 (www.beiotto.com; 1 Soi 20, Th Sukhumvit; mains 175-590B; ⊙9am-midnight; Ⓜ Sukhumvit exit 2, ⊟Asok exit 4) Claiming a Bangkok residence for nearly 30 years, Bei Otto's major culinary bragging point is its pork knuckles, reputedly the best in town. A good selection of German beers and an attached delicatessen with brilliant breads and super sausages makes it even more attractive to go Deutsch.

TENKAICHI YAKITON NAGIYA   JAPANESE $

Map p270 (www.nagiya.com; Nihonmachi 105, 115 Soi 26, Th Sukhumvit; mains 90-160B; ⊙5pm-midnight; Ⓜ Phrom Phong exit 4 & taxi) Originating in Tokyo, this is one of Bangkok's best *izakayas*, or Japanese tavern-style restaurants. The highlights here are the warming *nabe*, DIY hotpots, and the smokey *yaki-toshi*, grilled skewers of meat. Expect lots of Japanese-style welcoming (some might call it shouting) by the staff, and on weekends, a queue.

SOUL FOOD MAHANAKORN   THAI $

Map p270 (✆0 2714 7708; www.soulfoodmahanakorn.com; 56/10 Soi 55 (Thong Lor), Th Sukhumvit; mains 140-250B; ⊙5.30pm-midnight; ⊟Thong Lo exit 3) In less than a year, and despite being run by a *fa·ràng* from Pennsylvania, Soul Food has shot to the top of the heap of cool places to eat Thai food in Bangkok. The secret recipe? We reckon it's Soul Food's dual nature as both an inviting restaurant – the menu spans tasty but somewhat pricey takes on rustic Thai dishes – and a bar serving deliciously boozy, Thai-influenced cocktails. Reservations recommended.

SARAS INDIAN $

Map p270 (www.saras.co.th; Soi 20, Th Sukhumvit; mains 85-220B; ⊗8.30am-10.30pm; ⚙; ⓜSukhumvit exit 2, ⓡAsok exit 4) Describing yourself as a 'fast-food feast' may not be the most clever PR move we've ever encountered, but it's spot-on description of this new Indian restaurant. Order at the counter to be rewarded with crispy *dosai*, regional set meals or rich curries (dishes are brought to your table). There are shelves of Punjabi sweets and *chaat* (sweet and savoury snacks), and perhaps most endearingly, chai is served in earthenware cups. We wish all fast food could be this satisfying.

IMOYA JAPANESE $

Map p270 (2/17-19 Soi 24, Th Sukhumvit, 3rd fl, Terminal Shop Cabin; mains 40-400B; ⊗6pm-midnight; ⓡPhrom Phong exit 4) Temporarily set aside thoughts of Bangkok and whisk yourself back to 1950s-era Tokyo. A visit to this well-hidden Japanese restaurant, with its antique ads, wood panelling and wall of sake bottles, is like taking a trip in a time machine. Even the prices of the better-than-decent Japanese-style pub grub haven't caught up with modern times.

MYEONG GA KOREAN $$

Map p270 (Sukhumvit Plaza, cnr Soi 12 & Th Sukhumvit; mains 40-550B; ⊗dinner; ⓜSukhumvit exit 3, ⓡAsok exit 2) Located on the ground floor of Sukhumvit Plaza (the multistorey complex also known as Korean Town), this restaurant is the city's best destination for authentic Seoul food. Go for the tasty prepared dishes or, if you've got a bit more time, the excellent, DIY Korean-style barbecue.

PIZZA ROMANA PALA ITALIAN $

Map p270 (Th Sukhumvit; mains 40-250B; ⊗11.30am-10pm; ⓜSukhumvit exit 3, ⓡAsok exit 3) Strategically located at the intersection of BTS and MRT – ideal for that rush-hour snack – this place serves some of Bangkok's best pies. Pizzas are sold by the slice and are made using almost exclusively imported ingredients. Pala also boasts a deli: in addition to antipasti and simple pasta dishes you can also pick up a chunk of pecorino romano or some salami.

BACCO – OSTERIA DA SERGIO ITALIAN $$$

Map p270 (www.bacco-bkk.com; 35/1 Soi 53, Th Sukhumvit; antipasti 100-1200B; mains 250-850B; ⊗lunch & dinner; ⓡThong Lo exit 1) The slightly cheesy interior of this *osteria* (Italian-style wine bar) serves as something of a cover for one of Bangkok's better Italian menus. There's an abundance of delicious antipasti, but the emphasis here is on breads, from pizza to *piada*, all of which are done exceedingly well.

SNAPPER SEAFOOD $$

Map p270 (1/22 Soi 11, Th Sukhumvit; mains 160-650B; ⊗5pm-midnight; ⓡNana exit 3) Allegedly Bangkok's first restaurant serving New Zealand cuisine, Snapper specialises in Kiwi-style fish and chips. Choose from one of four sustainably harvested fish from New Zealand, your cut of fries, and the delicious homemade tartar sauce or a garlic aioli. A handful of other seafood dishes and salads and a brief wine list round out the selections.

NEW SRI FAH 33 CHINESE-THAI $$

Map p270 (www.newsrifa33.com; 12/19-21 Soi 33, Th Sukhumvit; mains 80-450B; ⊗5pm-3am; ⓡPhrom Phong exit 5) This former Chinatown shophouse restaurant, originally opened in 1955, has relocated to a tight but classy location in new Bangkok. Just about anything from the Thai-Chinese seafood-heavy menu is bound to satisfy, but we particularly love the stir-fried Chinese black olive with pork, and the stir-fried water mimosa.

BED SUPPERCLUB INTERNATIONAL $$$

Map p270 (☎0 2651 3537; www.bedsupperclub.com; 26 Soi 11, Th Sukhuvmit; mains 450-990B, set meals 790-1850B; ⊗7.30-10pm Tue-Thu, dinner 9pm Fri & Sat; ⓡNana exit 3) Within this sleek and futuristic setting – beds instead of tables and contemporary performances instead of mood music – the food stands up to the distractions with a changing menu described as 'modern eclectic cuisine'. Dining is à la carte, except on Fridays and Saturdays when there's a four-course surprise menu served at 9pm sharp.

CRÊPES & CO INTERNATIONAL $$

Map p270 (☎0 2653 3990; www.crepesnco.com; 18 Soi 12, Th Sukhumvit; mains 130-555B; ⊗9am-midnight Mon-Sat & 8am-midnight Sun; ☎; ⓜSukhumvit exit 3, ⓡAsok exit 2) Want to pretend you're part of Bangkok's expat community? This cute cottage crêperie is a good place to start. The homely setting and excellent service, not to mention a menu that offers much more than the restaurant's name suggests, keep the desperate housewives of

SUPER MARKETS

Are you an American in need of a peanut-butter fix or an Aussie craving Vegemite? Don't fret – Th Sukhumvit is home to many of Bangkok's international grocery stores.

Villa Market (Map p270; www.villamarket.com; Soi 33/1, Th Sukhumvit; ☺24hr) The main branch of Bangkok's most well-stocked international grocery store is the place to pick up necessities from Cheerios to cheddar cheese. Additional Th Sukhumvit branches include **Soi 11** (Map p270; Soi 11, Th Sukhumvit; ☺24hr), **Soi 49** (Map p270; Soi 49, Th Sukhumvit; ☺24hr) and **Soi 55 (Thong Lor)** (Map p270; Soi Thong Lor 15, Soi 55 (Thong Lor); ☺24hr); check the website for other locations.

Gourmet Market (Map p270; cnr Soi 24 & Th Sukhumvit, 5th fl, Emporium; ☺10am-10pm; ⊠Phrom Phong exit 2) Gourmet Market carries a wide range of Western-style staples.

Bangkok's diplomatic corps coming back again and again.

BHARANI
THAI **$**

Map p270 (Sansab Boat Noodle; 96/14 Soi 23, Th Sukhumvit; mains 50-200B; ☺lunch & dinner; Ⓜ Sukhumvit exit 2, ⊠Asok exit 3) This cosy Thai restaurant dabbles in a bit of everything, from ox-tongue stew to rice fried with shrimp paste, but the real reason to come is for the rich, meaty 'boat noodles' – so called because they used to be sold from boats plying the *klorng* (canals; also spelt *khlong*) of Ayuthaya.

FACE
INTERNATIONAL **$$**

Map p270 (✆0 2713 6048; www.facebars.com; 29 Soi 38, Th Sukhumvit; mains 310-670B; ☺lunch & dinner; ⊠Thong Lo exit 4) Housed in several interconnected Thai-style wooden structures, this handsome dining complex is essentially three very good restaurants in one. **Lan Na Thai** does flawless domestic with an emphasis on regional Thai dishes, **Misaki** handles the Japanese end of things and **Hazara** dabbles in exotic-sounding 'North Indian frontier cuisine'.

ROAST
INTERNATIONAL **$**

Map p270 (www.roastbkk.com; 251/5 Soi Thong Lor 13, 1st fl, SeenSpace 13; mains 160-350B; ☺10am-11pm Sun-Thu & 9am-1am Fri-Sat; ⊠Thong Lo exit 3 & taxi) Seemingly trying to woo the sophisticated brunch crowd, this new coffee roaster does specialist coffees and somewhat decadent takes on homey, American-style dishes. Yet the desserts, sandwiches (we particularly liked the Cubano), breakfast, many wines and an open and airy atmosphere make Roast a good choice for any time, day or night.

TAPAS CAFÉ
SPANISH **$$**

Map p270 (1/25 Soi 11, Th Sukhumvit; mains 75-750B; ☺11am-midnight; ⊠Nana exit 3) Although it's the least expensive of Bangkok's Spanish joints, a visit to this friendly restaurant is in no way a compromise. Tasty tapas, refreshing sangria and a jazzy Latin vibe make Tapas Café well worth the visit. Come before 7pm, when tapas are buy-two-get-one-free. Tapas Café is located nearly next door to Suk 11 hostel.

RUEA THONG
THAI **$**

Map p270 (331/2 Soi 55 (Thong Lor), Th Sukhumvit; mains 70-180B; ☺11.30am-2pm & 5-11pm Mon-Sat, 5-11pm Sun; ⊠Thong Lo exit 3) A tiny, homey restaurant serving a wide menu of Thai dishes, including some spicy southern Thai specialties. Expect a crowd of local and expat regulars. There's no English-language sign here, but Ruea Thong is located next door to Family Mart, near the corner of Soi Thong Lor 17.

LE PETIT ZINC
FRENCH **$$**

Map p270 (www.le-petit-zinc.com; 110/1 Soi Prasanmit, Th Sukhumvit; mains 240-670B; ☺11am-midnight Tue-Sat; Ⓜ Sukhumvit exit 2, ⊠Asok exit 6) Friendly French owners and an airy dining room that feels both modern and traditional separate Le Petit Zinc from the bistro cliché. Expect a short menu of mostly meaty country faves – think terrines, tartare and French salads – and come during the day for the excellent-value set lunches that include the tasty house desserts.

KUPPA
INTERNATIONAL **$$$**

Map p270 (www.kuppa.co.th; 39 Soi 16, Th Sukhumvit; mains 95-795B; ☺10am-11pm Tue-Sun; Ⓜ Sukhumvit exit 2, ⊠Asok exit 6) For Bangkok's ladies who lunch, Kuppa is something of a second home. Resembling an expansive living room, this place fancies itself as a 'tea and coffee trader' – the coffee is truly among the best in town. Thankfully the eats are just as good, in particular the spot-on Western-style pastries and sweets.

THONG LEE
THAI $

Map p270 (Soi 20, Th Sukhumvit; mains 50-100B; ☺9am-10pm, closed 3rd Sun of month; Ⓜ Sukhumvit exit 2, Ⓔ Asok exit 6) With the owners' possessions overflowing into the dining room, a heavily laden spirit shrine and tacky synthetic tablecloths, Thong Lee is the epitome of a typical Thai restaurant. However, in the sea of foreign food that is Th Sukhumvit, this is exactly what makes it stand out. Thong Lee offers a few dishes you won't find elsewhere, like *mŏo pàt gà·bì* (pork fried with shrimp paste) and *mèe gròrp* (sweet-and-spicy crispy fried noodles).

DUC DE PRASLIN
CAFE $

Map p270 (Soi 31/1, Th Sukhumvit, ground fl, RSU Tower; ☺8am-9pm; Ⓔ Phrom Phong exit 5) This Belgian-owned chocolatier has opened its classy European cafes at various locations around town. As well as the decadent bonbons, try a hot cocoa, made in front of your eyes with steaming milk and shards of rich chocolate.

SCAN DELI
SWEDISH $

Map p270 (www.scandeli.com; 21/3 Soi 18, Th Sukhumvit; mains 155-260B; ☺lunch & dinner; Ⓜ Sukhumvit exit 2, Ⓔ Asok exit 6) This tiny cafe, which also serves as the unofficial meeting point for Bangkok's Scandinavian community, serves a thick menu of dishes ranging from Swedish meatballs to *smörgås* (Swedish-style sandwiches). Come Thursdays after 7pm for all-you-can-eat *ärtsoppa*, (Swedish pea soup served with thin pancakes; 349B). An attached deli sells imported food items from Sweden.

CABBAGES & CONDOMS
THAI $$

Map p270 (www.pda.or.th/restaurant/; Soi 12, Th Sukhumvit; mains 100-450B; ☺11am-11pm; ☎; Ⓜ Sukhumvit exit 3, Ⓔ Asok exit 2) This long-standing garden restaurant is a safe place to gauge the Thai staples. It also stands for a safe cause: instead of after-meal mints, diners receive packaged condoms, and all proceeds go towards Population & Community Development Association (PDA), a sex education/AIDS prevention organisation.

SOI 38 NIGHT MARKET
THAI-CHINESE $

Map p270 (cnr Soi 38 & Th Sukhumvit; mains 30-60B; ☺8pm-3am; Ⓔ Thong Lo exit 4) It's not the best street food in town by a long shot, but after a hard night of clubbing on Sukhumvit, you can be forgiven for believing so. If you're going sober, stick to the knot of 'famous' vendors tucked into an alley on the right-hand side as you enter the street; the flame-fried *pàt tai* and herbal fish-ball noodles are standouts.

SUNDAY BRUNCH

Sunday brunch has become a Bangkok tradition, particularly among the members of the city's expat community, and the hotels along Th Sukhumvit offer some of the best spreads. Below are some of our favourites.

Rang Mahal (Map p270; ☎0 2261 7100; 19 Soi 20, Th Sukhumvit, 26th fl, Rembrandt Hotel; buffet 850B; ☺11am-2.30pm Sun; Ⓜ Sukhumvit exit 2, Ⓔ Asok exit 6) Couple views from this restaurant's 26th floor with an all-Indian buffet and a live band, and you have one of the most popular Sunday destinations for Bangkok's South Asian community.

Eugenia Hotel Weekend Brunch (Map p270; ☎0 2259 9017-19; www.theeugenia.com; 267 Soi 31 (Sawatdi), Th Sukhumvit; set meal 1590B; ☺11.30am-3pm Sat & Sun; Ⓔ Phrom Phong exit 6 & taxi) It's not a buffet, but we'll give a prize to anybody who can tackle this hotel's multi-course spread – which spans decadent egg dishes, a main course and dessert, not to mention coffee, juice and prosecco – and find it insufficient.

Sunday Jazzy Brunch (Map p270; ☎0 2649 8888; 250 Th Sukhumvit, 1st fl, Sheraton Grande Sukhumvit; adult/child 2600/1200B; ☺noon-3pm Sun; Ⓜ Sukhumvit exit 3, Ⓔ Asok exit 2) If you require more than just victuals, then consider the Sheraton's Sunday brunch, which unites all the hotel's restaurant outlets to a theme of live jazz.

Marriott Café (Map p270; ☎0 2656 7700; 4 Soi 2, Th Sukhumvit, ground fl, JW Marriott; buffet 1884B; ☺11.30am-3pm Sat & Sun; Ⓔ Nana exit 3) The feastlike weekend brunch at this American hotel chain is likened to Thanksgiving year-round.

DRINKING & NIGHTLIFE

TOP CHOICE WTF
BAR

Map p270 (www.wtfbangkok.com; 7 Soi 51, Th Sukhumvit; ⊙6pm-1am Tue-Sun; 🚇Thong Lo exit 3) No, not that WTF – Wonderful Thai Friendship is a funky and friendly neighbourhood bar that also packs in two floors of gallery space and a multipurpose event locale. Artsy locals and resident foreigners come for the old-school cocktails, live music and DJ events, poetry readings, art exhibitions and truly tasty bar snacks, whose influences range from Macau to Spain. And we, like them, give WTF our vote for Bangkok's best bar.

CHEAP CHARLIE'S
BAR

Map p270 (Soi 11, Th Sukhumvit; ⊙6pm-1am Mon-Sat; 🚇Nana exit 3) You're bound to have a mighty difficult time convincing your Thai friends to go to Th Sukhumvit only to sit at an outdoor wooden shack decorated with buffalo skulls and wagon wheels. Fittingly, Charlie's draws a staunchly foreign crowd who don't mind a bit of kitsch and sweat with their Singha.

SOI EKAMAI 5
NIGHTCLUB DISTRICT

Map p270 (cnr Soi Ekamai 5 & Soi 63 (Ekamai), Th Sukhumvit; admission free; ⊙8pm-2am; 🚇Ekkamai exit 2 & taxi) This open-air entertainment zone is the destination of choice for Bangkok's young and beautiful – for the moment at least. **Demo** (Map p270; admission free) combines blasting beats and a NYC warehouse vibe, while **Funky Villa** (Map p270; admission free), with its outdoor seating and Top 40 soundtrack, is more chilled.

BAR 23
BAR

Map p270 (Soi 16, Th Sukhumvit; ⊙7pm-1am Tue-Sat; 🚇Sukhumvit exit 2, 🚇Asok exit 6) The foreign NGO crowd and indie Thai types flock to this warehouse-like bar on weekends; cold Beerlao and a retro-rock soundtrack keep them there until the late hours. Bar 23 is located about 500m down Soi 16, which is accessible from Th Ratchadaphisek.

IRON FAIRIES
BAR

Map p270 (www.theironfairies.com; Soi 55 (Thong Lor), Th Sukhumvit; ⊙5pm-midnight Mon-Sat; 🚇Thong Lo exit 3) Imagine, if you can, an abandoned fairy factory in Paris c 1912, and you'll begin to get an idea of the vibe at this popular pub/wine bar. If you manage to wangle one of a handful of seats, you can test their claim of serving Bangkok's best burgers. There's live music after 9.30pm.

BANGKOK BAR
BAR

Map p270 (Soi Ekamai 2; ⊙8pm-1am; 🚇Ekkamai exit 1) Bounce with Thai indie kids at this fun but astonishingly uncreatively named bar. There's live music, and the eats are strong enough to make Bangkok Bar a dinner destination in itself. We double-dog-dare you to walk a straight line after downing two Mad Dogs, Bangkok Bar's infamous house drink.

LONG TABLE
BAR

Map p270 (www.longtablebangkok.com; 48 Soi 16, Th Sukhumvit, 25th fl, Column Building; ⊙5pm-2am; 🚇Sukhumvit exit 2, 🚇Asok exit 6) Come to this slick, 25th-floor balcony to sip fruity cocktails and gloat at the poor sods stuck in traffic below. In addition to views, there's a menu of Thai-inspired dishes and generous Happy Hour specials. Long Table is located about 200m down Soi 16, which is accessible via Th Ratchadaphisek.

6IXCRET
BAR

(www.6ixcret.com; 11 Soi Ekamai 6; ⊙5pm-1am; 🚇Ekkamai exit 1) The folks behind this new bar could have thrown us a bone by providing a less confounding name (it's a play on 'secret' and is pronounced much the same way), but they hit the mark with the bar's sophisticated yet chilled villa vibe. There's comfy outdoor seating, food and, of course, the Bangkok hipster trifecta of Thai bossa nova, sheeshas and draught Belgian beer.

HAPPY MONDAY
BAR

Map p270 (Soi Ekamai 10, Soi 63 (Ekamai), Th Sukhumvit, Ekkamai Shopping Mall; ⊙7pm-1am Mon-Sat; 🚇Ekkamai exit 1 & taxi) This somewhat concealed pub follows the tried and true Ekamai/Thong Lor formula of retro furniture, a brief bar-snack menu and bizarrely named house drinks. The diverse soundtrack, spun by local and visiting DJs, sets it apart.

BED SUPPERCLUB
NIGHTCLUB

Map p270 (www.bedsupperclub.com; 26 Soi 11, Th Sukhuvmit; admission from 600B; ⊙8pm-1am; 🚇Nana exit 3) Resembling an illuminated tube, Bed has basked in the Bangkok nightlife limelight for nearly a decade now, but has yet to lose any of its futuristic charm. Arrive at a decent hour to squeeze in dinner – or if you've only got dancing on your mind, come on Tuesday for the hugely popular hip-hop night.

TUBA
BAR, RESTAURANT

Map p270 (Soi Ekamai 21, Soi 63 (Ekamai), Th Sukhumvit, 34 Room 11-12 A; ⊘6pm-2am; ⊠Ekkamai exit 1 & taxi) Used-furniture shop by day, Italian restaurant-slash-bar by night; oddly enough, this business formula is not entirely unheard of in Bangkok. Pull up a leatherette lounge and take the plunge and buy a whole bottle for once. And don't miss the delicious chicken wings.

NEST
BAR

Map p270 (www.nestbangkok.com; 33/33 Soi 11, Th Sukhumvit, 8th fl, Le Fenix Hotel; ⊘5pm-2am; ⊠Nana exit 3) Perched eight floors aboveground on the roof of Le Fenix Hotel, Nest is a chic maze of cleverly concealed sofas and inviting day-beds. A DJ soundtrack and one of the more thoughtful pub grub menus in town keep things down to earth.

SHADES OF RETRO
BAR

Map p270 (Soi Thararom 2, Soi 55 (Thong Lor), Th Sukhumvit; ⊘2pm-1am Mon-Sat; ⊠Thong Lo exit 3 & taxi) As the name suggests, this eclectic place takes the current vintage fad to the max. You'll have to climb around Vespas and Naugahyde sofas to reach your seat, but you'll be rewarded with friendly service, an eclectic domestic soundtrack (the people behind Shades also run the domestic indie label Small Room) and free popcorn.

HOBS
BAR, RESTAURANT

Map p270 (House of Beers; 522/3 Soi 16, Soi 55 (Thong Lor), Th Sukhumvit; ⊘11am-midnight; ⊠Thong Lo exit 3 & taxi) Arguably the word's best brews, Belgian beers have been fleetingly available around Bangkok for a while now, but have found a permanent home at this pub. Be sure to accompany your beer with a bowl of crispy *frites*, served here Belgian-style, with mayonnaise.

BLACK SWAN
BAR, RESTAURANT

Map p270 (www.blackswanbkk.com; 326/8-9 Th Sukhumvit; ⊘8am-1am; ⓜSukhumvit exit 3, ⊠Asok exit 4) Liable to bring a tear to the eye of a homesick Brit, the combination of supping mates, dining families and bad decor make the Black Swan the most authentic of

DRINKING BUDDY

Bars, clubs and restaurants open and close faster than we can show on the printed page, but Th Thong Lo and Ekamai are arguably Bangkok's hippest strips for restaurants, bars and clubs. For up to date reviews, check out www.thonglor-ekamai.com.

Bangkok's numerous English pubs. If you're arriving hungry, a meaty pub-grub menu, with a few bar snacks and Thai dishes thrown in, is there for you.

Q BAR
NIGHTCLUB

Map p270 (www.qbarbangkok.com; 34 Soi 11, Th Sukhumvit; admission from 700B; ⊘8pm-2am; ⊠Nana exit 3) In club years, Q Bar is fast approaching retirement age, but a recent renovation has ensured that it still rules over Bangkok's club scene with slick industrial style. Most nights the dance floor is monopolised by working girls and their pot-bellied admirers, but theme nights and celebrity DJs bring in just about everybody else in town.

NUNG-LEN
NIGHTCLUB

Map p270 (www.nunglen.net; 217 Soi 63 (Ekamai), Th Sukhumvit; admission free; ⊘6pm-1am; ⊠Ekkamai exit 1 & taxi) Young, loud and Thai, Nung-Len (literally 'Sit and chill') is a ridiculously popular den of live music and uni students on buzzy Th Ekamai. Get there before 10pm or you won't get in at all.

GLOW
NIGHTCLUB

Map p270 (www.glowbkk.com; 96/415 Soi Prasanmit, Th Sukhumvit; admission from 300B; ⊘7pm-2am; ⓜSukhumvit exit 2, ⊠Asok exit 3) This self-proclaimed 'boutique' club starts things early in the evenings as a lounge boasting an impressive spectrum of vodkas. As the evening progresses, enjoy the recently upgraded sound system and tunes ranging from hip hop (Friday) to electronica (Saturday) and everything in between.

NARZ
NIGHTCLUB

Map p270 (112 Soi Prasanmit, Th Sukhumvit; admission 500B; ⊘9pm-3am; ⓜSukhumvit exit 2, ⊠Asok exit 3) The former Narcissus has undergone a nip and tuck and now consists of three separate zones boasting an equal variety of music. It's largely a domestic scene, but the odd guest DJ can pull a large crowd. Open later than most.

SCRATCH DOG NIGHTCLUB

Map p270 (8-10 Soi 20, Th Sukhumvit, basement, Windsor Suites Hotel; ⊘8pm-late; MSukhumvit exit 2, ⓓAsoke exit 4) It's pretty much as corny as the name and the Goofy-as-DJ logo suggest, but Scratch Dog pulls in a mixed crowd and is probably the least dodgy of Bangkok's late-night clubs. Don't bother showing up before 2am.

☆ ENTERTAINMENT

TOP CHOICE LIVING ROOM LIVE MUSIC

Map p270 (☏0 2649 8888; www.sheraton grandesukhumvit.com/en/thelivingroom; 250 Th Sukhumvit, Level 1, Sheraton Grande Sukhumvit; ⊘6pm-midnight; MSukhumvit exit 3, ⓓAsok exit) Don't let looks deceive you: every night this bland hotel lounge transforms into the city's best venue for live jazz. True to the name, there's comfy, sofa-based seating, all of it within earshot of the music. Enquire ahead of time to see which sax master or hide-hitter is in town.

TITANIUM LIVE MUSIC

Map p270 (2/30 Soi 22, Th Sukhumvit; ⊘8pm-1am; ⓓPhrom Phong exit 6) Most come to this cheesy 'ice bar' for the chill, the skimpily-

FAIR-TRADE FAIR

The twice-monthly **ThaiCraft Fair** (Map p270; www.thaicraft.org; cnr Soi 23 & Th Sukhumvit, 3rd fl, Jasmine City Building; ⊘10am-3pm; ⓓAsok exit 3, Sukhumvit exit 2) is a great chance to browse through the products of more than 60 community groups. For 20 years, ThaiCraft has marketed quality handicrafts made by artisans across all parts of Thailand, and recent fairs have seen products such as handmade baskets and mulberry-bark notebooks. Check the website to see if the next one is being held during your visit.

dressed working girls and the flavoured vodka, but we come for Unicorn, an all-female house band.

FAT GUT'Z LIVE MUSIC

Map p270 (www.fatgutz.com; 264 Soi 12, Soi 55 (Thong Lor), Th Sukhumvit; ⊘6pm-2am; ⓓThong Lo exit 3) This closet-sized 'saloon' combines live music and, er, fish and chips. Despite (or perhaps thanks to?) the odd whiff of chip oil, the odd combo works. Live blues every night from 9pm to midnight.

SOI COWBOY RED-LIGHT DISTRICT

Map p270 (btwn Soi 21 & Soi 23, Th Sukhumvit; ⊘7pm-2am; MSukhumvit exit 2, ⓓAsok exit 3) This single-lane strip of raunchy bars claims direct lineage to the post-Vietnam War R&R era. A real flesh trade functions amid the flashing neon.

NANA ENTERTAINMENTZ PLAZA RED-LIGHT DISTRICT

Map p270 (Soi 4 (Nana Tai), Th Sukhumvit; ⊘7pm-2am; ⓓNana exit 2) Nana is a three-storey go-go bar complex where the sexpats are separated from the gawking tourists. It's also home to a few *gà·teu·i* (also spelled *kathoey*; transgender person) bars.

🛍 SHOPPING

TOP CHOICE NANDAKWANG HANDICRAFTS

Map p270 (www.nandakwang.com; 108/2-3 Soi Prasanmit, Th Sukhumvit; ⊘9am-6.30pm Mon-Sat; MSukhumvit exit 2, ⓓAsok exit 3) The Bangkok satellite of a Chiang Mai store, Nandakwang sells a fun and colourful mix of cloth products. The cheery, chunky, hand-embroidered pillows, dolls and bags are particularly attractive.

ZUDRANGMA RECORDS MUSIC STORE

Map p270 (www.zudrangmarecords.com; 7/1 Soi 51, Th Sukhumvit; ⊘6-10pm Tue-Fri & 2-9pm Sat-Sun; ⓓThong Lo exit 1) Located next door to the popular bar WTF, the headquarters of this retro/world label is a chance to finally combine the university-era pastimes of record-browsing and drinking. Come to snicker at corny old Thai vinyl covers or invest in some of the label's highly regarded compilations of classic *mŏr lam* and *lôok tûng* (Thai-style country music).

BANGKOK'S SAVILE ROW

The strip of Th Sukhumvit between BTS stops Nana and Asok is is home to tonnes of tailors – both reputable and otherwise. We list some of the former below. For general tips on having bespoke clothes made, see p44.

Raja's Fashions (Map p270; 0 2253 8379; www.rajasfashions.com; 1/6 Soi 4, Th Sukhumvit; 10.30am-8pm Mon-Sat; Nana exit 2) With his photographic memory for names, Bobby will make you feel as important as the long list of ambassadors, foreign politicians and officers he's fitted over his family's decades in the business.

Rajawongse (Map p270; 0 2255 3714; www.dress-for-success.com; 130 Th Sukhumvit; 10.30am-8pm Mon-Sat; Nana exit 2) Another legendary Bangkok tailor; Jesse and Victor's creations are particularly renowned among American visitors and residents.

Ricky's Fashion House (Map p270; 0 2254 6887; www.rickysfashionhouse.com; 73/5 Th Sukhumvit; 11am-10pm Mon-Sat & 1-5.30pm Sun; Nana exit 1) Ricky gets positive reviews from locals and resident foreigners alike for his more casual styles of custom-made trousers and shirts.

Nickermann's (Map p270; 0 2252 6682; www.nickermanns.net; 138 Th Sukhumvit, basement, Landmark Hotel; 10am-8.30pm Mon-Sat & noon-6pm Sun; Nana exit 2) Corporate ladies rave about Nickermann's tailor-made power suits. Formal ball gowns are another area of expertise.

SOP MOEI ARTS HANDICRAFTS

Map p270 (www.sopmoeiarts.com; Soi 49/9, Th Sukhumvit; 9.30am-5pm Sun-Fri; Phrom Phong exit 3 & access by taxi) The Bangkok showroom of this non-profit organisation features the vibrant cloth creations of Karen weavers in Mae Hong Son, in northern Thailand. Located near the end of Soi 49/9, in the large Racquet Club complex.

EMPORIUM SHOPPING CENTRE

Map p270 (www.emporiumthailand.com; cnr Soi 24 & Th Sukhumvit; 10am-10pm; Phrom Phong exit 2) You might not have access to the beautiful people's nightlife scene, but you can observe their spending rituals at this temple to red-hot-and-classic cool. For something cheekily local, check out **Propaganda**, home to Mr P (brainchild of Thai designer Chaiyut Plypetch), who appears in anatomically correct cartoon lamps and other products.

THANON SUKHUMVIT MARKET MARKET

Map p270 (Th Sukhumvit, btwn Soi 13 & Soi 19; 11am-11pm; Nana exits 1 & 3) Leaving on the first flight out tomorrow morning? Never fear about gifts for those back home; here the street vendors will find you, with faux Fendi handbags, soccer kits, black-felt 'art', sunglasses and jewellery, to name a few. There are also ample stacks of nudie DVDs, Chinese throwing stars, penis-shaped lighters and other questionable gifts for your high-school-aged brother.

DASA BOOK CAFÉ BOOKSTORE

Map p270 (www.dasabookcafe.com; 714/4 Th Sukhumvit; 10am-8pm; Phrom Phong exit 4) Boasting more than 16,000 books, Dasa is one of Bangkok's best-stocked used bookstores. A frequently updated list of stock (also available online) makes it easy to find that book you've been searching for; an attached cafe provides an excuse to linger.

🏃 SPORTS & ACTIVITIES

PUSSAPA THAI MASSAGE SCHOOL MASSAGE

Map p270 (0 2204 2922; www.thaimassage-bangkok.com/nuat1_egl.htm; 25/8 Soi 26, Th Sukhumvit; tuition from 6000B; lessons 9am-4pm; Phrom Phong exit 4) Run by a longtime Japanese resident of Bangkok, the basic course in Thai massage here spans 30 hours over five days; there are shorter courses in foot massage and self massage. Thai massage is also available for 250B per hour.

HELPING HANDS COOKING COURSE

(08 4901 8717; www.cookingwithpoo.com; 1200B) This popular cooking course was started by a native of Khlong Toey's slums and is held in her neighbourhood. Courses, which must be booked in advance, span four dishes and include a visit to Khlong

SPA CENTRAL

Th Sukhumvit is home to many of Bangkok's recommended and reputable massage studios, including the following.

Health Land (Map p270; ☎0 2261 1110; www.healthlandspa.com; 55/5 Soi 21 (Asoke), Th Sukhumvit; 2hr Thai massage 450B; ⊙9am-midnight; ⊠Asok exit 5, Sukhumvit exit 1) A winning formula of affordable prices, expert treatments and pleasant facilities has created a small empire of Health Land centres, including branches on **Soi Ekamai 10** (Map p270; ☎0 2392 2233; www.healthlandspa.com; 96/1 Soi Ekamai 10; 2hr Thai massage 450B; ⊙9am-midnight; ⊠Ekkamai exit 2 & taxi) and Th Sathon Neua (p128).

Asia Herb Association (Map p270; ☎0 2260 8864; www.asiaherbassociation.com; 33/1 Soi 24, Th Sukhumvit; ⊙10am-9pm; ⊠Phrom Phong exit 4) With several branches along Th Sukhumvit, including **Sawasdee** (Map p270; ☎0 2261 2201; www.asiaherb association.com; 20/1 Soi 31 (Sawatdi), Th Sukhumvit; ⊙9am-midnight; ⊠Phrom Phong exit 5) and **Thong Lor** (Map p270; ☎0 2392 3631; www.asiaherbassociation.com; 58/19-25 Soi 55/ Thong Lor, Th Sukhumvit; ⊙9am-midnight; ⊠Thong Lo exit 3), this chain specialises in massage using *prà kóp*, traditional Thai herbal compresses filled with 18 different herbs.

Divana Massage & Spa (Map p270; ☎0 2261 6784; www.divanaspa.com; 7 Soi 25, Th Sukhumvit; spa treatments from 2350B; ⊙11am-9pm Mon-Fri, 10am-9pm Sat & Sun; ⊠Asok exit 6, Sukhumvit exit 2) Divana retains a unique Thai touch with a private and soothing setting in a garden house.

Coran (Map p270; ☎0 2651 1588; www.coranbangkok.com; 27/1-2 Soi 13, Th Sukhumvit; Thai massage per hr 400B; ⊙11am-10pm; ⊠Nana exit 3) A classy, low-key spa housed in a Thai villa. Aroma and Thai-style massage are also available.

Lavana (Map p270; ☎0 2229 4510; www.lavanabangkok.com; 4 Soi 12, Th Sukhumvit; Thai massage per hr 450B; ⊙9am-11pm; ⓂSukhumvit, ⊠Asok) Another spa with an emphasis on traditional Thai healing using *prà kóp*, a type of herbal compress.

Rakuten (Map p270; ☎0 2258 9433; www.rakutenspa.com; 94 Soi 33, Th Sukhumvit; Thai massage per hr 250B; ⊙noon-midnight; ⊠Phrom Phong exit 5) A Japanese-themed spa that gets good reports for its Thai-style massage.

Baan Dalah (Map p270; ☎0 2653 3358; www.baandalahmindbodyspa.com; 2 Soi 8, Th Sukhumvit; Thai massage per hr 350B; ⊙10am-midnight; ⊠Nana exit 4) A small, conveniently located spa with services ranging from foot massage to full-body Thai massage.

Toey Market (p131) and transportation to and from Emporium (p139).

BANGKOK BIKE RIDES
BICYCLE TOURS

Map p270 (☎0 2712 5305; www.bangkok bikerides.com; 14/1-B Soi Phrom Si 2, Th Sukhumvit; tours from 1000B; ⊙8.30am-6.30pm Tue-Sun; ⊠Phrom Phong exit 3) A division of tour company Spice Roads, this outfit offers a variety of cycling tours, both urban and rural, including a night tour of Bangkok. Pick-up is available.

WORLD FELLOWSHIP OF BUDDHISTS
MEDITATION

Map p270 (WFB; ☎0 2661 1284; www.wfb-hq.org; 616 Benjasiri Park, Soi Medhinevet, Th Sukhumvit; admission by donation; ⊙8.30am-4pm Sun-Fri; ⊠Phrom Phong exit 6) On the first Sunday of the month, this centre of Theravada Buddhism hosts meditation classes in English

from 2pm to 5pm. The fellowship also holds interesting forums on Buddhist issues.

ABC AMAZING BANGKOK CYCLISTS
BICYCLE TOURS

Map p270 (☎0 2665 6364; www.realasia.net; 10/5-7 Soi 26, Th Sukhumvit; tours from 1000B; ⊙daily tours at 8am, 10am & 1pm; ⊠Phrom Phong exit 4) A long-running operation offering morning, afternoon and all-day bike tours of Bangkok and its suburbs.

FUN-ARIUM
PLAY CENTRE

Map p270 (☎0 2665 6555; www.funarium. co.th; 111/1 Soi 26, Th Sukhumvit; adult/child under 105cm/child over 105cm (up to 13yr) 90/180/300B; ⊙9am-7pm Mon-Thu, 8.30am-8.30pm Fri & Sun; ☎) Bangkok's largest indoor playground, with coffee and wi-fi to keep parents happy while the kids play.

Greater Bangkok

Neighbourhood Top Five

1 Getting lost deep in the bowels of the **Chatuchak Weekend Market** (p143), one of the world's largest markets and a must-do Bangkok shopping experience.

2 Partying at the bars and clubs on Royal City Ave (RCA), such as **Cosmic Café** (p149) or **Slim/Flix** (p148).

3 Travelling back in time at retro-themed market **Talat Rot Fai** (p146).

4 Ditching the smog and traffic and heading to **Ko Kret** (p147) or **Ancient City** (p146).

5 Experiencing the charms of provincial Thailand at **Nonthaburi Market** (p146).

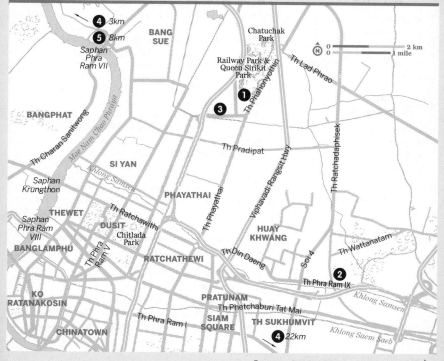

For more detail of this area, see sheet map ➡

Lonely Planet's Top Tip

Make a point of arriving at Chatuchak Weekend Market as early as possible – around 10am is a good bet – as the crowds are much thinner and the temperatures slightly lower.

Best Places to Eat

➡ Chatuchak Weekend Market (p143)

➡ Or Tor Kor Market (p147)

➡ Salt (p147)

➡ Nang Loeng Market (p147)

➡ Yusup (p147)

➡ Rosdee (p148)

For reviews, see p147 ➡

Best Places to Drink

➡ Cosmic Café (p149)

➡ Ratchada Soi 8 (p149)

➡ Parking Toys (p150)

For reviews, see p148 ➡

Best Markets

➡ Chatuchak Weekend Market (p143)

➡ Talat Rot Fai (p146)

➡ Nonthaburi Market (p146)

For reviews, see p146 ➡

Explore: Greater Bangkok

There are several reasons to visit Bangkok's suburbs, but most people come with markets in mind. Chatuchak Weekend Market draws tens of thousands of shoppers every weekend and is a hectic but must-do Bangkok experience. The Nonthaburi Market is an expansive wet market that shows the city's provincial side, while the retro-themed Talat Rot Fai is a magnet for Bangkok's hipsters. Other reasons to visit include nightlife, with the entertainment strip of RCA drawing thousands of partyers.

For the day markets, arrive as early as possible. Set aside at least half a day for Chatuchak. Getting to Nonthaburi Market by boat takes at least an hour and it has pretty much packed up by 9am. Talat Rot Fai is usually open until around 11pm. Most clubs and live music venues don't get going until 11pm and close at 2am.

Most of the markets are forgivingly located within easy access of the BTS (Skytrain) and/or MRT (Metro). Reaching other destinations in Bangkok's 'burbs often involves a taxi ride from BTS or MRT stations and a bit of luck. A mobile phone with a mapping function is a valuable tool in navigating the city.

Local Life

➡ **Chatuchak Weekend Market** (also known as JJ) may be a huge draw for tourists, but it's still very much a local affair, with tens of thousands of Thais shuffling between stalls and eating snacks every Saturday and Sunday.

➡ **RCA** For years, the strip of dance clubs, live-music clubs and bars known as Royal City Ave has been the first nightlife choice for most young Thais. In recent years the clientele has grown up and RCA now hosts locals and visitors of just about any age.

➡ **Local Style** Greasers, cowboys, hippies, punks and mods: Talat Rot Fai is the place to see the various cliques of modern Thai youth.

➡ **Full-Flavoured Eats** An excursion to Bangkok's suburbs can be a profoundly tasty experience. The northern reaches of the city in particular are home to heaps of restaurants that would never consider toning down their flavours for foreigners. The city's outskirts are also a great place to sample regional Thai cuisine.

Getting There & Away

➡ **BTS** Ari, Bang Chak, Chong Nonsi, Ekkamai, Mo Chit, Ratchathewi, Wongwian Yai.

➡ **MRT** Chatuchak Park, Kamphaeng Phet, Phahon Yothin, Phra Ram 9, Thailand Cultural Centre.

➡ **River ferry** Tha Nonthaburi, Saphan Phra Pin Klao.

TOP SIGHTS
CHATUCHAK WEEKEND MARKET

Imagine all of Bangkok's markets fused together in a seemingly never-ending commerce-themed barrio. Now add a little artistic flair, a saunalike climate and bargaining crowds and you've got a rough sketch of Chatuchak (also spelled 'Jatujak' or nicknamed 'JJ'). Everything is sold here, from live snakes to *mŏr lam* CDs. Once you're deep in the bowels, it will seem like there is no order and no escape, but Chatuchak is actually arranged into relatively coherent sections.

Antiques, Handicrafts & Souvenirs

Section 1 is the place to go for Buddha statues, old LPs and random antiques.

More secular arts and crafts, like musical instruments and hill-tribe items, can be found in Sections 25 and 26. **Meng** (Section 26, Stall 195, Soi 8) features a mish-mash of quirky antiques from Thailand and Myanmar (Burma).

Baan Sin Thai (Section 24, Stall 130, Soi 1) sells *kŏhn* masks and old-school Thai toys, and **Kitcharoen Dountri** (Section 8, Stall 464, Soi 15) specialises in Thai musical instruments, including flutes, whistles and drums, and CDs of Thai music.

Golden Shop (Section 17, Stall 19, Soi 1) is your standard souvenir shop, and boasts an equal blend of tacky and worthwhile items, ranging from traditionally dressed dolls to commemorative plates. Other quirky gifts available at Chatuchak include the lifelike plastic Thai fruit and vegetables at **Marché** (Section 17, Stall 254, Soi 1) or their scaled-down miniature counterparts nearby at **Papachu** (Section 17, Stall 23, Soi 1).

Section 7 is a virtual open-air art gallery; we particularly like the Bangkok-themed murals at **Pariwat A-nantachina** (Section 7, Stall 118, Soi 2).

Several shops in Section 10, including **Tuptim Shop** (Section 10, Stall 261, Soi 19) sell Burmese lacquerware.

DON'T MISS...

➡ Cheap clothes
➡ One-of-a-kind souvenirs
➡ A market meal

PRACTICALITIES

➡ ตลาดนัดจตุจักร | Talat Nat Jatujak
➡ www.chatuchak.org
➡ Th Phahonyothin
➡ ⊙9am-6pm Sat & Sun
➡ MChatuchak Park exit 1, Kamphaeng Phet exits 1 & 2, 🚇Mo Chit exit 1

IMPORTANT STUFF

There is an information centre and several banks with ATMs and foreign-exchange booths at the **Chatuchak Park offices**, near the northern end of the market's Soi 1, Soi 2 and Soi 3. Pay toilets are located sporadically throughout the market.

There are a few vendors out on weekday mornings, and open every day is nearby Or Tor Kor Market (p147), a vegetable, plant and flower market, which also has a decent food court, opposite the market's southern side.

FINDING YOUR WAY AROUND

Schematic maps are located throughout Chatuchak; if you need more detail, not to mention insider tips, consider purchasing Nancy Chandler's Map of Bangkok (p46), available at most Bangkok bookstores.

Arrive at Chatuchak early – ideally around 9am or 10am – to beat the crowds and heat.

Clothing & Accessories

Clothing dominates much of Chatuchak, starting in Section 8 and continuing through the even-numbered sections to 24. Sections 5 and 6 deal in used clothing for every Thai youth subculture, from punks to cowboys; Soi 7, where it transects Sections 12 and 14, is heavy on hip-hop and skate fashions. Tourist-sized clothes and textiles are found in sections 10 and 8.

Sections 2 and 3, particularly the tree-lined Soi 2 of the former, is the Siam Sq of Chatuchak, and is home to heaps of trendy independent labels. Moving north, Soi 4 in Section 4 boasts several shops selling locally designed T-shirts. In fact, Chatuchak as a whole is a particularly good place to pick up quirky T-shirts of all types. The shirts at **Real Gold** (Section 4, Stall 41, Soi 2) blend modern and traditional Thai designs, **Bang! Bang!** (Section 20, Stall 288, Soi 2) features custom-designed hand-drawn T-shirts of various celebrities, and there's even a stall selling **airline logo T-shirts** (Section 23, Stall 280, Soi 4). And if you thought there was a limit to Chatuchak's obscure clothing offerings, **Link** (Section 7, Stall 146, Soi 4) deals in 'retro underwear for men' and **Scout Story** (Section 21, Stall 66, Soi 2) specialises in scouting clothing and accessories from around the world.

For something more subdued, **Khaki-Nang** (Section 8, Stall 267, Soi 17) sells canvas clothing and tote bags, many featuring old-school Thai themes. And if you can't make it up to Chiang Mai, **One to Tree** (Section 26, Stall 235, Soi 8) or **Roi** (Section 25, Stall 268, Soi 4) is where you'll find hand-woven cotton scarves, clothes and other accessories from Thailand's north.

For accessories, several shops in Sections 24 and 26, such as **Orange Karen Silver** (Section 26, Stall 246, Soi 8) specialise in chunky silver jewellery and semi-precious uncut stones.

Eating & Drinking

Lots of Thai-style eating and snacking will stave off Chatuchak rage (cranky behaviour brought on by dehydration or hunger), and numerous food stalls set up shop throughout the market, particularly between Sections 6 and 8. Long-standing standouts include **Foon Talop** (Section 26, Stall 319, Soi 8), an incredibly popular Isan restaurant; **Café Ice** (Section 7, Stall 267, Soi 3), a Western-Thai fusion joint that does good *pàt tai* (fried noodles) and tasty fruit shakes; and **Saman Islam** (Section 16, Stall 34, Soi 24), a Thai-Muslim restaurant that serves a tasty chicken biriani. If you need air-con, pop into **Toh-Plue** (Th Kamphaengphet 2; ⊙11am-8pm; Ⓜ MRT Kamphaeng Phet) for all the Thai standards. And as evening draws near, down a beer at **Viva's** (Section 26, Stall 149, Soi 6), a

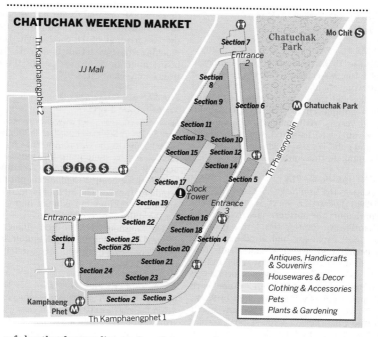

cafe-bar that features live music and stays open late, or cross Th Kamphaengphet 2 to the cosy whisky bars that keep nocturnal hours.

Housewares & Decor

The western edge of the market, particularly sections 8 to 26, specialises in all manner of housewares, from cheap plastic buckets to expensive brass woks. This area is a particularly good place to stock up on inexpensive Thai ceramics, ranging from celadon to the traditional rooster-themed bowls from Lampang. **N & D Tablewares** (Section 25, Stall 185, Soi 4) has a huge variety of stainless-steel flatware, and **Tan-Ta-Nod** (Section 22, Stall 61, Soi 5) deals in coconut- and sugar-palm derived plates, bowls and other utensils.

Those looking to spice up the house should stop by **Spice Boom** (Section 26, Stall 246, Soi 8), where you can find dried herbs and spices for both consumption and decoration. Other notable olfactory indulgences include the handmade soaps, lotions, salts and scrubs at **D-narn** (Section 19, Stall 204, Soi 1) and the fragrant perfumes and essential oils at **Karmakamet** (Section 2, Soi 3).

Pets

Possibly the most fun you'll ever have window-shopping will be petting puppies and cuddling kittens in sections 13 and 15. Soi 9 of the former features several shops that deal solely in clothing for pets.

Plants & Gardening

The interior perimeter of sections 2 to 4 features a huge variety of potted plants, flowers, herbs and fruits, and the accessories needed to maintain them. Many of these shops are also open on weekday afternoons.

TOP SIGHTS
CHATUCHAK WEEKEND MARKET

◉ SIGHTS

CHATUCHAK WEEKEND MARKET   MARKET
See p143.

TALAT ROT FAI   MARKET
(ตลาดรถไฟ; Th Kamphaengphet; ⊙6pm-midnight Sat & Sun; ⓂKamphaeng Phet exit 1) Set in a sprawling abandoned rail yard, this market is all about the retro, with goods ranging from antique enamel platters to second-hand Vespas. With mobile snack vendors, VW van–based bars and even a few land-bound pubs, it's also much more than just a shopping destination.

NONTHABURI MARKET   MARKET
(ตลาดนนทบุรี; Tha Nam Non; ⊙5-9am; ⚓Tha Nonthaburi) Located a short walk from Tha Nonthaburi, the northernmost extent of the Chao Phraya Express boats, this is one of the most expansive and atmospheric produce markets in the area. Exotic fruits, towers of dried chillies, smoky grills and the city's few remaining rickshaws form a very un-Bangkok backdrop here. Come early though, as most vendors are gone by 9am.

To get to the market, take any northbound Chao Phraya Express boat and get off at Tha Nonthaburi, the final stop. The market is a two-minute walk along the main road from the pier.

BANGKOK UNIVERSITY ART GALLERY   ART GALLERY
(BUG; http://fab.bu.ac.th/buggallery; 3rd fl, Bldg 9, City Campus, Th Phra Ram IV; ⊙9.30am-7pm Tue-Sat; ⚊Ekkamai exit 4 & taxi) This spacious new compound is located at what is currently the country's most cutting-edge art school. Recent exhibitions have encompassed a variety of media by some of the country's top names, as well as the work of internationally recognised artists.

ANCIENT CITY   MUSEUM
(เมืองโบราณ | Muang Boran; www.ancientcity.com; 296/1 Th Sukhumvit; adult/child 400/200B; ⊙8am-5pm) Don't have the time to see Thailand's most famous historic monuments? Then consider seeing scaled-down versions of them in what claims to be the largest open-air museum in the world. Covering more than 80 hectares of peaceful countryside, it is littered with 109 facsimiles of famous Thai monuments. It's an excellent place to explore by bicycle (daily rental 50B) as it is usually quiet and rarely crowded.

Ancient City lies outside Samut Prakan, an hour by road east of downtown. To get there, either negotiate with a taxi (about 1200B return) or take air-con bus 511 from the eastern end of Th Sukhumvit. Upon reaching the bus terminal at Pak Nam, board minivan 36, which passes the entrance to Ancient City.

ERAWAN MUSEUM (CHANG SAM SIAN)   MUSEUM
(พิพิธภัณฑ์ช้างเอราวัณ (ช้างสามเศียร); www.erawan-museum.com; Soi 119, Th Sukhumvit; adult/child 300/150B; ⊙8am-5pm) On the way to Ancient City and created by the same man, this museum is actually a five-storey sculpture of Erawan, Indra's three-headed elephant mount from Hindu mythology. The interior is filled with antique sculptures but is most impressive for the stained-glass ceiling.

The museum is 8km from Bangkok's Ekamai bus station and any Samut Prakan–bound bus can drop you off; just tell the driver.

BANG NAM PHEUNG MARKET   MARKET
(ตลาดบางน้ำผึ้ง; Bang Nam Pheung; ⊙8am-3pm Sat & Sun; ⚓Bang Na exit 2 & taxi) An easy escape from the city, this new and buzzy weekend-only market is on the Phra Pradaeng Peninsula, a vast rural-feeling district often referred to as Bangkok's 'green lung'. Although sometimes called a floating market, all of the stalls at Bang Nam Pheung are actually land-bound, and unfold at the edge of this lush, watery area's narrow coconut palm-lined canals. Because it's a Thai market, the emphasis is on food, and it's a great place for unrestrained snacking. The market is a stop on the many bike tours that criss-cross the peninsula, as are **Wat Bang Nam Pheung Nok** (admission free), a 250-year old temple near the pier, and **Si Nakhon Kheun Khan Park** (admission free; ⊙6am-7pm), a vast botanical garden with a large lake and bird-watching tower.

To get to the market, take the BTS to Bang Na and jump in a taxi for the short ride to the pier at Wat Bang Na Nork. From there, take the river-crossing ferry (4B) followed by a short motorcycle taxi (10B) ride.

ARDEL GALLERY OF MODERN ART   ART GALLERY
(www.ardelgallery.com; 99/45 Belle Ville, Moo 18, Th Boromaratchatchonanee; ⊙10.30am-7pm Tue-Sat, to 5.30pm Sun; ⚓Wongwian Yai exit 4 &

taxi) Despite its distance from the centre of town, Ardel is quickly becoming one of Bangkok's premier galleries. The expansive suburban compound unites two exhibition spaces, a print-making workshop, and a shop and cafe with a brand-new annex that includes an artists' residence and pool. Curated by Ajarn Thavorn Ko-Udomvit, a renowned lecturer at Silpakorn University, the collection often emphasises print and photos, but previous exhibitions have spanned a variety of media.

EATING

OR TOR KOR MARKET
THAI $

(Th Kamphaengphet; mains 30-60B; ⏰8am-6pm; Ⓜ Kamphaeng Phet exit 3) Or Tor Kor is Bangkok's highest-quality fruit and agricultural market, and sights such as toddler-sized mangoes and dozens of pots full of curries amount to culinary trainspotting. The vast majority of vendors' goods are takeaway only, but a small food court and a few informal restaurants exist, including **Rot Det**, which does tasty stir-fries and curries, and **Sut Jai Kai Yaang**, just south of the market, which does spicy northeastern-style Thai.

To get here, take the MRT to Kampheng Phet station and exit on the side opposite Chatuchak (the exit says 'Marketing Organization for Farmers').

SALT
INTERNATIONAL $$$

(www.saltbangkok.com; cnr Soi Ari 4 & Soi 7 (Ari), Th Phahonyothin; mains 180-1450B; ⏰5pm-midnight Mon-Sat; 🚇Ari exit 1) With a DJ booth flashing a strategically placed copy of *Larousse Gastronomique,* Salt is the kind of eclectic place that's currently shaping Bangkok's restaurant scene. Appropriately located in Ari, suburban Bangkok's trendiest 'hood, the menu here ranges from sushi to pizza, with a particular emphasis on grilled and smoked dishes. Seating is (loud) indoor or (sweaty) outdoor, and there's draught Belgian beer and house cocktails.

NANG LOENG MARKET
THAI $

(btwn Soi 8-10, Th Nakhon Sawan; mains 30-80B; ⏰10am-2pm Mon-Sat; 🚇Ratchathewi exit 3 & taxi) Dating back to 1899, this atmospheric fresh market is a wonderful glimpse of old Bangkok, not to mention a great place to grab a bite. Nang Loeng is renowned for its Thai sweets, and at lunchtime it is also an excellent place to fill up on savouries. Try a bowl of handmade egg noodles at Rung Rueng or the wonderful curries across the way at Ratana.

YUSUP
MUSLIM-THAI $

(Kaset-Navamin Hwy; mains 30-90B; ⏰11am-2pm; 🚇Mo Chit exit 3 & taxi) The Thai-language sign in front of this restaurant boldly

> **WORTH A DETOUR**
>
> ## KO KRET
>
> Bangkok's closest green getaway, **Ko Kret** (เกาะเกร็ด; adult/child 299/250B; ⏰10am-4.30pm; 🚢Tha Sathorn or Tha Maharaj) is an artificial 'island', the result of a canal being dug nearly 300 years ago to shorten an oxbow bend in the Chao Phraya. Today Ko Kret is known for its hand-thrown terracotta pots, which are sold at markets throughout Bangkok, and its food. This island and the pottery tradition date back to one of Thailand's oldest settlements of Mon people, who were a dominant tribe of central Thailand between the 6th and 10th centuries AD. From Wat Paramai Yikawat (Wat Mon), which has an interesting Mon-style marble Buddha, go in either direction to find working pottery centres on the east and north coasts.
>
> Even more prevalent than pottery is food. At weekends droves of Thais flock to Ko Kret to munch on deep-fried savouries, *kôw châa* (a Mon dish combining savoury/sweet titbits and chilled rice) and iced coffee. Arrive on a weekday and the eating options are much fewer, but you'll have the place to yourself.
>
> The most convenient way to get to Ko Kret is by taxi or bus (bus 33 from Sanam Luang) to Pak Kret, before boarding the cross-river ferry from Wat Sanam Neua. Going by river is more scenic; on Sundays you can join a busy weekend tour operated by Chao Phraya Express (p222), departing from Tha Maharaj or Tha Sathon (Central Pier); or take a regular express boat to Nonthaburi and then a taxi to Pak Kret.

LOCAL KNOWLEDGE

BANGKOK'S GREEN LUNG

Joey Tulyanond is Chief Greening Officer at the Bangkok Tree House, an ecofriendly resort on the Phra Pradaeng Peninsula.

How would you describe the Phra Pradaeng Peninsula? Serene and undisturbed. Geographically, the area is an island that is separated from Bangkok by the Chao Phraya River. Physically, it's as if the peninsula is lost in another time – in fact, if you wanted to see what Bangkok was like 200 years ago, this is the place to visit.

Why is it called Bangkok's 'green lung'? The people there are blessed with having a tropical jungle in their backyard, in addition to some very unique neighbours, from turquoise kingfishers to timid turtles.

What kind of people live there? Mostly local farmers and plantation owners, but more recently Bangkokians weary of city living and expats yearning for a slower and simpler life.

What kind of activities can visitors do there? A stroll through the lush green walkways along the fruit orchards always does it for me, but the weekend floating market [Bang Nam Pheung Market (p146)], the 200-*râi* (about 80 acres) botanical park [Si Nakhon Kheun Khan Park (p146)] and the dilapidated but stunning 250-year-old Bang Nam Pheung Nok temple are also worth a visit.

How does one get around? Bicycles, which can be rented at various locations, and which can be borrowed at the Bangkok Tree House (p186).

Is it difficult to get to there? A skip on the BTS [Skytrain], a hop on the taxi and a jump on the green ferry and you are there.

says *rah·chah kôw mòk* (King of Biriani) and Yusup backs it up with flawless biriani (try the unusual but delicious *kôw mòk Ƀlah;* fish biriani), not to mention mouthpuckering sour oxtail soup and decadent *gaang mát·sà·màn* (Muslim curry). For dessert try *roh·đi wǎhn,* a paratha-like crispy pancake topped with sweetened condensed milk and sugar – a dish that will send most carb-fearing Westerners running away screaming.

To get here, take a taxi heading north from BTS Mo Chit and tell the driver to take you to the Kaset intersection and turn right on Th Kaset-Navamin. Yusup is on the left-hand side about 1km past the first stop light.

ROSDEE
CHINESE-THAI **$**

(2357 Th Sukhumvit; mains 40-120B; ☺8am-9pm; ⛴Bang Chak exit 2) This stodgy family eating hall is never going to make it on to any international travel magazine's 'hot list' of places to dine, but the elderly bow-tied staff does give the place a certain element of charm. Instead, Rosdee is known for its consistently tasty, well-executed Chinese-Thai favourites such as the garlicky *or sòo·an* (oysters fried with egg and a sticky batter), or the house speciality, braised goose.

Rosdee is located on the corner with Soi 95/1, a short walk from the BTS stop at Bang Chak.

PHAT THAI ARI
THAI **$**

(Th Phahonyothin; mains 45-100B; ☺11am-10pm; ⛴Ari exit 4) One of the city's better-known *pàt tai* shops is located a couple blocks from the eponymous soi. Try the innovative 'noodle-less' version, where long strips of crispy green papaya are substituted for the traditional rice noodles from Chanthaburi.

Phat Thai Ari is located on the narrow soi that leads to Phaholyothin Center, just north of BTS Ari.

BAAN SUAN PAI
VEGETARIAN **$**

(Banana Family Park, Th Phahonyothin; mains 15-30B; ☺7am-3pm; ✏; ⛴Ari exit 1) This open-air vegie centre is worth the trip. Expect a wide variety of vendors selling meat-free Thai-style dishes, drinks and desserts.

To find it, take exit 1 at Ari BTS and turn right down the narrow alleyway just after the petrol station.

🍷 DRINKING & NIGHTLIFE

TOP CHOICE SLIM/FLIX
NIGHTCLUB

(29/22-32 Royal City Ave, off Th Phra Ram IX; admission free; ☺8pm-2am; ⓂPhra Ram 9 exit 3 & taxi) Ideal for the indecisive raver, this immense three-in-one complex dominating one end of RCA features chilled house on one side (Flix), while the other (Slim) does the hip-hop/R&B soundtrack found across much of the city. Oh, and there's a restaurant thrown in there somewhere as well. Despite its size, this place is positively packed on weekends.

TOP CHOICE COSMIC CAFÉ
BAR

(Block C, Royal City Ave, off Th Phra Ram IX; admission free; ⊙7pm-2am; ⓂPhra Ram 9 exit 3 & taxi) Blessedly more low-key than most places on RCA, Cosmic calls itself a cafe but looks a bar, and in recent years has become one of Bangkok's better live-music clubs. Despite the slight identity crisis, it's is a fun place to drink, rock to live music and meet people Thai-style.

TOP CHOICE RATCHADA SOI 8
GAY BAR

(www.ratchadasoi8.com; 76/4 Soi 8, Th Ratchadaphisek; admission free; ⊙8pm-1am; ⓂPhra Ram 9 exit 3) The upper age limit at this bar ,popular with gay Thais, seems to be 25, and everyone knows the moves to the K-Pop (Korean pop) soundtrack – and sometimes the words. There's the usual show with 'coyote boys' (skinny young guys in Speedos and boots).

TOP CHOICE ZETA
LESBIAN BAR

(29/67 Royal City Ave, off Phra Ram IX; admission 100B; ⊙8pm-2am; ⓂPhra Ram 9 exit 3 & taxi) At the time of writing Bangkok's only lesbian dance club, Zeta is an easy-going disco with a nightly band doing Thai and Western covers. Women only.

LED
NIGHTCLUB

(Block C, Royal City Ave, off Th Phra Ram IX; admission from 300B; ⊙9pm-2am; ⓂPhra Ram 9 exit 3 & taxi) The size of a warehouse and boasting one of the city's best sound systems, LED pulls in the big-name DJs from around the globe. The bad news is that outside of the big events, it can be virtually empty. Search for the Facebook page to see what's on.

ROUTE 66
NIGHTCLUB

(www.route66club.com; 29/33-48 Royal City Ave, off Th Phra Ram IX; admission 300B; ⊙8pm-2am; ⓂPhra Ram 9 exit 3 & taxi) This place has been around just about as long as RCA has, but a recent facelift has given it a new feel and a loyal following. Top 40 hip hop rules the main space here, although there are several

GREATER BANGKOK DRINKING & NIGHTLIFE

TAXI ALTARS: INSURANCE ON THE DASHBOARD

As your taxi races into Bangkok from the airport your delight at being able to do the 30km trip for less than US$10 is soon replaced by uneasiness, anxiety and eventually outright fear. Because 150km/h is fast, you're tailgating the car in front and there's no seatbelt. You can rest assured (or not), however, that your driver will share none of these concerns.

All of which makes the humble taxi trip an instructive introduction to Thai culture. Buddhists believe in karma and in turn that their fate is, to a large extent, predestined. Unlike Western ideas, which take a more scientific approach to road safety, many Thais believe factors such as speed, concentration, seatbelts and simple driver quality have no bearing whatsoever on your chances of being in a crash. Put simply, if you die a horrible death on the road, karma says you deserved it. The trouble is that when a passenger gets into a taxi they bring their karma and any bad spirits the passenger might have along for the ride. Which could upset the driver's own fate.

To counteract such bad influences most Bangkok taxi drivers turn the dashboard and ceiling into a sort of life-insurance shrine. The ceiling will have a *yantra* diagram drawn in white powder by a monk as a form of spiritual protection. This will often be accompanied by portraits of notable royals. Below this a red box dangling red tassels, beads and amulets hangs from the rear-vision mirror, while the dashboard is populated by Buddhist and royal statuettes, and quite possibly banknotes with the king's image prominent and more amulets. With luck (such as it exists in Thailand), the talismans will protect your driver from any bad karma you bring into the cab. Passengers must hope their driver's number is not up. If you feel like it might be, try saying *cháh cháh* soothingly – that is, ask your driver to slow down. For a look inside some of Bangkok's 100,000 or so taxis, check out *Still Life in Moving Vehicle* (www.lifeinmovingvehicle.blogspot.com).

A LITTLE BIG TIME

The suburbs north of Bangkok are home to handful of kid-oriented theme parks. All of the following lie north of Bangkok and are accessible via taxi from Mo Chit BTS station.

Safari World (☑0 2518 1000; www.safariworld.com; 99 Th Ramindra 1; adult/child 800/300B; ◷9am-5pm; 🚇Mo Chit exit 3 and taxi) Claiming to be the world's largest 'open zoo', Safari World is divided into two parts, a drive-through Safari Park and a Marine Park. In the Safari Park, visitors take a bus tour (windows remained closed) through an 'oasis for animals' separated into different habitats. The Marine Park focuses on stunts by dolphins and other trained animals; if that's not your thing you can go to the Safari Park only.

Siam Park City (☑0 2919 7200; www.siamparkcity.com; 203 Th Suansiam; admission 100-600B; ◷10am-6pm) Siam Park City features more than 30 rides and a water park with the largest wave pool in the world.

Dream World (☑0 2533 1152; www.dreamworld-th.com; 62 Moo 1, Th Rangsit-Nakornnay-ok; admission from 450B; ◷10am-6pm) Expansive amusement park that boasts a snow room.

different themed 'levels', featuring anything from Thai pop to live music.

FAKE CLUB   GAY BAR

(Th Kamphaengphet; ◷8pm-2am; 🚇Kamphaeng Phet exit 1) The area directly west of Chatuchak Weekend Market remains a popular destination for Thai gay men. You'll still find a few students here, but the crowd is generally older and more sophisticated, as is the decor and music. Fake Club has live music from 11.30pm.

ICK   GAY BAR

(www.ickbkk.com; Soi 89/2, Th Ramkhamhaeng; ◷8pm-1am; 🚇Phra Ram 9 exit 3 & taxi) Ramkhamhaeng is Bangkok's largest university, which means a lot of young gay guys. Dozens of gay pubs, karaoke bars and saunas have opened around the Lamsalee intersection, equivalent to Soi 89/2, Th Ramkhamhaeng, and ICK's scrawny coyote boys and cabaret shows are a cultural experience unto themselves.

 **ENTERTAINMENT**

TAWANDANG GERMAN BREWERY   LIVE MUSIC

(cnr Th Phra Ram III & Th Narathiwat Ratchanakharin; 🚇Chong Nonsi exit 2 & taxi) It's Oktoberfest all year round at this hangar-sized music hall. The Thai-German food is tasty, the house-made brews are entirely potable, and the nightly stage shows make

singing along a necessity. Music starts at 8.30pm.

PARKING TOYS   LIVE MUSIC

(☑0 2907 2228; 17/22 Soi Mayalap, Kaset-Navamin Hwy; 🚇Mo Chit exit 3 & taxi) Essentially a rambling shed stuffed with vintage furniture, Parking Toys is also one of Bangkok's best venues for live music, and hosts an eclectic revolving cast of fun bands ranging in genre from acoustic/classical ensembles to electro-funk jam acts.

To get here, take a taxi heading north from BTS Mo Chit and tell the driver to take you to the Kaset intersection and turn right on Th Kaset-Navamin. Upon passing the second stop light on this road, look for the small Heineken sign on your left.

MAMBO CABARET   THEATRE

Map p270 (☑0 2294 7381; 59/28 Yannawa Tat Mai; tickets 800-1000B; ◷show times 7.15pm, 8.30pm & 10pm; 🚇Chong Nonsi exit 2 taxi) This transgender cabaret venue hosts choreographed stage shows featuring Broadway high kicks and lip-synched pop tunes.

HOUSE   CINEMA

(www.houserama.com; 3rd fl, UMG Cinema, Royal City Ave, off Th Phra Ram IX; 🚇Phra Ram 9 exit 3 & taxi) Bangkok's first art-house cinema, House shows lots of foreign flicks of the non-Hollywood type.

HOLLYWOOD   LIVE MUSIC

(Soi 8, Th Ratchadaphisek; ◷8pm-2am; 🚇Phra Ram 9 exit 3) Like taking a time machine back to the previous century, Hollywood is a holdover from the days when a night out in Bangkok meant corny live stage shows, wiggling around the whiskey-set table and neon, neon, neon. As is the case with many of its remaining counterparts, you'll need to purchase a bottle of whiskey at the door to gain entry.

SIAM NIRAMIT   THEATRE

(☑0 2649 9222; www.siamniramit.com; 19 Th Thiam Ruammit; tickets 1500-2350B; ⊙shows 8pm; Ⓜ Thailand Cultural Centre exit 1 & access by shuttle bus) A cultural theme park, this enchanted kingdom transports visitors to a Disneyfied version of ancient Siam with a technicoloured stage show of traditional performance depicting the Lanna Kingdom, the Buddhist heaven and Thai festivals. Elaborate costumes and sets are guaranteed to be spectacular both in their grandness and their indigenous interpretation.

The show is predominately popular with tour groups, but if you're visiting independently, a free shuttle-bus service is available at Thailand Cultural Centre MRT station every 15 minutes from 6pm to 7.45pm.

🛍 SHOPPING

FORTUNE TOWN   ELECTRONICS

(Th Ratchadaphisek; ⊙10am-9pm; Ⓜ Phra Ram 9 exit 1) If you need to supplement your digital life with cheap software, a camera or computer peripherals, this multistorey mall is a much saner alternative to Pantip Plaza.

ÁMANTEE   ANTIQUES

(☑0 2982 8694; www.amantee.com; 131/3 Soi 13, Th Chaeng Wattana; ⊙9am-8pm, cafe 9am-5pm; 🚇Mo Chit exit 3 & taxi) Although well outside of the city centre, this 'repository of Oriental and Tibetan art and antiques' is well worth the trip. Consisting of several interconnecting wooden Thai houses holding a variety of classy items, the peaceful compound also boasts a cafe, accommodation and occasional cultural events.

A Thai-language map for taxi drivers can be downloaded from the website.

🏃 SPORTS & ACTIVITIES

BAIPAI THAI COOKING
SCHOOL   COOKING COURSE

(☑0 2561 1404; www.baipai.com; 8/91 Soi 54, Th Ngam Wong Wan; lessons 1800B; ⊙9.30am-1.30pm & 1.30-5.30pm Tue-Sat) Housed in an attractive suburban villa, and taught by a small army of staff, Baipai offers two daily lessons of four dishes each. Transportation is available.

MANOHRA CRUISES   CRUISE

(☑0 2477 0770; www.manohracruises.com; 257/1-3 Th Charoennakorn, Thonburi, Bangkok Marriott Resort & Spa; 3-day trip 69,000B) The nautical equivalent of the *Eastern & Oriental Express* train, the *Mahnora Song* is a restored teak rice barge decorated with antiques, Persian carpets and four luxury sleeping berths. The trip is a three-day, two-night excursion to Ayuthaya, and the package price is all-inclusive except for tax and service.

HOUSE OF DHAMMA   MEDITATION

(☑0 2511 0439; www.houseofdhamma.com; 26/9 Soi 15, Th Lat Prao; Ⓜ Phahon Yothin exit 5) Helen Jandamit has opened her suburban Bangkok home to meditation retreats and classes in *vipassana* (insight meditation). Check the website to see what workshops are on offer, and be sure to call ahead before making a visit.

MUAYTHAI INSTITUTE   THAI BOXING

(☑0 2992 0096; www.muaythai-institute.net; Rangsit Stadium, 336/932 Th Prachatipat, Pathum Thani; tuition for 1st level 8000B; 🚇Mo Chit exit 3 & taxi) Associated with the respected World Muay Thai Council, the institute offers a fundamental Thai boxing course (consisting of three levels of expertise), as well as courses for instructors, referees and judges.

FAIRTEX MUAY THAI   THAI BOXING

(☑0 2755 3329; www.fairtexbangplee.com; 99/5 Mu 3, Soi Buthamanuson, Th Thaeparak; tuition & accommodation per day from 1100B; 🚇Chong Nonsi exit 2 & taxi) A popular, long-running Thai boxing camp south of Bangkok.

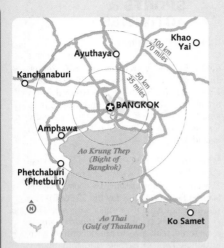

Day Trips from Bangkok

Ayuthaya Historical Park p153
Thailand's heroic former capital, Ayuthaya is a Unesco World Heritage site and a major pilgrimage site for anyone interested in ancient history.

Ko Samet p156
This island, only a few hours from Bangkok, has famously squeaky sand beaches and a range of accommodation to fit any budget.

Amphawa p159
Amphawa's canal-side setting and ancient wooden houses look like they are straight out of a movie set, and homestays can provide a firsthand experience of this unique community.

Phetchaburi (Phetburi) p161
Phetchaburi's temples and peak-roofed wooden houses combine to form the epitome of central Thai life.

Kanchanaburi p165
History is only a train ride away in Kanchanaburi, where museums and touching monuments bring home the area's past as a WWII labour camp.

Khao Yai p170
This area is home to Khao Yai National Park, one of Thailand's biggest and best preserves, where mountainous monsoon forests boast hundreds of resident species.

Ancient ruins, the vibe of rural Thailand, tasty food, good-value accommodation – and all of it only 70km from Bangkok: Ayuthaya is the easiest and most worthwhile escape from the Big Mango.

The riverside city served as the seat of one of ancient Thailand's most powerful former kingdoms until 1767, when it was destroyed in warfare by the Burmese. Today, the ruins of the former capital, Ayuthaya Historical Park, are one of Thailand's biggest tourist sites. They're separated into two distinct districts: ruins 'on the island' , in the central park of town west of Th Chee Kun, are most easily visited by bicycle (50B per day) or motorbike (200B per day); those 'off the island', opposite the river from the centre, are best visited by way of an evening boat tour (200B per hour). For more detailed descriptions of the ruins, you can pick up the *Ayuthaya* booklet from the Tourist Information Centre.

On the Island

Wat Phra Si Sanphet

Once the largest **temple** (วัดพระศรีสรรเพชญ์; admission 50B; ⊘8am-7pm) in Ayuthaya, this was used as the royal palace by several kings. Built in the 14th century, the compound contained a 16m standing Buddha coated with 250kg of gold, which was melted down and carted off by the Burmese conquerors. Its three Ayuthaya-style *chedi* (stupas) are identified with Thai art more than any other style. The adjacent **Wat Phra Mongkhon Bophit** (วัดพระมงคลบพิตร; admission free; ⊘8am-7pm) houses one of the largest bronze seated Buddhas in Thailand.

Wat Lokayasutharam

This **temple** (วัดโลกยสุธาราม; off Th Khlong Thaw; admission free; ⊘8am-7pm) features an impressive 28m-long reclining Buddha, ostensibly dating back to the early Ayuthaya period. A visit is worth the short bike trip it takes to reach it.

Wat Phra Mahathat

This **wat** (วัดพระมหาธาตุ; cnr Th Chee Kun & Th Naresuan; admission 50B; ⊘8am-7pm) has one of the first *prang* (Khmer-style tower) built in the capital and an evocative Buddha head engulfed by fingerlike tree roots – the most photographed site in Ayuthaya.

DON'T MISS...

➡ Wat Phra Si Sanphet

➡ Riverside setting at Wat Chai Wattanaram

➡ Reclining Buddha at Wat Lokayasutharam

➡ Ancient murals at Wat Ratburana

PRACTICALITIES

➡ อุทยานประวัติศาสตร์อยุธยา

➡ admission to individual sites 20B to 50B, day pass 220B

➡ ⊘8am-6pm

SLEEPING IN AYUTHAYA

➡ **Baan Lotus Guest House** (☑0 3525 1988; 20 Th Pamaphrao; s 200B, d 400-600B; ✳🛜) Set in large, leafy grounds, this converted teak schoolhouse has a cool, clean feel and remains our favourite place to crash. Staff are as charmingly old-school as the building itself.

➡ **Promtong Mansion** (☑0 3524 2459; www.promtong.com; off Th Dechawat; s/d/tr 500/700/1100B; ✳🛜) Tucked away off the main road, Promtong Mansion is a four-storey guesthouse that has a distinctive buzz thanks to its enthusiastic staff.

➡ **Tony's Place** (☑0 3525 2578; www.tonyplace-ayutthaya.com; 12/18 Soi 2, Th Naresuan; r 200-1200B; ✳🛜) Budget rooms offer just the basics, but the true flashpacker can hang out in renovated rooms that verge on the palatial, relatively speaking.

GETTING THERE & AWAY

Ayuthaya is 85km north of Bangkok and getting there takes about one or two hours. Minivans depart from east of Bangkok's Victory Monument (Map p263) every hour from 5.30am to 7pm (60B, one hour); buses depart Bangkok's Northern & Northeastern Bus Terminal (p220) (also called Mo Chit) every 20 minutes between 4.30am and 7.15pm (50B, 1½ hours); and northbound trains leave from Bangkok's Hualamphong Station (p221) roughly every 30 minutes between 6.20am and 9.30am, less frequently until about 4pm, then every 30 minutes or so between 5pm and 9pm (15B to 315B, 1½ hours). A taxi to Ayuthaya will cost around 1000B.

Most visitors to Ayuthaya do so on a big bus on a tight schedule, but we suggest exploring the ruins by túk-túk tour, boat or our favourite, hired bicycle.

INFORMATION

Ayuthaya's **Tourist Information Centre** (📞0 3524 6076; 108/22 Th Si Sanphet; ⊗8.30am-4.30pm) is housed in an art-deco building west of the historical park.

Wat Ratburana

Located across from Wat Phra Mahathat, **Wat Ratburana** (วัดราชบูรณะ; admission 50B; ⊗8am-7pm) dates back to the early 15th century and contains *chedi* and faded murals that are among the oldest in the country.

Wat Thammikarat

Also nearby, **Wat Thammikarat** (วัดธรรมิกราช; admission free; ⊗8am-7pm) features overgrown *chedi* ruins and lion sculptures.

Chao Sam Phraya National Museum

The city's largest **museum** (พิพิธภัณฑสถานแห่งชาติเจ้าสามพระยา; cnr Th Rotchana & Th Si Sanphet; adult/child 150B/free; ⊗9am-4pm Wed-Sun) has 2400 items on show, ranging from a 2m-high bronze-cast Buddha head to glistening treasures found in the crypts of Wat Phra Mahathatand and Wat Ratburana.

Wat Suwannaram

The two main structures of this **wat** (วัดสุวรรณาราม; off Th U Thong; admission free; ⊗8am-7pm) boast attractive murals, including a modern-era depiction of a famous Ayuthaya-era battle in the *wí·hǎhn* (central sanctuary), and classic *Jataka* (stories from the Buddha's lives) in the adjacent *bòht* (ordination hall). Nearby **Pom Phet** (ป้อมเพชร) served as the island's initial line of defence for centuries. Only crumbling walls remain today, but the spot features breezy views and is also home to a ferry to the mainland.

Ayuthaya Historical Study Centre

This **centre** (ศูนย์ศึกษาประวัติศาสตร์อยุธยา; Th Rotchana; adult/student 100/50B; ⊗9am-4.30pm Mon-Fri, to 5pm Sat & Sun) offers informative, professional displays, ranging from dioramas to videos, that paint a very clear picture of the ancient city.

Chantharakasem National Museum

Inside this national **museum** (พิพิธภัณฑสถานแห่งชาติจันทรเกษม; Th U Thong; admission 100B; ⊗9am-4pm Wed-Sun) is a collection of Buddhist art, ancient weapons and lacquered cabinets. The museum is within the grounds of Wang Chan Kasem (Chan Kasem Palace), which was built for King Naresuan by his father in 1577.

Off the Island

Wat Chai Whattanaram

The ruined Ayuthaya-style tower and *chedi* of **Wat Chai Wattanaram** (วัดไชยวัฒนาราม; admission 50B; ⊗8am-7pm), on the western bank of Mae Nam Chao Phraya, boast the most attractive setting of any of the city's temples. The manicured Thai-style compound across the river belongs to the Thai royal family.

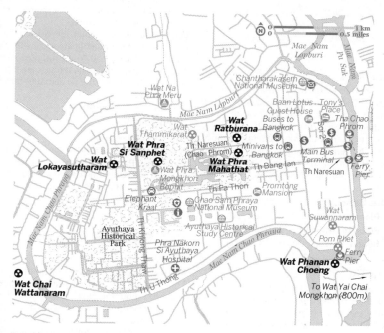

Wat Phanan Choeng

Southeast of town on Mae Nam Chao Phraya, this **wat** (วัดพนัญเชิง; admission 20B; ☺8am-7pm) was built before Ayuthaya became a Siamese capital. The temple's builders are unknown, but it appears to have been constructed in the early 14th century, so it's possibly Khmer. The main *wí·hǎhn* contains a highly revered, 19m sitting Buddha image from which the wát derives its name.

Elephant Kraal

North of the city, the **Elephant Kraal** (เพนียดคล้องช้าง; admission free) is a restoration of the wooden stockade once used for the annual roundup of wild elephants. A fence of huge teak logs enclosed the elephants. The king had a raised observation pavilion for the thrilling event.

Wat Yai Chai Mongkhon

Southeast of town, this **wat** (วัดใหญ่ชัยมงคล; admission 20B) is a quiet place built in 1357 by King U Thong and was once famous as a meditation centre. The compound contains a large *chedi*, and a community of *mâa chee* (Buddhist nuns) lives here.

Wat Na Phra Meru

This **temple** (วัดหน้าพระเมรุ; admission 20B) is notable because it escaped destruction when the Burmese army overran and sacked the city in 1767. The main *bòht* was built in 1546 and features fortresslike walls and pillars. The *bòht* interior contains an impressive carved wooden ceiling and a splendid 6m-high sitting Buddha in royal attire. Inside a smaller *wí·hǎhn* behind the *bòht* is a green-stone, European-pose (sitting in a chair) Buddha from Ceylon, said to be 1300 years old. The walls of the *wí·hǎhn* show traces of 18th- or 19th-century murals.

TOP SIGHTS
AYUTHAYA HISTORICAL PARK

Ko Samet

เกาะเสม็ด

Explore

It takes at least five hours to reach Ko Samet from Bangkok, so schedule in at least two nights if you really want to experience the island's famously fine sands. Long weekends can be particularly busy, with thousands of Bangkokians beelining for the island; arrive on a weekday and you'll probably have Ko Samet to yourself.

The Best...

➡ **Place to Eat** Jep's Restaurant (p159)
➡ **Place to Drink** Naga Bar (p159)
➡ **Beach** Ao Wong Deuan

Top Tip

Ko Samet is a relatively dry island, making it an excellent place to visit during the rainy season (approximately June to October) when other tropical paradises might be under water.

Getting There & Away

Minivan Minivans depart from just east of Bangkok's Victory Monument to Ban Phe – the pier for ferries to Ko Samet – every hour from 7am to 6pm (250B, four hours).

Bus Buses to Ban Phe leave from Bangkok's Eastern Bus Terminal (p220; Ekamai), taking about four hours (158B).

Boat Boats to Ko Samet leave from Ban Phe's many piers. Most boats go to Tha Na Dan (return 100B, 30 to 45 minutes each way). You can also charter a speedboat (about 2500B depending on demand) for up to 10 people.

Need to Know

➡ **Area Code** ☏038
➡ **Location** 200km southeast of Bangkok
➡ **National Parks Main Office** (btwn Na Dan & Hat Sai Kaew; ☺sunrise-sunset). There's another office at Ao Wong Deuan.

◉ SIGHTS

MERMAID STATUE   STATUE

Ko Samet earned a permanent place in Thai literature when classical Thai poet Sunthorn Phu set part of his epic *Phra Aphaimani* on its shores. The story follows the travails of a prince exiled to an undersea kingdom governed by a lovesick female giant. A mermaid assists the prince in his escape to Ko Samet, where he defeats a giant by playing a magic flute. Today the poem is immortalised on the island by the mermaid statue built on the rocky point separating Ao Hin Khok and Hat Sai Kaew.

SLEEPING IN KO SAMET

Due to the high demand, Ko Samet's prices can seem elevated compared with the amenities on offer, especially on weekends. A ramshackle hut starts at about 300B and with air-con this can climb to 800B. Reservations aren't always honoured, so at peak times (most weekends and especially public-holiday weekends) it is advisable to arrive early, poised for the hunt.

➡ **Tubtim Resort** (☏0 3864 4025; www.tubtimresort.com; Ao Phutsa; r 600-2500B; ✳🛜) Tubtim has dozens of bungalows climbing up a rugged hill from the beach. The pick of the bunch are the modern, stylish bungalows with big windows and balconies that look straight down the beach; midpriced rooms are thoroughly comfortable, too. The resort's restaurant serves some of the best food on the island.

➡ **Saikaew Villa** (☏0 3864 4144; r 800-2000B; ✳) The closest option to the pier, Saikaew Villa has big rooms or small rooms, fan or air-con and conjures up a holiday-camp atmosphere. Quality and privacy varies with each room.

➡ **Tok's** (☏0 3864 4072; r 1500B; ✳) Snazzy villas climb up a landscaped hillside with plenty of shade and flowering plants, making Tok's a respectable midranger.

A CHEAT SHEET TO KO SAMET'S BEACHES

Ko Samet is shaped like a golf tee, with the wide part in the north tapering away along a narrow strip to the south. Most boats from the mainland arrive at Tha Na Dan in the north, which is little more than a transit point for most visitors. Starting just south of Tha Na Dan and moving clockwise, the island's most noteworthy beaches include:

➡ **Hat Sai Kaew (Diamond Beach)** On the northeastern coast is the most developed stretch of beaches and the best place for nightlife. Wealthy Bangkokians file straight into Hat Sai Kaew's air-con bungalows.

➡ **Ao Hin Khok, Ao Phai** Scattered south along the eastern shore are a scruffier set of beaches that were once populated solely by backpackers but are increasingly catering to flashpackers and Bangkok expats.

➡ **Ao Phutsa (Ao Tub Tim)** This wide and sandy beach is a favourite for solitude seekers, families and gay men who need access to 'civilisation' but not a lot of other stimulation.

➡ **Ao Nuan, Ao Cho (Chaw)** Less voluptuous beaches that appeal more to romantics than crowds.

➡ **Ao Wong Deuan** Immediately to the south is the prom queen of the bunch, with a graceful stretch of sand that is home to an entourage of sardine-packed sunworshippers, package tourists, screaming jet skis and honky-tonk bars.

➡ **Ao Thian (Candlelight Beach)** This beach is punctuated by big boulders that shelter small sandy spots, creating a castaway feel. Thai college kids claim these for all-night guitar jam sessions. If you're also on a tight budget, this is your best bet.

➡ **Ao Phrao (Coconut Beach)** The only developed beach on the steeper western side of the island, it hosts three upmarket resorts and moonlights as 'Paradise Beach' to those escaping winter climates.

➡ **Ao Noi Na, Ao Klang** Along the oft-overlooked northern shore are several decent midrange resorts and guesthouses.

KHAO LAEM YA/MU KO SAMET NATIONAL PARK

(☏ 0 3865 3034; reserve@dnp.go.th; adult/child 200/100B; ☺8.30am-4.30pm) In the early 1980s, Ko Samet began receiving its first visitors: young Thais in search of a retreat from city life. It was made a national marine park in 1981 and at that time there were only about 40 houses on the island. Rayong and Bangkok speculators saw the sudden interest in Ko Samet as a chance to cash in on an up-and-coming Phuket and began buying up land along the beaches. No one bothered about the fact that it was a national marine park. When *fa·ràng* (Westerners) soon followed, spurred on by rumours that Ko Samet was similar to Ko Samui '10 years ago' (one always seems to miss it by a decade), the National Parks Division stepped in and built a visitors' office on the island, ordered that all bungalows be moved back behind the tree line and started charging admission to the park.

However, the regulating hand of the National Parks Division is almost invis-

ible beyond its revenue-raising role at the **admission gate** (Hat Sai Kaew; ☺sunrise-sunset). One successful measure, however, is a ban on new accommodation except where it replaces old sites, ensuring that bungalows remain thinly spread over most of the island.

🍴 EATING & DRINKING

Every hotel and guesthouse on Ko Samet has a restaurant and choosing one is as difficult as a walk along the beach inspecting menus along the way. There are several food stalls along the main drag between Tha Na Dan and Hat Sai Kaew, and it's worth looking out for the nightly beach barbecues, particularly along Ao Hin Khok and Ao Phai.

Likewise, every hotel has a beachside bar, and there are plenty of stand-alone barrestaurants that occupy the beachfront at Hat Sai Kaew and Ao Wong Deuan.

Ko Samet

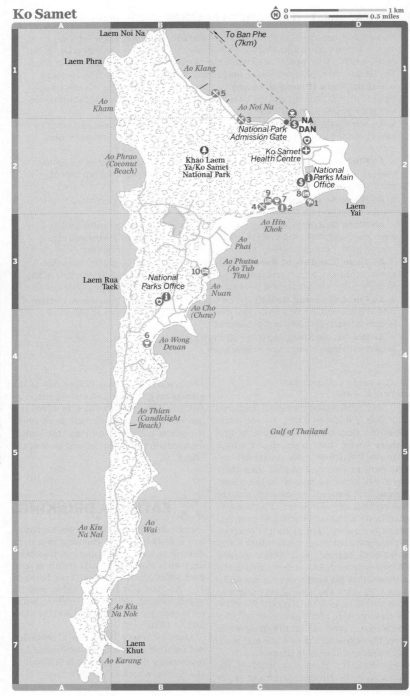

N 0 _____ 1 km
0 _____ 0.5 miles

Laem Noi Na

To Ban Phe
(7km)

Laem Phra

Ao Klang

Ao
Kham

Ao Noi Na

3

5

National Park
Admission Gate

NA
DAN

Ao Phrao
(Coconut
Beach)

Khao Laem
Ya/Ko Samet
National Park

Ko Samet
Health Centre

National
Parks
Main Office

9

7

4

8

1

2

Laem Yai

Ao Hin
Khok

Ao Phai

Laem Rua
Taek

National
Parks Office

10

Ao Phutsa
(Ao Tub
Tim)

Ao
Nuan

Ao Cho
(Chaw)

6

Ao Wong
Deuan

Ao Thian
(Candlelight
Beach)

Gulf of Thailand

Ao Kiu
Na Nai

Ao
Wai

Ao Kiu
Na Nok

Laem
Khut

Ao Karang

Ko Samet

◉ **Sights**

✕ **Eating**

◒ **Drinking**

▣ **Sleeping**

JEP'S RESTAURANT   INTERNATIONAL **$**

(Ao Hin Khok; mains 60-150B; ⊘7am-11pm) Canopied by the branches of an arching tree decorated with pendant lights, this pretty place does a little of everything right on the beach.

SUMMER RESTAURANT   INTERNATIONAL **$$**

(Baan Puu Paan, Ao Noi Na; dishes 250-400B; ⊘dinner) In a crisp setting overlooking the harbour, Summer's menu resembles a globetrotters' culinary scrapbook, from Indian-style chicken tikka to Cajun chicken breasts.

BAN PLOY SAMED   THAI **$$**

(☏0 3864 4188; Ao Noi Na; dishes 300-600B; ⊘11am-9pm) Better than having to haul in your meal, you are hauled to this floating restaurant by a boat-and-pulley system. Fresh seafood dishes, especially the whole steamed fish variety, await. Reservations are recommended.

NAGA BAR   BAR

(Ao Hin Khok) This beachfront bar specialises in drinking games: coin tosses, Thai boxing bouts and whisky buckets to give you courage.

BAYWATCH BAR   BAR, RESTAURANT

(Ao Wong Deuan) Pam Anderson is nowhere to be found but the delicious cocktails and international dishes (mains 190-290B) are a decent consolation prize.

Amphawa
อัมพวา

Explore

Amphawa is located within day-trip distance from Bangkok, but is probably best approached as an overnighter. The trip can be done quite conveniently via bus or minivan, or via a more circuitous route. After you've seen the town, Amphawa is also a good jumping-off point for other floating markets (p167) such as Damnoen Saduak and Tha Kha.

The Best...

➡ **Sight** Amphawa (p160)

➡ **Place to Eat** Amphawa Floating Market (p161)

➡ **Place to Stay** Ploen Amphawa Resort (p161)

Top Tip

Amphawa is mobbed with tourists from Bangkok every weekend. For cheaper accommodation and a calmer environment, make a point of hitting the town during the week.

Getting There & Away

Minivan Frequent minivans leave from just north of Bangkok's Victory Monument (Map p263) to Samut Songkhram (70B, one hour, from 5.30am to 8pm). From there, you can hop in a *sŏrng·tăa·ou* (pick-up minibus; 8B) near the market for the 10-minute ride to Amphawa. From Friday to Sunday, minivans depart from and head to Amphawa for slightly more.

Bus From Bangkok's Southern Bus Terminal (p221), board any bus bound for Damnoen Saduak and ask to get off at Amphawa (80B, two hours, every 20 minutes from 6am to 9pm).

Need to Know

➡ **Area Code** ☏034

➡ **Location** 80km southwest of Bangkok

➡ **Tourist Office** (☏0 3475 2847; ⊘8.30am-4.30pm)

THE LONG WAY TO AMPHAWA

Amphawa is only 80km from Bangkok, but if you play your cards right, you can reach the town via a multihour journey involving trains, boats, a motorcycle ride and a short jaunt in the back of a truck. Why? Because sometimes the journey is just as important as the destination.

The adventure begins at Thonburi's Wong Wian Yai (p221) train station. Just past the traffic circle (Wong Wian Yai) is a fairly ordinary food market that camouflages the unspectacular terminus of this commuter line. Hop on one of the hourly trains (10B, one hour, from 5.30am to 8.10pm) to Samut Sakhon and you're on your way.

After 15 minutes on the rattling train the city density yields to squat villages. From the window you can peek into homes, temples and shops built a carefully considered arm's length from the passing trains. Further on, palm trees, patchwork rice fields and marshes filled with giant elephant ears and canna lilies line the route, punctuated by whistle-stop stations.

The backwater farms evaporate quickly as you enter Samut Sakhon, popularly known as Mahachai because it straddles the confluence of Mae Nam Tha Chin and Khlong Mahachai. This is a bustling port town, several kilometres upriver from the Gulf of Thailand, and the end of the first rail segment. Before the 17th century it was called Tha Jiin (Chinese Pier) because of the large number of Chinese junks that called here.

After working your way through one of the most hectic fresh markets in the country, you'll come to a vast harbour clogged with water hyacinths and wooden fishing boats. A few rusty cannons pointing towards the river testify to the existence of the town's crumbling fort, built to protect the kingdom from sea invaders.

Take the ferry across to Baan Laem (3B to 5B), jockeying for space with motorcycles that are driven by school teachers and errand-running housewives. If the infrequent 5B ferry hasn't already deposited you there, take a motorcycle taxi (10B) for the 2km ride to Wat Chawng Lom, home to the Jao Mae Kuan Im Shrine, a 9m-high fountain in the shape of the Mahayana Buddhist Goddess of Mercy that is popular with regional tour groups. Beside the shrine is Tha Chalong, a train stop with three daily departures for Samut Songkhram at 10.10am, 1.30pm and 4.40pm (10B, one hour). The train rambles out of the city on tracks that the surrounding forest threatens to engulf, and this little stretch of line genuinely feels a world away from the big smoke of Bangkok.

The jungle doesn't last long, and any illusion that you've entered a parallel universe free of concrete is shattered as you enter Samut Songkhram. And to complete the seismic shift you'll emerge directly into a hubbub of hectic market stalls. Between train arrivals and departures these stalls set up directly on the tracks, and must be hurriedly cleared away when the train arrives – it's quite an amazing scene.

Commonly known as Mae Klong, Samut Songkhram is a tidier version of Samut Sakhon and offers a great deal more as a destination. Owing to flat topography and abundant water sources, the area surrounding the provincial capital is well suited to the steady irrigation needed to grow guava, lychee and grapes. From Mae Klong Market pier (*tâh dà·làht mâa glorng*), you can charter a boat (800B) or hop in a *sŏrng·tăa·ou* (passenger pick-up truck; 8B) near the market for the 10-minute ride to Amphawa.

◉ SIGHTS

AMPHAWA   VILLAGE

(อัมพวา) This canal-side village has become a popular destination among city folk who wish to seek out what many consider its quintessentially 'Thai' setting. This urban influx has sparked quite a few signs of gentrification, but the canals, old wooden buildings, atmospheric cafes and quaint water-borne traffic still retain heaps of charm. At weekends, Amphawa puts on a fun floating market (p167).

WAT AMPHAWAN
CHETIYARAM   BUDDHIST TEMPLE

(วัดอัมพวันเจติยาราม; admission free; ◎7am-7pm) Steps from Amphawa's central footbridge is this graceful temple thought to be located at the place of the family home of Rama II (King Phraphutthaloetla Naphalai; r 1809–24), and which features accomplished murals.

KING BUDDHALERTLA (PHUTTHA LOET LA) NAPHALAI MEMORIAL PARK — MUSEUM

(อุทยานพระบรมราชานุสรณ์ พระบาทสมเด็จพระพุทธเลิศหล้านภาลัย อุทยาน ร. 2); admission 20B; ⊗8.30am-5pm) A short walk from Wat Amphwan Chetiyaram is an open-air museum consisting of a collection of traditional central-Thai houses set on four landscaped acres. Dedicated to Rama II, the houses contain rare books and antiques from early-19th-century Siam.

FIREFLIES — GUIDED TOUR

(หิ่งห้อย) At night long-tail boats zip through Amphawa's sleeping waters to watch the Christmas-tree-like light dance of the *hìng hôy* (fireflies), most populous during the wet season. From Friday to Sunday, several operators from several piers lead tours, charging 60B for a seat. Outside of these days, it costs 500B for a two-hour charter.

DON HOI LOT — BEACH

(ดอนหอยหลอด) The area's second-most famous tourist attraction is a bank of fossilised shells at the mouth of Mae Nam Mae Klong, not far from Samut Songkhram. These shells come from *hŏy lòrt* (clams with a tubelike shell). While nearby seafood restaurants are popular with city folk year-round, the shell bank is best seen during April and May when the river surface has receded to its lowest level. To get there hop into a *sŏrng·tăa·ou* (10B, about 15 minutes) in front of Samut Songkhram's Somdet Phra Phuttalertla Hospital at the intersection of Th Prasitpattana and Th Tamnimit. Or charter a boat from Mae Klong Market pier *(tâh dà·làht mâa glorng)*, a scenic journey of around 45 minutes (about 1000B).

EATING

There are several basic Thai restaurants in Amphawa; many more open on weekends.

AMPHAWA FLOATING MARKET — MARKET $

(dishes 20-40B; ⊗4-9pm Fri-Sun) If you're in town on a weekend, plan your meals around this fun market where *pàt tai* and other noodle dishes are served directly from boats.

SEAFOOD RESTAURANTS — SEAFOOD $

(Samut Songkhram; mains 70-200B; ⊗lunch & dinner) The road leading to Don Hoi Lot is lined with seafood restaurants, nearly all serving dishes made with *hŏy lòrt*, the area's eponymous shellfish.

Phetchaburi (Phetburi)

เพชรบุรี

Explore

Phetchaburi (colloquially known as Phetburi) is only about two hours from Bangkok, but is probably best approached as an overnighter, although it's worth noting that the town's hotels are a dreary lot. Regardless, despite the number of worthwhile sights, very few foreign tourists make to Phetburi, and you'll most likely have the town to yourself.

SLEEPING IN AMPHAWA

Amphawa is popular with Bangkok's weekend warriors and virtually every other house opens as a homestays. These can range from little more than a mattress and a mosquito net to upscale guesthouses. Fan rooms start at about 200B while air-con rooms, many of which share bathrooms, begin at about 1000B. Prices are half this on weekdays. If you prefer something a bit more private, consider one of the following.

➜ **Ploen Amphawa Resort** (☏08 1458 9411; www.ploenamphawa.com; Th Rim Khlong; r incl breakfast 1400-2500B; ❀☏) Not a resort at all, but rather a scant handful of rooms in a refurbished wooden home in the thick of the canal area.

➜ **ChababaanCham Resort** (☏08 1984 1000; Th Rim Khlong; r incl breakfast 1900-2400B; ❀☏) A compound with modern but somewhat overpriced rooms and bungalows just off the canal.

➜ **Baan Ku Pu** (☏0 3472 5920; Th Rim Khlong; d 1000B; ❀) A longstanding collection of wooden bungalows a brief walk from the market area.

161

DAY TRIPS FROM BANGKOK PHETCHABURI (PHETBURI)

Phetchaburi (Phetburi)

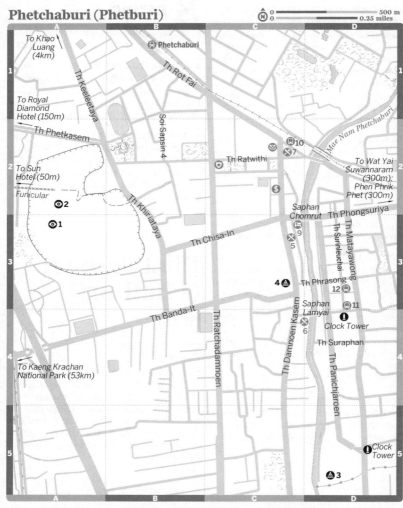

DAY TRIPS FROM BANGKOK PHETCHABURI (PHETBURI)

If you've got a bit more time, consider extending your stay to take in the jungle at Kaeng Krachan National Park or the beach at Hat Chao Samran.

The Best...

→ **Sight** Khao Wang (p163)
→ **Place to Eat** Phen Phrik Phet (p164)
→ **Place to Stay** Sun Hotel (p165)

Top Tip

The train is the slowest but arguably the most scenic way to reach Phetburi.

Getting There & Away

Minivan Frequent minivans ply from just east of Bangkok's Victory Monument to Phetburi (90B, two hours, every 45 minutes from 5am to 7.30pm).

Bus Air-con buses run to/from Bangkok's Southern bus terminal (p221), with frequent departures during the morning hours (120B, two hours).

Train There are frequent services from Bangkok's Hualamphong Train Station (p94), and fares vary depending on the train and class (3rd class 84B to 144B, 2nd class 188B to 358B, three hours).

Phetchaburi (Phetburi)

....

Need to Know

➡ **Area Code** ✍ 032
➡ **Location** 166km south of Bangkok

◎ SIGHTS

FREE **WAT MAHATHAT**   BUDDHIST TEMPLE

(วัดมหาธาตุวรวิหาร; Th Damnoen Krasem; ⊘7am-6pm) Complete with its late Ayuthaya-early Ratanakosin adaptation of the *prang* of Lopburi and Phimai, Wat Mahathat is Phetburi's most imposing temple. The beautiful murals inside the *wí·hăhn* illustrate the *Jataka* and also show vivid snippets of everyday Thai life during the 19th century. The roof of the adjacent *bòht* holds some fine examples of stucco work, which is characteristic of the Phetburi school of art that can be seen on many of the city's temples.

WAT YAI SUWANNARAM   BUDDHIST TEMPLE

(วัดใหญ่สุวรรณาราม; Th Phongsuriya; admission free; ⊘7am-6pm) This expansive temple compound was originally built in Ayuthaya during the 17th century and was moved to Phetburi and renovated during the reign of Rama V (King Chulalongkorn; r 1868–1910). Legend has it that the gash in the ornately carved wooden doors of the lengthy

wooden *săh·lah* dates to the Burmese attack. The faded murals inside the *bòht* date back to the 1730s. Next to the *bòht,* set on a murky pond, is a beautifully designed old *hŏr đrai* (Tripitaka library), though these days it's home only to pigeons.

KHAO WANG   HISTORICAL SITE

(เขาวัง) Phetburi lives in the shadow of a looming hill studded with *wát* and topped by various components of Rama IV's (King Mongkut; r 1851–68) 1860 palace, **Phra Nakhon Khiri** (พระนครคีรี; admission 150B; ⊘9am-4pm). The mountaintop is divided into three sections; the east peak bears a scaled-down version of Wat Phra Kaew (p58; the Temple of the Emerald Buddha) and an unusual *chedi* made of granite blocks; the middle peak is dominated by a 40m-high *chedi* that affords panoramic views from its upper level, while the western peak is home to Mongkut's palace, his observatory and other palace essentials built in Thai and Sino-European styles. To get here, make the strenuous upward climb or head to the west side of the hill and take a **funicular** (return adult/child 40/15B; ⊘9am-4pm) straight up to the peak.

WAT KO KAEW SUTHARAM   BUDDHIST TEMPLE

(วัดเกาะแก้วสุทธาราม|Wat Ko; off Th Matayawong; ⊘7am-6pm) Located at the edge of town, this temple compound dates back to the Ayuthaya era, and the *bòht* features early-18th-century murals that are among the oldest in Thailand. One panel depicts what appears to be a Jesuit priest wearing the robes of a Buddhist monk, while another shows other foreigners undergoing Buddhist conversions. You'll probably have to ask the caretaker to open it for you.

FREE **KHAO LUANG**   CAVE

(เขาหลวง; ⊘9am-4pm Mon-Fri, to 5pm Sat & Sun) About 4km north of town is this cave sanctuary, which has three caverns filled with dozens of Buddha images in various poses – some of them originally placed by Rama IV. The best time to visit Khao Luang is around 5pm, when the school groups should have gone and the evening light pierces the ceiling, surrounding artefacts below with an ethereal glow. A round-trip *săhm·lór* from town should cost about 150B.

⊙ Around Phetchaburi (Phetburi)

KAENG KRACHAN NATIONAL PARK

NATIONAL PARK

(อุทยานแห่งชาติแก่งกระจาน; ☏0 3245 9293; www.dnp. go.th; admission 200B) The largest national park in Thailand and home to the gorgeous Pala-U waterfalls, Kaeng Krachan National Park is easily reached from Phetburi. There are caves to explore, mountains, a huge lake and excellent bird-watching opportunities in the evergreen forest blanketing the park. Kaeng Krachan has fantastic trekking, and it is one of the few places to see Asian elephants roaming wild (if you're lucky).

Tourist infrastructure in the park is somewhat limited and the roads can be rough. The park rangers can help arrange camping-gear rental, food and transport. The best months to visit are between November and April. The folks at **Rabieng Rim Num** (p165) can arrange trekking and birding tours from 1950B per person, ranging from one day to multiple days.

There are various **bungalows** (☏0 2562 0760; www.dnp.go.th/parkreserve) within the park, mainly near the reservoir. There are also **campsites** (60-90B per person), including a pleasant grassy one near the reservoir at the visitors centre. On the road leading to the park entrance are several simple resorts and bungalows.

The park is 50km from Phetburi. A single daily *sŏrng tăa·ou* (50B, 9.30am) departs from Phetburi's market area and stops 4km from the park headquarters. To get to the higher campgrounds you'll have to charter a vehicle from the headquarters (1600B) or hitch.

> ### PRIMATE WARNING
>
> Note that Khao Wang is home to hundreds of cheeky monkeys that are, according to numerous signs, 'not afraid anyone'. You make yourself a particular target of their aggression by carrying any sort of food or drink. If you're hungry or thirsty, consume your food or drink at the stalls (the vendors are armed with slingshots and can defend against attacks) and be sure to discard any cans, peels or wrappers before proceeding.

HAT CHAO SAMRAN

BEACH

(หาดเจ้าสำราญ) Lying 18km east of Phetburi, Hat Chao Samran is one of Thailand's oldest beach resorts, dating back to the reign of Rama VI (King Vajiravudh; r 1910–25). It's a pleasant enough place to laze your way through a day or two, punctuating your naps with cheap seafood binges. A recent resurgence in popularity has brought with it 'boutique'-style bungalow accommodation. **Blue Sky** (☏0 3244 1399; www.bluesky resort.com; 5 Moo 2, Hat Chao Samran; bungalows 1800-5000B; ☏☀) offers cute bungalows and rooms overlooking the garden or the sea. When you can relax no more, stumble next door to the ramshackle **Jaa Piak** (mains 50-280B; ⊙9am-9pm), which serves all manner of seafood including a mean horseshoe crab egg salad (*yam kài maang dah tálair*).

To reach Hat Chao Samran, hop on a morning or afternoon *sŏrng tăa·ou* (30B, 35 minutes) across from Phetburi's clock tower (the one just east of Saphan Lamyai).

✕ EATING

Phetburi is especially famous for its desserts, many of which can claim a royal pedigree and obtain their sweet taste from the fruit of the sugar palms that dot the countryside around here. Two of the most famous sweets on offer include *môr gaang* (an egg and coconut-milk custard) and *kà·nŏm đahn* (bright yellow steamed buns sweetened with sugar-palm kernels).

PHEN PHRIK PHET

NOODLES $

(173/1 Th Phongsuriya; mains from 35B; ⊙9am-3pm Wed-Mon) Located directly across from the entrance to Wat Yai Suwannaram, this local noodle legend makes delicious *gŏo·ay đĕe·o mŏo nám daang* (pork noodles in a fragrant dark broth). There's no English-language sign; look for the umbrellas, pots and potted plants.

KHAO CHAE NANG RAM

CENTRAL THAI $

(Th Damnoen Kasem; dishes 20B; ⊙8am-5pm) *Kôw châa* (camphor-scented chilled rice served with sweet/savoury titbits) is a dish associated with Phetburi, and this roadside stall in front of a noodle restaurant is considered one of the best places to try it. There's no English-language sign; look for the cart under the old blue awning.

> **SLEEPING IN PHETCHABURI (PHETBURI)**
>
> There is not much to choose from in the accommodation department, so don't get too excited.
>
> ➡ **Sun Hotel** (📞0 3240 0000; www.sunhotelthailand.com; 43/33 Soi Phetkasem; r 790-890B, ste 1390B; ❄@🛜) Probably the best place to stay in town, the rooms here are huge, and come with TV, fridge, air-con and warm water, but not much character. The Sun is located opposite the back entrance to Phra Nakhon Khiri.
>
> ➡ **Royal Diamond Hotel** (📞0 3241 1061; www.royaldiamondhotel.com; 555 Th Phetkasem; r 1200-2000B, ste 2500B, all incl breakfast; ❄🛜) The Royal Diamond is an imposing if somewhat abandoned-feeling hotel, also located near the back entrance to Phra Na-khon Khiri. Rooms are big and functional, but lack character and can be musty.
>
> ➡ **Rabieng Rimnum Guesthouse** (📞0 3242 5707; www.rabiengrimnum.com; 1 Th Chisa-In; s/d with shared bathroom 120/240B) The cheapest place in town, this wooden house is straight out of the shoestring guides of the '80s. The tiny fan rooms have walls that cut out little of the traffic noise passing across the bridge. The people who run it also do tours and can provide local information.

MONDEE CENTRAL THAI $

(dishes 25-100B; ⊙10am-midnight) During the day, this cosy wooden shack beside the river serves *kà·nŏm jeen* (fresh rice noodles served with a variety of curries). At night Mondee takes full advantage of the breezes and river view and serves decent central Thai fare with an emphasis on seafood. There's no English-language sign; it's located at the foot of the bridge.

NIGHT MARKET CENTRAL THAI $

(Th Ratwithi; dishes 25-60B; ⊙4-11pm) Located near the Bangkok-bound bus station, this busy night market does a variety of tasty Thai dishes, from noodles to curries.

Kanchanaburi
กาญจนบุรี

Explore

There are multiple ways to approach Kanchaburi's sights. Many choose to charter a boat, which for 800B will take up to six people on a two-hour tour of the area's big sights. With a bit more time, bike (40B per day) and motorcycle (150B to 200B per day) are cheaper, but still viable ways to get around. And if you've got more time, there are tourist trains that (slowly) whisk visitors to Nam Tok, over the Death Railway Bridge

and via Hellfire Pass. In fact, it's worth staying overnight in Kanchanaburi, as there's good-value accommodation, and after the sun sets the river boom-booms its way through the night with disco and karaoke barges packed with Bangkokians looking to let their hair down, especially at weekends.

The Best...

➡ **Sight** Death Railway Bridge (Bridge Over the River Kwai; p166)

➡ **Place to Eat** Keeree Tara Restaurant (p170)

➡ **Place to Drink** Resort (p170)

Top Tip

Try as you might, you will find few Thais who have ever heard of the River Kwai. The river over which the Death Railway trundled is pronounced like 'quack' without the '-ck'.

Getting There & Away

Travel Time About three hours

Minivan Frequent minivans depart from just west of Bangkok's Victory Monument (Map p263) to Kanchanaburi (120B, two hours, hourly from 6am to 7.30pm).

Bus Buses leave from the Southern Bus Terminal (p221) in Thonburi (77B to 99B, about two hours, every 20 minutes from 5am to 10.30pm) and the Northern & Northeastern Bus Terminal (p220; 95B to 122B, about three hours, hourly from 5am to 4pm).

Train Trains leave Bangkok Noi Train Station in Thonburi at 7.45am and 1.35pm (100B, about three hours). To return to

Kanchanaburi

To U Inchantree / Kanchanaburi (200m)

To Wat Pa Luangta Bua Yannasampanno (Tiger Temple; 45km); Erawan National Park (50km); Hellfire Pass Memorial (75km)

Th Saengchuto

Th Mae Nam Khwae

Mae Nam Khwae Yai

Kanchanaburi

Th Jaokannun

Th Kratai Thong

Market

City Gate

Tourism Authority of Thailand (TAT)

Mae Nam Khwae Noi

Mae Nam Mae Klong

To Chung Kai Allied War Memorial (1.3km)

Bangkok, trains depart Kanchanaburi at 7.19am, 2.44pm and 5.41pm.

Need to Know

➡ **Area Code** ☏ 034

➡ **Location** 130km west of Bangkok

➡ **Tourism Authority of Thailand (TAT) Office** (☏ 0 3451 1200; Th Saengchuto; ◷ 8.30am-4.30pm)

⊙ SIGHTS

TOP CHOICE DEATH RAILWAY BRIDGE (BRIDGE OVER THE RIVER KWAI)   HISTORICAL SITE

(สะพานข้ามแม่น้ำแคว; Th Mae Nam Khwae) Despite its unspectacular appearance (it's an iron bridge), the bridge across Mae Nam Khwae is one of Kanchanaburi's most popular attractions. Indeed, Kanchanaburi can thank

FLOATING MARKETS

Pictures of floating markets *(dà·làht nám)* jammed full of wooden canoes pregnant with colourful exotic fruits have defined the official tourist profile of Thailand for decades. The idyllic scenes are as iconic as the Grand Palace or the Reclining Buddha, but they are also almost completely contrived for, and dependent upon, foreign and domestic tourists – roads and motorcycles have long moved Bangkokians' daily errands onto dry ground. That said, if you can see them for what they are, a few of Thailand's floating markets are worth a visit.

➡ **Tha Kha Floating Market** (ตลาดน้ำท่าคา; Samut Songkhram; ⏰7am-noon, 2nd, 7th & 12th day of waxing & waning moons & Sat-Sun) This, the most 'real' feeling floating market, is also the most difficult to reach. A handful of vendors coalesce along an open rural *klorng* (canal, also spelt *khlong*) lined with coconut palms and old wooden houses. Boat rides (20B per person, 45 minutes) can be arranged along the canal, and there are lots of tasty snacks and fruits for sale. Take one of the morning *sŏrng·tǎa·ou* (passenger pick-up trucks) from Samut Songkhram's market area (20B, 45 minutes); for details on getting to Samut Songkhram see p159.

➡ **Amphawa Floating Market** (p161) The Amphawa Floating Market, located in Samut Songkhram Province, convenes near Wat Amphawa. The emphasis is on edibles and tourist knick-knacks, and because the market is only on weekends and is popular among tourists from Bangkok, things can get pretty hectic. For details on getting to Amphawa see p159.

➡ **Taling Chan Floating Market** (ตลาดน้ำตลิ่งชัน; Nonthaburi; ⏰7am-4pm Sat & Sun) Just outside Bangkok on the access road to Khlong Bangkok Noi, Taling Chan looks like any other fresh-food market, busy with produce vendors from nearby farms. But the twist emerges at the canal where several floating docks serve as informal dining rooms, and the kitchens are canoes tethered to the docks. Taling Chan is in Thonburi and can be reached from Bangkok's Th Ratchadamnoen Klang (map p254) via air-con bus 79 (16B, 25 minutes). Long-tail boats from any large Bangkok pier can also be hired for a trip to Taling Chan and the nearby Khlong Chak Phra.

➡ **Damnoen Saduak Floating Market** (ตลาดน้ำดำเนินสะดวก; Ratchaburi; ⏰7am-noon) This 100-year-old floating market – the country's most famous – is now essentially a floating souvenir stand filled with package tourists. This in itself can be a fascinating insight into Thai culture, as the vast majority of tourists here are Thais, and watching the approach to this cultural 'theme park' is instructive. But beyond the market, the residential canals are quite peaceful and can be explored by hiring a boat (100B per person) for a longer duration. Trips stop at small family businesses, including a Thai candy maker, a pomelo farm and a knife crafter. Air-con buses 78 and 996 go direct from the Southern Bus Terminal in Thonburi (see p220) to Damnoen Saduak (80B, two hours, every 20 minutes from 6am to 9pm).

➡ **Don Wai Market** (ตลาดดอนหวาย; Talat Don Wai; ⏰6am-6pm) Not technically a swimmer, this market claims a riverbank location in Nakhon Pathom Province, having originally started out in the early 20th century as a floating market for pomelo and jackfruit growers and traders. The main attraction here is food, including fruit, traditional sweets and *bètpah·lóh* (five-spice stewed duck), which can be consumed aboard large boats that cruise Mae Nam Nakhorn Chaisi (60B, one hour). The easiest way to reach Don Wai Market is to take a minibus (45B, 35 minutes) from beside Central Pinklao in Thonburi, accessible via Saphan Phra Pin Klao..

director David Lean and his Hollywood epic *The Bridge on the River Kwai* for a good proportion of the city's foreign visitors. The bridge, 2km north of town, was taken from Java by the Japanese and reassembled here with work beginning in 1942.

It was bombed repeatedly during WWII and today only the curved spans are original; the two square sections were rebuilt with Japanese reparation money in 1946.

A rainbow-coloured mini train runs regular trips (20B, 11am to 2pm) across the bridge. Three trains daily (7.12am, 2.36pm and 5.31pm; 50B, about two hours) also cross the bridge en route to Nam Tok, via the infamous Hellfire Pass. During the last week of November and first week of December a nightly sound-and-light show marks the Allied attack on the Death Railway in 1945.

TOP CHOICE THAILAND-BURMA RAILWAY CENTRE MUSEUM MUSEUM

(ศูนย์รถไฟไทย-พม่า; www.tbrconline.com; 73 Th Jaokannun; adult/child 120/60B; ⊙9am-5pm) The pick of Kanchanaburi's war museums, where interactive exhibits, short films and clear descriptions provide the context of the Japanese aggression in Southeast Asia, detail their plans for the railway and describe the horrors faced by those prisoners who worked and died constructing it. Give yourself a full hour to read through the museum, and stop for a coffee upstairs for sweeping views across the cemetery.

TOP CHOICE ALLIED WAR CEMETERY HISTORICAL SITE

(สุสานทหารพันธมิตรดอนรัก; Th Saengchuto; admission free; ⊙8am-6pm) This cemetery is the final resting place of about 7000 prisoners who died while working on the railway. The cemetery is meticulously maintained by the Commonwealth War Graves Commission, and the rows of headstones are identical except for the names and the short, moving epitaphs. It's just around the corner from the riverside guesthouses.

JEATH WAR MUSEUM MUSEUM

(พิพิธภัณฑ์สงคราม; Th Wisuttharangsi; admission 30B; ⊙8am-5pm) The simple Jeath War Museum operates in the grounds of a local temple and is housed in a re-creation of the long bamboo huts used by the POWs as shelter. Inside are various photographs, drawings, maps, weapons, paintings by POWs and other war memorabilia. The acronym Jeath represents the ill-fated meeting of Japan, England, Australia/America, Thailand and Holland at Kanchanaburi during WWII.

WWII MUSEUM MUSEUM

(พิพิธภัณฑ์สงครามโลกครั้งที่สอง; Th Mae Nam Khwae; admission 40B; ⊙8am-6.30pm) This museum beside the bridge has a picture-postcard view and a vast and eclectic assortment of war and peace memorabilia, from rusting guns to mural-sized portraits of WWII-era political figures. Oddly contrasting with these is a permanent exhibit to former Thai beauty queens. If you enjoy sifting through junk shops you'll love this place.

CHUNG KAI ALLIED WAR CEMETERY HISTORICAL SITE

(สุสานทหารพันธมิตรช่องไก่; admission free; ⊙7am-6pm) This less-visited cemetery, where about 1700 graves are kept, is a short and scenic bike ride from central Kanchanaburi. Take the bridge across the river through picturesque corn and sugarcane fields until you reach the cemetery on your left.

⊙ Around Kanchanaburi

HELLFIRE PASS MEMORIAL MUSEUM

(ช่องเขาขาด; Rte 323; admission by donation; ⊙9am-4pm) Viewing the bridge and war museums doesn't quite communicate the immense task of bending the landscape with human muscle that was involved in building the Death Railway. A better understanding comes from a visit to the excellent Hellfire Pass Memorial, an Australian-Thai Chamber of Commerce memorial and museum dedicated to the POW labourers, 75km north of Kanchanaburi. A crew of 1000 prisoners worked for 12 weeks to cut a pass through the mountainous area dubbed Hellfire Pass. Nearly 70% of them died in the process. An interactive museum is enhanced by several short films. Below the museum is a walking trail along the track itself and through Hellfire Pass.

Hellfire Pass and the Tiger Temple are accessed via the road running west from Kanchanaburi to Sangkhlaburi and the Myanmar border. It's easy to arrange tours from Kanchanaburi, or take a bus towards Sangkhlaburi (145-175B; 1½ hours; 6am, 8.40am, 10.20am and noon) and ask the driver to drop you near your destination. The last return bus leaves Sangkhlaburi at 1.15pm, pulling in to Hellfire Pass around 5pm, and takes five hours to reach Kanchanaburi. Alternatively, hire a motorbike (150B per day) or taxi (return to Hellfire Pass, about 1300B; to Tiger Temple, 600B).

WAT PA LUANGTA BUAYANNASAMPANNO (TIGER TEMPLE) BUDDHIST TEMPLE

(วัดป่าหลวงตาบัว ญาณสัมปันโน; www.tigertemple.org; admission 500B; ⊙8.30am-noon & 1.30-5pm) This is one of Kanchanaburi's more bizarre tourist destinations, colloquially known as the Tiger Temple. After gaining a reputation as a refuge for wounded animals, the temple received its first tiger cub in 1999 and has accumulated dozens more since. During visiting hours, the cats are led around a quarry and, for a hefty fee, will pose for photos with tourists. Although the efforts are undeniably the result of goodwill, there's something disconcerting (not to mention surreal) about seeing monks leading full-grown tigers around on leashes and tourists posing for pictures with said huge cats lying in their laps. It's 45km outside town; detailed directions are on the website. To see the tigers close-up, time your visit for around noon.

ERAWAN NATIONAL PARK   NATIONAL PARK
(อุทยานแห่งชาติเอราวัณ; admission 200B; ☺8am-4pm) Northwest of Kanchanaburi town is the area's natural playground. Erawan National Park sports a watery mane of waterfalls and is visited by locals and tourists out for a day trip of photographs, picnics and swimming. **Sai Yok National Park** has more variety: waterfalls, limestone caves, hot springs and accommodation. Tour organisers in Kanchanaburi can arrange day outings to these parks on various expeditions: river kayaking, elephant trekking, waterfall spotting and bamboo rafting.

The limestone hills surrounding Kanchanaburi are famous for their temple caves, an underground communion of animistic spirit worship and traditional Buddhism. Winding arteries burrow into the guts of the caves past bulbous calcium deposits and altars for reclining or meditating Buddhas, surrounded by offerings from pilgrims. **Wat Tham Khao Pun** is one of the closest cave temples, and is best reached by bicycle. The temple is about 4km from the TAT office and 1km southwest of the Chung Kai cemetery across the railroad tracks and midway up the hill.

✖ EATING & DRINKING

Kanchanaburi is not a culinary destination, and guesthouse-style and touristoriented restaurants serving bland Thai standards seem to dominate. It is, however, something of a nightlife town, and bars extend nearly the entire length of Th Mae Nam Khwae. Of these, tacky hostess bars dominate the southern end, backpackerfriendly pubs define the middle, and openair bar-restaurants for the Thai crowd can be found at the street's northern end.

THE DEATH RAILWAY

Kanchanaburi's history includes a brutal cameo (later promoted to starring) role in WWII. The town was home to a Japanese-run prisoner of war camp, from which Allied soldiers and many others were used to build the notorious Death Railway, linking Bangkok with Burma (now Myanmar). Carving a rail bed out of the 415km stretch of rugged terrain was a brutally ambitious plan by the Japanese, intended to meet an equally remarkable goal of providing an alternative supply route for the Japanese conquest of Burma and other countries to the west. Japanese engineers estimated that the task would take five years to complete. But the railway was completed in a mere 14 months, entirely by forced labour that had little access to either machines or nutrition. A Japanese brothel train inaugurated the line.

Close to 100,000 labourers died as a result of the hard labour, torture or starvation; 13,000 of them were POWs, mainly from Britain, Australia, the Netherlands, New Zealand and America, while the rest were Asians recruited largely from Burma, Thailand and Malaysia. The POWs' story was chronicled in Pierre Boulle's novel *The Bridge on the River Kwai* and later popularised by the movie of the same name. Many visitors come here specifically to pay their respects to the fallen POWs at the Allied cemeteries.

The original bridge was used by the Japanese for 20 months before it was bombed by Allied planes in 1945. As for the railway itself, only the 130km stretch from Bangkok to Nam Tok remains. The rest was either carted off by Karen and Mon tribespeople for use in the construction of local buildings and bridges, recycled by Thai Railways or reclaimed by the jungle.

SLEEPING IN KANCHANABURI

There are lots of budget places along Th Mae Nam Khwae, although standards vary greatly; we've listed our favourite midrange and top-end places below.

➡ **Ploy Guesthouse** (☑0 3451 5804; www.ploygh.com; 79/2 Th Mae Nam Khwae; r 750-1000B; ❄☎) The rooms here don't have views of the adjacent river, but are located in an attractive garden and are stylishly simple. The cheaper rooms lack TV and fridge, but all feature air-con and comfy beds on an elevated platform. There's a single riverside bungalow. Very good value.

➡ **U Inchantree Kanchanaburi** (☑0 3452 1584; www.ukanchanaburi.com; 443 Th Mae Nam Khwae; r/ste incl breakfast 2943/4120B; ❄@☎☒) Granted, the rooms here are pretty small for the price tag, but they're packed with clever amenities (an iPod and wide-screen TV) and the hotel's location, on an attractive bend in Mae Nam Khwae within eyeshot of the famous bridge, is probably the best in town. Located 300m north of the Death Railway Bridge.

➡ **Apple's Retreat** (☑0 3451 2017; www.applenoi-kanchanaburi.com; 153/4 Moo 4, Ban Tamakham; r 490-690B; ❄☎) For a quiet, countryside atmosphere, head to this tidy compound just across Mae Nam Khwae. Staff are helpful, rooms are exceedingly tidy (though they lack TV and fridge) and the one-day Thai cooking courses get good reports. Call for free pick-up from the bus or train station.

KEEREE TARA RESTAURANT   THAI $$

(Th Rong Hip Oi; dishes 45-500B; ⊙11am-11pm) Couple decent Thai food with nightly live music and stunning views of the famous bridge at this, Kanchanaburi's most sophisticated eatery. Located just north of the Death Railway Bridge.

NIGHT MARKET   MARKET $

(Th Saengchuto; dishes 30-60B; ⊙6-11pm) An expansive market featuring everything from Thai-Muslim nosh to *pàt tai* unfolds every night in front of the bus station.

FLOATING RESTAURANTS   THAI $$

(Th Song Khwae; dishes 80-200B; ⊙6-11pm) Down on the river are several large floating restaurants where the quality of the food varies, but it's hard not to enjoy the atmosphere.

SITTHISANG COFFEE SHOP   CAFE

(Th Pak Phraek; ⊙9am-7pm) In a historic yellow-painted shophouse Sitthisang is a cosy cafe with friendly staff and real coffee (from 35B).

RESORT   BAR

(318/2 Th Mae Nam Khwae) A faux-colonial-era veranda bar, the Resort is a favourite for visiting Bangkokians and boasts a nightly live band and attractive outdoor seating.

Khao Yai
เขาใหญ่

Explore

Khao Yai is only about 200km from Bangkok, but the area is best approached as an overnight trip. There are two strategies to doing this, depending on your interests. If you've come for the nature, the logical option is to sleep at the park (or at a guesthouse that provides tours to the park), which can be reached via public transport. If you're looking for a more leisurely weekend getaway of taking in the restaurants, resorts, wineries and other attractions that surround the actual park, you'll need a hire car.

The Best...

➡ **Sight** Khao Yai National Park (p171)
➡ **Place to Eat** Khrua Khao Yai (p172)
➡ **Place to Stay** Hotel des Artists (p172)

Top Tip

The best time to visit the park is in the dry season (December to June), but during the rainy season river rafting and waterfall-spotting will be more dramatic.

Getting There & Away

Travel Time Three hours

Minivan Frequent minivans ply from just north of Bangkok's Victory Monument to Pak Chong (160B, 2½ hours, hourly 6am to 8pm) and, upon request, to Khao Yai National Park (300B).

Bus From Bangkok's Northern & Northeastern Bus Terminal, buses to Khorat (Nakhon Ratchasima) stop in Pak Chong (60B to 70B, about two hours). From Pak Chong, take a *sǒrng · tǎa·ou* (35B, 40 minutes, from 6am to 3pm) to the park entrance. From there, it's another 14km to the visitor centre, which can be reached by hitchhiking or chartering a vehicle (500B).

Hire Car For more freedom, hire a car (p223) and drive.

Need to Know

➤ **Area Code** 044

➤ **Location** 196km northeast of Bangkok

➤ **Tourist Office** (0 3731 2282; tatnayok@tat.or.th; 182/88 Moo 1, Th Suwannason)

◉ SIGHTS

KHAO YAI NATIONAL PARK NATIONAL PARK
(อุทยานแห่งชาติเขาใหญ่; adult/child 400/200B; 8am-4pm) Cool and lush, Khao Yai National Park is an easy escape into the primordial jungle. The 2168-sq-km park, part of a Unesco World Heritage site, spans five forest types, from rainforest to monsoon, and is the primary residence of, among many others, shy tigers and elephants, noisy gibbons, colourful tropical birds and countless audible, yet invisible, insects. Khao Yai is a major birding

destination with large flocks of hornbills and several migrators, including the flycatcher from Europe. Caves in the park are the preferred resting place for wrinkle-lipped bats. In the grasslands, batik-printed butterflies dissect flowers with their surgical tongues.

The park has several accessible trails for self-tours, but birders or animal trackers should consider hiring a jungle guide to increase the appreciation of the environment and to spot more than the tree-swinging gibbons and blood-sucking leeches (the rainy season is the worst time for the latter). In total, there are 12 maintained trails criss-crossing the entire park; not ideal if you want to walk end to end. Access to transport is another reason why a tour might be more convenient, although Thai visitors with cars are usually happy to pick up pedestrians.

A two-hour walk from the **visitor centre** (08 6092 6529; 8am-8pm) leads to the **Nong Pak Chee Observation Tower** (หอส่อง สัตว์หนองผักชี), which is a good early-morning spot for seeing insect-feeding birds, occasional thirsty elephants and sambar deer; make reservations at the visitor centre. It's important to understand that spotting the park's reclusive tigers and elephants is considered a bonus, with most people happy just to admire the frothy waterfalls that drain the peaks of Big Mountain. The park's centrepiece is **Nam Tok Haew Suwat** (น้ำตก เหวสุวัต), a 25m-high cascade that puts on a thundering show in the rainy season. **Nam Tok Haew Narok** (น้ำตกเหวนรก) is its larger cousin with three pooling tiers and a towering 150m drop.

PALIO SHOPPING CENTRE
(www.palio-khaoyai.com; Km 17 Th Thanarat; 10am-7pm Mon-Fri, 9am-9pm Sat-Sun) We can't imagine a more jarring contrast to one

DAY TRIPS FROM BANGKOK KHAO YAI

THAILAND'S NAPA VALLEY

The cool highlands surrounding Khao Yai are also home to a nascent wine industry. These have been dubbed the 'New Latitude' wines because, at between 14 and 18 degrees north, they fall far outside the traditional wine-grape growing latitudes of between 30 and 50 degrees north or south of the equator. **PB Valley Khao Yai Winery** (www.khaoyaiwinery.com; 102 Moo 5, Phaya Yen, Pak Chong; winery day tour incl meal 730-1100B; tours 10.30am, 1.30pm & 3.30pm) and **GranMonte Estate** (www.granmonte.com; 52 Th Phansuk-Kud Khala; tours Sat & Sun) are among the wine makers managing to coax shiraz and chenin blanc grapes from the relatively tropical climate. The wines do seem to improve year by year, though they still have a way to go. Both offer free tastings and GranMonte also has some appealing rooms overlooking the vineyards from 3550B.

SLEEPING IN KHAO YAI

Th Thanarat is home to several midrange to upscale resorts targeted at Thai tourists.

➡ **Hotel des Artists** (✆0 4429 7444; www.hotelartists.com; Km17, Th Thanarat; r/bungalow incl breakfast 4000/6000B; ❄@🔁⛵) Eschewing the Tuscan and jungle themes that seem to define every other resort in the area, this place resembles a French-colonial-era mansion. Expect style, mod cons, mountain views, and by the time you read this, eight new villa-like bungalows.

➡ **Greenleaf Guesthouse** (✆0 4436 5073; www.greenleaftour.com; Km7.5, Th Thanarat; d 200-300B; 🔁) The extremely basic but clean rooms here are virtually the area's only budget option. Greenleaf isn't located near anything of interest, but the folks who run it do half- and full-day tours of Khao Yai National Park.

➡ **Park Lodging** (✆0 2562 0760; www.dnp.go.th/parkreserve; 2-6 person tents 150-400B; r & bungalows 800-3500B) The Department of National Parks provides a range of clean, simple lodgings scattered through the park. It's best to book online, where you can also get more detail on locations and facilities, though bookings are also possible at the information centre.

of the world's premier protected natural areas than this wacky open-air shopping centre. Modelled after a Tuscan village, Palio is indicative of what the Khao Yai area has increasingly become over the last decade: a weekend playground for upper middle-class Thais. Inside, you'll find shops, cafes, bars and hordes of Thais taking photos of each other with digital SLRs. There's plenty to eat, and on weekends, live music until 9pm.

✗ EATING

In recent years, the area surrounding Khao Yai National Park has become a minor culinary destination, with restaurants featuring cuisines ranging from upmarket Italian to Muslim-Thai. The towns that surround the park have lively night markets but if you don't have a car, you'll find restaurants within the park.

KHRUA KHAO YAI INTERNATIONAL-THAI $
(Km 13.5, Th Thanarat; mains 60-150B; ☺9am-8pm Sun-Thu, to 10pm Fri & Sat) This open-air hut is hugely popular with visiting Bangkokians because it serves a hefty menu of satisfying Thai and fa·ràng dishes. The English-language menu is limited, so we

recommend pointing to whatever the table next to you is eating, which is likely to be the delicious home-smoked ham or a mushroom dish. There's no signage in English; Khrua Khao Yai is located roughly halfway between Pak Chong and the entrance to Khao Yai, near the well-posted turn off to Belle Villa and several other resorts.

DAIRY HOME INTERNATIONAL-THAI $
(Km 144, Th Mitraphab/Rte 2; mains 50-300B; ☺9am-8pm) If a weekend of intense jungle exploring or wine tasting has left you with a need for meat, stop by this organic dairy for steak or homemade sausages, or of course, a milky shake or ice cream. Arrive earlier in the day and it also does basic breakfasts and real coffee drinks.

NARKNAVA MUSLIM-THAI $
(Khao Mok Hi So; www.narknavafarm.com; Km 8, Th Phansuk-Kud Khala; mains 50-150B; ☺8am-7pm Tue-Sun) Muslim and even Middle Eastern fare are unexpected cuisines in this neck of the woods, but Narknava is an established favourite for its infamous chicken biryani – infamous, because at 100B it's superexpensive by Thai standards. Unusually, the food is much better than the website images suggest.

🛏 Sleeping

If your idea of the typical Bangkok hotel was influenced by The Hangover Part II, you'll be pleased to learn that the city is home to a diverse spread of modern hostels, guesthouses and hotels. To make matters better, much of Bangkok's accommodation offers excellent value, and competition is so intense that fat discounts are almost always available.

Hostels

Those counting every baht can get a fan-cooled dorm bed (or a closet-like room) with a shared bathroom for between 150B and 300B. The latest trend in Bangkok is slick 'flashpacker' hostels that blur the line between budget and midrange. A bed at these starts at about 500B.

Guesthouses

In Bangkok, this designation usually refers to any sort of budget accommodation rather than a room in a family home, although we use it to describe the latter. Guesthouses are generally found in somewhat inconveniently located corners of old Bangkok (Banglamphu, Chinatown and Thewet), which means that the money you're saving in rent will probably go for taxi fares. Rates begin at about 600B.

Hotels

Bangkok's midrange hotels often have all the appearance of a Western-style hotel, but without the predictability. If you're on a lower-midrange budget, and don't care much about aesthetics, some very acceptable rooms can be had for between 1500B and 2000B. If your budget is higher, it really pays to book ahead, as online discounts here can be substantial. You'll find several midrange hotels at lower Th Sukhumvit and in Banglamphu.

Luxury, Business & Boutique Hotels

Bangkok is home to a huge number of hotels ranging from boutique (small but cosy) to luxury (big and brash). Most hotels of this type are located on Th Sukhumvit and Th Silom, or along the Chao Phraya River. Rooms start between 6000B and 9000B before hefty online discounts.

Amenities

Wi-fi is nearly universal across the spectrum, but air-conditioning and lifts are not.

BUDGET

The cheapest hostels and guesthouses often share bathrooms and may not even supply a towel. Many will be fan-cooled or will only run the air-con between certain hours. Wi-fi, if available, is often free. Breakfast at most Bangkok hostels and budget hotels is little more than instant coffee and white bread.

MIDRANGE

Increasingly, midrange has come to mean a room with air-con, a fridge, hot water, wi-fi and TV. It's not uncommon for a room to boast all of these but lack a view, or even windows. Breakfast can range from 'buffets' based around white bread and oily fried eggs to more thoughtful meals involving yoghurt or tropical fruit.

TOP END

Top-end hotels in Bangkok supply all the amenities you'd expect. The more thoughtful places have amenities such as en suite computers and free wi-fi; otherwise, expect to pay a premium for the privilege. In sweaty Bangkok, pools are almost standard, not to mention fitness and business centres, restaurants and bars. Breakfast is often buffet-style.

NEED TO KNOW

Price Ranges

Accommodation in this book is broken down into three categories. We've listed high-season walk-in rates, excluding the 'plus-plus' that most top-end places charge, which in Thailand is made up of 10% service and 7% government tax.

$ less than 1000B a night

$$ 1000B to 3000B a night

$$$ more than 3000B a night

Accommodation Websites

The best time for discounts is outside of Bangkok's peak seasons, which are November to March and July and August.
Lonely Planet's Hotels & Hostels (www.hotels.lonelyplanet.com) Find reviews and make bookings.
Travelfish (www.travelfish.org) Independent reviews with lots of reader feedback.

Lonely Planet's Top Choices

Siam Heritage (p181) Homey touches and warm service make this the closest you may come to sleeping in a Thai home.

AriyasomVilla (p183) Sumptuous refurbished villa with a classy B&B vibe.

Arun Residence (p176) The best river views in town; the funky, loft-like rooms aren't too shabby, either.

Phra-Nakorn Norn-Len (p178) An artsy, fun hotel compound in a refreshingly untouristed 'hood.

Lamphu Treehouse (p176) Cheerful budget vibe meets top-end quality at a midrange price.

Best by Budget

$
Lub*d (p179)
NapPark Hostel (p179)
Sam Sen Sam Place (p179)
Suk 11 (p185)
Fortville Guesthouse (p177)

$$
Napa Place (p185)
72 Ekamai (p184)
Baan Dinso (p179)
Rose Hotel (p182)
Swan Hotel (p181)

$$$
Metropolitan (p181)
Mandarin Oriental (p181)
Peninsula Hotel (p181)
Bhuthorn (p176)
Eugenia (p184)

Best for Romantics

Old Bangkok Inn (p176)
Mandarin Oriental (p181)
Baan Pra Nond (p182)
Heritage Baan Silom (p182)

Best Contemporary Cool

Metropolitan (p181)
Siam@Siam (p178)
Ma Du Zi (p184)
LUXX XL (p180)
72 Ekamai (p184)
Refill Now! (p187)

Best Affordable Luxury

Hansar (p180)
Silq (p187)
Shangri-La Hotel (p181)
Aurum: The River Place (p176)

Best Artsy Stays

Mystic Place (p188)
Lit (p180)
Diamond House (p176)
Seven (p185)
Shanghai Mansion (p178)

Best Rooms with Views

Peninsula Hotel (p181)
Millennium Hilton (p182)
Navalai River Resort (p177)
Le Meridien Bangkok (p182)

Best for Time Travel

Bhuthorn (p176)
Praya Palazzo (p177)
Hotel Muse (p180)
Eugenia (p184)
Chakrabongse Villas (p176)

Where to Stay

Neighbourhood	For	Against
Historical Centre: Ko Ratanakosin & Thonburi	Bangkok's most famous sights at your door; occasional river views; (relatively) fresh air; old-school Bangkok feel.	Difficult to reach; few budget options; lack of dining and drinking venues; touts.
Old Bangkok: Banglamphu	Close to main sights; proximity to a classic Bangkok 'hood; lots of good-value budget beds; fun, intergalactic melting-pot feel; virtually interminable dining options; one of the city's best nightlife areas.	Getting to and from the area can be troublesome; Th Khao San can be noisy and rowdy; budget places can have low standards; relentless touts.
Dusit Palace Park & Around: Thewet & Dusit	Good budget options; riverside village feel; fresh air; close to a handful of visit-worthy sights.	Few midrange and upscale options; not very convenient access to rest of Bangkok; relatively few dining and drinking options; comatose at night.
Chinatown	Some interesting budget and midrange options; off the beaten track; easy access to worthwhile sights and some of the city's best food; close to Bangkok's main train station.	Noisy; polluted; touts; hectic; few non-eating-related nightlife options; access to rest of Bangkok not very convenient.
Shopping District: Siam Square, Pratunam, Ploenchit & Ratchathewi	Wide spread of accommodation alternatives; mega-convenient access to shopping (and air-conditioning); steps away from BTS.	Touts; un-pristine environment; relative lack of dining and entertainment options in immediate area; lacks character.
Riverside, Silom & Lumphini	Some of the city's best upscale accommodation; river boats and river views; super-convenient access to BTS and MRT; lots of dining and nightlife options; gay-friendly.	Can be noisy and polluted; budget options can be pretty dire; hyper-urban feel away from the river.
New Bangkok: Thanon Sukhumvit	Some of city's most sophisticated hotels; lots of midrange options; easy access to BTS and MRT; international dining; easy access to some of the city's best bars; home to to several reputable spas and massage parlours.	Annoying street vendors and sexpat vibe; noisy; hyper-touristy.
Greater Bangkok	Less hectic setting; good value; depending on location, convenient airport access.	Transportation can be inconvenient; lack of drinking and entertainment options.

SLEEPING

🛏 Ko Ratanakosin & Thonburi

TOP CHOICE ARUN RESIDENCE BOUTIQUE HOTEL $$$

Map p252 (📞0 2221 9158; www.arunresidence. com; 36-38 Soi Pratu Nokyung; incl breakfast r 4000-4200B, ste 5800B; ✳@🛜; 🚤Tha Tien) Although strategically located across from Wat Arun, this multilevel wooden house on the river boasts much more than just brilliant views. The six rooms here manage to feel both homey and stylish, some being tall and loftlike, while others join two rooms (the best is the top-floor Arun Suite, with its own balcony). There are also inviting communal areas, including a library, rooftop bar and restaurant. Reservations essential.

CHAKRABONGSE VILLAS BOUTIQUE HOTEL $$$

Map p252 (📞0 2622 3356; www.thaivillas.com; 396/1 Th Maha Rat; incl breakfast r 5000B, ste 10,000-40,000B; ✳@🏊; 🚤Tha Tien) The grounds of Prince Chakrabongse Bhuvanath's 19th-century mansion have been adapted to become one of the city's classiest, most discreet boutique properties. The compound incorporates three sumptuous but cramped rooms and six larger suites and villas. The best pick are those nearer to the river, which combine a modern Zen feel with luxuries in Thai and Chinese styles. There's a pool, jungle-like gardens and an elevated deck for romantic riverside dining.

AURUM: THE RIVER PLACE BOUTIQUE HOTEL $$$

Map p252 (📞0 2622 2248; www.aurum-bangkok. com; 394/27-29 Soi Pansook; r incl breakfast 3700-4600B; ✳@🛜; 🚤Tha Tien) At the river end of a row of old Chinese warehouses, the Aurum manages to feel homey despite its rather ostentatious faux-Parisian facade. The 12 tastefully furnished rooms are by no means big, but the windows are, and they make the most of the not-wholly-uninterrupted river views. Breakfast is included, though there's a riverside cafe right next door.

🛏 Banglamphu

TOP CHOICE LAMPHU TREEHOUSE HOTEL $$

Map p254 (📞0 2282 0991; www.lamphutree hotel.com; 155 Wanchat Bridge, Th Prachatipatai; r incl breakfast 1500-3000B; ✳@🛜🏊; 🚤Tha Phan Fah) Despite the name, this very attractive midranger has its feet firmly on land, and as such represents brilliant value. The wood-panelled rooms are attractive and inviting, and the rooftop bar, pool, internet cafe, restaurant and quiet canal-side location ensure that you may never feel the need to leave. A new annexe a couple blocks away increases your odds of snagging an elusive reservation. Highly recommended.

OLD BANGKOK INN BOUTIQUE HOTEL $$$

Map p254 (📞0 2629 1787; www.oldbangkokinn. com; 609 Th Phra Sumen; r incl breakfast 3190-6590B; ✳@🛜; 🚤Tha Phan Fah) Occupying several adjoining shophouses that were once a neighbourhood noodle restaurant, this boutique hotel is now pleasingly decorated in colours that conjure up visions of desserts: crème-caramel walls, dark-cocoa furnishings, persimmon silk bedspreads and flowing white mosquito nets. The 10 rooms occupy unconventional and sometimes cramped spaces, but are all done with class and style, and the enduring vibe is that of the perfect honeymoon hotel.

DIAMOND HOUSE BOUTIQUE HOTEL $$

Map p254 (📞0 2629 4008; www.thaidiamond house.com; 4 Th Samsen; r/ste 2000-2800/3600; ✳@🛜; 🚤Tha Phra Athit (Banglamphu)) Despite sharing real estate with a rather brash Chinese temple, there's no conflict of design at this eccentric, funky hotel. Most rooms are loft-style, with beds on raised platforms, and are outfitted with stained glass, dark, lush colours and chic furnishings. There's a lack of windows, and some of the suites aren't that much larger than the cheaper rooms, but a rooftop sunbathing deck and an outdoor jacuzzi make up for this. Generous online rates are available.

BHUTHORN BOUTIQUE HOTEL $$$

Map p254 (📞0 2622 2270; thebhuthorn.com; 96-98 Th Phraeng Bhuthon; r incl breakfast 3600-5000B; ✳@🛜; 🚤Tha Phan Fah) Travel a century back in time by booking one of the three rooms in this beautiful antique shophouse located in a classic Bangkok neighbourhood. They're not particularly huge, but are big on atmosphere and boast classic touches such as four-poster beds, antique cupboards and lamps, old photographs and Arabesque prints, not to mention modern amenities such as flat-screen TVs, DVD players and free wi-fi. The corner 'Bhuthorn' room is the best pick.

FORTVILLE GUESTHOUSE BUDGET HOTEL $

Map p254 (☑0 2282 3932; www.fortvilleguest house.com; 9 Th Phra Sumen; r 720-1050B; ❄@🛜; 🚢Tha Phra Athit (Banglamphu)) With an exterior that combines elements of a modern church and/or castle and an interior that relies on mirrors and industrial themes, the design concept of this unique new hotel is tough to pin down. Rooms are small, but the more expensive ones include perks such as a fridge, balcony and free wi-fi. A quirky, stylish good value hotel.

HOTEL DÉ MOC HOTEL $$$

Map p254 (☑0 2282 2831; www.hoteldemoc. com; 78 Th Prachathipatai; r incl breakfast 3000-3500B; ❄@🛜⛲; 🚢Tha Phan Fah) The rooms at this classic, '60s-era hotel are large, with high ceilings and generous windows and balconies, although it must be noted that a recent renovation failed to purge all of the less-desirable original furnishings. That said, we really do like the funky, breezy feel of the place, and complimentary transport to Th Khao San and free bike rental are thoughtful perks. Avoid inflated rack rates by booking online.

SOURIRE BOUTIQUE HOTEL $$

Map p254 (☑0 2280 2180; www.sourirebangkok. com; Soi Chao Phraya Si Phiphat; r incl breakfast 1500-3500B; ❄@🛜; 🚢Tha Phan Fah) More home than hotel, the 38 rooms here exude a calming, matronly feel. Soft lighting, comfortable, sturdy wood furniture and the friendly, aged owners round out the package. To reach the hotel, follow Soi Chao Phraya Si Phiphat to the end and knock on the tall, brown wooden door immediately on your left.

PRAYA PALAZZO BOUTIQUE HOTEL $$$

(☑0 2883 2998; www.prayapalazzo.com; 757/1 Somdej Prapinklao Soi 2; r/ste incl breakfast 6000-11,900/16,500-26,500B; ❄🛜⛲; 🚢from Tha Phra Athit/Banglamphu) After lying dormant for nearly 30 years, this elegant 19th-century mansion has been reborn as an attractive riverside boutique hotel. The 17 rooms can feel rather tight and river views can be elusive, but the meticulous renovation, handsome antique furnishings and bucolic atmosphere convene in a hotel with genuine old-world charm. Praya Palazzo is located on the Thonburi side of the river, roughly across from Tha Phra Athit.

FEUNG NAKORN BALCONY HOTEL $$

Map p254 (☑0 2622 1100; www.feungnakorn. com; 125 Th Fuang Nakhon; incl breakfast dm 700B, r 1800-2500B, ste 3500-4200B; ❄@🛜; 🚢Tha Phan Fah) Located in a former school, the 42 rooms here surround an inviting garden courtyard and are large, bright and cheery, if still retaining slight reminders of the classrooms they used to be. Amenities such as a free minibar, safe and flat-screen TV come standard, and it has a quiet and secluded location away from the strip and capable staff. A charming if not extremely great-value place to stay.

NAVALAI RIVER RESORT HOTEL $$$

Map p254 (☑0 2280 9955; www.navalai.com; 45/1 Th Phra Athit; r incl breakfast 2900-4800B; ❄@🛜⛲; 🚢Tha Phra Athit (Banglamphu)) Perched between the banks of Mae Nam Chao Phraya and arty Th Phra Athit, this busy 74-room boutique hotel delivers on location, style and space. The rooms are big, have cheeky peep-show bathrooms and are decorated in an edgy-if-not-wild range of colours and artworks to complement sweeping river views. Upping the ante are the rooftop pool and riverside restaurant.

BUDDY BOUTIQUE HOTEL HOTEL $$$

Map p254 (☑0 2629 4477; www.buddylodge.com; 256 Th Khao San; r incl breakfast 4000-4500B; ❄@🛜⛲; 🚢Tha Phra Athit (Bangamphu)) This gigantic complex, which includes a pool, fitness room and, ahem, a branch of McDonald's, is – as far as we're aware – the most expensive place to stay on Th Khao San. Correspondingly, rooms are comfortable, well equipped and evocative of a breezy, tropical manor house. Wi-fi is 60B an hour; non-guests can use the pool for 200B.

NEW SIAM RIVERSIDE HOTEL $$

Map p254 (☑0 2629 3535; www.newsiam.net; 21 Th Phra Athit; r incl breakfast 1390-2990B; ❄@⛲; 🚢Tha Phra Athit (Banglamphu)) One of a couple of newish places along Th Phra Athit taking advantage of the riverside setting, this hotel has comfortable rooms with tiny bathrooms. But the real value comes from the amenities (internet, travel agent, restaurant) and the location on one of the city's more pleasant streets. Book ahead.

VILLA CHA-CHA HOTEL $$

Map p254 (☑0 2280 1025; www.villachacha.com; 36 Th Tani; r 1000-3200B; ❄@🛜⛲; 🚢Tha Phra Athit (Banglamphu)) Wind your way between

Balinese statues, lounging residents, a rambling restaurant and a tiny pool to emerge at this seemingly hidden, but popular, hotel. Rooms are capable – bar the clumsy stabs made at interior design (think topless portraits) – but the real draw is the super-social, resort-like atmosphere.

PANNEE RESIDENCE HOTEL $$

Map p254 (📞0 2629 4560; 117 Th Din So; incl breakfast s 880B, d 1200-1360B; ❋@🛜; 🚤Tha Phan Fah) Pannee is a new multistorey hotel offering tidy, if somewhat character-anaemic, rooms. The cheapest rooms are pretty tiny, but like all the others include a safe, TV and fridge. An upper-floor patio with outdoor rain showers and daybeds for sunbathing provides a bit more room to stretch, and convenient proximity to Bangkok's big sights makes the decision easy.

🛏 Thewet & Dusit

🔝CHOICE PHRA-NAKORN
NORN-LEN BOUTIQUE HOTEL $$

Map p257 (📞0 2628 8188; www.phranakorn-nornlen.com; 46 Soi Thewet 1; incl breakfast s 1800B, d 2200-2400B, tr 3600B; ❋@🛜; 🚤Tha Thewet) Set in an expansive garden compound decorated like the Bangkok of yesteryear, this bright and cheery hotel is a hyper-atmospheric – if not necessarily great-value – place to stay. Rooms come with a minimum of functional furniture, but are generously decorated with vintage bits and bobs and floor-to-ceiling wall paintings. Communal facilities include a living room, restaurant/ cafe, and a children's play room; breakfast is vegetarian and massage is offered.

SHANTI LODGE BUDGET HOTEL $

Map p257 (📞0 2281 2497; www.shantilodge. com; 37 Th Si Ayuthaya; dm 200B, r 300-1950B; ❋@🛜; 🚤Tha Thewet) Shanti Lodge is the sort of place where you might find barefooted backpackers engaging in long, languid conversations about the philosophy of travel and their dislike of Th Khao San, while a fellow backpacker strums a guitar and waits for fresh coffee. The dark corridors lead to surprisingly bright rooms, which are made even livelier by myriad colours, and bathrooms decked out in psychedelic tiles and stones. But it's the blissed-out garden cafe downstairs where you'll spend most of your time.

🛏 Chinatown

SHANGHAI MANSION BOUTIQUE HOTEL $$

Map p258 (📞0 2221 2121; www.shanghaimansion.com; 479-481 Th Yaowarat; r 2000-3000B, ste 4000B; ❋@🛜; Ⓜ Hua Lamphong exit 1 & taxi; 🚤Tha Ratchawong) Shanghai Mansion is easily the most consciously stylish place to stay in Chinatown, if not in all of Bangkok. This award-winning boutique hotel screams China c 1935 via stained glass, an abundance of lamps, bold colours and tongue-in-cheek Chinatown kitsch. If you're willing to splurge, ask for one of the bigger, street-side rooms, with tall windows that allow more natural light.

BAAN HUALAMPONG GUESTHOUSE $

Map p258 (📞0 2639 8054; www.baanhualampong.com; 336/20-21 Trok Chalong Krung; incl breakfast dm 250B, r 290-800B; ❋@🛜; Ⓜ Hua Lamphong exit 1) Off a quiet soi a brief walk from the station, this old-style wood-and-concrete guesthouse has developed a loyal following among those seeking a mix of family atmosphere and backpacker self-sufficiency. The tiny rooftop garden is a great place to get to know your baan-mates over a sundowner – you'll probably spend more time there and in the ground-floor communal space than in the simple rooms.

SIAM CLASSIC GUESTHOUSE $

Map p258 (📞0 2639 6363; www.siamclassic-hostel.com; 336/10 Trok Chalong Krung; r 450-1400B; ❋@🛜; Ⓜ Hua Lamphong exit 1) This homey-feeling place is just across the street from Bangkok's main train station. Rooms here are relatively bare, but exceedingly tidy, and a genuine effort has been made at making them feel comfortable. An inviting ground-floor communal area encourages meeting and chatting.

🛏 Siam Square, Pratunam, Ploenchit & Ratchathewi

SIAM@SIAM BOUTIQUE HOTEL $$$

Map p260 (📞0 2217 3000; www.siamatsiam.com; 865 Th Phra Ram I; r incl breakfast 4750-8000B; ❋@🛜🏊; 🚈National Stadium exit 1) Siam@ Siam has taken the concept of industrial design pretty much as far as it can go. Wire sculptures stand on polished concrete and railway sleepers cover every exposed pylon – thanks to a thoughtful design and liberal

BATHROOMLESS IN BANGKOK

If you don't require your own en suite bathroom, Bangkok has heaps of options for you, ranging from hi-tech dorm beds in a brand new hostel to private bedrooms in a hundred-year-old wooden house. Some of our picks:

Lub*d (Map p260; ✆0 2634 7999; www.lubd.com; Th Pha Ram I; dm 550-600B, r 1400-2000B; ✳@⧂; ⧆National Stadium exit 1) The title is a play on the Thai *làp dee,* meaning 'sleep well', but the fun atmosphere at this bright new backpacker hostel might make you want to stay up all night. There are 14 dorm rooms (including eight ladies-only dorms) here, each with only four beds, and a few private rooms, both with and without bathrooms. There's an inviting communal area stocked with free internet, games and a bar, and thoughtful facilities ranging from washing machines to a theatre room. If this one's full, there's another branch just off **Th Silom** (Map p264; ✆0 2634 7999; www.lubd.com; 4 Th Decho, Th Surawong; dm 370-450B, r 1050-1550B; ✳@⧂; ⧆Chong Nonsi exit 2).

NapPark Hostel (Map p254; ✆0 2282 2324; www.nappark.com; 8 Th Tani; dm 480-650B; ✳@⧂; ⧅Tha Phra Athit (Banglamphu)) This exceedingly well-run hostel features dorm rooms of various sizes, the smallest and most expensive of which boasts six pod-like beds outfitted with power points, mini-TV, reading lamp and wi-fi. Daily cultural-based activities, including bike trips and volunteer opportunities, and inviting communal areas ensure that you may not actually get the chance to plug in.

Baan Dinso (Map p254; ✆0 2622 0560; www.baandinso.com; 113 Trok Sin; r incl breakfast 1200-2900B; ✳@⧂; ⧅Tha Phan Fah) The four cheapest rooms in this beautiful and award-winning antique wooden villa share a row of exceedingly tidy bathrooms. If exploring the classic Bangkok neighbourhood doesn't appeal, there's a basement-level communal area with TV, DVD, computers, books, games and a fridge. It's not the best value in Bangkok, but for accommodation with a homey feel and palpable sense of place, it's almost impossible to beat.

HQ Hostel (Map p264; ✆0 2233 1598; www.hqhostel.com; 5/3-4 Soi 3, Th Silom; dm/r 380-599/1300-1700B; ✳@⧂; ⧆Sala Daeng, Si Lom) HQ is a flashpacker hostel in the polished-concrete-and-industrial-style mould. It includes four- to 10-bed dorms, a few doubles and inviting communal areas in a narrow multistorey building in the middle of Bangkok's financial district.

Sam Sen Sam Place (Map p257; ✆0 2628 7067; www.samsensam.com; 48 Soi 3, Th Samsen; r incl breakfast 590-2400B; ✳@⧂; ⧅Tha Phra Athit (Banglamphu)) Built almost a hundred years ago and once part of a nursery, this welcoming guesthouse is now a palette of pastels, with 17 rooms sharing names and colours with grapes, bananas, kiwis, peaches and strawberries, among others. The smallest rooms share bathrooms, but all have polished floorboards and teak furnishings.

Niras Bankoc (Map p254; ✆0 2221 4442; www.nirasbankoc.com; 204-208 Th Mahachai; dm 400B, r 1000-1700B; ✳@⧂; ⧅Tha Phan Fah) The rooms in this beautifully refurbished shophouse tend to lack windows and aren't amazing value, but the dorms, which share recently refurbished bathrooms, are worth considering. A downstairs cafe and cozy communal area provide a bit more leg space.

Shambara (Map p254; ✆0 2282 7968; www.shambarabangkok.com; 138 Th Khao San; r 300-700B; ✳@⧂; ⧅Tha Phra Athit (Banglamphu)) Just 50m from the noise and neon of Khao San, Shambara feels a world away. The century-old traditional wooden home has nine tiny but appealing rooms that share two clean showers and toilets. Price includes coffee and toast; wi-fi is 50B per day.

Lamphu House (Map p254; ✆0 2629 5861; www.lamphuhouse.com; 75-77 Soi Ram Buttri; r 200-950B; ✳@⧂; ⧅Tha Phra Athit (Banglamphu)) A refreshing oasis, Lamphu House creates a mellow mood with its hidden, relatively quiet location and service that is more personal thazn that of some of its neighbours. Rooms are clean, and some have balconies overlooking the green courtyard; cheaper fan rooms with shared bathrooms are also available.

SLEEPING

splashes of warm, earthy tones, it works. The 203 rooms occupy the 14th to 25th floors; they're not huge, but all have city views and are well equipped. Ask for one overlooking the National Stadium.

HANSAR
BOUTIQUE HOTEL **$$$**

Map p260 (✆0 2209 1234; www.hansarbangkok. com; 3 Soi Mahadlekluang 2, Th Ratchadamri; r incl breakfast 5500-24,000B; ✳@🛜❄; 🚆Ratchadamri exit 4) The brand-new Hansar can claim that elusive intersection of style and value. All 94 rooms here are handsome and feature huge bathrooms and giant desks, but the smallest (and cheapest) studios are probably the best deal, as they have a kitchenette, washing machine, stand-alone tub, free wi-fi and balcony. Located a short walk from BTS Ratchadamri.

HOTEL MUSE
BOUTIQUE HOTEL **$$$**

Map p260 (✆0 2630 4000; www.hotelmusebang kok.com; 55/555 Soi Lang Suan; incl breakfast r 5500-6300B; ste 11,500-35,500B; ✳@🛜❄; 🚆Ratchadamri exit 2) Gaining inspiration from the golden era of travel of the late-19th century, this new hotel straddles the past and the present. Rooms feel dark and decadent – the vibe set by the faux-antique furniture, textured wallpaper and clawfoot tubs – but also feature modern amenities and great city views. It's run by Accor, so the service is on par with the surroundings.

FOUR SEASONS HOTEL
LUXURY HOTEL **$$$**

Map p260 (✆0 2126 8866; www.fourseasons. com/bangkok; 155 Th Ratchadamri; r 7300-23,100B; ste 27,300-82,950B; ✳@🛜❄; 🚆Ratchadamri exit 4) A spectacular mural descending a grand staircase, ceilings adorned with neck-craning artwork…the initial classy impression continues into rooms here, which combine Thai elements with heavy hardwood furniture and modern yet subtle amenities. If you've got deep pockets, consider the two-room Explorers Suite, decked out with beautiful swathes of Jim Thompson Thai silk. This being a Four Seasons hotel, you can rest assured that service is first-rate.

LUXX XL
BOUTIQUE HOTEL **$$$**

Map p260 (✆0 2684 1111; www.staywithluxx.com; 82/8 Soi Lang Suan; incl breakfast r 2500-7000B, ste 13,000-22,000B; ✳@🛜❄; 🚆Ratchadamri exit 2) LUXX XL is indeed extra-large compared with the original 13-room LUXX hotel near Th Silom, but aside from the

4m-high front door it appeals more for its minimalist style than its size. The 50 rooms range from 33-sq-metre studios to suites three times that size. Teak dominates the decor, with wooden floors and furniture and elegantly simple corrugated wainscoting accompanied by open bathrooms, flatscreen TVs, DVD players and free wi-fi. The rack rates are extra large, too – be sure to book online.

LIT
HOTEL **$$$**

Map p260 (✆0 2612 3456; www.litbangkok.com; 36/1 Soi Kasem San 1; r incl breakfast 7000-10,000B; ✳@🛜❄; 🚆National Stadium exit 1) This architecturally striking new hotel has a variety of room styles united by a light theme. Check out a few, as they vary significantly – some features, including a shower that can be seen from the living room, aren't necessarily for everybody. Try the website for online discounts.

WENDY HOUSE
HOSTEL **$$**

Map p260 (✆0 2214 1149; www.wendyguest house.com; 36/2 Soi Kasem San 1; incl breakfast s 900B, d 1050-1200B; ✳@🛜; 🚆National Stadium exit 1) Wendy is a cheery backpacker joint with small but well-scrubbed rooms and tiled bathrooms. Desk staff are sweet and really try hard, while the well-lit lobby is the sort of place where you're likely to end up swapping stories with fellow travellers. Breakfast is included and the wi-fi is free.

PULLMAN BANGKOK
KING POWER
BUSINESS HOTEL **$$$**

Map p263 (✆0 2680 9999; www.pullmanbang kokkingpower.com; 8/2 Th Rang Nam; incl breakfast r 3860-4330B, ste 6800-7275B; ✳@🛜❄; 🚆Victory Monument exit 2) The Pullman is a great choice for those who want to stay in a business-class hotel but would rather not stay downtown. Rooms are smart and modern, and the Pullman's restaurants are among the best-value Western dining options in town. Located a brief walk from the BTS stop at Victory Monument.

RENO HOTEL
HOTEL **$$**

Map p260 (✆0 2215 0026; www.renohotel.co.th; 40 Soi Kasem San 1; r incl breakfast 1280-2150B; ✳@🛜❄; 🚆National Stadium exit 1) This Vietnam War veteran has embraced the 21st century with colour and flair, making the best of its retro features (check out the monogrammed pool) and funking up the foyer and cafe, in particular. The 58 rooms remain fairly simple, the best being those with a balcony overlooking the pool. Service can be reluctant, but for a midrange choice strategically located within striking distance of the shopping, the Reno delivers.

VIP GUEST HOUSE/ GOLDEN HOUSE
HOTEL **$$**

Map p260 (☑0 2252 9535; www.goldenhouses. net; 1025/5-9 Th Ploenchit; r incl breakfast 1800-2000B; ✴@✿; ⬛Chit Lom exit 1) The 27 clean, quiet and mainly bright rooms make this a decent midrange choice in this otherwise pricey part of town. Rooms vary, so ask to see more than one.

🛏 Riverside, Silom & Lumphini

TOP CHOICE **SIAM HERITAGE**
BOUTIQUE HOTEL **$$$**

Map p264 (☑0 2353 6101; www.thesiamherit age.com; 115/1 Th Surawong; incl breakfast r 2700B, ste 3300-8200B; ✴@✿; ⬛Sala Daeng exit 1, ⓂSi Lom exit 2) Tucked off busy Th Surawong, this classy boutique hotel oozes with homey Thai charm – most likely because the owners also live in the same building. The 73 rooms are decked out in silk and dark woods with genuinely thoughtful design touches, not to mention considerate amenities. There's an inviting rooftop garden/pool/spa, which, like the rest of the hotel, is looked after by a team of charming and professional staff. Highly recommended.

METROPOLITAN
HOTEL **$$$**

Map p268 (☑0 2625 3333; www.metropolitan. bangkok.como.bz; 27 Th Sathon Tai; incl breakfast r 8500-10,500B; ste 11,500-78,000B; ✴@✿; ⓂLumphini exit 2) The very essence of urban cool, the Metropolitan was reborn from the ashes of – wait for it – a YMCA. The techno-cool lobby sets the tone for sleek, modern rooms with sexy furniture and earthy tones. But the ghost of hostels past is still apparent in the cramped City rooms, though the bathrooms remain big enough for rock-star primping. Studio rooms are more humane, and the two-storey suites are the ultimate in expansive, expensive luxury. An impending renovation at the time of research should see all rooms having been given a facelift by the time you read this.

MANDARIN ORIENTAL
LUXURY HOTEL **$$$**

Map p266 (☑0 2659 9000; www.mandarin oriental.com/bangkok; 48 Soi 40/Oriental, Th Charoen Krung; r 15,000-26,000B; ste 26,000-150,000B; ✴@✿❆; ⬛hotel shuttle boat from Tha Sathon/Central Pier) Dating to 1876, the Oriental Hotel is one of Southeast Asia's grand colonial-era hotels and one of the most luxurious and respected in the region. The management prides itself on highly personalised service – once you've stayed here the staff will remember your name and what you like to eat for breakfast. The majority of the 393 rooms are in the more modern River and Tower wings, but we prefer the original Authors' Wing, with its larger rooms and palpable sense of history.

SWAN HOTEL
HOTEL **$$**

Map p266 (☑0 2235 9271; www.swanhotelbkk. com; 31 Soi 36, Th Charoen Krung; r incl breakfast 1200-2000B; ✴@✿❆; ⬛Tha Oriental) Hidden among shade trees and quiet riverside lanes, the Swan Hotel has been around almost long enough (nearly 50 years) to have earned its own place in the lore of this historic neighbourhood. The 67 rooms are clean, bright and airy, with decor that is very clearly original but remains in good condition. But the main attractions are the delightful pool and surrounding garden that most rooms look onto, and the excellent value for this area. Wi-fi is 300B a day; rooms are 20% cheaper online.

PENINSULA HOTEL
LUXURY HOTEL **$$$**

Map p266 (☑0 2861 2888; www.peninsula.com; 333 Th Charoen Nakhon, Thonburi; r 14,000-15,000B; ste 20,000-102,000B; ✴@✿❆; ⬛hotel shuttle boat from Tha Sathon (Central Pier)) The Peninsula's location, style, dependable-but-unpretentious service and pure class make it one of Bangkok's top hotels. Being on the Thonburi side of the river, the hotel enjoys views of both the river and the skyline beyond – an incandescent combination so picturesque it can sear a sultry sunset into the mind forever. The 370 rooms are larger than most in town and boast heaps of clever techie comforts, such as a TV in the bathroom and a clever shoeshine box.

SHANGRI-LA HOTEL
HOTEL **$$$**

Map p266 (☑0 2236 7777; www.shangri-la.com; 89 Soi 42/1/Wat Suan Phlu; r 7900-10,300B; ste 10,300-105,000B; ✴@✿❆; ⬛Saphan Taksin exit 1) A recent renovation has this riverside, resort-feeling hotel looking much younger than its nearly 30 years. An understated, New Asia aesthetic dominates in the main wing, where the curved sides ensure everyone gets a river view; rooms in the Krungthep Wing are older and slightly less chic, but have low-rise terraces overlooking the river. It's within the luxury sphere, yet families won't feel like bulls in a china shop and compared with its neighbours it's positively cheap.

MILLENNIUM HILTON HOTEL $$$

Map p266 (☎0 2442 2000; www.bangkok.hilton. com; 123 Th Charoen Nakorn, Thonburi; r 8000-9800B, ste 10,400-33,000B; ✳@☕≈; ⛴hotel shuttle boat from Tha Sathon (Central Pier)) As soon as you enter the dramatic lobby, it's obvious that this is Bangkok's youngest-feeling, most modern riverside hotel. Rooms, all of which boast widescreen river views, carry on the theme and are decked out with funky furniture and Thai-themed photos. A glass elevator and an artificial beach are just some of the fun touches. Discounts are available for longer stays and for booking three weeks ahead.

BAAN PRA NOND BOUTIQUE HOTEL $$$

Map p264 (☎0 2212 2242; www.baanpranond. com; 18/1 Th Charoen Rat; r incl breakfast 3100-5400; ✳@☕≈; ⊟Surasak exit 2) The nine small-but-bright rooms in two yellow-washed colonial-style villas feature classic 1930s decor: floor tiles, four-poster beds, overhead fans, wind-up alarm clocks and crisp white linen. The ground floor boasts a communal space that is perfect for chatting with helpful hosts Tasma and Jason; there's a pint-sized pool in the courtyard. This would be one of our favourite places in town if it weren't for its characterless location between two noisy roads.

LE MERIDIEN BANGKOK HOTEL $$$

Map p264 (☎0 2232 8888; www.lemeridien. com/bangkoksurawong; 40/5 Th Surawong; r 6000-8000B, ste 15,000-29,000B; ✳@☕≈; ⊟Sala Daeng exit 1, Ⓜ Si Lom exit 2) The look at this new, design-oriented hotel is modern Asian, with bamboo, dark timber and earthy colours delivered in clean lines throughout the 282 rooms and edgy restaurants. The location is convenient, if somewhat hectic, and floor-to-ceiling windows ensure uninterrupted views of the Patpong action and make the rooms seem bigger than they are.

TRIPLE TWO SILOM BOUTIQUE HOTEL $$$

Map p264 (☎0 2627 2222; www.tripletwosi lom.com; 222 Th Silom; r/ste incl breakfast 3800/5500B; ✳@☕; ⊟Chong Nonsi exit 3) Rooms here resemble sleek modern offices – in a good way. But don't worry, with huge bathrooms and inviting-looking beds, you'll be inspired to relax, not work. Guests can use the rooftop garden, but have to go next door to the sister Narai Hotel for the swimming pool and fitness centre.

HERITAGE BAAN SILOM BOUTIQUE HOTEL $$

Map p264 (☎0 2236 8388; www.theheritage baansilom.com; 669 Soi 19, Th Silom, Baan Silom Shopping Centre; r incl breakfast 2100-3400B; ✳@☕; ⊟Surasak exit 3) Tucked behind a 'lifestyle arcade' (ie shopping centre), this wannabe top-ender is a modern interpretation of an English colonial-era mansion. Carefully designed with attractive wood and wicker furnishings, the rooms here are bright and airy, each featuring a different colour theme and custom wall prints.

SUKHOTHAI HOTEL HOTEL $$$

Map p268 (☎0 2344 8888; www.sukhothai.com; 13/3 Th Sathon Tai; r 11,000-14,000B, ste 15,000-90,000B; ✳@☕≈; Ⓜ Lumphini exit 2) If you're sick of cookie-cutter international hotels where you need to remind yourself what city you're in, stay at the Sukhothai. As the name suggests, this hotel employs brick stupas, courtyards and antique sculptures to create a historical, temple-like atmosphere. The recently remodelled superior rooms contrast this with hi-tech TVs, phones and yes, digital toilets from Japan.

ROSE HOTEL HOTEL $$

Map p264 (☎0 2266 8272, 0 2266 8268; www. rosehotelbkk.com; 118 Th Surawong; r/ste incl breakfast 1950/3300B; ✳@☕≈; Ⓜ Si Lom exit 2, ⊟Sala Daeng exit 1) Hidden down a lane beside the landmark Montien Hotel, the Rose is yet another of Bangkok's Vietnam War vets. A refurbishment sees the 70 spacious rooms sporting a stylish mix of coloured walls, dark tiles and sleek bathrooms, and the Rose also boasts an oasis-like pool, a small gym (three machines) and a sauna. With breakfast included and wi-fi for 300B a day, it's one of the best deals in town.

BAAN SALADAENG BOUTIQUE HOTEL $$

Map p268 (☎0 2636 3038; www.baansaladaeng. com; 69/2 Th Sala Daeng; r incl breakfast 1000-1950B; ✳@☕; Ⓜ Si Lom exit 2, ⊟Sala Daeng exit 4)

Of the handful of pint-sized boutique hotels along Th Sala Daeng, Baan Saladaeng is most welcoming. The lobby's cheery primary colour theme carries on into the 11 rooms, with those on the upper floors being the largest and airiest. Gay-friendly.

BANGKOK CHRISTIAN GUEST HOUSE
BUDGET HOTEL **$$**

Map p262 (☎0 2233 2206; www.bcgh.org; 123 Soi Sala Daeng 2; s/d/tr incl breakfast 1100/1540/1980B; ❄@⚛; ⓂSi Lom exit 2 ⓢSala Daeng exit 2) Located just steps from Patpong's go-go bars, this lower midrange but thoroughly wholesome (no beer, free water) place proves that vice and morality are never far apart. The 58 rooms are comfortable and spotlessly clean, with cable TV and air-con standard. The style is more Christian simplicity than global Zen, but at these prices you can't complain.

ALL SEASONS SATHORN
BUDGET HOTEL **$$**

Map p268 (☎0 2343 6333; www.allseasons-sathorn.com; 31 Th Sathon Tai; r incl breakfast 1800-2500B; ❄@⚛; ⓂLumphini exit 2) The former King's Hotel has been reborn as this modern, attractive budget choice, right in the middle of the embassy district. The primary colours and bold lines of the design scheme make up for the lack of natural light in some rooms. Superior and deluxe rooms are best; the rooftop 'Exclusive' rooms are small but include a 6pm checkout.

NEW ROAD GUESTHOUSE
BUDGET HOTEL **$**

Map p266 (☎0 2630 9371; www.newroadguesthouse.com; 1216/1 Th Charoen Krung; dm fan/air-con 160/250B, r 900-2500B; ❄@⚛; ⓢTha Si Phraya) For those on tight budgets, the clean, fan-equipped dorms here are among the cheapest accommodation in all of Bangkok. Run by young Danish guys whose main gig is operating budget-priced (and oft-recommended) tours around Thailand, the atmosphere is amiable and the evenings-only bar is a great place to meet other travellers.

Thanon Sukhumvit

ᴛᴏᴘ ᴄʜᴏɪᴄᴇ ARIYASOMVILLA
BOUTIQUE HOTEL **$$$**

Map p270 (☎0 2254 880; www.ariyasom.com; 65 Soi 1, Th Sukhumvit; r incl breakfast 5050-12,100B; ❄@⚛; ⓡPhloen Chit exit 3) At the end of Soi 1 and hidden behind a virtual wall of frangipani, this beautifully renovated 1940s-era villa is one of the worst-kept accommodation secrets in Bangkok. If you can score a reservation, you'll be privy to one of 24 spacious rooms, meticulously outfitted with thoughtful Thai design touches and classy antique furniture. There's a spa and an inviting tropical pool; breakfast is vegetarian and is served in the original villa's stunning, glass-encased dining room.

FROM LITERATI TO GLITTERATI

Now a famous grand dame, the Mandarin Oriental (p181) started its career as the seafarers' version of a Th Khao San guesthouse. The original owners, two Danish sea captains, traded the nest to Hans Niels Andersen, the founder of the formidable East Asiatic Company. Andersen transformed the hotel into a civilised palace of grand architecture and luxury standards. He hired an Italian architect, S Cardu, to design what is now the Authors' Wing, which was the city's most fantastic building not constructed by the king.

The rest of the hotel's history relies on its famous guests. A Polish-born sailor named Joseph Conrad stayed here in 1888. The hotel brought him good luck: he got his first command on the ship *Otago*, from Bangkok to Port Adelaide, which in turn gave him ideas for several early stories. W Somerset Maugham stumbled into the hotel with an advanced case of malaria. In his feverish state, he heard the German manager arguing with the doctor about how a death in the hotel would hurt business. Maugham's overland Southeast Asian journey is recorded in *Gentleman in the Parlour: A Record of a Journey from Rangoon to Haiphong*, which gave literary appeal to the hotel. Other notable guests have included Noel Coward, Graham Greene, John le Carré, James Michener, Gore Vidal and, er, Barbara Cartland. Some modern-day writers claim that an Oriental stay will overcome writer's block – though we suspect any writer staying these days would need a very generous advance indeed.

72 EKAMAI
HOTEL **$$**

Map p270 (0 2714 7327; www.72ekamai.com; 72 Soi 63 (Ekamai), Th Sukhumvit; incl breakfast r 2750-3100B, ste 3250-4100B; ⊠⊛@🛜⊠; ⓔEkkamai exit 1) The neighbourhood off Sukhumvit's Soi 63 (Soi Ekamai) is a magnet for young hipsters, so it's no surprise that a stylish, sophisticated, retro-sleek hotel has opened here. The lobby sets the tone with a glowing red counter and '60s-era TV set. The rooms maintain the theme with, for example, Fab Four walking dolls striding along a shelf. What is surprising, however, is how big the studios and one-bedroom suites are – from 30 to 62 sq metres. All up, a top choice that's even better with regular online discounts.

EUGENIA
BOUTIQUE HOTEL **$$$**

Map p270 (0 2259 9017-19; www.theeugenia. com; 267 Soi 31 (Sawatdi), Th Sukhumvit; ste incl breakfast 7200-9000B; ⊛@🛜⊠; ⓔPhrom Phong exit 6 & taxi) The Eugenia is one unique boutique. Think Livingstone/Hemingway/Indian Raj, with the rooms and public spaces packed full of art, books, antique furniture, beaten-copper bathtubs and dead animals (we counted zebra, warthog, crocodile, various antelope, peacock and duck). It's not, however, devoid of modern luxuries, with wi-fi internet, VoIP telephony and minibar all included in the rate. Our only criticism is that the rooms aren't huge, especially the tiny Siam suites. Ask about airport trips in the vintage Mercedes.

MA DU ZI
BOUTIQUE HOTEL **$$$**

Map p270 (0 2615 6400; www.maduzihotel. com; cnr Th Ratchadapisek & Soi 16, Th Sukhumvit; incl breakfast r 5000-12,000B; ste 12,000B; ⊛@🛜; ⓜSukhumvit exit 3, ⓔAsok exit 6) The name is a play on the Thai phrase for 'come take a look', somewhat of a misnomer for this reservations-only, no walk-ins hotel. Behind its towering gate you'll find a chic, modern hotel steeped in dark, minimalist tones and designs. Rooms are huge, starting at 49 sq metres and climbing to 79 sq metres, and come with perks such as free minibar, late checkout and early check-in, and fast-track airport pick-ups.

LUXURY FOR LESS IN EXECUTIVE APARTMENTS

Bangkok is loaded with serviced apartment buildings aimed at the executive market, ranging from midrange comfort to no-sacrifice-is-too-great luxury. But what few people realise is that most apartments are happy to take short-term guests as well as longer stayers – and that by booking ahead you can get a luxury apartment with much more space than a hotel room for the same or less money. It's really a great way to stay, especially if you are a family who needs more room than two hotel rooms.

Several luxury buildings are on centrally located Soi Lang Suan, between Chit Lom BTS station and Lumphini Park, while others gather on the other side of Lumphini Park in the Silom business district, and along Th Sukhumvit. The **Centrepoint** (www. centrepoint.com) group is the biggest manager of serviced apartments, with eight buildings across Bangkok. Others we like:

Fraser Place Urbana Langsuan (Map p260; 0 2250 6666; www.bangkok.fraser shophospitality.com; 55 Th Lang Suan; daily 3000-7000B; ⊛@🛜⊠; ⓔChit Lom exit 4) Architecturally stunning, with decor, facilities, service and location to match. Fraser has three other properties in Bangkok, with great online deals.

Siri Sathorn (Map p268; 0 2266 2345; www.sirisathorn.com; 27 Soi Sala Daeng 1, Th Silom; daily 6000-14,000, per month 80,000-200,000B; ⊛@🛜⊠; ⓜSi Lom exit 2 , ⓔSala Daeng exit 2) Chic modern apartments starting at 60 sq metres; also includes shuttle bus, spa and satisfying service.

House by the Pond (Map p270; 0 2259 3543; www.housebythepond.com; 230/3 Soi Sainumthip 2, Soi 20, Th Sukhumvit; daily 1200-2000B, per month 17,500-34,000B; ⊛@🛜⊠; ⓔPhrom Phong exit 6) More affordable, older-style apartments.

For more options try these websites:

➡ **www.sabaai.com** Most professional site for apartments.

➡ **www.mrroomfinder.com** Wide range, detailed search options.

➡ **www.bangkokapartments.info** Cheap places.

➡ **www.airbnb.com** Apartment rentals.

FUSION SUITES
BOUTIQUE HOTEL $$

Map p270 (☑0 2665 2644; www.fusionbangkok. com; 143/61-62 Soi 21 (Asoke), Th Sukhumvit; r incl breakfast 1800-3500B; ❄@☎; MSukhumvit exit 1, ⓐAsok exit 1) It's hard to classify exactly what's going on in this seven-storey, 35-room boutique hotel. Dark rooms with polished concrete floors are embellished with Persian carpets, Indian wooden furniture, parlour-room buttoned leather couches, Buddhist iconography and a head-spinning array of hi-tech gadgetry. It sounds dizzying, but somehow seems to work. The one small downside is that only the standard and deluxe rooms have windows; deluxe rooms are the pick.

ALOFT
BOUTIQUE HOTEL $$$

Map p270 (☑0 2207 7000; www.alofthotels. com/bangkoksukhumvit11; 35 Soi 11, Th Sukhumvit; r incl breakfast 3150-6500B; ❄@☎❈; ⓐNana exit 5) Fun seems to be the operative term for this new, young-feeling hotel – even down to its seemingly strategic location on Soi 11, steps from some of the city's best clubs and bars. The lobby sets the theme with bold colours, a fusball table and lots of TVs, while free wi-fi, a fun bar and generous online specials prove that the sentiment runs more than just skin deep.

SEVEN
BOUTIQUE HOTEL $$$

Map p270 (☑0 2662 0951; www.sleepatseven. com; 3/15 Soi 31 (Sawatdi), Th Sukhumvit; r incl breakfast 4708-7062B; ❄@☎; ⓐPhrom Phong exit 5) Thais believe each day has its own colour, and each of the seven rooms here is themed accordingly. Rooms are tight, but well appointed with free mobile phones, wifi and iPods. Seven will appeal to hip young singles and couples looking for design and informal-but-well-informed service. Hefty online discounts available.

NAPA PLACE
HOTEL $$

Map p270 (☑0 2661 5525; www.napaplace.com; 11/3 Soi Napha Sap 2; incl breakfast r 2200-2400B; ste 3400-4100B; ❄@☎; ⓐThong Lo exit 2) Tucked away in a quiet soi off Soi 36 and a short walk to BTS Thong Lo, Napa offers a genuinely homey atmosphere. It appeals especially to families because the apartment-like rooms are huge (36 to 67 sq metres), there is plenty of living room–like communal space and solid security, and cable broadband and buffet breakfasts are included in the price.

SUK 11
BUDGET HOTEL $

Map p270 (☑0 2253 5927; www.suk11.com; 1/33 Soi 11, Th Sukhumvit; r incl breakfast 500-2000B; ❄@☎; ⓐNana exit 3) Extremely well run and equally popular, this rambling building is an oasis of wood and greenery in the urban jungle that is Th Sukhumvit. The cheaper rooms have shared bathrooms, and although they've somehow managed to stuff nearly 100 rooms in there, you'll still need to book at least two weeks ahead.

SHERATON GRANDE SUKHUMVIT
HOTEL $$$

Map p270 (☑0 2649 8888; www.luxurycollection. com/bangkok; 250 Th Sukhumvit; r incl breakfast 8000-10,000B, ste 16,500-55,000B; ❄@☎❈; MSukhumvit exit 3, ⓐAsok exit 2) The Sheraton is a hit with corporate travellers because it's arguably the most professionally managed hotel in Bangkok. Its 420 large (from 45 sq metres) and meticulously appointed rooms come with handy details such as irons, extra-large deposit boxes and big tubs as standard. Ask for a lake-view room.

CITADINES SOI 23
HOTEL $$

Map p270 (☑0 2204 4777; www.citadines.com; 37 Soi 23, Th Sukhumvit; r 2475-3870B; ❄@☎❈; MSukhumvit exit 2, ⓐAsok exit 6) Of the four Citadines 'Apart-Hotels' on this stretch of Sukhumvit, this is our pick. In both the studio (28 sq metres) and one-bedroom (45 sq metres) options the decor is bright with orange and lime flavours, and the design makes the most of the space. Expect a kitchenette you can actually cook in, a living area and bedroom (separated by a partition in the studio).

FEDERAL HOTEL
HOTEL $$

Map p270 (☑0 2253 0175; www.federalbangkok. com; 27 Soi 11, Th Sukhumvit; r incl breakfast 1100-1500B; ❄@☎❈; ⓐNana exit 4) You wouldn't know it from the exterior, but after 40 years 'Club Fed' finally decided to get a makeover. All rooms are equipped with air-con, fridge and TV, but our tip is to go for the more spacious-feeling poolside rooms on the 1st floor. A solid, if not sexy, midrange choice if you want to stay near the restaurants, bars and clubs of 'downtown'.

BANGKOK BOUTIQUE HOTEL
BOUTIQUE HOTEL $$$

Map p270 (☑0 2261 2850; www.bangkokbou tiquehotel.com; 241 Soi Asoke, Th Sukhumvit; incl breakfast r 2900-6000B, ste 6000-7500B; ❄@☎; MPhetchaburi exit 2) At the north end of noisy Soi Asoke, BB features rooms that combine ancient Thai themes with minimalist, polished-concrete aesthetic. The high-ceilinged superior rooms are best; ask for one away from the street. The rack rates are asking a bit much, but massive discounts are available online.

DREAM BOUTIQUE HOTEL $$$

Map p270 (☑0 2254 8500; www.dreambkk.com; 10 Soi 15, Th Sukhumvit; incl breakfast r 2500-3800B, ste 4000-8000B; 🕸@🛜🌊; MSukhumvit exit 3, 🚇Asok exit 5) The 195 rooms in two buildings are a rock-star world of cream leather, mirrors, silver and blue motifs and, in the uberchic lounge-bar-cum-restaurant, a white tiger (yes, blue stripes) and pink leopard. Rooms come with free wi-fi, coffee machines and big flat-screen TVs. Equally indulgent discounts are available online.

HI-SUKHUMVIT HOSTEL $

Map p270 (☑0 2391 9338; www.hisukhumvit.com; 23 Soi 38, Th Sukhumvit; incl breakfast dm/s 350/650B, d 900-1300B, tr 1200-1650B; 🕸@🛜; 🚇Thong Lo exit 4) Seemingly lost in a galaxy where budget lodgings usually fear to go, the clean, simple dorms and rooms and welcoming family owners make this budget place a real find. The breezy rooftop is a good place to chill out, wash clothes and watch another Bangkok condo emerge from the ground, and the nearby night market is a great place to eat.

S31 HOTEL $$$

Map p270 (☑0 2260 1111; www.s31hotel.com; 545 Soi 31, Th Sukhumvit; incl breakfast r 6000B, ste 7000-10,000B; 🕸🛜🌊; 🚇Phrom Phong exit 5) The bold patterns and graphics of its interior and exterior make the S31 a fun, young feeling choice. Thoughtful touches like kitchenettes with large fridge, superhuge beds and free courses (cooking, Thai boxing and yoga) prove that the style also has substance. Significant discounts can be found online, and additional branches can be found on Soi 15 and Soi 33.

NA NA CHART HOSTEL $

Map p270 (☑0 2259 6908; www.thailandhostel.com; cnr Soi 25 & Th Sukhumvit; incl breakfast dm 500-600B, s/d/tr 1200/1500/1800B; 🕸@🛜; MSukhumvit exit 2, 🚇Asok exit 6) This HI-affiliated place looks a bit institutional, but it's spotless and very convenient to transport, and a good value in this part of town. Dorms range from three to six beds and

feature en suite bathroom, cable TV, fridge and air-con – although you need three occupants before the latter is turned on. Membership costs 200B per person and is granted on the spot, saving up to 300B on the more expensive rooms.

RAMADA HOTEL & SUITES HOTEL $$$

Map p270 (☑0 2664 7000; www.ramadasuitesbangkok.com; 22 Soi 12, Th Sukhumvit; incl breakfast r 3000-3800B, ste 3800-4200B; 🕸@🛜🌊; MSukhumvit exit 3, 🚇Asok exit 5) Tucked into a quiet residential area, there are no surprises here, just an attractive and low-key hotel with long-stay options and professional service. Go for the suites, which for only a bit more have a kitchenette and sitting room.

ATLANTA HOTEL $

Map p270 (☑0 2252 1650; www.theatlantahotelbangkok.com; 78 Soi 2, Th Sukhumvit; incl breakfast r 500-600B, ste 750-1700B; 🕸@🛜🌊; 🚇Nana exit 2) While the Atlanta looks thoroughly grim from outside, the perfectly preserved mid-century lobby, complete with old-fashioned writing desks and a grand entrance staircase sweeping up five floors (there's no lift), makes you want to hang around waiting for Bogart to slip in. Unfortunately, the simple rooms (the cheapest of which are fan-cooled) don't live up to the standard set by the lobby. Note: the Atlanta does not welcome sex tourists and does not try to be polite about it.

STABLE LODGE BUDGET HOTEL $$

Map p270 (☑0 2653 0017; www.stablelodge.com; 39 Soi 8, Th Sukhumvit; r 1400-1600B; 🕸@🛜🌊; 🚇Nana exit 4) To be honest, we were slightly disappointed that the faux-Tudor theme of the downstairs restaurant didn't carry on into the rooms, but could find no other faults. A recent renovation has given a bit of life to the simple rooms here, and the spacious balconies still offer great city views.

🛏 Greater Bangkok

BANGKOK TREE HOUSE BOUTIQUE HOTEL $$$

(☑08 2995 1150; www.bangkoktreehouse.com; near Wat Bang Nam Pheung Nork; r incl breakfast 6000-10,000B; 🕸@🛜🌊; 🚇Bang Na exit 2 & taxi) Although construction on this resort at the edge of the Phra Pradaeng Peninsula, Bangkok's 'green lung', wasn't yet finished at research time, it's already impressed us as one of the area's more intriguing places to stay. The 12 multilevel bungalows are stylishly sculpted from sustainable and recycled materials, resulting in a vibe that calls to mind a sophisticated, eco-friendly summer camp. Thoughtful amenities include en suite computers equipped with movies, free mobile phone and bicycle use, and free ice cream. And if the remote location smacks of rural purgatory, there are heaps of activities in the area, ranging from cooking courses to the Bang Nam Pheung Market, to keep you occupied.

To get to Bangkok Tree House, take the BTS to Bang Na and jump in a taxi for the short ride to the pier at Wat Bang Na Nork. From there, take the river-crossing ferry (4B, ☺5am to 9.30pm), and continue by motorcycle taxi (10B) or on foot (call in advance for directions).

REFILL NOW! HOSTEL **$**

(☑0 2713 2044; www.refillnow.co.th; 191 Soi Pridi Bhanom Yong 42, Soi 71, Th Sukhumvit; dm 515B, r 980-3900B; ✳@🛜🖳; 🚇Phra Khanong exit 3 & taxi) This is the kind of place that might make you think twice about sleeping in a dorm. Rooms and dorms are stylishly minimalist and the latter have flirtatious pull screens between each double-bunk; women-only dorms are also available. There's an achingly hip chill-out area and, upstairs, a massage centre.

Refill Now! is near trendy Th Thong Lo and only 20 minutes from the airport by taxi, or 15 minutes by City Link to Ramkamhaeng Station, then a 50B taxi. On the BTS, get off at Phra Khanong and take a taxi or moto taxi down Soi 71, turn right on Soi 42 and left; or best of all come by

MIDRANGE MANIA

Bangkok's noughties building boom has seen Th Sukhumvit become a forest of good-value, wannabe-boutique hotels. Most are located near the office towers of Soi 21 (aka Soi Asoke), and most have embraced the global Zen style so popular in this range – think faux-wooden floors in smallish rooms, white linens, hanging silks, arty prints, compact bathrooms with rain showers, flat-screen TVs and subtle, earthy colours; all very pleasing if not particularly original. Competition is fierce, and fantastic deals are often available online. Following is a list of those we liked.

Silq (Map p270; ☑0 2252 6800; www.silqbkk.com; 54 Soi 19, Th Sukhumvit; r incl breakfast 2800-3700B; ✳@🛜; ⓂSukhumvit exit 1, 🚇Asok exit 1) The eight-storey, 46-room Silq offers bright rooms that feel larger than they are thanks to big windows (in most rooms). Service is friendly and wi-fi is free; the buffet and à la carte breakfast is the clincher.

CitiChic (Map p270; ☑0 2342 3888; www.citichichotel.com; 34 Soi 13, Th Sukhumvit; r incl breakfast 2700-3000B; ✳@🖳; 🚇Nana exit 3) Everything (except the TVs) in this 37-room, five-storey place is small, but the space is attractive and well utilised. There's a small rooftop pool, small rooms with small desks and small bathrooms. The ground-floor rooms have small outdoor patios.

Sacha's Hotel Uno (Map p270; ☑0 2651 2180; www.sachas.hotel-uno.com; 28/19 Soi 19, Th Sukhumvit; r incl breakfast 1800-2500B; ✳@🛜; ⓂSukhumvit exit 1 , 🚇Asok exit 1) These 56 rooms in adjacent buildings are pretty compact, and are neither the 'five-star' promised in the marketing nor quite as impressive as the lobbies suggest. Still, they are very well wired for business, and the 'Deluxe' rooms in the main building, in particular, won't disappoint at these prices.

On8 (Map p270; ☑0 2254 8866; www.on8bangkok.com; 162 Th Sukhumvit; r incl breakfast 1900-2800B; ✳@🛜; 🚇Nana exit 4) Literally on the doorstep of Nana BTS station, in the heart of the action near the corner of Soi 8, On8 is a highly designed 40-room hotel where space is at a premium. Over four floors, the three categories of room differ only in size and outlook (ie none or an opaque window, which is appropriate given what you'd be looking at). They all have big flat-screen TVs, small desks and appealing decor.

Baan Sukhumvit (Map p270; ☑0 2258 5622; www.baansukhumvit.com; 392/38-39 Soi 20, Th Sukhumvit; r 1540-1650B; ✳@🛜; 🚇Nana exit 3) With only 12 rooms, this hotel exudes a cosy feel. Rooms lack bells and whistles, but are subtly attractive; the more expensive ones include a bit more space, a bathtub and a safe.

AIRPORT ACCOMMODATION

If you have a super-early departure or late arrival it's worth considering a hotel near Suvarnabhumi International Airport. That said, it's worth keeping in mind that Bangkok taxis are cheap and early-morning traffic means the trip doesn't take that long.

Novotel Suvarnabhumi Airport Hotel (☑0 2131 1111; www.novotel.com; r incl breakfast from 7146B; ❄@⊛) With 600-plus luxurious rooms; in the airport compound.

Grand Inn Come Hotel (☑0 2738 8189-99; www.grandinncome-hotel.com; 99 Moo 6, Th Kingkaew; r incl breakfast from 1800B; ❄@⊛) Solid midranger 10km from the airport, with airport shuttle and 'lively' karaoke bar.

Refill Now! (p187) Nearest good budget option.

klorng (canal, also spelt *khlong*) taxi to Tha Khlong Tong and walk.

MYSTIC PLACE   BOUTIQUE HOTEL $$

(☑0 2270 3344; www.mysticplacebkk.com; 224/5-9 Th Pradiphat; r incl breakfast 2500-3500B; ❄@⊛; 🚇Saphan Khwai exit 2 & taxi) The 36 rooms here have each been styled by a different artist, designer or celebrity, making Mystic Place the most arty and kitschy hotel in Thailand. A 10-minute walk from BTS Saphan Khwai in a hectic Thai neighbourhood, rooms are Starbucks-sized: 'small' is really big and 'large' is mega. Each is fitted with a DVD player and free wi-fi. Check out the rooms online to book the one you want; street-side rooms are noisy.

BE MY GUEST BED & BREAKFAST   GUESTHOUSE $$

(☑0 2692 4037; www.bemyguestbnb.com; 212/4 Soi 1, Soi 7 (Na Thong), Th Ratchadaphisek; s/d incl breakfast 900/1400B; ❄@⊛; 🅼Thailand Cultural Centre exit 4 & taxi) With only four rooms and the owner living upstairs, you really are the eponymous guest at this friendly, tidy guesthouse. Rooms are neat but simple, and are supplemented by user-friendly communal areas, personal service and a genuinely homey feel. Be sure to contact in advance, both to ensure vacancy and to ask for detailed instructions on locating the place.

Understand Bangkok

Bangkok Today

As the vortex of Thailand's power and a hotbed of political activism, Bangkok entered 2012 bruised and battered. Already shaken by street protests and clashes between pro-monarchy forces and supporters of deposed Prime Minister Thaksin Shinawatra, in June 2011 the capital was struck by devastating floods resulting in the loss of 600 lives, and a staggering US$45 billion in economic costs to farms and factories. Prime Minister Yingluck Shinawatra fared poorly in flood management, but won sympathy for her accountability and hard work.

Best on Film

Monrak Transistor (directed by Pen-Ek Ratanaruang; 2001) An aspiring *loôk tûng* (Thai country music) singer trades his bucolic provincial life for one of struggle in the big city.

Nang Nak (directed by Nonzee Nimibutr; 1999) This classic Thai tale is a fascinating peek at Thai beliefs, not to mention at the provincial village that existed before Bangkok was taken over by concrete.

Best in Print

Sightseeing (Rattawut Lapcharoensap; 2004) Written by an American-born Thai who later moved to Bangkok, the short stories in this book provide a look at the lives of normal Thais who live in the type of suburbs and towns most visitors will never see.

Four Reigns (Kukrit Pramoj; Thai 1953, English 1981) *Four Reigns* follows the fictional life of Phloi, a minor courtier during the Bangkok palace's last days of absolute monarchy.

Democratic Stalemate

The floods of 2011 became Yingluck's political baptism. Her post-flood learning curve has been steep, but she has gained much in stature and confidence as she holds the electoral ground in lieu of her controversial older brother. Yingluck hails from the Shinawatra family business and made it to the premiership in 45 days on the coat-tails of Thaksin's resilient popularity and populist platform that, a decade ago, provided a sense of upward mobility to the neglected masses and addressed long-standing grievances of Thailand's rural heartlands. Thaksin's pro-establishment opponents, clad in royalist yellow, have done all they can to keep him at bay since the coup, but he keeps hovering over them as Thailand's undefeated election winner so far this century. Thaksin's years in power were characterised by corruption allegations, conflicts of interest, abuses of power and human rights violations. As a corruption conviction and two years in jail await his return, Thaksin and his loyalists have pinned their hopes on a general amnesty, or constitutional amendments based on the Yingluck government's majority in the national assembly.

The titanic tussle between Thaksin's red shirts and Thailand's yellow-shirted traditional elites has yielded a political stalemate. The exiled former prime minister can win elections but is not allowed to rule, while his opponents can call the shots but are unable to triumph at the polls. A truce has been put in place for the interim. Establishment centres have allowed Yingluck to rule in Thaksin's name without the street protests that rocked Bangkok in 2008 (most spectacularly the takeover of Bangkok's airports). In return, the pro-Thaksin red shirts stay in line, Thaksin agrees to remain abroad, the Yingluck government leaves the army's high command untouched, and anti-monarchy elements are suppressed.

Royal Twilight

Those who have followed the topsy-turvy Thai politics in recent years have witnessed a gruelling transformation from kingdom to democracy where loyal subjects are increasingly becoming informed citizens. The uneasy truce between the populist red shirts and the establishment yellow shirts is untenable: Thailand is in flux during the twilight of the remarkable 65-year reign of respected monarch, 84-year-old King Bhumibol Adulyadej (Rama IX), who presided over Thailand's transformation from a village backwater to a modernised nation with ubiquitous concrete townhouses and gleaming skyscrapers. His passing will spell the end of Thailand as we know it, raising the spectre of a murky succession. The next monarch is unlikely to command as much moral authority and the institution will need to be recalibrated to fit democratic times.

The transformation of economy and society has brought undeniable political liberalisation and electoral democracy, giving rise to new demands for and expectations of accountability and a greater share of the pie for the downtrodden masses. As elections become imperative and military coups increasingly obsolete, it appears that the royalist elites may have lost the battle. The dilemma for Thailand is to ensure that democratic institutions become the ultimate winner in this ongoing struggle for Thailand's soul.

Thai Resilience

Thailand has weathered innumerable storms in recent years: scores of military coups during the 20th century, an economic crisis in the 1990s, ongoing political turmoil as the establishment yellow shirts battle the populist red shirts, devastating and politically challenging natural disasters and the uncertainty of a new order as the reign of beloved King Bhumibol Adulyadej comes to an end. No visitor is foolish enough to ask what is to be Thailand's next crisis.

No answer is definitive, except that all will transpire against the backdrop of a revered king's passing and the wrenching political transformation in the interim and in its wake. Still, visitors continue to flock to Bangkok. Suvarnabhumi, Bangkok's main international airport, teems with passengers. Bangkok's nearby beaches are crowded. And the economy manages to find a way to grow in the face of nasty politics, thanks to Thailand's geography, natural endowments, and a resourceful and hospitable people who take life and its manifestations in their stride. Thailand has found a way to sufficiently decouple its existential socio-political crisis from its tourist attractions and future economic development.

– Thitinan Pongsudhirak, Professor of International Political Economy and Director of the Institute of Security and International Studies at Chulalongkorn University, Bangkok.

if Bangkok were 100 people

75 would be Thai
14 would be Chinese
11 would be Other

belief systems
(% of population)

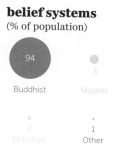

94
Buddhist

3
Muslim

2
Christian

1
Other

population per sq km

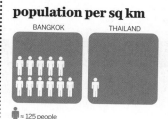

BANGKOK   THAILAND

≈ 125 people

History

Since the late 18th century, the history of Bangkok has essentially been the history of Thailand. Many of the country's defining events have unfolded here, and today the language, culture and food of the city have come to represent those of the entire country. This situation may once have seemed impossible, given the city's origins as little more than an obscure Chinese trading port, but, today boasting a population of more than 10 million, Bangkok will most likely continue to shape Thailand's history for some time to come.

FROM THE BEGINNING

Ayuthaya & Thonburi

Before it became the capital of Siam – as Thailand was then known – in 1782, the tiny settlement known as Bang Makok was merely a backwater village opposite the larger Thonburi Si Mahasamut on the banks of Mae Nam Chao Phraya, not far from the Gulf of Siam.

Thonburi had been founded by a group of wealthy Siamese during the reign of King Chakkaphat (r 1548–68) as an important relay point for sea- and river-borne trade between the Gulf of Siam and Ayuthaya, 86km up-river. Ayuthaya served as the royal capital of Siam from 1350 to 1767, and throughout this time European powers tried without success to colonise the kingdom.

Eventually, an Asian power subdued the capital when the Burmese sacked Ayuthaya in 1767. Many Siamese were marched off to Pegu (Bago, Myanmar today), where they were forced to serve the Burmese court. However, the remaining Siamese regrouped under Phraya Taksin, a half-Chinese, half-Thai general who decided to move the capital further south along Mae Nam Chao Phraya, closer to the Gulf of Siam. Thonburi was a logical choice for the new capital.

The Chakri Dynasty & the Birth of Bangkok

Taksin eventually succumbed to mental illness and was executed, and one of his key generals, Phraya Chakri, came to power and was crowned in

> King Taksin's execution was in the custom reserved for royalty – sealing him inside a velvet sack to ensure no royal blood touched the ground before beating him to death with a scented sandalwood club.

TIMELINE	1548–68	1768	1779
	Thonburi Si Mahasamut, at the time little more than a Chinese trading post on the right bank of Mae Nam Chao Phraya, is founded.	King Taksin the Great moves the Thai capital from Ayuthaya to Thonburi Si Mahasamut, a location he regarded as beneficial for both trade and defence.	After a brutal war of territorial expansion, the Emerald Buddha, Thailand's most sacred Buddha image, is brought to Bangkok from Laos, along with hundreds of Laotian slaves.

1782 as Phraphutthayotfa. Fearing Thonburi to be vulnerable to Burmese attack from the west, Chakri moved the Siamese capital across the river to Bang Makok (Olive Plum riverbank), named for the trees that grew there in abundance. As the first monarch of the new Chakri royal dynasty – which continues to this day – Phraya Chakri was posthumously dubbed Rama I.

The first task set before the planners of the new city was to create hallowed ground for royal palaces and Buddhist monasteries. Astrologers divined that construction of the new royal palace should begin on 6 May 1782, and ceremonies consecrated Rama I's transfer to a temporary new residence a month later.

In time, Ayuthaya's control of tribute states in Laos and western Cambodia was transferred to Bangkok, and thousands of prisoners of war were brought to the capital to work. Bangkok also had ample access to free Thai labour via the *prâi lõo•ang* (commoner/noble) system, under which all commoners were required to provide labour to the state in lieu of taxes.

Using this immense pool of labour, Rama I augmented Bangkok's natural canal and river system with hundreds of artificial waterways feeding into Thailand's hydraulic lifeline, the broad Mae Nam Chao Phraya. Rama I also ordered the construction of 10km of city walls and *klorng rôrp grung* (canals around the city) to create a royal 'island' – Ko Ratanakosin – between Mae Nam Chao Phraya and the canal loop.

Temple and canal construction remained the highlight of early development in Bangkok until the reign of Rama III (King Phranangklao; r 1824–51), when attention turned to upgrading the port for international sea trade. The city soon became a regional centre for Chinese trading ships, slowly surpassing in importance even the British port at Singapore.

Water-borne traffic dominated Bangkok, supplemented by a meagre network of footpaths, well into the middle of the 19th century.

TRAFFIC

THE AGE OF POLITICS
European Influence & the 1932 Revolution

Facing increasing pressure from British colonies in neighbouring Burma and Malaya, in 1855 Rama IV (King Mongkut; r 1851–68) signed the Bowring Treaty with Britain. This agreement marked Siam's break from exclusive economic involvement with China, a relationship that had dominated the previous century.

The signing of this document, and the subsequent ascension of Rama V (King Chulalongkorn; r 1868–1910) led to the largest period of European influence on Siam. Wishing to head off any potential invasion plans, Rama V ceded Laos and Cambodia to the French and northern

Rama IV was the first monarch to show his face to the Thai public.

1782	1785	1821	1851
Rama I re-establishes the Siamese court across the river from Thonburi, resulting in the creation of both the current Thai capital and the Chakri dynasty.	The majority of the construction of Ko Ratanakosin, Bangkok's royal district, including famous landmarks such as the Grand Palace and Wat Phra Kaew, is finished.	A boatload of opium marks the visit of the first Western trader to Bangkok; the trade of this substance is eventually banned nearly 20 years later.	Rama IV, the fourth king of the Chakri dynasty, comes to power, courts relations with the West and encourages the study of modern science in Siam.

Malaya to the British between 1893 and 1910. The two European powers, for their part, were happy to use Siam as a buffer state between their respective colonial domains.

Rama V gave Bangkok 120 new roads during his reign, inspired by street plans from Batavia (the Dutch colonial centre now known as Jakarta), Calcutta, Penang and Singapore. Germans were hired to design and build railways emanating from the capital, while the Dutch contributed the design of Bangkok's Hualamphong Train Station, today considered a minor masterpiece of civic art deco.

In 1893 Bangkok opened its first railway line, extending 22km from Bangkok to Pak Nam, where Mae Nam Chao Phraya enters the Gulf of Siam. A 20km electric tramway opened the following year, paralleling the left bank of Mae Nam Chao Phraya.

Americans established Siam's first printing press along with the kingdom's first newspaper in 1864. The first Siamese-language newspaper, *Darunovadha,* came along in 1874, and by 1900 Bangkok boasted three daily English-language newspapers: the *Bangkok Times, Siam Observer* and *Siam Free Press.*

As Bangkok prospered, many wealthy merchant families sent their children to study in Europe. Students of humbler socioeconomic status who excelled at school had access to government scholarships for overseas study as well. In 1924 a handful of Siamese students in Paris formed the Promoters of Political Change, a group that met to discuss ideas for a future Siamese government modelled on Western democracy.

A bloodless revolution in 1932, initiated by the Promoters of Political Change and a willing Rama VII (King Prajadhipok; r 1925–35), transformed Siam from an absolute monarchy into a constitutional one. Bangkok thus found itself the nerve centre of a vast new civil service, which, coupled with its growing success as a world port, transformed the city into a mecca for Siamese seeking economic opportunities.

WWII & the Struggle for Democracy

Phibul Songkhram, appointed prime minister by the People's Party in December 1938, changed the country's name from Siam to Thailand and introduced the Western solar calendar. Phibul, who in 1941 allowed Japanese regiments access to the Gulf of Thailand, resigned in 1944 under pressure from the Thai underground resistance, and was eventually exiled to Japan. Bangkok resumed its pace towards modernisation, even after Phibul returned to Thailand in 1948 and took over the leadership again via a military coup. Over the next 15 years, bridges were built over Mae Nam Chao Phraya, canals were filled in to provide

In 1861 Bangkok's European diplomats and merchants delivered a petition to Rama IV requesting roadways so they could enjoy horse riding for physical fitness and pleasure. The royal government acquiesced, and established a handful of roads suitable for horse-drawn carriages and rickshaws.

HORSES

RICHARD NEBESKY / LONELY PLANET IMAGES ©

Coat of arms for the reigning Chakri dynasty of King Bhumibol

EXTENDED FAMILIES IN THAILAND'S ROYAL COURT

Until polygamy was outlawed by Rama VI (King Vajiravudh; r 1910–25), it was expected of Thai monarchs to maintain a harem consisting of numerous 'major' and 'minor' wives and the children of these relationships. This led to some truly vast families: Rama I (King Phraphutthayotfa; r 1782–1809) had 42 children by 28 mothers; Rama II (King Phraphutthaloetla Naphalai; r 1809–24), 73 children by 40 mothers; Rama III (King Phranangklao; r 1824–51), 51 children by 37 mothers (he would eventually accumulate a total of 242 wives and consorts); Rama IV (King Mongkut; r 1851–68), 82 children by 35 mothers; and Rama V (King Chulalongkorn; r 1868–1910), 77 children by 40 mothers. In the case of Rama V, his seven 'major' wives were all half-sisters or first cousins, a conscious effort to maintain the purity of the bloodline of the Chakri dynasty. Other consorts or 'minor' wives were often the daughters of families wishing to gain greater ties with the royal family.

In contrast to the precedent set by his predecessors, Rama VI had one wife and one child, a girl born only a few hours before his death. As a result, his brother, Prajadhipok, was appointed as his successor. Rama VII also had only one wife and failed to produce any heirs. After abdicating in 1935 he did not exercise his right to appoint a successor, so lines were drawn back to Rama V, and the grandson of one of his remaining 'major' wives, nine-year-old Ananda Mahidol, was chosen to be the next king.

space for new roads, and multistorey buildings began crowding out traditional teak structures.

From 1964 to 1973 – the peak years of the second Indochina War – Thai army officers Thanom Kittikachorn and Praphat Charusathien ruled Thailand and allowed the US to establish several army bases within Thai borders to support the US campaign in Indochina. During this time Bangkok gained notoriety as a 'rest and recreation' (R&R) spot for foreign troops stationed in Southeast Asia.

In October 1973 the Thai military brutally suppressed a large pro-democracy student demonstration at Thammasat University in Bangkok, but Rama IX (King Bhumibol Adulyadej; r 1946–present) and General Krit Sivara, who sympathised with the students, refused to support further bloodshed, forcing Thanom and Praphat to leave Thailand. Oxford-educated Kukrit Pramoj took charge of a 14-party coalition government and steered a leftist agenda past the conservative parliament.

The military regained control in 1976 after right-wing, paramilitary civilian groups assaulted a group of 2000 students holding a sit-in at Thammasat. Officially, 46 people died in the incident, although the num

1893	1910	1917	1932
After a territorial dispute, France sends gunboats to threaten Bangkok, forcing Siam to give up most of its territory east of the Mekong River; Siam gains its modern boundaries.	Vajiravudh becomes the sixth king of the Chakri dynasty after the death of his older brother; he fails to produce a male heir during his reign.	Chulalongkorn University, the country's first Western-style institute of higher education, is founded; it's still regarded as the most prestigious in the country.	A bloodless coup transforms Siam from an absolute to a constitutional monarchy; Rama VII remains on the throne until his resignation three years later.

RAMA IX

If you see a yellow Rolls-Royce flashing by along city avenues, accompanied by a police escort, you've just caught a glimpse of Thailand's longest-reigning monarch – and the longest-reigning living monarch in the world – King Bhumibol Adulyadej. Also known in English as Rama IX (the ninth king of the Chakri dynasty), Bhumibol Adulyadej was born in 1927 in the USA, where his father Prince Mahidol was studying medicine at Harvard University.

Fluent in English, French, German and Thai, Bhumibol ascended the throne in 1946 following the death of his brother Rama VIII (King Ananda Mahidol; r 1935–46), who reigned for just over 11 years before dying under mysterious circumstances.

An ardent jazz composer and saxophonist when he was younger, Rama IX has hosted jam sessions with the likes of jazz greats Woody Herman and Benny Goodman. His compositions are often played on Thai radio. The king is also recognised for his extensive development projects, particularly in rural areas of Thailand. For an objective English-language biography of the king's accomplishments, *King Bhumibol Adulyadej: A Life's Work* (Editions Didier Millet, 2010) is available in most Bangkok bookstores.

Rama IX and Queen Sirikit have four children: Princess Ubol Ratana (b 1951), Crown Prince Maha Vajiralongkorn (b 1952), Princess Mahachakri Sirindhorn (b 1955) and Princess Chulabhorn (b 1957).

After more than 60 years in power, and having recently reached his 84th birthday, Rama IX is preparing for his succession. For the last few years the Crown Prince has performed most of the royal ceremonies the king would normally perform, such as presiding over the Royal Ploughing Ceremony, changing the attire on the Emerald Buddha and handing out academic degrees at university commencements.

Along with nation and religion, the monarchy is very highly regarded in Thai society – negative comment about the king or any member of the royal family is a social as well as legal taboo.

Thailand (PLAT), an armed communist insurgency based in the hills, which had been active in Thailand since the 1930s.

Bangkok continued to seesaw between civilian and military rule for the next 15 years. Although a general amnesty in 1982 brought an end to the PLAT, and students, workers and farmers returned to their homes, a new era of political tolerance exposed the military once again to civilian fire.

In May 1992 several huge demonstrations demanding the resignation of the next in a long line of military dictators, General Suchinda Kraprayoon, rocked Bangkok and the large provincial capitals. Charismatic Bangkok governor Chamlong Srimuang, winner of the 1992 Magsaysay Award (a humanitarian service award issued in the Philippines) for his role in galvanising the public to reject Suchinda, led the protests.

1935–46	1939	1946	1951–63
Ananda Mahidol, a grandson of one of Rama V's wives, is appointed king; his reign ends abruptly when he is found shot dead in his room under mysterious circumstances.	The country's name is changed from Siam to Thailand.	Pridi Phanomyong becomes Thailand's first democratically elected prime minister; after a military coup, Pridi is forced to flee Thailand, returning only briefly one more time.	Field marshal Sarit Thanarat wrests power from Phibun Songkhram, abolishes the constitution and embarks on one of the most authoritarian regimes in modern Thai history.

After confrontations between the protesters and the military near the Democracy Monument resulted in nearly 50 deaths and hundreds of injuries, Rama IX summoned both Suchinda and Chamlong for a rare public scolding. Suchinda resigned, having been in power for less than six weeks.

A mere 13 sq km in 1900, Bangkok grew to an astounding metropolitan area of more than 330 sq km by the end of the 20th century. Today the greater city encompasses not only Bangkok proper, but also the former capital of Thonburi across Mae Nam Chao Phraya to the west, along with the densely populated 'suburb' provinces, Samut Prakan to the east and Nonthaburi to the north. More than half of Thailand's urban population lives in Bangkok.

THE RECENT PAST

The Crisis & the People's Constitution

Bangkok approached the new millennium riding a tide of events that set new ways of governing and living in the capital. The most defining moment occurred in July 1997 when – after several months of warning signs that nearly everyone in Thailand and the international community ignored – the Thai currency fell into a deflationary tailspin and the national economy screeched to a virtual halt. Bangkok, which rode at the forefront of the 1980s double-digit economic boom, suffered more than elsewhere in the country in terms of job losses and massive income erosion.

Two months after the crash, the Thai parliament voted in a new constitution that guaranteed – at least on paper – more human and civil rights than had ever been granted in Thailand previously. The so-called 'people's constitution' fostered great hope in a population left emotionally battered by the 1997 economic crisis.

Thaksin Shinawatra: CEO Prime Minister

In January 2001, billionaire and former police colonel Thaksin Shinawatra became prime minister after winning a landslide victory in nationwide elections – the first in Thailand under the strict guidelines established in the 1997 constitution. Thaksin's new party, called Thai Rak Thai (TRT; Thais Love Thailand), swept into power on a populist agenda that seemed at odds with the man's enormous wealth and influence.

The sixth-richest ruler in the world as of late 2003, Thaksin owned the country's only private TV station through his family-owned Shin Corporation, the country's largest telecommunications company. Shin

Historical Reads

Thailand: A Short History (David K Wyatt)
. . . .
A History of Thailand (Chris Baker & Pasuk Phongpaichit)
. . . .
Chronicle of Thailand (Editions Didier Millet)
. . . .
Reading Thai Murals (David K Wyatt)

1962	1973	1981	1985
US involvement in the Indochina War leads to economic expansion of Bangkok; dissatisfaction with the authoritarian Thai government leads to a period of communist insurgency.	Student protests lead to violent military suppression; 1971 coup leader Thanom Kittikachorn is exiled by Rama IX; Kukrit Pramoj's civilian government takes charge.	General Prem Tinsulanonda is appointed prime minister after a military coup and is largely able to stabilise Thai politics over the next eight years.	Chamlong Srimuang is elected mayor of Bangkok; three years later, after forming his own largely Buddhist-based political group, the Palang Dharma Party, he is elected mayor again.

Corporation also owned Asia's first privately owned satellite company, Shin Satellite, and a large stake in Thai AirAsia, a subsidiary of the Malaysia-based airline AirAsia.

Despite numerous controversies, during the February 2005 general elections Thaksin became the first Thai leader in history to be re-elected to a consecutive second term.

However, time was running short for Thaksin and his party. The final straw came in January 2006, when Thaksin announced that his family had sold off its controlling interest in Shin Corporation to a Singaporean investment firm. Since deals made through the Stock Exchange of Thailand (SET) were exempt from capital-gains tax, Thaksin's family paid no tax on the US$1.9 billion sale, which enraged Bangkok's middle class.

Many of the PM's most highly placed supporters also turned against him. Most prominently, media mogul and former friend, Sondhi Limthongkul organised a series of anti-Thaksin rallies in Bangkok, culminating in a rally at Bangkok's Royal Plaza on 4 and 5 February 2006 that drew tens of thousands of protestors.

Thaksin's ministers responded by dissolving the national assembly and scheduling snap elections for 2 April 2006, three years ahead of schedule. Thaksin initially claimed victory, but after a conference with the king, announced that he would take a break from politics.

The Coup & the Red/Yellow Divide

On the evening of 19 September 2006, while Thaksin was attending a UN conference in New York City, the Thai military took power in a bloodless coup. Calling themselves the Council for Democratic Reform under the Constitutional Monarch, the junta cited the TRT government's alleged lese-majesty (treason), corruption, interference with state agencies and creation of social divisions as justification for the coup. Thaksin quickly flew to London, where he remained in exile until his UK visa was revoked in 2008.

In a nationwide referendum held on 19 August 2007, Thais approved a military-drafted constitution. Under the new constitution, elections were finally held in late 2007. After forming a loose coalition with several other parties, parliament chose veteran politician and close Thaksin ally Samak Sundaravej as prime minister.

Not surprisingly, Samak was regarded as little more than a proxy of Thaksin by his opponents, and shortly after taking office he became the target of a series of large-scale protests held by the Peoples' Alliance for Democracy (PAD), the same group of mostly Bangkok-based middle-class royalists who had called for Thaksin's resignation in the lead up to

In 2005, Thaksin Shinawatra became the first prime minister in Thai history to complete a four-year term of office.

1992	1997	1999
Protests led by Chamlong Srimuang against 1991 coup leader Suchinda Kraprayoon lead to violent confrontations; Suchinda resigns following a public scolding by Rama IX.	Thailand devalues its currency, the baht, triggering the Asian economic crisis; massive unemployment and debt, and a significant crash of the Thai stock market, follow.	The BTS (Skytrain), Bangkok's first expansive metro system, opens in commemoration of Rama IX's 72nd birthday; the system is currently in the process of being expanded.

PETER STUCKINGS / LONELY PLANET IMAGES ©

Thai baht, featuring the king

THAILAND'S COLOURS OF PROTEST

Most Thais are aware of the day of the week they were born, and in Thai astrology each day is associated with a particular colour. However, in the aftermath of the 2006 coup, these previously benign hues started to take on a much more political meaning.

To show their alleged support for the royal family, the anti-Thaksin Peoples' Alliance for Democracy (PAD) adopted yellow as their uniform. This goes back to 2006, when in an effort to celebrate the 60th anniversary of Rama IX's ascension to the throne, Thais were encouraged to wear yellow, the colour associated with Monday, the king's birthday.

To differentiate themselves, the pro-Thaksin United Front for Democracy against Dictatorship (UDD) began to wear red, and soon thereafter became known colloquially as the 'red shirts'. To add to the political rainbow, during the riots of April 2009 that disrupted an Asean summit in Pattaya, a blue-shirted faction emerged, apparently aligned with a former Thaksin ally and allegedly sponsored by the Ministry of the Interior. And during the subsequent political crisis of 2010, a 'no colour' group of peace activists and a 'black shirt' faction, believed to consist of rogue elements of the Thai military, also emerged.

Because of the potential political associations, many have become wary about sporting the divisive colours, and on Rama IX's birthday in 2009, pink seemingly became the new yellow when Thais wore the colour as a nod to a previous occasion when the king safely emerged from a lengthy hospital visit wearing a bright pink blazer.

the 2006 coup. By this point, the PAD had already begun wearing their trademark yellow to show their allegiance to the king.

In August 2008, several thousand yellow-shirted PAD protesters invaded and took over Government House in Bangkok. The takeover was followed by sporadic violent clashes between the PAD and the United Front for Democracy against Dictatorship (UDD), a loose association of red-shirted Thaksin supporters who had set up camp nearby at Sanam Luang.

On 25 November, hundreds of armed PAD protesters stormed Bangkok's Suvarnabhumi and Don Muang Airports, entering the passenger terminals and seizing control of the control towers. Thousands of additional PAD sympathisers eventually flooded Suvarnabhumi, leading to the cancellation of all flights and leaving as many as 230,000 domestic and international passengers stranded. The stand-off lasted until 2 December, when the Supreme Court wielded its power yet again in order to ban Samak's successor, Prime Minister Somchai Wongsawat, from politics and ordering his political party and two coalition parties dissolved.

2001	2004	9 June 2006	19 September 2006
Thaksin Shinawatra, Thailand's richest man, is elected prime minister on a populist platform in what some have called the most open, corruption-free election in Thai history.	The MRT, Bangkok's first underground public transport system, is opened; an accident the next year injures 140 and causes the system to shut down for two weeks.	Thailand celebrates the 60th anniversary of Rama IX's ascension to the throne; the Thai king continues to be the longest-serving monarch in the world.	A bloodless coup sees the Thai military take power from Thaksin while he is at a UN meeting in New York; he remains in exile.

In addition to financial loss, the events of 2008 also had a significant social cost in that Thailand, a country that had mostly experienced a relatively high level of domestic stability and harmony throughout its modern history, was now effectively polarised between the predominately middle- and upper-class, urban-based PAD and the largely working-class, rural UDD.

In December 2008, a tenuous new coalition was formed, led by Oxford-educated Abhisit Vejjajiva, leader of the Democrat Party. Despite Abhisit being young, photogenic, articulate and allegedly untainted by corruption, his perceived association with the PAD did little to placate the UDD, and in February 2010, 'red shirts' and self-proclaimed prodemocracy activists united to demand that Prime Minister Abhisit Vejjajiva stand down.

In April 2010 there were violent clashes between police and protesters (numbering up to tens of thousands), resulting in 25 deaths. Redshirted protesters barricaded themselves into an area stretching from Lumphini Park to the shopping district near Siam Square, effectively shutting down parts of central Bangkok. In May the protesters were dispersed by force, but not before at least 36 buildings were set alight and at least 15 people killed. The death toll from the 2010 conflicts amounted to nearly 100 people, making it Thailand's most violent political unrest in 20 years.

Yingluck Shinawatra and the 2011 Floods

Parliamentary elections in 2011 saw the election of Yingluck Shinawatra, the younger sister of the still-exiled Thaksin. A former businesswoman who is also Thailand's first female and youngest prime minister, Yingluck has no prior political experience and has been described by her older brother as his 'clone'. Yingluck's leadership was tested in late 2011, when the outskirts of Bangkok were hit by the most devastating floods in decades. Although nearly all of central Bangkok was spared from flooding, it was largely perceived that this was done at the expense of upcountry regions.

Although much of Yingluck's tenure has been free of the large-scale colour-coded protests of previous years, many Thais suspect she intends to facilitate the return of her brother to Thailand, possibly inciting yet another round of political turmoil.

August 2007	November 2008	April 2010	5 August 2011
In a nationwide referendum, voters agree to approve a military-drafted constitution, Thailand's 17th since becoming a constitutional monarchy in 1932.	Thousands of yellow-shirted anti-Thaksin protesters calling themselves the Peoples' Alliance for Democracy take over Bangkok's airports; tourist numbers drop.	Pro-Thaksin supporters clash with troops in central Bangkok, leading to 25 deaths, several hundred injuries and the torching of several buildings.	Thai parliament approves the election of Yingluck Shinawatra, younger sister of deposed former prime minister Thaksin Shinawatra, and the country's first female prime minister.

People & Culture

Bangkok is both utterly Thai and totally foreign. Old and new ways clash and mingle, constantly redrawing the lines of what it means to be 'Thai'. But despite the international veneer, a Thai value system – built primarily on religious and monarchical devotion – is ticking away, guiding every aspect of life. Almost all Thais, even the most conspicuously consuming, are dedicated Buddhists who aim to be reborn into a better life by making merit (giving donations to temples or feeding monks), regarding merit-making as the key to their earthly success.

PEOPLE OF BANGKOK

Bangkok accommodates every rung of the economic ladder, from the aristocrat to the slum dweller. It is the new start for the economic hopefuls and the last chance for the economic refugees. The lucky ones from the bottom rung form the working-class backbone of the city – taxi drivers, food vendors, maids, nannies and even prostitutes. Many hail from the northeastern provinces and send hard-earned baht back to their families in small rural villages. At the very bottom are the dispossessed, who live in squatter communities on marginal, often polluted land. While the Thai economy has surged, a social net has yet to be constructed. Meanwhile, Bangkok is also the great incubator for Thailand's new generation of young creatives, from designers to architects, and has long nurtured the archetype of the country's middle class.

The city has also represented economic opportunity for foreign immigrants. Approximately a quarter of its population claims some Chinese ancestry, be it Cantonese, Hainanese, Hokkien or Teochew. Although the first Chinese labourers faced discrimination from the Thais, their descendants' success in business, finance and public affairs helped to elevate the status of Chinese and Thai-Chinese families.

Immigrants from South Asia also migrated to Bangkok and comprise the second-largest Asian minority. Sikhs from northern India typically make their living in tailoring, while Sinhalese, Bangladeshis, Nepalis and Pakistanis can be found in the import-export or retail trade.

THE THAI CHARACTER

Much of Thailand's cultural value system is hinged upon respect for the family, religion and monarchy. Within that system each person knows his or her place and Thai children are strictly instructed in the importance of group conformity, respecting elders and suppressing confrontational views. In most social situations, establishing harmony often takes a leading role and Thais take personal pride in making others feel at ease.

Other notable cultural characteristics include a strong belief in the concept of saving face and an equally strong regard for *sà·nùk*, Thai-style fun.

Thailand Demographics

Population: 66.7 million

Fertility rate: 1.6

Percentage of people over 65: 9.2%

Urbanisation rate: 34%

Life expectancy: 73 years

RELIGION

Theravada Buddhism

Around 90% of Bangkokians are Buddhists, who believe that individuals work out their own paths to *nibbana* (nirvana) through a combination of good works, meditation and study of the *dhamma* (Buddhist philosophy).

The social and administrative centre for Thai Buddhism is the wát (temple or monastery), a walled compound containing several buildings constructed in the traditional Thai style with steep, swooping roof lines and colourful interior murals; the most important structures contain solemn Buddha statues cast in bronze.

Walk the streets of Bangkok early in the morning and you'll catch the flash of shaved heads bobbing above bright ochre robes, as monks all over the city engage in *bin·tá·bàht,* the daily house-to-house alms food-gathering. Thai men are expected to shave their heads and don monastic robes temporarily at least once in their lives.

Guardian Spirits

Animism predates the arrival of all other religions in Bangkok, and it still plays an important role in the everyday life of most city residents. Believing that *prá poom* (guardian spirits) inhabit rivers, canals, trees and other natural features, and that these spirits must be placated whenever humans trespass upon or make use of these features, the Thais build spirit shrines to house the displaced spirits. These dollhouse-like structures perch on wood or cement pillars next to their homes and receive daily offerings of rice, fruit, flowers and water.

Cultural Readings

Being Dharma:
The Essence of
the Buddha's
Teachings (2001;
Ajahn Chah)

Very Thai: Every-
day Pop Culture
(2006; Philip
Cornwel-Smith)

Thai Folk Wisdom:
Contemporary
Takes on Tradi-
tional Proverbs
(2010; Tulaya
Pornpiriyakulchai
& Jane Vejjaviva)

Sacred Tattoos of
Thailand (2011;
Joe Cummings)

THE CHINESE INFLUENCE

In many ways Bangkok is a Chinese, as much as a Thai, city. The presence of the Chinese in Bangkok dates back to before the founding of the city, when Thonburi Si Mahasamut was little more than a Chinese trading outpost on Mae Nam Chao Phraya. In the 1780s, during the construction of the new capital under Rama I (King Phraphutthayotfa; r 1782–1809), Hokkien, Teochew and Hakka Chinese were hired as labourers. The Chinese already living in the area were relocated to the districts of Yaowarat and Sampeng, today known as Bangkok's Chinatown.

During the reign of Rama I, many Chinese began to move up in status and wealth. They controlled many of Bangkok's shops and businesses, and because of increased trading ties with China, were responsible for an immense expansion in Thailand's market economy. Visiting Europeans during the 1820s were astonished by the number of Chinese trading ships on Mae Nam Chao Phraya, and some assumed that the Chinese formed the majority of Bangkok's population.

The newfound wealth of certain Chinese trading families created one of Thailand's first elite classes that was not directly related to royalty. Known as *jâo sŭa*, these 'merchant lords' eventually obtained additional status by accepting official posts and royal titles, as well as offering their daughters to the royal family. At one point, Rama V (King Chulalongkorn; r 1868–1910) took a Chinese consort. Today it is believed that more than half of the people in Bangkok can claim some Chinese ancestry. The current Thai king is also believed to have partial Chinese ancestry.

During the reign of Rama III (King Phranangklao; r 1824–51), the Thai capital began to absorb many elements of Chinese food, design, fashion and literature. This growing ubiquity of Chinese culture, coupled with the tendency of the Chinese men to marry Thai women and assimilate into Thai culture, had, by the beginning of the 20th century, resulted in relatively little difference between the Chinese and their Siamese counterparts.

Other Religions

Thai royal ceremony remains almost exclusively the domain of one of the most ancient religious traditions still functioning in the kingdom, Brahmanism. White-robed, topknotted priests of Indian descent keep alive an arcane collection of rituals that, it is generally believed, must be performed at regular intervals to sustain the three pillars of Thai nationhood: sovereignty, religion and the monarchy.

Green-hued onion domes looming over rooftops belong to mosques and mark the immediate neighbourhood as Muslim, while brightly painted and ornately carved cement spires indicate a Hindu temple. Wander down congested Th Chakraphet in the Phahurat district to find Sri Gurusingh Sabha, a Sikh temple where visitors are very welcome. A handful of steepled Christian churches, including a few historic ones, have been built over the centuries and can be found near the banks of Mae Nam Chao Phraya. In Chinatown, large round doorways topped with heavily inscribed Chinese characters and flanked by red paper lanterns mark the location of *săhn jôw*, Chinese temples dedicated to the worship of Buddhist, Taoist and Confucian deities.

MONARCHY

The Thais' relationship with their king is deeply spiritual and intensely personal. Many view him as a god (all Thai kings are referred to as 'Rama', one of the incarnations of the Hindu god Vishnu) and as a father figure (the king's birthday is the national celebration of Father's Day). The reigning monarch, King Bhumibol Adulyadej, also known as Rama IX, inherited automatic reverence when he assumed the throne in 1946, but he captured the Thai people's hearts with his actions.

In June 2006, the king celebrated his 60th year on the throne, an event regarded by many Thais as bittersweet because the ageing king may soon leave the helm of the Thai nation. His son, Crown Prince Maha Vajiralongkorn, has been chosen to succeed him, but it is the king's daughter, Princess Mahachakri Sirindhorn, that many Thais feel a deeper connection with because she has followed in her father's philanthropic footsteps.

It's worth mentioning that, in Thai society, not only is criticising the monarchy an extreme social faux pas, it's also illegal.

VISUAL ARTS

Divine Inspiration

The wát served as a locus for the highest expressions of Thai art for roughly 800 years, from the Lanna to Ratanakosin eras. Accordingly, Bangkok's 400-plus Buddhist temples are brimming with the figuratively imaginative, if thematically formulaic, art of Thailand's foremost muralists. Always instructional in intent, such painted images range from the depiction of the *jataka* (stories of the Buddha's past lives) and scenes from the Indian Hindu epic *Ramayana*, to elaborate scenes detailing daily life in Thailand.

The Modern Era

Although the origins of Thai art can be traced back to religion, today's cultural currents are as likely to be swayed by Korean soap operas, Japanese manga comics, Chinese mass merchandising, European fashion and American street culture as traditional Thai life. These influences are fuelling introspection among artists, with more art being created that pertains to the condition of the self and the societal constraints

Recommended Arts Reading

Flavours: Thai Contemporary Art (2005; Steven Pettifor)

Bangkok Design: Thai Ideas in Textiles & Furniture (2006; Brian Mertens)

Buddhist Temples of Thailand: A Visual Journey Through Thailand's 40 Most Historic Wats (2010; Joe Cummings)

The Thai House: History and Evolution (2002; Ruethai Chaichongrak)

The Arts of Thailand (1998; Steve Van Beek)

WHAT'S A WÁT?

Bangkok is home to hundreds of wáts, temple compounds that have traditionally been at the centre of community life.

Buildings & Structures

Even the smallest wát will usually have a *bóht*, *wí·hăhn* and monks' living quarters.

➡ **Bóht** The most sacred prayer room at a wát, similar in size and shape to the *wí·hăhn*. Aside from the fact it does not house the main Buddha image, you'll know the *bóht* because it is more ornately decorated and has eight cornerstones to ward off evil.

➡ **Chedi (stupa)** A large bell-shaped tower usually containing five structural elements symbolising (from bottom to top) earth, water, fire, wind and void; depending on the wát, relics of the Buddha, a Thai king or some other notable are housed inside.

➡ **Drum Tower** Elevates the ceremonial drum beaten by novices.

➡ **Mon·dòp** An open-sided, square building with four arches and a pyramidal roof, used to worship religious objects or texts.

➡ **Prang** A towering phallic spire of Khmer origin serving the same religious purpose as a *chedi*.

➡ **Săh·lah (sala)** A pavilion, often open-sided, for relaxation, lessons or miscellaneous activities.

➡ **Wí·hăhn (vihara)** The sanctuary for the temple's main Buddha image and where laypeople come to make their offerings. Classic architecture typically has a three-tiered roof representing the triple gems: the Buddha (the teacher), Dharma (the teaching) and Brotherhood (the followers).

Buddha Images

Elongated earlobes, no evidence of bone or muscle, arms that reach to the knees, a third eye: these are some of the 32 rules, originating from 3rd-century India, that govern the depiction of the Buddha in sculpture and denote his divine nature. Other symbols to be aware of are the various hand positions and 'postures', which depict periods in the life of the Buddha.

➡ **Sitting** Teaching or meditating. If the right hand is pointed towards the earth, the Buddha is subduing the demons of desire. If the hands are folded in the lap, the Buddha is meditating.

➡ **Reclining** The exact moment of the Buddha's passing into *parinibbana* (postdeath nirvana).

➡ **Standing** Bestowing blessings or taming evil forces.

➡ **Walking** The Buddha after his return to earth from heaven.

imposed upon it. Whereas a decade ago artists seemed to be the defenders of a precious national identity, now themes have become more personal and reflective. Though such approaches seem more aligned to the modern Western artist's mindset, there still remains an inextricable leaning towards a more spiritual, and ostensibly Buddhist, path.

MUSIC

Classical Thai

Classical central-Thai music *(pleng tai deum)* features a dazzling array of textures and subtleties, hair-raising tempos and pastoral melodies. The classical orchestra *(bèe-pâht)* can include as few as five players or might have more than 20. Leading the band is *bèe*, a straight-lined woodwind instrument with a reed mouthpiece and an oboe-like tone; you'll hear it most at *moo·ay tai* (Thai boxing; also spelt *muay thai*) matches. The four-stringed *phin*, plucked like a guitar, lends subtle counterpoint, while *rá·nâht èhk*, a bamboo-keyed percussion instrument resembling the xylophone, carries the main melodies. The slender *sor*, a bowed instrument with a coconut-shell soundbox, provides soaring embellishments, as does the *klòo•i*, a wooden Thai flute.

Lôok Tûng & Mŏr Lam

Popular Thai music has borrowed much from Western music, particularly in instrumentation, but retains a distinct flavour of its own. The bestselling of all modern musical genres in Thailand remains *lôok tûng*. Literally 'children of the fields', *lôok tûng* dates back to the 1940s, is comparable to country and western in the USA, and is a genre that tends to appeal most to working-class Thais. Subject matter almost always cleaves to tales of lost love, tragic early death and the dire circumstances of farmers who work day in and day out and, at the end of the year, still owe money to the bank.

Another genre more firmly rooted in northeastern Thailand, and nearly as popular in Bangkok, is *mŏr lam*. Based on the songs played on the Lao-Isan *kaan*, a wind instrument devised of a double row of bamboo-like reeds fitted into a hardwood soundbox, *mŏr lam* features a simple but insistent bass beat and plaintive vocal melodies.

Songs for Life

The 1970s ushered in a new music style inspired by the politically conscious folk rock of the US and Europe, which the Thais dubbed *pleng pêu·a chee·wít* (literally 'music for life') after Marxist Jit Phumisak's earlier Art for Life movement. Closely identified with the Thai band Caravan – which still performs regularly – the introduction of this style was the most significant musical shift in Thailand since *lôok tûng* arose in the 1940s.

Pleng pêua chee·wít has political and environmental topics rather than the usual love themes. During the authoritarian dictatorships of the '70s many of Caravan's songs were banned. Following the massacre of student demonstrators in 1976, some members of the band fled to the hills to take up with armed communist groups.

T-Pop & Indie

In recent years, Thailand has also developed a thriving teen-pop industry – sometimes referred to as T-Pop – centred on artists who have been chosen for their good looks, and then matched with syrupy song arrangements. Labels GMM Grammy and RS Productions are the heavyweights of this genre, and their rivalry has resulted in a flood of copycat acts.

In the 1990s an alternative pop scene – known as *glorng sĕh·ree* ('free drum'); also *pleng dâi din* ('underground music') – grew in Bangkok. Modern Dog, a Britpop-inspired band of four Chulalongkorn University graduates, is generally credited with bringing independent Thai music into the mainstream, and their success prompted an explosion of similar bands and indie recording labels.

Recommended Playlist

GMM Memory Hits Vol 1 (various artists)

Da Jim Rap Thai (Dajim)

Big Ass Begins (Big Ass)

Ruam Hit Pleng Thai Amata Lukthung 2 (Chai Mueang Sing)

Palmy (Palmy)

GMM Country Hits Vol 1 (various artists)

Mint (Silly Fools)

CINEMA

Thailand has a lively homespun movie industry and produces nearly 50 comedies, dramas and horror films every year. Cinema is possibly the country's most significant contemporary cultural export, and several Thai films of the last two decades have emerged as international film festival darlings.

Bangkok Film launched Thailand's film industry with the first Thai-directed silent movie, *Chok Sorng Chan*, in 1927. Silent films proved to be more popular than talkies right into the 1960s, and as late as

1969 Thai studios were still producing them from 16mm stock. Perhaps partially influenced by India's famed masala movies – which enjoyed a strong following in post-WWII Bangkok – film companies blended romance, comedy, melodrama and adventure to give Thai audiences a little bit of everything.

The Thai movie industry almost died during the '80s and '90s, swamped by Hollywood extravaganzas and the boom era's taste for anything imported. From a 1970s peak of about 200 releases per year, the Thai output shrank to an average of only 10 films a year by 1997. The Southeast Asian economic crisis that year threatened to further bludgeon the ailing industry, but the lack of funding coupled with foreign competition brought about a new emphasis on quality rather than quantity. The current era boasts a new generation of seriously good Thai directors, several of whom studied film abroad during Thailand's '80s and early '90s boom period. Thai and foreign critics alike speak of a current Thai 'new wave', who, avoiding the soap operatics of the past, favour gritty realism, artistic innovation and a strengthened Thai identity.

Recommended Thai Movies

Mon Rak Transistor (2001; directed by Pen-Ek Ratanaruang)

Sud Sanaeha (Blissfully Yours; 2002; directed by Apichatpong Weerasethakul)

Ong Bak (2003; directed by Prachya Pinkaew)

Satree Lex (Iron Ladies; 2000; directed by Yongyoot Thongkongtoon)

Fah Talai Jone (Tears of the Black Tiger; 2000; directed by Wisit Sasantieng)

Suriyothai (2001; directed by Chatrichalerm Yukol)

Nang Nak (1999; directed by Nonzee Nimibutr)

BANGKOK FICTION

First-time visitors to virtually any of Bangkok's English-language bookstores will notice an abundance of novels with titles such as The Butterfly Trap, Confessions of a Bangkok Private Eye, Even Thai Girls Cry, Fast Eddie's Lucky 7 A Go Go, Lady of Pattaya, The Go Go Dancer Who Stole My Viagra, My Name Lon You Like Me?, The Pole Dancer, and Thai Touch. Welcome to the Bangkok school of fiction, a genre, as the titles suggest, defined by its obsession with crime, exoticism and Thai women.

The birth of this genre can be traced back to Jack Reynolds' 1956 novel, A Woman of Bangkok. Although long out of print, the book is still an acknowledged influence for many Bangkok-based writers, and Reynolds' formula of Western-man-meets-beautiful-but-dangerous-Thai-woman – occasionally spiced up with a dose of crime – is a staple of the modern genre.

Standouts include John Burdett's Bangkok 8 (2003), a page-turner in which a half-Thai, half-fa·ràng (Westerner) police detective investigates the python-and-cobras murder of a US marine in Bangkok. Along the way we're treated to vivid portraits of Bangkok's gritty nightlife scene and insights into Thai Buddhism. A film version of the novel is in the early stages of production, and its sequels, Bangkok Tattoo and Bangkok Haunts, have sold well in the US.

Christopher G Moore, a Canadian who has lived in Bangkok for the last two decades, has authored more than 20 mostly Bangkok-based crime novels to positive praise both in Thailand and abroad. His description of Bangkok's sleazy Thermae Coffee House (called 'Zeno' in A Killing Smile) is the closest literature comes to evoking the perpetual male adolescence to which such places cater.

Private Dancer, by popular English thriller author Stephen Leather, is another classic example of Bangkok fiction, despite having only been available via download until recently.

Jake Needham's 1999 thriller The Big Mango provides tongue-in-cheek references to the Bangkok bargirl scene and later became the first expat novel to be translated into Thai.

TRADITIONAL THEATRE & DANCE

Kŏhn

Scenes performed in traditional *kŏhn* (and *lá·kon* performances) – a dance drama formerly reserved for court performances – come from the 'epic journey' tale of the *Ramakien* (the Thai version of the Hindu epic, the *Ramayana*), with parallels in the Greek Odyssey and the myth of Jason and the Argonauts. In all *kŏhn* performances, four types of characters are represented – male humans, female humans, monkeys and demons. Monkey and demon figures are always masked with the elaborate head coverings often seen in tourist promo material. Behind the masks and make-up, all actors are male. Traditional *kŏhn* is very expensive to produce – Ravana's retinue alone (Ravana is the Ramakian's principal villain) consists of more than 100 demons, each with a distinctive mask.

Lá · kon

The more formal *lá·kon nai* (inner *lá·kon,* which means that it is performed inside the palace) was originally performed for lower nobility by all-female ensembles. Today it's a dying art, even more so than royal *kŏhn.* In addition to scenes from the Ramakian, *lá·kon nai* performances may include traditional Thai folk tales; whatever the story, text is always sung. *Lá·kon nôrk* (outer *lá·kon,* performed outside the palace) deals exclusively with folk tales and features a mix of sung and spoken text, sometimes with improvisation. Male and female performers are permitted. Like *kŏhn* and *lá·kon nai,* performances of *lá·kon nôrk* are increasingly rare.

A variation on *lá·kon* that has evolved specifically for shrine worship, *lá·kon gâa bon* involves an ensemble of about 20, including musicians. At an important shrine such as Bangkok's Lak Meuang, four *gâa bon* troupes may alternate each week, as a performance lasts from 9am to 3pm and there is usually a long list of worshippers waiting to hire them.

Lí · gair

In outlying working-class neighbourhoods of Bangkok you may be lucky enough to come across the gaudy, raucous *lí·gair.* This theatrical art form is thought to have descended from drama-rituals brought to southern Thailand by Arab and Malay traders. The first native public performance in central Thailand came about when a group of Thai Muslims staged *lí·gair* for Rama V in Bangkok during the funeral commemoration of Queen Sunantha. *Lí·gair* grew very popular under Rama VI, peaked in the early 20th century and has been fading slowly since the 1960s.

Lá · kon Lék

Lá·kon lék (little theatre; also known as *hùn lŏo·ang,* or royal puppets), like *kŏhn,* was once reserved for court performances. Metre-high marionettes made of *kòi* paper and wire, wearing elaborate costumes modelled on those of the *kŏhn,* were used to convey similar themes, music and dance movements.

Two to three puppet masters were required to manipulate each *hùn lŏo·ang* – including arms, legs, hands, even fingers and eyes – by means of wires attached to long poles. Stories were drawn from Thai folk tales, particularly Phra Aphaimani (a classical Thai literary work), and occasionally from the *Ramakian.* Surviving examples of a smaller, 30cm court version called *hùn lék* (little puppets) are occasionally used in live performances; only one puppeteer is required for each marionette in *hùn lék.*

Another form of Thai puppet theatre, *hùn grà·bòrk* (cylinder puppets) is based on popular Hainanese puppet shows. It uses 30cm hand puppets carved from wood and viewed only from the waist up.

E-BOOKS

Eating in Thailand

There's an entire universe of amazing dishes once you get beyond 'pad thai' and green curry, and for many visitors food is one of the main reasons for choosing Thailand as a destination. Even more remarkable, however, is the love for Thai food among the locals: Thais become just as excited as tourists when faced with a bowl of well-prepared noodles or when seated at a renowned hawker stall. This unabashed enthusiasm for eating, not to mention an abundance of fascinating ingredients and influences, has generated one of the most fun and diverse food scenes anywhere in the world.

HOW THAIS EAT

Aside from the occasional indulgence in deep-fried savouries, most Thais sustain themselves on a varied and healthy diet of many fruits, rice and vegetables mixed with smaller amounts of animal protein and fat. Satisfaction seems to come not from eating large amounts of food at any one meal, but rather from nibbling at a variety of dishes with as many different flavours as possible throughout the day.

The author of Eating Thai Food (www.eating thaifood.com) has put together an 88-page illustrated PDF guide to identifying and ordering Thai dishes for foreign visitors.

Nor are certain kinds of food restricted to certain times of day. Practically anything can be eaten first thing in the morning, whether it's sweet, salty or chilli-ridden. *Kôw gaang* (curry over rice) is a very popular morning meal, as are *kôw nĕe·o mŏo tôrt* (deep-fried pork with sticky rice) and *kôw man gài* (sliced chicken cooked in chicken broth and served over rice).

Lighter morning choices, especially for Thais of Chinese descent, include *ʿbah·tôrng·gŏh* (deep-fried bits of dough) dipped in warm *nám dôw hôo* (soy milk). Thais also eat noodles, whether fried or in soup, with great gusto in the morning, or as a substantial snack at any time of day or night.

As the staple with which almost all Thai dishes are eaten (noodles are still seen as a Chinese import), *kôw* (rice) is considered an indispensable part of the daily diet. Most Bangkok families will put on a pot of rice, or start the rice cooker, just after rising in the morning to prepare a base for the day's menu.

Thai Food by David Thompson is widely considered the most authoritative English-language book on Thai cooking. Thompson's latest book, Thai Street Food, focuses on less-formal street cuisine.

Finding its way into almost every meal is *ʿblah* (fish), even if it's only in the form of *nám ʿblah* (a thin amber sauce made from fermented anchovies), which is used to salt Thai dishes, much as soy sauce is used in eastern Asia. Pork is undoubtedly the preferred protein, with chicken in second place. Beef is seldom eaten in Bangkok, particularly by Thais of Chinese descent who subscribe to a Buddhist teaching that forbids eating 'large' animals.

Thais are prodigious consumers of fruit. Vendors push glass-and-wood carts filled with a rainbow of fresh sliced papaya, pineapple, watermelon and mango, and a more muted palette of salt-pickled or candied seasonal fruits. These are usually served in a small plastic bag with a thin bamboo stick to use as an eating utensil.

Because many restaurants in Thailand are able to serve dishes at an only slightly higher price than they would cost to make at home, Thais dine out far more often than their Western counterparts. Dining with others is always preferred because it means everyone has a chance to sample several dishes. When forced to fly solo by circumstances – such as during lunch breaks at work – a single diner usually sticks to one-plate dishes such as fried rice or curry over rice.

THE FOUR FLAVOURS

Simply put, sweet, sour, salty and spicy are the parameters that define Thai food, and although many associate the cuisine with spiciness, virtually every dish is an exercise in balancing these four tastes. This balance might be obtained by a squeeze of lime juice, a spoonful of sugar and a glug of fish sauce, or a tablespoon of fermented soybeans and a strategic splash of vinegar. Bitter also factors into many Thai dishes, and often comes from the addition of a vegetable or herb. Regardless of the source, the goal is the same: a favourable balance of four clear, vibrant flavours.

STAPLES & SPECIALITIES
Rice & Noodles

Rice is so central to Thai food culture that the most common term for 'eat' is *gin kôw* (literally, 'consume rice') and one of the most common greetings is *Gin kôw rěu yang?* (Have you consumed rice yet?). To eat is to eat rice, and for most of the country, a meal is not acceptable without this staple.

Rice is customarily served alongside main dishes like curries, stir-fries or soups, which are lumped together as *gàp kôw* (with rice). When you order plain rice in a restaurant you use the term *kôw plòw* ('plain rice') or *kôw sŏo·ay* ('beautiful rice').

You'll find four basic kinds of noodle in Thailand. Hardly surprising, given the Thai fixation on rice, is the overwhelming popularity of *sên gŏo·ay děe·o*, noodles made from rice flour mixed with water to form a paste, which is then steamed to form wide, flat sheets. The sheets are folded and sliced into various widths.

Also made from rice, *kà·nŏm jeen* is produced by pushing rice-flour paste through a sieve into boiling water, much the way Italian-style pasta is made. *Kà·nŏm jeen* is a popular morning market meal that is eaten doused with various spicy curries and topped with a self-selection of fresh and pickled vegetables and herbs.

The third kind of noodle, *bà·mèe*, is made from wheat flour and egg. It's yellowish in colour and sold only in fresh bundles.

Maintained by a Thai woman living in the US, She Simmers (www.shesimmers.com) is a good source of recipes that cover the basics of Thai cooking.

NOODLE MIXOLOGY

If you see a steel rack containing four lidded glass bowls or jars on your table, it's proof that the restaurant you're in serves *gŏo·ay děe·o* (rice noodle soup). Typically these containers offer four choices: *nám sôm prík* (sliced green chillies in vinegar), *nám plah* (fish sauce), *prík pòn* (dried red chilli, flaked or ground to a near powder) and *nám·dahn* (plain white sugar).

In typically Thai fashion, these condiments offer three ways to make the soup hotter – hot and sour, hot and salty, and just plain hot – and one to make it sweet.

The typical noodle-eater will add a teaspoonful of each one of these condiments to the noodle soup, except for the sugar, which in sweet-tooth Bangkok usually rates a full tablespoon. Until you're used to these strong seasonings, we recommend adding them a small bit at a time, tasting the soup along the way to make sure you don't go overboard.

Finally there's *wún·sên*, an almost clear noodle made from mung-bean starch and water. Often sold in dried bunches, *wún·sên* (literally 'jelly thread') is prepared by soaking in hot water for a few minutes. The most common use of the noodle is in *yam wún sên*, a hot and tangy salad made with lime juice, fresh sliced *prík kêe nŏo* (tiny chillies), shrimp, ground pork and various seasonings.

Curries & Soups

In Thai, *gaang* (it sounds somewhat similar to the English 'gang') is often translated as 'curry', but it actually describes any dish with a lot of liquid and can thus refer to soups (such as *gaang jèut*) as well as the classic chilli-paste-based curries for which Thai cuisine is famous. The preparation of the latter begins with a *krê·uang gaang*, created by mashing, pounding and grinding an array of fresh ingredients with a stone mortar and pestle to form an aromatic, extremely pungent-tasting and rather thick paste. Typical ingredients in a *krê·uang gaang* include dried chilli, galangal, lemon grass, kaffir lime zest, shallots, garlic, shrimp paste and salt.

Another food celebrity that falls into the soupy category is *dôm yam*, the famous Thai spicy and sour soup. Fuelling the fire beneath *dôm yam*'s often velvety surface are fresh *prík kêe nŏo* (tiny chillies) or, alternatively, half a teaspoonful of *nám prík pŏw* (a roasted chilli paste). Lemon grass, kaffir lime leaf and lime juice give *dôm yam* its characteristic tang.

Stir-Fries & Deep-Fries

The simplest dishes in the Thai culinary repertoire are the various *pàt* (stir-fries), introduced to Thailand by the Chinese, who are world famous for being able to stir-fry a whole banquet in a single wok.

The list of *pàt* dishes seems endless. Many cling to their Chinese roots, such as the ubiquitous *pàt pàk bûng fai daang* (morning glory flash-fried with garlic and chilli), while some are Thai-Chinese hybrids, such as *pàt pèt* (literally 'hot stir-fry'), in which the main ingredients, typically meat or fish, are quickly stir-fried with red curry paste.

Tôrt (deep-frying in oil) is mainly reserved for snacks such as *glôo·ay tôrt* (deep-fried bananas) or *pò·pée·a* (egg rolls). An exception is *plah tôrt* (deep-fried fish), which is a common way to prepare fish.

Hot & Tangy Salads

Standing right alongside curries in terms of Thai-ness is the ubiquitous *yam*, a hot and tangy 'salad' typically based around seafood, meat or vegetables.

Lime juice provides the tang, while the abundant use of fresh chilli generates the heat. Most *yam* are served at room temperature or just slightly warmed by any cooked ingredients. The dish functions equally well as part of a meal, or on its own as *gàp glâam*, snack food to accompany a night of boozing.

Nám Prík

Although they're more home than restaurant food, *nám prík*, spicy chilli-based 'dips' are, for the locals at least, among the most emblematic of all Thai dishes. Typically eaten with rice and steamed or fresh vegetables and herbs, they're also among the most regional of Thai dishes, and you could probably pinpoint the province you're in by simply looking at the *nám prík* on offer.

HAWKER

Thai Hawker Food by Kenny Yee and Catherine Gordon is an illustrated guide to recognising and ordering street food in Thailand.

Fish Sauce

Westerners might scoff at the all-too-literal name of this condiment, but for much of Thai cooking, fish sauce is more than just another ingredient, it is *the* ingredient.

Essentially the liquid obtained from fermented fish, fish sauce takes various guises depending on the region. In northeastern Thailand, discerning diners prefer a thick, pasty mash of fermented freshwater fish and sometimes rice. Elsewhere, where people have access to the sea, fish sauce takes the form of a thin liquid extracted from salted anchovies. In both cases the result is highly pungent, but generally salty (rather than fishy) in taste, and used much the same way as the salt-shaker in the West.

Fruits

Being a tropical country, Thailand excels in the fruit department. *Má·môo·ang* (mangoes) alone come in a dozen varieties that are eaten at different stages of ripeness. Other common fruit include *sàp·bà·rót* (pineapple), *má·lá·gor* (papaya) and *đaang moh* (watermelon), all of which are sold from ubiquitous vendor carts and are accompanied by a dipping mix of salt, sugar and ground chilli.

Some of the more unusual types of fruit you're likely to come across in Bangkok's fresh markets and supermarkets:

➡ **Kà·nŭn** – Jackfruit hails from India. The giant green pod conceals dozens of waxy yellow sections that taste like a blend of pineapple and bananas (it reminds us of Juicy Fruit chewing gum). At its peak from January to May.

➡ **Tú·ree·an** – Due to its intense odour and weaponlike appearance, the durian is possibly Southeast Asia's most infamous fruit, the flesh of which can suggest everything from custard to onions. Available from May to August.

➡ **Lín·jèe** – The pink skin of the lychee conceals an addictive translucent flesh similar in flavour to a grape. Available from April to June.

➡ **Ngó** – Known in English as rambutan, *ngó* has a tough hairy skin (*rambut* is the Malay word for hair) that holds a clear, sweet-tasting flesh and a large pit. Available from May to September.

➡ **Lam yai** – This indigenous fruit, known in English as longan, hides a sweet and fragrant flesh under its brittle shell. Often dried and used in juices or as a snack. Available from June to August.

Written, photographed and maintained by the author of this chapter, www.austinbushphotography.com/ blog details food and dining in both Bangkok and provincial Thailand.

EATING IN THAILAND STAPLES & SPECIALITIES

(CON)FUSION CUISINE

A popular dish at restaurants across Thailand is *kôw pàt à·me·rí·gan*, 'American fried rice'. Taking the form of rice fried with ketchup, raisins and peas, sides of ham and deep-fried hot dogs, and topped with a fried egg, the dish is, well, every bit as revolting as it sounds. But at least there's an interesting history behind it: American fried rice apparently dates back to the Vietnam War era, when thousands of US troops were based in northeastern Thailand. A local cook apparently decided to take the ubiquitous 'American Breakfast' (also known as ABF: fried eggs with ham and/or hot dogs, and white bread, typically eaten with ketchup) and make it 'Thai' by frying the various elements with rice.

This culinary cross-pollination is only a recent example of the tendency of Thai cooks to pick and choose from the variety of cuisines at their disposal. Other (significantly more palatable) examples include *gaang mát·sà·màn*, 'Muslim curry', a now classic blend of Thai and Middle Eastern cooking styles, and the famous *pàt tai*, essentially a blend of Chinese cooking methods and ingredients (frying, rice noodles) with Thai flavours (fish sauce, chilli, tamarind).

MUITO OBRIGADO

Try to imagine a Thai curry without the chillies, *pàt tai* without the peanuts, or papaya salad without the papaya. Many of the ingredients used on a daily basis by Thais are recent introductions courtesy of European traders and missionaries. During the early 16th century, while Spanish and Portuguese explorers were first reaching the shores of Southeast Asia, there was also subsequent expansion and discovery in the Americas. The Portuguese in particular were quick to seize the exciting products coming from the New World and market them in the East, thus most likely having introduced such modern-day Asian staples as tomatoes, potatoes, corn, lettuce, cabbage, chillies, papayas, guavas, pineapples, pumpkins, sweet potatoes, peanuts and tobacco.

Chillies in particular seem to have struck a chord with Thais, and are thought to have first arrived in Ayuthaya via the Portuguese around 1550. Before their arrival, the natives got their heat from bitter-hot herbs and roots such as ginger and pepper.

And not only did the Portuguese introduce some crucial ingredients to the Thai kitchen, but also some enduring cooking techniques, particularly in the area of sweets. The bright-yellow duck egg and syrup-based treats you see at many Thai markets are direct descendants of Portuguese desserts known as *fios de ovos* ('egg threads') and *ovos moles*. And in the area surrounding the Church of Santa Cruz (p97), a former Portuguese enclave, you can still find *kà·nǒm fa·ràng,* a bunlike snack baked over coals.

→ **Má·feuang** – An import from the Americas, the starfruit or carambola is refreshingly crispy and slightly tart. Available from October to December.

→ **Chom·pôo** – Resembling a small pear, the indigenous rose apple is a delicate and crispy fruit with a slightly bitter flavour and a mild rose scent. Available from February to June.

→ **Nóy nàh** – Known in English as custard apple, this native of the Americas has a soft and slightly gritty texture and predominantly sweet flavour. Available from June to September.

→ **Mang·kút** – Known as mangosteen in English, the thick purple skin of this Queen of Fruit conceals a creamy white flesh that is equal parts rich and tangy. Available from May to October.

→ **Sôm oh** – The flesh of this indigenous fruit, known in English as pomelo, comes in large sections and is generally sweeter than the grapefruit it resembles. Available August to November.

Thai Food Master (www.thaifood master.com), maintained by a long-time foreign resident of Thailand, contains helpful step-by-step photos that illustrate the making of a variety of Thai dishes.

Sweets

English-language Thai menus often have a section called 'Desserts', but the concept takes two slightly different forms in Thailand. *Kǒrng wǎhn,* which translates as 'sweet things', are small, rich sweets that often boast a slightly salty flavour. Prime ingredients for *kǒrng wǎhn* include grated coconut, coconut milk, rice flour (from white rice or sticky rice), cooked sticky rice, tapioca, mung-bean starch, boiled taro and various fruits.

Thai sweets similar to the European concept of pastries are called *kà·nǒm.* Probably the most popular type of *kà·nǒm* are the bite-sized items wrapped in banana leaves, especially *kôw đôm gà·tí* and *kôw đôm mát.* Both consist of sticky rice grains steamed with *gà·tí* (coconut milk) inside a banana-leaf wrapper to form a solid, almost taffylike, mass.

Although foreigners don't seem to immediately take to most Thai sweets, two dishes few visitors have trouble with are *roh·dee,* the backpacker staple 'banana pancakes' slathered with sugar and condensed milk, and *ai·đim gà·tí,* Thai-style coconut ice cream. At more traditional shops, the ice cream is garnished with toppings such as kidney beans or sticky rice, and is a brilliant snack on a sweltering Thai afternoon.

DRINKS

Coffee, Tea & Fruit Drinks

Thais are big coffee drinkers, and good-quality arabica and robusta are cultivated in the hilly areas of northern and southern Thailand. The traditional filtering system is nothing more than a narrow cloth bag attached to a steel handle. This type of coffee is served in a glass, mixed with sugar and sweetened with condensed milk – if you don't want either, be sure to specify *gah·faa dam* (black coffee) followed with *mâi sài nám·đahn* (without sugar).

Black tea, both local and imported, is available at the same places that serve real coffee. *Chah tai,* Thai-style tea, derives its characteristic orange-red colour from ground tamarind seed added after curing.

Fruit drinks appear all over Thailand and are an excellent way to rehydrate after water becomes unpalatable. Most *nám pŏn·lá·mái* (fruit juices) are served with a touch of sugar and salt and a whole lot of ice. Many foreigners object to the salt, but it serves a metabolic role in helping the body to cope with tropical temperatures.

VEGETARIANS & VEGANS

Vegetarianism isn't a widespread trend in Thailand, but many of the tourist-oriented restaurants cater to vegetarians, and there are also a handful of *ráhn ah·hăhn mang·sà·wí·rát* (vegetarian restaurants) in Bangkok where the food is served buffet-style and is very inexpensive. Dishes are almost always 100% vegan (ie no meat, poultry, fish or fish sauce, dairy or egg products).

During the Vegetarian Festival, celebrated by Chinese Buddhists in October, many restaurants and street stalls in Bangkok go meatless for one month. During the remainder of the year, the downloadable *Vegetarian Thai Food Guide* (http://www.eatingthaifood.com/vegetarian -thai-food-guide) is a handy resource.

The phrase 'I'm vegetarian' in Thai is *pŏm gin jair* (for men) or *dì·chăn gin jair* (for women). Loosely translated this means 'I eat only vegetarian food', which includes no eggs and no dairy products – in other words, total vegan.

HABITS & CUSTOMS

Like most of Thai culture, eating conventions appear relaxed and informal but are orchestrated by many implied rules.

Whether at home or in a restaurant, Thai meals are always served 'family-style', that is, from common serving platters, and the plates appear in whatever order the kitchen can prepare them. When serving yourself from a common platter, put no more than one spoonful onto your plate at a time. Heaping your plate with all 'your' portions at once will look greedy to Thais unfamiliar with Western conventions.

Bangkok's Top 50 Street Food Stalls, by Chawadee Nualkhair, also functions well as a general introduction and guide to Thai-style informal dining.

STREET FOOD

REGIONAL VARIATIONS

One particularly unique aspect of Thai food is its regional diversity. Despite having evolved in a relatively small area, Thai cuisine is anything but a single entity, and takes a slightly different form every time it crosses a provincial border. For a description of the dishes, flavours and ingredients that comprise Bangkok-style Thai food, and the best places to sample it, see our Eating chapter (p25).

Another important factor in a Thai meal is achieving a balance of flavours and textures. Traditionally, the party orders a curry, a steamed or fried fish, a stir-fried vegetable dish and a soup, taking great care to balance cool and hot, sour and sweet, salty and plain.

Originally Thai food was eaten with the fingers, and it still is in certain regions of the kingdom. In the early 1900s, Thais began setting their tables with fork and spoon to affect a 'royal' setting, and it wasn't long before fork-and-spoon dining became the norm in Bangkok and later spread throughout the kingdom. To use these tools the Thai way, use a serving spoon, or alternatively your own, to take a single mouthful of food from a central dish, and ladle it over a portion of your rice. The fork is then used to push the now food-soaked portion of rice back onto the spoon before entering the mouth.

If you're not offered chopsticks, don't ask for them. When *fa·ràng* (Westerners) ask for chopsticks to eat Thai food, it only puzzles the restaurant proprietors.

Chopsticks are reserved for eating Chinese-style food from bowls, or for eating in all-Chinese restaurants. In either case you will be supplied with chopsticks without having to ask. Unlike their counterparts in many Western countries, restaurateurs in Thailand won't assume you don't know how to use them.

Keep up with the ever-changing food scene in Bangkok by following the dining section of CNNGo's Bangkok pages (www.cnngo.com/bangkok/eat) and BK's restaurant section (http://bk.asia-city.com/restaurants).

The Sex Industry in Thailand

Thailand has had a long and complex relationship with prostitution that persists today. It is also an international sex tourism destination, a designation that began around the time of the Vietnam War. The industry targeted to foreigners is very visible with multiple red-light districts in Bangkok alone, but there is also a more clandestine domestic sex industry and myriad informal channels of sex-for-hire.

Prostitution is illegal in Thailand. However, anti-prostitution laws are often ambiguous and unenforced. Some analysts have argued that the high demand for sexual services in Thailand limits the likelihood of the industry being curtailed; however, limiting abusive practices within the industry is the goal of many activists and government agencies.

It is difficult to determine the number of sex workers in Thailand, the demographics of the industry or its economic strength. This is because there are many indirect forms of prostitution, because the illegality of the industry makes research difficult, and because different organisations use different approaches to collect data. In 2003, measures to legalise prostitution cited the Thai sex industry as being worth US$4.3 billion (about 3% of GDP), employing roughly 200,000 sex workers. A study conducted in 2003 by Thailand's Chulalongkorn University estimated 2.8 million sex workers, of which 1.98 million were adult women, 20,000 were adult men and 800,000 were children, defined as any person under the age of 18. By China Williams

Help stop child-sex tourism by reporting suspicious behaviour on a dedicated hotline (☎1300), or by reporting the individual directly to the embassy of their nationality.

The Coalition Against Trafficking in Women (CATW; www.catwinternational.org) is an NGO that works internationally to combat prostitution and trafficking in women and children.

HISTORY & CULTURAL ATTITUDES

Prostitution has been widespread in Thailand since long before the country gained a reputation among international sex tourists. Throughout Thai history the practice was accepted and common among many sectors of society, though it has not always been respected by society as a whole.

Due to international pressure from the UN, prostitution was declared illegal in 1960, though entertainment places (go-go bars, beer bars, massage parlours, karaoke bars and bathhouses) are governed by a separate law passed in 1966. These establishments are licensed and can legally provide nonsexual services (such as dancing, massage); sexual services occur through these venues but they are not technically the primary purpose.

With the arrival of the US military forces in Southeast Asia during the Vietnam War era, enterprising forces adapted the existing framework to suit foreigners, in turn creating an international sex-tourism industry that persists today. Indeed, this foreigner-oriented sex industry is still a prominent part of Thailand's tourist economy.

In 1998 the International Labour Organization, a UN agency, advised Southeast Asian countries, including Thailand, to recognise prostitution as an economic sector and income generator. It is estimated that one-third of the entertainment establishments are registered with the government and the majority pay an informal tax in the form of police bribes.

ECONOMIC MOTIVATIONS

Regardless of their background, most women in the sex industry are there for financial reasons: many find that sex work is one of the highest-paying jobs for their level of education, and they have financial obligations (be it dependents or debts). The most comprehensive data on the economics of sex workers comes from a 1993 survey by Kritaya Archavanitkul. The report found that sex workers made a mean income of 17,000B per month (US$18 per day), the equivalent of a mid-level civil servant job, a position acquired through advanced education and family connections. At the time of the study, most sex workers did not have a high-school degree.

The International Labour Organization estimates a Thai sex workers' salary at 270B (US$9) a day, the average wage of a Thai service-industry worker.

These economic factors provide a strong incentive for rural, unskilled women (and to a lesser extent, men) to engage in sex work.

As with many in Thai society, a large percentage of sex workers' wages are remitted back to their home villages to support their families (parents, siblings and children). Kritaya's 1993 report found that between 1800B and 6100B per month was sent back home to rural communities. The remittance-receiving households typically bought durable goods (TVs and washing machines), bigger houses and motorcycles or automobiles. Their wealth displayed their daughters' success in the industry and acted as free advertisement for the next generation of sex workers.

MUSEUM

Created by a sex workers' advocacy group, This is Us: Empower Foundation National Museum (☎ 0 2526 8311; 57/60 Th Ti-wanon; ☺ Mon-Fri) leads visitors through the history and working conditions of sex workers in Thailand.

WORKING CONDITIONS

The unintended consequence of prostitution prohibitions is the lawless working environment it creates for women who enter the industry. Sex work becomes the domain of criminal networks that are often involved in other illicit activities and circumvent the laws through bribes and violence.

Sex workers are not afforded the rights of other workers: there is no minimum wage; no required vacation pay, sick leave or break time; no deductions for social security or employee-sponsored health insurance; and no legal redress.

Bars can set their own punitive rules that fine a worker if she doesn't smile enough, arrives late or doesn't meet the drink quota. Empower, an NGO that fights for safe and fair standards in the sex industry, reported that most sex workers will owe money to the bar at the end of the month through these deductions. In effect, the women have to pay to be prostitutes and the fines disguise a pimp relationship.

Through lobbying efforts, groups such as Empower hope that lawmakers will recognise all workers at entertainment places (including dish washers and cooks as well as 'working girls') as employees subject to labour and safety protections.

HIV/AIDS

Thailand was lauded for its rapid and effective response to the AIDS epidemic through an aggressive condom-use campaign in the 1990s. Infection rates of female sex workers declined to 5% by 2007 but rates have recently doubled among informal sex workers (street prostitutes). Analysts warn that the country is on the verge of a resurgence as public education efforts have declined and cultural attitudes towards sex have changed. Of the country's 610,000 people living with HIV/AIDS, intravenous drug users make up the largest portion (30–50% in 2007).

THE EXPERTS' VIEWS: THAILAND'S SEX INDUSTRY

In an effort to provide alternate viewpoints on one of Thailand's most contentious issues, we approached members of Empower (www.empowerfoundation.org), a Thailand-based NGO that fights for safe and fair standards in the sex industry and equal rights in society, and Associate Professor Virada Somswasdi, Head of the Women's Studies Center, Chiang Mai University, with a few of the most common questions we've heard from visitors to Bangkok about Thailand's sex industry.

Why does the sex industry appear to be so open and tolerated in Thailand? Are Thai attitudes regarding the sex trade different than those of the West?

➡ Professor Virada: In any society – West, East and beyond, Thailand is no exception – where a deep-rooted and dominant patriarchal social structure controls sexuality and abuses women's bodies, combined with the huge vested interests of 'the industry' and a highly corruptible level of law enforcement, any 'illegal' deeds will go untouched or with a low response.

➡ Empower: Because it is so open and many people are in the business and they seem to make no harm to the public, and because the work is an economic opportunity for many women who need a job that pays enough to support herself and her family.

What are the biggest problems with the sex industry as it exists now in Thailand?

➡ Professor Virada: Degradation of women and their wellbeing, sexual exploitation, violence against women, gender inequality and sex tourism. The thin and very blurred line between trafficking in women and prostitution.

➡ Empower: Applying criminal laws to try and enforce moral judgment turns workers and the business into criminals to be punished, not humans to be supported.

Why do Thai women (and to a lesser extent, men) become sex workers?

➡ Professor Virada: It's about dominance of male sexuality that 'the industry' continues and expands to serve its clients, taking advantage of lower economic, social and political capabilities of women and girls to traffic and lure them into prostitution under the name of 'choice' or 'consent'.

➡ Empower: It's the job they chose over other jobs because it offers the most freedom, variety and opportunities.

Many people in the West tend to associate Thailand with child prostitution – is this still a significant problem in the country?

➡ Professor Virada: Yes, the establishments involved in commercial sexual exploitation and prostitution still target girls more and more, focusing on those from neighbouring countries of Thailand.

➡ Empower: As far as Empower's 25 years of experience, we have been working with adult women and have only seen child prostitution if we watch a documentary.

Should prostitution in Thailand be legalised? What are the potential positives and negatives of this?

➡ Professor Virada: Legalising prostitution will merely benefit pimps, traffickers and the sex industry; it will increase child prostitution, clandestine, hidden, illegal and street prostitution; it does not promote women's health, nor enhance women's choices; women in systems of prostitution do not want the sex industry legalised.

➡ Empower: We don't think that there should be law to either legalise or criminalise sex work, but rather that [sex workers] should be considered workers or employers under the labour protection law.

As told to Austin Bush.

Other commentators, such as the Coalition Against Trafficking in Women (CATW), argue that legalising prostitution is not the answer, because such a move would legitimise a practice that is always going to be dangerous and exploitative for the women involved. Instead, these groups focus on how to enable the women to leave prostitution and make their way into different types of work.

CHILD PROSTITUTION & HUMAN TRAFFICKING

According to Ecpat (End Child Prostitution & Trafficking), there are currently 30,000 to 40,000 children involved in prostitution in Thailand, though estimates are unreliable. According to Chulalongkorn University, the number of children is as high as 800,000.

In 1996, Thailand passed a reform law to address the issue of child prostitution (defined into two tiers: 15 to 18 years old and under 15). Fines and jail time are assigned to customers, establishment owners and even parents involved in child prostitution (under the old law only prostitutes were culpable). Many countries also have extraterritorial legislation that allows nationals to be prosecuted in their own country for such crimes committed in Thailand.

Urban job centres such as Bangkok have large populations of displaced and marginalised people (Burmese immigrants, ethnic hill-tribe members and impoverished rural Thais). Children of these fractured families often turn to street begging, which is an entryway into prostitution usually through low-level criminal gangs.

Thailand is also a conduit and destination for people trafficking (including children) from Myanmar (Burma), Laos, Cambodia and China. According to the UN, human trafficking is a crime against humanity and involves recruiting, transporting, transferring, harbouring and receiving a person through force, fraud or coercion for purposes of exploitation. In 2007, the US State Department labelled Thailand as not meeting the minimum standards of prevention of human trafficking.

It is difficult to obtain reliable data about trafficked people, including minors, but a 1997 report on foreign child labour, by Kritaya Archavanitkul, found that there were 16,423 non-Thai prostitutes working in the country and that 30% were children under the age of 18 (a total of 4900). Other studies estimated that there were 100,000 to 200,000 foreign-born children in the Thai workforce but these figures do not determine the type of work being done.

This chapter was written by China Williams, Lonely Planet author

Organisations working across borders to stop child prostitution include Ecpat (End Child Prostitution & Trafficking; www.ecpat.net) and its Australian affiliate Child Wise (www.childwise.net).

Survival Guide

Transport

GETTING TO BANGKOK

Most travellers will arrive in Bangkok via air, but for those entering the city on ground transport, or who have plans to move onward, below is a summary of the city's major transport hubs.

Flights, tours and rail tickets can be booked online at lonelyplanet.com/bookings.

Air

Just about everybody flying to Bangkok comes through **Suvarnabhumi International Airport** (☑0 2132 1888; www.bangkokairportonline.com). The unofficial website has real-time details of airport arrivals and departures. **Left-luggage facilities** (⊘24 hr) are available on level 2, beside the helpful Tourism Authority of Thailand office.

Travel to/from Suvarnabhumi International Airport

TRAIN
In 2010 the **Airport Rail Link** (www.airportraillink.railway.co.th) connecting central Bangkok and Suvarnabhumi Airport was finally completed. The system is comprised of a local service, which makes six stops before terminating at Phaya Thai station (30 minutes, 45B), connected by a walk-

way to the BTS (Skytrain) of the same name, as well as an express service that runs without stopping between the airport and Makkasan or Phaya Thai stations (15 to 17 minutes, 150B). Makkasan, also known as Bangkok City Air Terminal, is a short walk from Phetchaburi MRT (metro) station, and if you show up at least three hours before your departure, also has check-in facilities for passengers flying on Thai Airways. Both lines run from 6am to midnight.

TAXI
➡ Metered taxis are available kerbside at the 1st floor – ignore the 'official airport taxi' touts who approach you inside the terminal.

➡ Typical metered fares from the airport are as follows: 200B to 250B to Th Sukhumvit; 250B to 300B to Th Khao San; 400B to Mo Chit. Toll charges (paid by the passengers) vary between 25B and 45B. Note that there's an additional 50B surcharge added to all fares departing from the airport, payable directly to the driver.

➡ You can hail a taxi directly from the street for airport trips or you can arrange one through the hotels or by calling ☑1681 (which charges a 20B dispatch surcharge).

BUS
➡ A public transport centre is 3km from the airport and includes a bus terminal with buses to a handful of provinces and inner-city-bound buses and minivans. An airport shuttle connects the transportation centre with the passenger terminals.

➡ Bus lines city-bound tourists are likely to use include 551 (Victory Monument), 554 (Don Mueang) and 556 (Th Khao San), and minivan line 552 (On Nut BTS station, 25B). From these points, you can continue by public transport or taxi to your hotel.

Bus

Buses using government bus stations are far more reliable and less prone to incidents of theft than minibuses or coaches departing from Th Khao San or other tourist centres.

➡ **Eastern Bus Terminal** (Ekamai; ☑0 2391 2504; Soi 40, Th Sukhumvit; ℝEkkamai exit 2) Go to this station for buses to cities on or near the eastern gulf coast including Ban Phe (for Ko Samet), Pattaya, Rayong, Chanthaburi and Trat.

➡ **Northern & Northeastern Bus Terminal** (Mor Chit; ☑for northeastern routes 0 2936 2852, ext 611/448, for

CLIMATE CHANGE & TRAVEL

Every form of transport that relies on carbon-based fuel generates CO_2, the main cause of human-induced climate change. Modern travel is dependent on airplanes, which might use less fuel per kilometer per person than most cars but travel much greater distances. The altitude at which aircraft emit gases (including CO_2) and particles also contributes to their climate change impact. Many websites offer 'carbon calculators' that allow people to estimate the carbon emissions generated by their journey and, for those who wish to do so, to offset the impact of the greenhouse gases emitted with contributions to portfolios of climate-friendly initiatives throughout the world. Lonely Planet offsets the carbon footprint of all staff and author travel.

northern routes 0 2936 2841, ext 311/442; Th Kamphaeng Phet; MKamphaeng Phet exit 1 & taxi, MMo Chit exit 3 & taxi) Commonly called Mor Chit, this station serves destinations in northern and northeastern Thailand.

➡ **Southern Bus Terminal** (Sai Tai Mai; 0 2435 1199; Th Bromaratchachonanee) Located across Saphan Phra Pinklao (Map p252) in the far western suburbs, Sai Tai Mai serves all points south – hello Phuket, Surat Thani, Krabi, Hat Yai – as well as Kanchanaburi and western Thailand. The easiest way to reach the station is by taxi, or you can take bus 79, 159, 201 or 516 from Th Ratchadamnoen Klang (Map p254) or bus 40 from the **Victory Monument** (อนุสาวรีย์ชัย; Map p263; cnr Th Ratchawithi & Th Phayathai; ordinary 12 & 62, Victory Monument).

Minivan

Privately run minivans, called *rót đôo*, are a fast and relatively comfortable way to get between Bangkok and its neighbouring provinces. Several minivans depart from various points surrounding the **Victory Monument** (อนุสาวรีย์ชัย; Map p263; cnr Th Ratchawithi & Th Phayathai; ordinary 12 & 62, Victory Monument).

Train

➡ **Hualamphong** (0 2220 4334, nationwide call centre 1690; www.railway.co.th; Th Phra Ram IV) The city's main train terminus. It's advisable to ignore all touts here and avoid the travel agencies. To check timetables and prices for other destinations call the **State Railway of Thailand** (SRT; 1690; www.railway.co.th) or visit the website.

➡ **Wong Wian Yai** (off Th Phra Jao Taksin; Wongwian Yai & taxi) This tiny hidden station is the jumping-off point for the commuter line to Samut Sakhon (also known as Mahachai).

➡ **Bangkok Noi** (off Th Itsaraphap; Wongwian Yai & taxi) A miniscule train station with departures for Kanchanaburi.

GETTING AROUND

Bangkok may seem chaotic at first, but its transport system is improving, and although you'll almost certainly find yourself stuck in traffic at some point, the jams aren't as legendary as they used to be. For most of the day and night, Bangkok's 70,000 clean and dirt-cheap taxis are the most expedient choice – although it's important to note that Bangkok traffic is anything if not unpredictable. During rush hour, the BTS, MRT, river ferries, *klorng* (canal, also spelt *khlong*) ferries are much wiser options. Locals and

many expats swear by the ubiquitous motorcycle taxis, but the accidents we've seen suggest that they're not really worth the risk.

BTS & MRT

The elevated **BTS** (0 2617 7300, tourist information 0 2617 7340; www.bts.co.th), also known as the Skytrain (*rót fai fáa*), whisks you through 'new' Bangkok (Silom, Sukhumvit and Siam Sq). The interchange is at Siam station, and trains run frequently from 6am to midnight. Fares range from 15B to 40B, or 120B for a one-day pass. Most ticket machines only accept coins, but change is available at the information booths.

Bangkok's **MRT** (www.bangkokmetro.co.th) or metro is helpful for people staying in the Sukhumvit or Silom area to reach the train station at Hualamphong. Otherwise the system is mainly a suburban commuter line. Fares cost 15B to 40B, or 120B for a one-day pass. The trains run frequently from 6am to midnight.

Taxi

Although many first-time visitors are hesitant to use them, in general, Bangkok's taxis are new and spacious and the drivers are courteous and helpful, making them an excellent way to get around.

All taxis are required to use their meters, which start at 35B, and fares to most places within central Bangkok cost 60B to 90B. Freeway tolls – 25B to 45B depending on where you start – must be paid by the passenger.

Taxi Radio (☎1681; www.taxiradio.co.th) and other 24-hour 'phone-a-cab' services are available for 20B above the metered fare.

If you leave something in a taxi your best chance of getting it back (still pretty slim) is to call ☎1644.

Boat

River Ferries

The **Chao Phraya Express Boat** (☎0 2623 6001; www.chaophrayaexpressboat.com) operates the main ferry service along Mae Nam Chao Phraya. The central pier is known as Sathon, Saphan Taksin or Central Pier, and connects to the BTS at Saphan Taksin station.

The service runs from 6am to 8pm on weekdays and from 6am to 7pm on weekends. You can buy tickets (10B to 32B) at the pier or on board; hold on to your ticket as proof of purchase (an occasional formality).

Boats with yellow or red-and-orange flags are express boats. These run only during peak times and don't make every stop. A yellow-flagged tourist boat (30B, every 30 minutes from 9.30am to 4pm) runs from **Tha Sathon (Central Pier)** to **Tha Phra Athit (Banglamphu)** with stops at 10 major sightseeing piers and barely comprehensible English-language commentary.

There are also dozens of cross-river ferries, which charge 3B and run every few minutes until late at night.

Private long-tail boats can be hired for sightseeing trips (p50) at **Tha Phra Athit (Banglamphu)**, **Tha Chang**, **Tha Tien** and **Tha Oriental**.

Klorng Boats

Canal taxi boats run along Khlong Saen Saep (Banglamphu to Ramkhamhaeng) and are an easy way to get between Banglamphu and Jim Thompson's House, the Siam Sq shopping centres (get off at **Tha Hua Chang** for both) and other points further east along Th Sukhumvit – after a manda-

tory change of boat at **Tha Pratunam**. These boats are mostly used by daily commuters and pull into the piers for just a few seconds – jump straight on or you'll be left behind. Fares range from 9B to 21B and boats run from 6.15am to 7.30pm.

Motorcycle Taxi

Motorcycle taxis (known as motorsai) serve two purposes in Bangkok. Most commonly and popularly they form an integral part of the public-transport network, running from the corner of a main thoroughfare, such as Th Sukhumvit, to the far ends of sois that run off that thoroughfare. Riders wear coloured, numbered vests and gather at either end of their soi, usually charging 10B to 20B for the trip (without a helmet unless you ask).

Their other purpose is as a means of beating the traffic. You tell your rider where you want to go, negotiate a price (from 20B for a short trip up to about 150B going across town), strap on the helmet (they will insist for longer trips) and say a prayer to whichever god you're into.

Túk-Túk

Bangkok's iconic túk-túk (pronounced đúk đúk; a type of motorised rickshaw) are used by Thais for short hops not worth paying the taxi flag fall for. For foreigners, however, these emphysema-inducing machines are part of the Bangkok experience, so despite the fact they overcharge outrageously and you can't see anything due to the low roof, pretty much everyone takes a túk-túk at least once. It's worth knowing, however, that túk-túk are notorious for taking little 'detours' to commission-paying gem and silk shops and massage parlours. En route to

---

BANGKOK TAXI TIPS

➡ Never agree to take a taxi that won't use the meter; these drivers park outside hotels and in tourist areas. Simply get one that's passing by instead.

➡ Bangkok taxi drivers will generally not try to 'take you for a ride' as happens in some other countries; they make more money from passenger turnover.

➡ It's worth keeping in mind that many Bangkok taxi drivers are in fact seasonal labourers fresh from the countryside and may not know their way around.

➡ If a driver refuses to take you somewhere, it may because he needs to return his rental cab before a certain time, not because he doesn't like you.

➡ Very few Bangkok taxi drivers speak much English; an address written in Thai can help immensely.

➡ Older cabs may be less comfortable but typically have more experienced drivers because they are driver-owned, as opposed to the new cabs, which are usually rented.

MOTORCYCLE MADNESS

It's Friday rush hour in Bangkok and traffic is bumper-to-bumper as far as the eye can see. You need to be somewhere – fast. Assuming you don't have a police escort, the only way out is to hop on the back of a fearless motorcycle taxi, known as a *motorsai*. Hang on tight as your orange-vested driver weaves past belching trucks, zips down tiny back-alleys and, when all else fails, treats the pavement as a bike lane.

Motorsai are an essential lubricant for Bangkok's congested streets, with an estimated 200,000 on the road. They gather at street corners in ranks known as *win*. As well as transporting people and goods, they double as messengers for private companies. Since they can drive down narrow sois, motorsai are often the only form of public transport in parts of the city.

Not all motorsai journeys are mad dashes across town, but their finest hours come when traffic is so backed up that a regular taxi or bus just won't do – there's something exhilarating about passing a $50,000 BMW caught in a snarl-up. 'They make space where there is no space,' says Claudio Sopranzetti, an anthropology student at Harvard who spent a year researching motorsai drivers for his PhD.

Yet while nearly everyone relies on them, motorsai have a mixed reputation. Bangkokians swap hair-raising stories of drunken or reckless drivers who should be behind bars. Then there's the underworld aspect: motorsai ranks are typically run by moonlighting cops or soldiers, a shady practice that former Prime Minister Thaksin Shinawatra tried to stamp out in 2003. He didn't quite succeed, but he won the loyalty of drivers who were fed up of paying their bosses for protection.

This loyalty to Thaksin is why motorsai drivers were so active in the red-shirt protests that convulsed Bangkok in 2009 and 2010. As well as joining mass demonstrations, drivers used their bikes to transport supplies into protest camps, bring red-shirt guards to the front lines and to keep tabs on troop movements. Journalists also relied on nimble motorsai to get them in and out of danger zones.

Since then, some drivers have tried to steer a more neutral path through Thailand's colour-coded politics. They prefer to be seen as orange shirts, not red shirts (or yellow shirts). Their orange vests can be valuable property. Although each numbered vest is supposed to stay with its registered owner, drivers trade or sell them, fetching prices of up to 150,000 baht on busy corners or in posh neighbourhoods. Sopranzetti says that an average motorsai earns 400 to 500 baht a day. That isn't far off the salary of an office worker, but the hours are longer and the work more hazardous.

Motorsai first became popular in the 1980s as the city spread rapidly outwards and commuters found themselves stranded far from public transport. The peculiar layout of Bangkok – narrow sois, big roads, lots of dead ends – meant that motorcycles had the edge. Like so much of Bangkok's workings, it was an ad hoc response to a failure of central urban planning. Bangkok may be the world's least planned yet most livable city – and its motorsai drivers are the unsung heroes who help make it that way.
Simon Montlake, Bangkok-based journalist

'special' temples, you'll meet 'helpful' locals who will steer you to even more rip-off opportunities (229). Ignore anyone offering too-good-to-be-true 10B trips.

The vast majority of túk-túk drivers ask too much from tourists (expat *fa·ràng* never use them). Expect to be quoted a 100B fare, if not more, for even the shortest trip. Try bargaining them down to about 50B for a short trip, preferably at night when the pollution (hopefully) won't be quite so bad. Once you've done it, you'll find taxis are cheaper, cleaner, cooler and quieter.

Car

For short-term visitors, you will find parking and driving a car in Bangkok more trouble than it is worth. If you need private transport, consider hiring a car and driver through your hotel or hire a taxi driver that you find trustworthy. One reputable operator is **Julie Taxi** (☎08 1846 2014; www.julietaxitour. com), which offers a variety of vehicles and excellent service.

But if you still want to give it a go, all the big car-hire companies have offices in Bangkok and Suvarnabhumi

BANGKOK ADDRESSES

Any city as large and unplanned as Bangkok can be tough to get around. Street names often seem unpronounceable to begin with, compounded by the inconsistency of romanised Thai spellings. For example, the street often spelt as 'Rajdamri' is actually pronounced 'Ratchadamri' (with the appropriate tones, of course), or in abbreviated form as Rat damri. The 'v' in Sukhumvit should be pronounced like a 'w'... One of the most popular locations for foreign embassies is known both as Wireless Rd and Th Witthayu (wí·tá·yú is Thai for 'radio').

Many street addresses show a string of numbers divided by slashes and hyphens, for example, 48/3-5 Soi 1, Th Sukhumvit. The reason is that undeveloped property in Bangkok was originally bought and sold in lots. The number before the slash refers to the original lot number. The numbers following the slash indicate buildings constructed within that lot. The pre-slash numbers appear in the order in which they were added to city plans, while the post-slash numbers are arbitrarily assigned by developers. As a result numbers along a given street don't always run consecutively.

The Thai word tà·nǒn (usually spelt 'thanon') means road, street or avenue. Hence Ratchadamnoen Rd (sometimes referred to as Ratchadamnoen Ave) is always called Thanon (Th) Ratchadamnoen in Thai.

A soi is a small street or lane that runs off a larger street. In our example, the address referred to as 48/3-5 Soi 1, Th Sukhumvit will be located off Th Sukhumvit on Soi 1. Alternative ways of writing the same address include 48/3-5 Th Sukhumvit Soi 1, or even just 48/3-5 Sukhumvit 1. Some Bangkok soi have become so large that they can be referred to both as thanon and soi, eg Soi Sarasin/Th Sarasin and Soi Asoke/Th Asoke. Smaller than a soi is a tròrk (usually spelt 'trok') or alley. Well-known alleys in Bangkok include Chinatown's Trok Itsaranuphap and Banglamphu's Trok Rong Mai.

Joe Cummings, Lonely Planet author

airport. Rates start at around 1800B per day for a small car. A passport plus a valid licence from your home country (with English translation if necessary) or an International Driving Permit are required for all rentals.

Reliable car-hire companies include the following, all of which also have counters at Suvarnabhumi International Airport:

Avis (☏0 2251 1131; www. avisthailand.com; 2/12-13 Th Withayu; ⓜPhloen Chit exit 1) Cars and motorcycles can be hired through this international chain. Rates start at around 1000B per day, excluding insurance. An International Driving Permit and passport are required for all rentals.

Budget (☏0 2203 9222; www. budget.co.th; 19/23 Bldg A, Royal City Ave, Th Phetchaburi Tat Mai; ⓜPhra Ram 9 exit 3 & taxi) A reliable car-hire place.

Thai Rent A Car (☏0 2737 8888; www.thairentacar.com; 2371 Th Petchaburi Tat Mai; ⓜThong Lo exit 3 & taxi) If you're not dissuaded, cars and motorcycles can be rented through this local chain, which has a branch at Suvarnabhumi International Airport. Rates start at around 1000B per day, excluding insurance. An International Driving Permit and passport are required for all rentals.

Bus

Bangkok's public buses are run by the **Bangkok Mass Transit Authority** (☏0 2246 0973; www.bmta. co.th). As the routes are not always clear, and with Bangkok taxis being such a good deal, you'd really have to be pinching pennies to rely on buses as a way to get around Bangkok. However, if you're determined, air-con bus fares range from 11B to 23B, and fares for fan-cooled buses start at 7B or 8B. Most of the bus lines run between 5am and 10pm or 11pm, except for the 'all-night' buses, which run from 3am or 4am to midmorning. You'll most likely require the help of thinknet's *Bangkok Bus Guide*.

TOURS

Bangkok has a variety of walking, bicycle or guided tours (p49).

Directory
A–Z

Business Hours

Opening hours for businesses in this book are listed only if they differ from the following.

➡ **Banks** From 8.30am to 3.30pm Monday to Friday; banks in shopping centres and tourist areas are often open longer hours (generally until 8pm), including weekends.

➡ **Bars & Clubs** Open until midnight or 1am, although those in designated entertainment zones can stay open until 2am or 3am.

➡ **Shops** Large shops usually open from 10am to 7pm; shopping centres open until 10pm.

➡ **Government Offices** From 8.30am to 4.30pm Monday to Friday. There's a strong chance of disappointment if you expect to get anything done between noon and 1pm.

➡ **Restaurants** Local Thai places often serve food from morning until night (10am to 8pm or 9pm), while more formal restaurants serve only during lunch (from around 11am to 2pm) and dinner (6pm to 10pm).

Customs Regulations

➡ Customs officers prohibit the import or export of the usual array of goods – porn, weapons, drugs. If you're caught with drugs in particular, expect life never to be the same again. The usual 200 cigarettes or 250g of tobacco are

allowed in without duty, along with up to 1L of wine or spirits.

➡ For customs details, check out www.customs.go.th.

➡ Licences are required for exporting religious images and other antiquities (p43).

Discount Cards

The Th Khao San trade in fake student cards and press passes is still bubbling along 20 years after it began. Not surprisingly, Bangkok institutions don't accept these cards as proof of anything.

Electricity

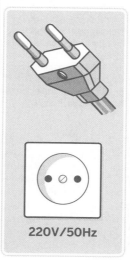

220V/50Hz

220V/50Hz

Embassies & Consulates

Australian Embassy (📞0 2344 6300; www.thailand.embassy.gov.au; 37 Th Sathon Tai; ⓂLumphini exit 2)

Burmese (Myanmar) Embassy (📞0 2233 2237; www.mofa.gov.mm/myanmar missions/thailand.html; 132 Th Sathon Neua; 🚇Surasak exit 3)

Cambodian Embassy (📞0 2957 5851; 518/4 Th Pracha Uthit, aka Soi Ramkhamhaeng 39; ⓂPhra Ram 9 exit 3 & taxi)

Canadian Embassy (📞0 2636 0540; www.canadainterna

tional.gc.ca/thailand-thailande; 15th fl, Abdulrahim Pl, 990 Th Phra Ram IV; MSi Lom exit 2, Sala Daeng exit 4) Consulate only at Chiang Mai.

Dutch Embassy (0 2309 5200; www.netherlands embassy.in.th; 15 Soi Tonson; Chit Lom exit 4)

French Embassy (0 2266 8250-56; www.ambafrance-th. org; 35 Soi 36, Th Charoen Krung; Tha Oriental)

French Consulate (0 2287 1592; 29 Th Sathon Tai; MLumphini exit 2)

German Embassy (0 2287 9000; www.bangkok. diplo.de; 9 Th Sathon Tai; MLumphini exit 2)

Irish Consulate (0 2632 6720; www.irelandinthailand. com; 4th fl, Thaniya Bldg, 62 Th Silom; MSi Lom exit 2, Sala Daeng exit 1)

Laotian Embassy (0 2539 6667; www.bkklao embassy.com; 502/1-3 Soi Sahakarnpramoon, Th Pracha Uthit, aka Soi Ramkhamhaeng 39; MPhra Ram 9 exit 3 & taxi)

Malaysian Embassy (0 2629 6800; www.kln.gov.my/ web/tha_bangkok/home; 35 Th Sathon Tai; MLumphini exit 2)

New Zealand Embassy (0 2254 2530; www.nz embassy.com/thailand; 14th fl, M Thai Tower, All Seasons Pl, 87 Th Witthayu/Wireless Rd; Phloen Chit exit 5)

UK Embassy (0 2305 8333; www.ukinthailand.fco. gov.uk.uk; 14 Th Witthayu/

Wireless Rd; Phloen Chit exit 5) Consulate only in Chiang Mai.

US Embassy (0 2205 4000; http://bangkok.use mbassy.gov; 120/22 Th Wit-thayu/Wireless Rd; Phloen Chit exit 5)

Emergency

Ambulance (via police 191) In a medical emergency, it's probably best to call a hospital direct, and it will dispatch an ambulance. See Medical Services (p228) for recommended hospitals.

Fire (199) You're unlikely to find an English-speaker at this number, so it's best to use the default 191 emergency number.

Police (191)

Tourist Police (24hr hotline 1155) The best way to deal with most problems requiring police (usually a rip-off or theft) is to contact the tourist police, who are used to dealing with foreigners and can be very helpful in cases of arrest. The English-speaking unit investigates criminal activity involving tourists and can act as a bilingual liaison with the regular police. Although they typically have no jurisdiction over the kinds of cases handled by regular cops, they should be able to help with translation, contacting your embassy and/ or arranging a police report you can take to your insurer.

Health

While urban horror stories can make a trip to Bangkok seem frighteningly dangerous, few travellers experience anything more than an upset stomach and the resulting clenched-cheek waddles to the bathroom. If you do have a problem, Bangkok has some very good hospitals.

Air Pollution

Bangkok has a bad reputation for air pollution, and on bad days the combination of heat, dust and motor fumes can be a powerful brew of potentially toxic air. The good news is that more-efficient vehicles, fewer of them thanks to the BTS (Skytrain) and MRT (Metro), and less industrial pollution mean Bangkok's skies are much cleaner than they were.

Flu

Thailand has seen a number of nasty influenza strains in recent years, most notably the bird (H5N1) and swine (H1N1) varieties. That said, it's no worse than any other country in the region and is probably better prepared than most of the world for any major outbreak because the government has stock-piled tens of millions of Tami-flu doses.

Food

If a place looks clean and well run and the vendor also looks clean and healthy, then the food is probably safe.

PRACTICALITIES

➡ Bangkok's predominant English-language newspapers are the **Bangkok Post** (www.bangkokpost.com) and the business-heavy **Nation** (www.nationmultimedia.com).

➡ The *International Herald Tribune* and weeklies such as the *Economist* and *Time* are sold at numerous newsstands.

➡ **Bangkok 101** (www.bangkok101.com) is a tourist-friendly listings magazine.

➡ The metric system is used for weights and measures.

➡ Smoking in restaurants and bars has been banned since 2008.

In general, the food in busy restaurants is cooked and eaten quite quickly with little standing around, and is probably not reheated. The same applies to street stalls.

Heat

By the standards of most visitors, Bangkok is somewhere between hot and seriously (expletive) hot all year round. Usually that will mean nothing more than sweat-soaked clothing, discomfort and excessive tiredness. However, heat exhaustion is not uncommon, and dehydration is the main contributor. Symptoms include feeling weak, headache, irritability, nausea or vomiting, sweaty skin, a fast, weak pulse and a normal or slightly elevated body temperature. Treatment involves getting out of the heat and/or sun and cooling the victim down by fanning and applying cool, wet cloths to the skin, laying the victim flat with their legs raised and rehydrating with electrolyte drinks or water containing a quarter teaspoon of salt per litre. Heatstroke is more serious and requires more urgent action. Symptoms come on suddenly and include weakness, nausea, a hot, dry body with a temperature of more than 41°C, dizziness, confusion, loss of coordination, seizures and, eventually, collapse and loss of consciousness. Seek medical help and begin cooling by getting the victim out of the heat, removing their clothes, fanning them and applying cool, wet cloths or ice to their body, especially to the groin and armpits.

HIV & AIDS

In Thailand around 95% of HIV transmission occurs through sexual activity, and the remainder through natal transmission or illicit intravenous drug use. HIV/AIDS can also be spread through infected blood transfusions, although this risk is virtually nil in Thailand due to

rigorous blood-screening procedures. If you want to be pierced or tattooed, be sure to check that the needles are new.

Water & Ice

Don't drink tap water, but do remember that all water served in restaurants or to guests in offices or homes in Bangkok comes from purified sources. It's not necessary to ask for bottled water in these places unless you prefer it. Ice is generally produced from purified water under hygienic conditions and is therefore theoretically safe.

Internet Access

➡ There's no shortage of internet cafes in Bangkok competing to offer the cheapest and fastest connection. Rates vary depending on the concentration and affluence of net-heads – Banglamphu is cheaper than Sukhumvit or Silom, with rates as low as 20B per hour.

➡ Many internet shops are adding Skype and headsets to their machines so international calls can be made for the price of surfing the web.

➡ A convenient place to take care of your communication needs is the **TrueMove Shop** (www.truemove.com; Soi 2, Siam Sq; ⏱7am-10pm; 🚇Siam). It has high-speed internet computers equipped with Skype, sells phones and mobile subscriptions, and can also provide information on city-wide wi-fi access for computers and phones.

➡ Wi-fi, mostly free of charge, is becoming more and more ubiquitous around Bangkok. For relatively authoritative lists of wi-fi hot spots in Bangkok, go to www.bkkpages.com (under 'Bangkok Directory') or www.stickmanweekly.com/WiFi/BangkokFreeWirelessInternetWiFi.htm.

Legal Matters

➡ Thailand's police don't enjoy a squeaky clean reputation, but as a foreigner, and especially a tourist, you probably won't have much to do with them. While some expats will talk of being targeted for fines while driving, most anecdotal evidence still suggests most Thai police will usually go out of their way not to arrest a foreigner breaking minor laws.

➡ Most Thai police view drug-takers as a social scourge and consequently see it as their duty to enforce the letter of the law; for others it's an opportunity to make untaxed income via bribes. Which direction they'll go often depends on drug quantities; small-time offenders are sometimes offered the chance to pay their way out of an arrest, while traffickers usually go to jail.

➡ Smoking is banned in all indoor spaces, including bars and pubs. The ban extends to open-air public spaces, which means lighting up outside a shopping centre, in particular, might earn you a polite request to butt out. If you throw your cigarette butt on the ground, however, you could then be hit with a hefty littering fine.

➡ If you are arrested for any offence, police will allow you to make a phone call to your embassy or consulate if you have one, or to a friend or relative. There's a whole set of legal codes governing the length of time and manner in which you can be detained before being charged or put on trial. Police have a lot of discretion and are more likely to bend these codes in your favour than the reverse. However, as with police worldwide, if you don't show respect you will only make matters worse, so keep a cool head and avoid being confrontational.

Medical Services

More than Thailand's main health-care hub, Bangkok has become a major destination for medical tourism, with patients flying in for surgery and treatment from all over the world.

Hospitals

The following hospitals have English-speaking doctors.

BNH (📞0 2686 2700; www. bnhhospital.com; 9 Th Convent; 🚇Sala Daeng, 🚇Si Lom)

Bangkok Christian Hospital (📞0 2235 1000; www. bkkchristianhosp.th.com; 124 Th Silom; 🚇Sala Daeng, 🚇Si Lom)

Bumrungrad International Hospital (📞0 2667 1000; www.bumrungrad. com; 33 Soi 3, Th Sukhumvit; 🚇Phloen Chit exit 3)

Samitivej Hospital (📞0 2711 8000; www.samitivej hospitals.com; 133 Soi 49, Th Sukhumvit, access by taxi; 🚇Phrom Phong)

Dentists

Business is good in the teeth game, partly because so many fa·ràng are cleverly combining their holiday with a spot of cheap root canal surgery or some 'personal outlook' care – a sneaky teeth-whitening treatment by any other name. Prices are a bargain compared with Western countries, and the quality of dentistry is generally good.

Bangkok Dental Spa (📞0 2651 0807; www.bangkok dentalspa.com; 2nd fl, Metha-wattana Bldg, 27 Soi 19, Th Sukhumvit; 🚇Sukhumvit exit 3, 🚇Asok exit 1) This is not a typo. Combines oral hygiene with spa services (foot and body massage).

DC-One the Dental Clinic (📞0 2240 2800; www.dc-one. com; 31 Th Yen Akat; 🚇Lum-phini exit 2 & taxi) Reputation for excellent work and relatively high prices; popular with UN staff and diplomats.

Dental Hospital (📞0 2260 5015, 0 2260 5000; www. dentalhospitalbangkok.com; 88/88 Soi 49, Th Sukhumvit; 🚇Phrom Phong exit 3 & taxi) A private dental clinic with fluent English-speaking dentists.

Siam Family Dental Clinic (📞0 8197 7700; www. siamfamilydental.com; 209 Th Phayathai; 🚇Siam exit 2) Teeth-whitening is big here.

Pharmacies

Pharmacies are plentiful, and in central areas most pharmacists will speak English. If you don't find what you need in a Boots, Watsons or local pharmacy, try one of the hospitals.

Money

The basic unit of Thai currency is the baht. There are 100 satang in one baht – though the only place you'll be able to spend them is in the ubiquitous 7-Elevens. Coins come in denominations of 25 satang, 50 satang, 1B, 2B, 5B and 10B. Paper currency comes in denominations of 20B (green), 50B (blue), 100B (red), 500B (purple) and 1000B (beige).

ATMs

You won't need a map to find an ATM in Bangkok – they're literally everywhere. Bank ATMs accept major international credit cards and many will also cough up cash (Thai baht only) if your card is affiliated with the international Cirrus or Plus networks (typically for a fee of 150B). You can withdraw up to 20,000B per day from most ATMs.

Changing Money

Banks or legal moneychangers offer the optimum foreign-exchange rates. When buying baht, US dollars and euros are the most readily accepted currencies, and travellers cheques receive better rates than cash. British pounds, Australian dollars, Singapore dollars and Hong Kong dollars are also widely accepted. As banks often charge commission and duty for each travellers cheque cashed, you'll save on commissions if you use larger cheque denominations.

Credit Cards

Credit cards as well as debit cards can be used for purchases at many shops and pretty much any hotel or restaurant, though you'll have to pay cash for your pàt tai. The most commonly accepted cards are Visa and MasterCard, followed by Amex and JCB. To report a lost or stolen card, call the following numbers:

Amex (📞0 2273 5544)
MasterCard (📞001 800 11887 0663)
Visa (📞001 800 11 535 0660)

Tipping

Tipping is not a traditional part of Thai life and, except in big hotels and posh restaurants, tips are appreciated but not expected.

Post

Thailand has an efficient postal service, and both domestic and international rates are very reasonable.

Main Post Office (Communications Authority of Thailand, CAT; 📞0 2233 1050; Th Charoen Krung; ⏰8am-8pm Mon-Fri, to 1pm Sat & Sun; 🚤Tha Si Phraya) Near Soi 35.

Public Holidays

Government offices and banks close their doors on the following national public holidays. For the precise dates of lunar holidays, see the Tourism Authority of

Thailand (TAT) website www.
tourismthailand.org/travel
-information.
New Year's Day 1 January
Makha Bucha Day
January/March (lunar)
Chakri Day Commemorates
the founding of the royal
Chakri dynasty; 6 April
Songkran Thai New Year;
13–15 April
Labor Day 1 May
Coronation Day Commemo-
rating the 1950 coronation of
the current king and queen;
5 May
Visakha Bucha Day
May/June (lunar)
Khao Phansa Beginning of
the Buddhist rains retreat,
when monks refrain from
travelling away from their
monasteries; July/August
(lunar)
Queen's Birthday 12 August
King Chulalongkorn Day
23 October
Ok Phansa End of Buddhist
rains retreat; October/
November (lunar)
King's Birthday 5 December
Constitution Day
10 December
New Year's Eve
31 December

Safe Travel

Bangkok is a safe city
and incidents of violence
against tourists are rare.
That said, there are
enough well-rehearsed
scams that there's an en-
tire website (www.bangkok
scams.com) dedicated to
them.

But don't be spooked by
the stories; commit the following to memory and you'll
most likely enjoy a scam-free
visit:

➡ **Gem scam** We are begging
you, if you aren't a gem trader
or expert, then please don't buy
unset stones in Thailand –
period (see p44).

➡ **Closed today** Ignore any
'friendly' local who tells you
that an attraction is closed for a
Buddhist holiday or for cleaning.

These are set-ups for trips to a
bogus gem sale.

➡ **Túk-túk rides for 10B** Say
goodbye to your day's itinerary if you climb aboard this
ubiquitous scam. These alleged
'tours' bypass all the sights and
instead cruise to all the fly-by-
night gem and tailor shops that
pay commissions.

➡ **Flat-fare taxi ride** Flatly
refuse any taxi driver who
quotes a flat fare (usually
between 100B and 150B for
in-town destinations), which
will usually be three times more
expensive than the reasonable
meter rate. Walking beyond the
tourist area will usually help in
finding an honest driver. If the
driver has 'forgotten' to put the
meter on, just say, 'Meter, kha/
khap'.

➡ **Friendly strangers** Be wary
of smartly dressed and well-
spoken men who approach you
asking where you're from and
where you're going. Their opening gambit is usually followed
with: 'Ah, my son/daughter is
studying at university in (your
home city)' – they seem to have
an encyclopaedic knowledge
of the world's major universities. As the tourist authorities
here pointed out, this sort of
behaviour is out of character
for Thais and should be treated
with suspicion.

Taxes & Refunds

➡ Thailand has a 7% value-
added tax (VAT) on many goods
and services. Midrange and
top-end hotels and restaurants
might also add a 10% service
tax. When the two are combined
this becomes the 17% king hit
known as 'plus plus', or '++'
(see p45).

➡ You can get a refund on VAT
paid on shopping, though not on
food or hotels, as you leave the
country.

Telephone
Domestic & International Calling

➡ Inside Thailand you must dial
the area code no matter where
you are. In effect, that means
all numbers are nine digits; in
Bangkok they begin with ☎02,
then a seven-digit number. The
only time you drop the initial
0 is when you're calling from
outside Thailand. Calling the
provinces will usually involve a
three-digit code beginning with
0, then a six-digit number.

➡ To direct-dial an international
number from a private phone,
you can first dial ☎001 then
the country code. However,
you wouldn't do that, because
☎001 is the most expensive
way to call internationally
and numerous other prefixes
give you cheaper rates. These
include ☎006, ☎007, ☎008
and ☎009, depending on
which phone you're calling from.
If you buy a local mobile phone
SIM card, which we recommend
doing, the network provider will
tell you which prefix to use; read
the fine print.

USEFUL NUMBERS
Thailand country code
☎66
Bangkok city code ☎02
Mobile numbers ☎08
**Operator-assisted interna-
tional calls** ☎100
**Free local directory assist-
ance call** ☎1133

Internet Phone & Phonecards

➡ The cheapest way to call
internationally is via the internet, and many internet cafes in
Bangkok are set up for phone
calls. Some have Skype loaded
and (assuming there's a working headset) you can use that
for just the regular per-hour
internet fee, plus Skype credit if
calling to a phone.

➜ CAT offers the PhoneNet card, which comes in denominations of 200B, 300B, 500B and 1000B and allows you to call overseas via VoIP (Voice over Internet Protocol) for less than regular rates. You can call from any phone (landline, your mobile etc). Quality is good and rates represent excellent value; refills are available. Cards are available from any CAT office or online at www.thaitelephone. com, from which you get the necessary codes and numbers immediately. See www.thaitel ephone.com/EN/RateTable for rates.

Mobile Phones

➜ If you have a GSM phone you will probably be able to use it on roaming in Thailand. If you have endless cash, or you only want to send text messages, you might be happy to do that. Otherwise, think about buying a local SIM card.

➜ If your phone is locked, head down to MBK Center (p109) to get it unlocked or to shop for a new or cheap used phone (they start at less than 2000B).

➜ Buying a prepaid SIM is as difficult as finding a 7-Eleven. The market is super-competitive and deals vary so check websites first, but expect to get a SIM for as little as 49B. More expensive SIMs might come with pre-loaded talk time; if not, recharge cards are sold at the same stores and range from 100B to 500B. Domestic per-minute rates start at less than 50 satang. Calling internationally, the network will have a promotional code (eg ☎006 instead of ☎001) that affords big discounts on the standard international rates.

➜ The main networks:
AIS (www.ais.co.th/12call/th)
DTAC (www.dtac.co.th)
TrueMove (www.truemove. com)

Time

➜ Thailand is seven hours ahead of GMT/UTC. Thus, noon in Bangkok is 9pm the previous night in Los Angeles, midnight the same day in New York, 5am in London, 6am in Paris, 1pm in Perth and 3pm in Sydney. Times are an hour later in countries or regions that are on Daylight Saving Time (DST). Thailand does not use daylight saving.

➜ The official year in Thailand is reckoned from the Western calendar year 543 BC, the beginning of the Buddhist Era (BE), so that AD 2011 is 2554 BE, AD 2012 is 2555 BE etc. All dates in this book refer to the Western calendar.

Toilets

➜ If you don't want to pee against a tree like the túk-túk drivers, you can stop in at any shopping centre, hotel or fast-food restaurant for facilities. Shopping centres typically charge 2B to 3B for a visit.

➜ In older buildings and wát you'll still find squat toilets, but in modern Bangkok expect to be greeted by a throne.

➜ Toilet paper is rarely provided, so carry an emergency stash. Even in places where sit-down toilets are installed, the septic system may not be designed to take toilet paper. In such cases there will be a waste basket where you're supposed to place used toilet paper and feminine hygiene products. Many toilets also come with a small spray hose – Thailand's version of the bidet.

Tourist Information

Bangkok has two organisations that handle tourism matters: the Tourism Authority of Thailand (TAT) for country-wide information, and Bangkok Information Center for city-specific information. Also be aware that travel agents in the train station and near tourist centres co-opt 'T.A.T.' and 'Information' as part of their name to lure in commissions. These places are not officially sanctioned information services, but just agencies registered with the TAT. So how can you tell the difference? Apparently it's all in the full stops – 'T.A.T.' means agency; 'TAT' is official.

Bangkok Information Center (☎0 2225 7612-4; www.bangkoktourist.com; 17/1 Th Phra Athit; ⊙8am-7pm Mon-Fri, 9am-5pm Sat-Sun; ⛴Tha Phra Athit) City-specific tourism office provides maps, brochures and directions. Kiosks and booths are found around town; look for the green-on-white symbol of a mahout on an elephant.

Tourism Authority of Thailand (TAT) (☎1672; www.tourismthailand.org) head office (☎0 2250 5500; 1600 Th Phetchaburi Tat Mai; ⊙8.30am-4.30pm; Ⓜ Phetchaburi exit 2); Banglamphu (☎0 2283 1500; cnr Th Ratchadamnoen Nok & Th Chakrapatdipong; ⊙8.30am-4.30pm; ⛴Phan Fah); Suvarnabhumi International Airport (☎0 2134 0040; 2nd fl, btwn Gates 2 & 5, Suvarnabhumi International Airport; ⊙24hr)

Travellers with Disabilities

➜ Bangkok presents one large, ongoing obstacle course for the mobility-impaired, with its high kerbs, uneven pavements and nonstop traffic. Many of the city's streets must be crossed via pedestrian bridges flanked with steep stairways, while buses and boats don't stop long enough to accommodate even the mildly disabled. Aside from at some BTS and MRT stations, ramps or other access points for wheelchairs are rare.

➡ A few top-end hotels make consistent design efforts to provide disabled access. Other deluxe hotels with high employee-to-guest ratios are usually good about providing staff help where building design fails. For the rest, you're pretty much left to your own resources.

➡ The following companies and websites might be useful:
Asia Pacific Development Centre on Disability (www.apcdfoundation.org)
Society for Accessible Travel & Hospitality (SATH; www.sath.org)
Wheelchair Tours to Thailand (www.wheelchairtours.com)

Visas

➡ Thailand's **Ministry of Foreign Affairs** (www.mfa.go.th) oversees immigration and visa issues. In the past five years there have been new rules nearly every year regarding visas and extensions; the best online monitor is **Thaivisa** (www.thaivisa.com).

➡ Citizens of 41 countries (including most European countries, Australia, New Zealand and the USA) can enter Thailand at no charge. These citizens are issued a 30-day visa if they arrive by air or 15 days by land.

Visa Extensions

➡ If you need more time in the country, apply for a 60-day tourist visa prior to arrival at a Thai embassy or consulate abroad. For business or study purposes, you can obtain 90-day non-immigrant visas but you'll need extra documentation. Officially, on arrival you must prove you have sufficient funds for your stay and proof of onward travel, but visitors are rarely asked about this.

➡ If you overstay your visa the penalty is 500B per day, with a 20,000B limit; fines can be paid at any official exit point or at the **Bangkok immigration office** (✉0 2141 9889; Bldg B, Government Center, Soi 7, Th Chaeng Watthana; ⏱8.30am-noon & 1-4.30pm Mon-Fri; 🚇Mo Chit & acess by taxi). Dress in your Sunday best when doing official business in Thailand and do all visa business yourself (don't hire a third party). Bring

along two passport-sized photos and a copy of the photo and visa pages of your passport.

➡ You can extend your stay, for the normal fee of 1900B, at the immigration office. Those issued with a standard stay of 15 or 30 days can extend their stay for seven to 10 days (depending on the immigration office) if the extension is handled before the visa expires. The 60-day tourist visa can be extended by up to 30 days at the discretion of Thai immigration authorities.

Women Travellers

➡ Everyday incidents of sexual harassment are much less common in Thailand than in India, Indonesia or Malaysia, and this might lull women familiar with those countries into thinking that Thailand is safer than it is. If you're a woman travelling alone it's worth pairing up with other travellers when moving around at night or, at the least, avoiding quiet areas.

➡ Whether it's tampons or any other women-specific product, you'll have no trouble finding it in Bangkok.

Language

Thailand's, and therefore Bangkok's official language is effectively the dialect spoken and written in central Thailand, which has successfully become the lingua franca of all Thai and non-Thai ethnic groups in the kingdom.

In Thai the meaning of a single syllable may be altered by means of different tones. In standard Thai there are five: low tone, mid tone, falling tone, high tone and rising tone. The range of all five tones is relative to each speaker's vocal range, so there is no fixed 'pitch' intrinsic to the language.

➡ **low tone** – 'Flat' like the mid tone, but pronounced at the relative bottom of one's vocal range. It is low, level and has no inflection, eg bàht (baht – the Thai currency).

➡ **mid tone** – Pronounced 'flat', at the relative middle of the speaker's vocal range, eg dee (good). No tone mark is used.

➡ **falling tone** – Starting high and falling sharply, this tone is similar to the change in pitch in English when you are emphasising a word, or calling someone's name from afar, eg mâi (no/not).

➡ **high tone** – Usually the most difficult for non-Thai speakers. It's pronounced near the relative top of the vocal range, as level as possible, eg máh (horse).

➡ **rising tone** – Starting low and gradually rising, sounds like the inflection used by English speakers to imply a question – 'Yes?', eg sǎhm (three).

WANT MORE?

For in-depth language information and handy phrases, check out Lonely Planet's *Thai Phrasebook*. You'll find it at **shop.lonelyplanet.com**, or you can buy Lonely Planet's iPhone phrasebooks at the Apple App Store.

The Thai government has instituted the Royal Thai General Transcription System (RTGS) as a standard method of writing Thai using the Roman alphabet. It's used in official documents, road signs and on maps. However, local variations crop up on signs, menus etc. Generally, names in this book follow the most common practice.

In our coloured pronunciation guides, the hyphens indicate syllable breaks within words, and some syllables are further divided with a dot to help you pronounce compound vowels, eg mêu·a·rai (when).

The vowel a is pronounced as in 'about', aa as the 'a' in 'bad', ah as the 'a' in 'father', ai as in 'aisle', air as in 'flair' (without the 'r'), eu as the 'er' in 'her' (without the 'r'), ew as in 'new' (with rounded lips), oh as the 'o' in 'toe', or as in 'torn' (without the 'r') and ow as in 'now'.

Most consonants correspond to their English counterparts. The exceptions are b (a hard 'p' sound, almost like a 'b', eg in 'hip-bag'); d (a hard 't' sound, like a sharp 'd', eg in 'mid-tone'); ng (as in 'singing'; in Thai it can occur at the start of a word) and r (as in 'run' but flapped; in everyday speech it's often pronounced like 'l'). If you read our coloured pronunciation guides as if they were English, you shouldn't have problems being understood.

BASICS

The social structure of Thai society demands different registers of speech depending on who you're talking to. To make things simple we've chosen the correct form of speech appropriate to the context of each phrase.

When being polite, the speaker ends his or her sentence with kráp (for men) or kâ (for women). It is the gender of the speaker that is being expressed here; it is also the common way to answer 'yes' to a question or show agreement.

In this chapter the masculine and feminine forms of phrases are indicated where relevant with 'm/f'.

Signs

ทางเข้า	Entrance
ทางออก	Exit
เปิด	Open
ปิด	Closed
ห้าม	Prohibited
ห้องสุขา	Toilets
ชาย	Men
หญิง	Women

Hello.	สวัสดี	sà-wàt-dee
Goodbye.	ลาก่อน	lah gòrn
Yes.	ใช่	châi
No.	ไม่	mâi
Please.	ขอ	kŏr
Thank you.	ขอบคุณ	kòrp kun
You're welcome.	ยินดี	yin dee
Excuse me.	ขออภัย	kŏr à-pai
Sorry.	ขอโทษ	kŏr tôht

How are you?
สบายดีไหม — sà-bai dee măi

Fine. And you?
สบายดีครับ/ค่ะ — sà-bai dee kráp/
แล้วคุณล่ะ — kâ láa-ou kun lâ (m/f)

What's your name?
คุณชื่ออะไร — kun chêu à-rai

My name is ...
ผม/ดิฉันชื่อ... — pŏm/dì-chăn chêu ... (m/f)

Do you speak English?
คุณพูดภาษา — kun pôot pah-săh
อังกฤษได้ไหม — ang-grìt dâi măi

I don't understand.
ผม/ดิฉัน ไม่ เข้าใจ — pŏm/dì-chăn mâi kôw jai (m/f)

ACCOMMODATION

Where's a ...? — ... อยู่ที่ไหน — ... yòo têe năi

campsite	ค่ายพักแรม	kâi pák raam
guesthouse	บ้านพัก	bâhn pák
hotel	โรงแรม	rohng raam
youth hostel	บ้าน	bâhn
	เยาวชน	yow-wá-chon

Do you have a ... room? — มีห้อง ... ไหม — mee hôrng ... măi

single	เดี่ยว	dèe·o
double	เตียงคู่	đee·ang kôo
twin	สองเตียง	sŏrng đee·ang

air-con	แอร์	aa
bathroom	ห้องน้ำ	hôrng nám
laundry	ห้องซักผ้า	hôrng sák pâh
mosquito net	มุ้ง	múng
window	หน้าต่าง	nâh đàhng

DIRECTIONS

Where's ...?
... อยู่ที่ไหน — ... yòo têe năi

What's the address?
ที่อยู่คืออะไร — têe yòo keu à-rai

Could you please write it down?
เขียนลงให้ได้ไหม — kĕe·an long hâi dâi măi

Can you show me (on the map)?
ให้ดู (ในแผนที่) — hâi doo (nai păan têe)
ได้ไหม — dâi măi

Turn left/right.
เลี้ยวซ้าย/ขวา — lée·o sái/kwăh

It's ... — อยู่ ... — yòo ...

behind	ที่หลัง	têe lăng
in front of	ตรงหน้า	đrong nâh
near	ใกล้ๆ	glâi glâi
next to	ข้างๆ	kâhng kâhng
straight ahead	ตรงไป	đrong bai

EATING & DRINKING

I'd like (the menu), please.
ขอ (รายการ — kŏr (rai gahn
อาหาร) หน่อย — ah-hăhn) nòy

What would you recommend?
คุณแนะนำอะไรบ้าง — kun náa-nam à-rai bâhng

That was delicious!
อร่อยมาก — à-ròy mâhk

Cheers!
ไชโย — chai-yoh

Please bring the bill.

ขอบิลหน่อย		kŏr bin nòy
I don't eat ...	ผม/ดิฉัน	pŏm/dì-chăn
	ไม่กิน ...	mâi gin ... (m/f)
eggs	ไข่	kài
fish	ปลา	blah
red meat	เนื้อแดง	néu·a daang
nuts	ถั่ว	tòo·a

Key Words

bottle	ขวด	kòo·at
bowl	ชาม	chahm
breakfast	อาหารเช้า	ah-hăhn chów
cafe	ร้านกาแฟ	ráhn gah-faa
chopsticks	ไม้ตะเกียบ	mái dà-gèe·ap
cold	เย็น	yen
cup	ถ้วย	tôo·ay
dessert	ของหวาน	kŏrng wăhn
dinner	อาหารเย็น	ah-hăhn yen
drink list	รายการ	rai gahn
	เครื่องดื่ม	krêu·ang dèum
fork	ส้อม	sôrm
glass	แก้ว	gâa·ou
hot	ร้อน	rórn
knife	มีด	mêet
lunch	อาหาร	ah-hăhn
	กลางวัน	glahng wan
market	ตลาด	dà-làht
plate	จาน	jahn
restaurant	ร้านอาหาร	ráhn ah-hăhn
spicy	เผ็ด	pèt
spoon	ช้อน	chórn
vegetarian	คนกินเจ	kon gin jair
with/without	มี/ไม่มี	mee/mâi mee

Meat & Fish

beef	เนื้อ	néu·a
chicken	ไก่	gài
crab	ปู	boo
duck	เป็ด	bèt
fish	ปลา	blah
meat	เนื้อ	néu·a
pork	หมู	mŏo
seafood	อาหารทะเล	ah-hăhn tá-lair
squid	ปลาหมึก	blah mèuk

Fruit & Vegetables

banana	กล้วย	glôo·ay
beans	ถั่ว	tòo·a
coconut	มะพร้าว	má-prów
eggplant	มะเขือ	má-kĕu·a
fruit	ผลไม้	pŏn-lá-mái
guava	ฝรั่ง	fa-ràng
lime	มะนาว	má-now
mango	มะม่วง	má-môo·ang
mangosteen	มังคุด	mang-kút
mushrooms	เห็ด	hèt
nuts	ถั่ว	tòo·a
papaya	มะละกอ	má-lá-gor
potatoes	มันฝรั่ง	man fa-ràng
rambutan	เงาะ	ngó
tamarind	มะขาม	má-kăhm
tomatoes	มะเขือเทศ	má-kĕu·a têt
vegetables	ผัก	pàk
watermelon	แตงโม	đaang moh

Other

chilli	พริก	prík
egg	ไข่	kài
fish sauce	น้ำปลา	nám blah

Question Words

What?	อะไร	à-rai
When?	เมื่อไร	mêu·a-rai
Where?	ที่ไหน	têe năi
Who?	ใคร	krai

noodles	เส้น	sên
oil	น้ำมัน	nám man
pepper	พริกไทย	prík tai
rice	ข้าว	kôw
salad	ผักสด	pàk sòt
salt	เกลือ	gleu·a
soup	น้ำซุป	nám súp
soy sauce	น้ำซีอิ๊ว	nám see·éw
sugar	น้ำตาล	nám đahn
tofu	เต้าหู้	đow hôo

Drinks

beer	เบียร์	bee·a
coffee	กาแฟ	gah-faa
milk	นมจืด	nom jèut
orange juice	น้ำส้ม	nám sôm
soy milk	น้ำเต้าหู้	nám đow hôo
sugar-cane juice	น้ำอ้อย	nám ôy
tea	ชา	chah
water	น้ำดื่ม	nám dèum

EMERGENCIES

Help!	ช่วยด้วย	chôo·ay dôo·ay
Go away!	ไปให้พ้น	bai hâi pón

Call a doctor!
เรียกหมอหน่อย — rêe·ak mŏr nòy

Call the police!
เรียกตำรวจหน่อย — rêe·ak đam·ròo·at nòy

I'm ill.
ผม/ดิฉันป่วย — pŏm/di·chăn bòo·ay (m/f)

I'm lost.
ผม/ดิฉัน — pŏm/di·chăn
หลงทาง — lŏng tahng (m/f)

Where are the toilets?
ห้องน้ำอยู่ที่ไหน — hôrng nám yòo têe năi

SHOPPING & SERVICES

I'd like to buy ...
อยากจะซื้อ ... — yàhk jà séu ...

How much is it?
เท่าไร — tôw-rai

That's too expensive.
แพงไป — paang bai

Can you lower the price?
ลดราคาได้ไหม — lót rah-kah dâi măi

There's a mistake in the bill.
บิลใบนี้ผิด — bin bai née pìt ná
นะครับ/ค่ะ — kráp/kâ (m/f)

TIME & DATES

What time is it?
กี่โมงแล้ว — gèe mohng láa·ou

morning	เช้า	chów
afternoon	บ่าย	bài
evening	เย็น	yen
yesterday	เมื่อวาน	mêu·a wahn
today	วันนี้	wan née
tomorrow	พรุ่งนี้	prûng née

Monday	วันจันทร์	wan jan
Tuesday	วันอังคาร	wan ang-kahn
Wednesday	วันพุธ	wan pút
Thursday	วันพฤหัสฯ	wan pá-réu-hàt
Friday	วันศุกร	wan sùk
Saturday	วันเสาร์	wan sŏw
Sunday	วันอาทิตย์	wan ah-tít

TRANSPORT

Public Transport

bicycle rickshaw	สามล้อ	săhm lór
boat	เรือ	reu·a
bus	รถเมล์	rót mair
car	รถเก๋ง	rót gĕng
motorcycle	มอร์เตอร์ไซค์	mor-đeu-sai
taxi	รับจ้าง	ráp jâhng
plane	เครื่องบิน	krêu·ang bin
train	รถไฟ	rót fai
túk-túk	ตุ๊ก ๆ	đúk đúk

When's the ... bus?	รถเมล์คัน ... มาเมื่อไร	rót mair kan ... mah mêu·a rai
first	แรก	râak
last	สุดท้าย	sùt tái
A ... ticket, please.	ขอตั๋ว ...	kŏr đŏo·a ...
one-way	เที่ยวเดียว	têe·o dee·o
return	ไปกลับ	bai glàp
I'd like a/an ... seat.	ต้องการที่นั่ง ...	đôrng gahn têe nâng ...
aisle	ติดทางเดิน	đìt tahng deun
window	ติดหน้าต่าง	đìt nâh đàhng
ticket window	ช่องขายตั๋ว	chôrng kăi đŏo·a
timetable	ตารางเวลา	đah-rahng wair-lah

What time does it get to (Chiang Mai)?

ถึง (เชียงใหม่) กี่โมง — tĕung (chee·ang mài) gèe mohng

Does it stop at (Saraburi)?

รถจอดที่ (สระบุรี) ไหม — rót jòrt têe (sà-rà-bù-ree) măi

I'd like to get off at (Saraburi).

ขอลงที่(สระบุรี) — kŏr long têe (sà-rà-bù-ree)

Driving & Cycling

I'd like to hire a/an ...	อยากจะ เช่า ...	yàhk jà chôw ...
4WD	รถโฟร์วีล	rót foh ween
car	รถเก๋ง	rót gĕng
motorbike	รถมอร์เตอร์ไซค์	rót mor-đeu-sai
I'd like ...	ต้องการ ...	đôrng gahn ...
my bicycle repaired	ซ่อมรถจักรยาน	sôrm rót jàk-gà-yahn
to hire a bicycle	เช่ารถจักรยาน	chôw rót jàk-gà-yahn

Numbers

1	หนึ่ง	nèung
2	สอง	sŏrng
3	สาม	săhm
4	สี่	sèe
5	ห้า	hâh
6	หก	hòk
7	เจ็ด	jèt
8	แปด	bàat
9	เก้า	gôw
10	สิบ	sìp
11	สิบเอ็ด	sìp-èt
20	ยี่สิบ	yêe-sìp
21	ยี่สิบเอ็ด	yêe-sìp-èt
30	สามสิบ	săhm-sìp
40	สี่สิบ	sèe-sìp
50	ห้าสิบ	hâh-sìp
60	หกสิบ	hòk-sìp
70	เจ็ดสิบ	jèt-sìp
80	แปดสิบ	bàat-sìp
90	เก้าสิบ	gôw-sìp
100	หนึ่งร้อย	nèung róy
1000	หนึ่งพัน	nèung pan
1,000,000	หนึ่งล้าน	nèung láhn

Is this the road to (Ban Bung Wai)?

ทางนี้ไป (บานบุงหวาย) ไหม — tahng née bai (bâhn bùng wăi) măi

Where's a petrol station?

ปั๊มน้ำมันอยู่ที่ไหน — bâm nám man yòo têe năi

How long can I park here?

จอดที่นี่ได้นานเท่าไร — jòrt têe née dâi nahn tôw-rai

I need a mechanic.

ต้องการช่างรถ — đôrng gahn châhng rót

I have a flat tyre.

ยางแบน — yahng baan

I've run out of petrol.

หมดน้ำมัน — mòt nám man

GLOSSARY

baht – Thai currency

BTS – Bangkok Mass Transit System (Skytrain)

CAT – Communications Authority of Thailand

fa·ràng – foreigner of European descent

Isan – isăan; general term for northeastern Thailand, from the Sanskrit name for the medieval kingdom Isana, which encompassed parts of Cambodia and northeastern Thailand.

klorng or khlong – canal

rai – Thai unit of measurement (area); 1 rai = 1600 sq metres

Ratanakosin – style of architecture present in the late 19th to early 20th century, which combines traditional Thai and European forms; also known as 'old Bangkok'

rót fai fáa – BTS Skytrain

soi – sawy; lane or small road

TAT – Tourist Authority of Thailand

tha – thâa; pier

THAI – Thai Airways International

thanon – thanŏn (abbreviated 'Th' in this guide); road or street

trok – tràwk; alleyway

wàt – Buddhist temple, monastery

Behind the Scenes

SEND US YOUR FEEDBACK

We love to hear from travellers – your comments keep us on our toes and help make our books better. Our well-travelled team reads every word on what you loved or loathed about this book. Although we cannot reply individually to postal submissions, we always guarantee that your feedback goes straight to the appropriate authors, in time for the next edition. Each person who sends us information is thanked in the next edition – the most useful submissions are rewarded with a selection of digital PDF chapters.

Visit **lonelyplanet.com/contact** to submit your updates and suggestions or to ask for help. Our award-winning website also features inspirational travel stories, news and discussions.

Note: We may edit, reproduce and incorporate your comments in Lonely Planet products such as guidebooks, websites and digital products, so let us know if you don't want your comments reproduced or your name acknowledged. For a copy of our privacy policy visit lonelyplanet.com/privacy.

OUR READERS

Many thanks to the travellers who used the last edition and wrote to us with helpful hints, useful advice and interesting anecdotes:

Yvonne Brennan, Juergen Huber, Matt Price, Lora Sweeney, Don Turner.

AUTHOR THANKS

Austin Bush

I'd like to thank the folks at Lonely Planet, including the patient and helpful Ilaria Walker, David Connolly and Bruce Evans; the authors of previous editions, Andrew Burke and Joe Cummings; fellow Lonely Planeteer China Williams; not to mention people on the ground here in Bangkok, including Prempreeda Na Ayutthaya, Prasuputh Chainikom (Kosalo), Nima Chandler, Liz and Noi and the other helpful ladies at EMPOWER, Robert Halliday, Richard Hermes, Thitinan Pongsudhirak, Wesley Hsu, Natchaphat Itthi-chaiwarakom, Gene Kasidit, Chomploy Leeraphante, Maher Sattar, Associate Professor Virada Somswasdi, David Thompson, Joey Tulyanond and Patrick Winn.

ACKNOWLEDGMENTS

Cover photograph: Traders on their boats at the floating market, Damnoen Saduak, Bangkok, Thailand, Chris Mellor/Lonely Planet Images.

Many of the images in this guide are available for licensing from Lonely Planet Images: www.lonelyplanetimages.com.

THIS BOOK

This 10th edition of Lonely Planet's *Bangkok* guidebook was researched and written by Austin Bush: Bangkok resident, Thai food guru, rockstar photographer and overall great guy. The Bangkok Today chapter was written by Dr Thitinan Pongsudhirak, celebrated analyst, journalist and Director of the Institute of Security and International Studies, Chulalongkorn University. David Thompson, celebrity chef, bestselling author and owner of nahm restaurant, wrote Bangkok's Best Bites. Motorcycle Madness box was written by journalist and Bangkok expert Simon Montlake. The sex industry chapter was written by China Williams

and repurposed by Austin Bush. The previous two editions were written by Andrew Burke and Austin Bush. This guidebook was commissioned in Lonely Planet's Melbourne office, and produced by the following:

Commissioning Editor
Ilaria Walker

Coordinating Editors
Paul Harding, Briohny Hooper, Andi Jones, Ali Lemer

Coordinating Cartographer
Valentina Kremenchutskaya

Coordinating Layout Designer
Mazzy Prinsep

Managing Editors
Bruce Evans, Dianne Schallmeiner, Angela Tinson

Managing Cartographers
David Connolly, Corey Hutchison, Anthony Phelan, Amanda Sierp

Managing Layout Designer
Jane Hart

Assisting Editors Samantha Forge, Kim Hutchins, Karyn Noble, Charlotte Orr, Gabbi Stefanos

Assisting Layout Designer
Paul Iacono

Cover Research
Naomi Parker

Internal Image Research
Rebecca Skinner

Language Content
Branislava Vladisavljevic

Thanks to Daniel Corbett, Laura Crawford, Janine Eberle, Ryan Evans, Larissa Frost, Liz Heynes, Laura Jane, David Kemp, Trent Paton, Piers Pickard, Lachlan Ross, Michael Ruff, Peter Shearman, Julie Sheridan, Laura Stansfeld, John Taufa, Gerard Walker, Clifton Wilkinson.

BEHIND THE SCENES

Index

See also separate subindexes for:

🍴 **EATING P246**

🍷 **DRINKING & NIGHTLIFE P247**

☆ **ENTERTAINMENT P248**

🛍 **SHOPPING P248**

🏃 **SPORTS & ACTIVITIES P248**

🛏 **SLEEPING P249**

Sights 000
Map Pages **000**
Photo Pages **000**

✕ **EATING**

INDEX DRINKING & NIGHTLIFE

Bangkok Maps

Map Legend

Sights
- Beach
- Buddhist
- Castle
- Christian
- Hindu
- Islamic
- Jewish
- Monument
- Museum/Gallery
- Ruin
- Winery/Vineyard
- Zoo
- Other Sight

Eating
- Eating

Drinking & Nightlife
- Drinking & Nightlife
- Cafe

Entertainment
- Entertainment

Shopping
- Shopping

Sports & Activities
- Diving/Snorkelling
- Canoeing/Kayaking
- Skiing
- Surfing
- Swimming/Pool
- Walking
- Windsurfing
- Other Sports & Activities

Sleeping
- Sleeping
- Camping

Information
- Bank
- Embassy/Consulate
- Hospital/Medical
- Internet
- Police
- Post Office
- Telephone
- Toilet
- Tourist Information
- Other Information

Transport
- Airport
- Border Crossing
- Bus
- Cable Car/Funicular
- Cycling
- Ferry
- Metro
- Monorail
- Parking
- S-Bahn
- Taxi
- Train/Railway
- Tram
- Tube Station
- U-Bahn
- Other Transport

Routes
- Tollway
- Freeway
- Primary
- Secondary
- Tertiary
- Lane
- Unsealed Road
- Plaza/Mall
- Steps
- Tunnel
- Pedestrian Overpass
- Walking Tour
- Walking Tour Detour
- Path

Boundaries
- International
- State/Province
- Disputed
- Regional/Suburb
- Marine Park
- Cliff
- Wall

Geographic
- Hut/Shelter
- Lighthouse
- Lookout
- Mountain/Volcano
- Oasis
- Park
- Pass
- Picnic Area
- Waterfall

Hydrography
- River/Creek
- Intermittent River
- Swamp/Mangrove
- Reef
- Canal
- Water
- Dry/Salt/Intermittent Lake
- Glacier

Areas
- Beach/Desert
- Cemetery (Christian)
- Cemetery (Other)
- Park/Forest
- Sportsground
- Sight (Building)
- Top Sight (Building)

MAP INDEX

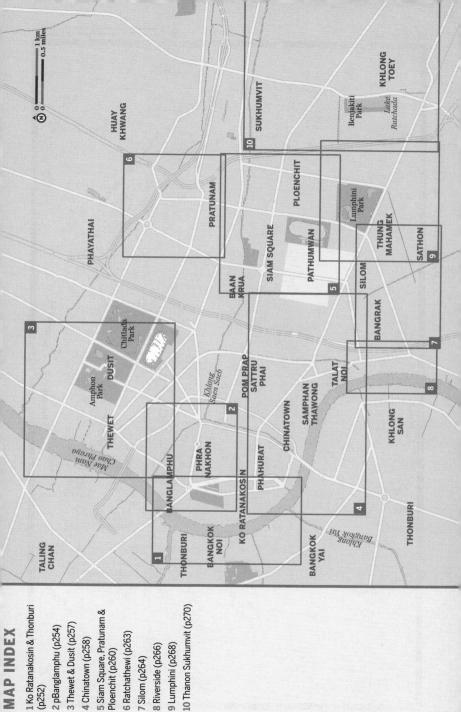

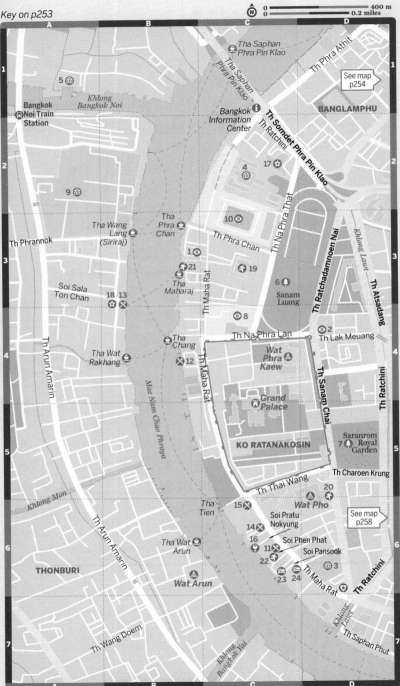

KO RATANAKOSIN & THONBURI

0   400 m
0   0.2 miles

BANGLAMPHU

See map p254

Tha Saphan Phra Pin Klao

Tha Saphan Phra Pin Klao

Th Phra Athit

Th Phra Pin Klao

Bangkok Information Center

Th Somdet Phra Pin Klao

Th Ratchini

Bangkok Noi Train Station

Khlong Bangkok Noi

Th Phrannok

Tha Wang Lang (Siriraj)

Tha Phra Chan

Th Phra Chan

Th Na Phra That

Th Ratchadamnoen Nai

Khlong Lawt

Th Atsadang

Soi Sala Ton Chan

Tha Maharaj

Th Maha Rat

Sanam Luang

Th Lak Meuang

Th Ratchini

Tha Wat Rakhang

Tha Chang

Th Na Phra Lan

Th Sanam Chai

Mae Nam Chao Phraya

Wat Phra Kaew

Grand Palace

KO RATANAKOSIN

Saranrom Royal Garden

Th Charoen Krung

Khlong Mon

Th Arun Amarin

Th Thai Wang

Wat Pho

See map p258

Tha Tien

Soi Pratu Nokyung

Soi Phen Phat

Soi Pansook

Tha Wat Arun

Th Maha Rat

Th Ratchini

THONBURI

Wat Arun

Th Wang Doem

Khlong Bangkok Yai

Th Saphan Phut

KO RATANAKOSIN & THONBURI *Map on p252*

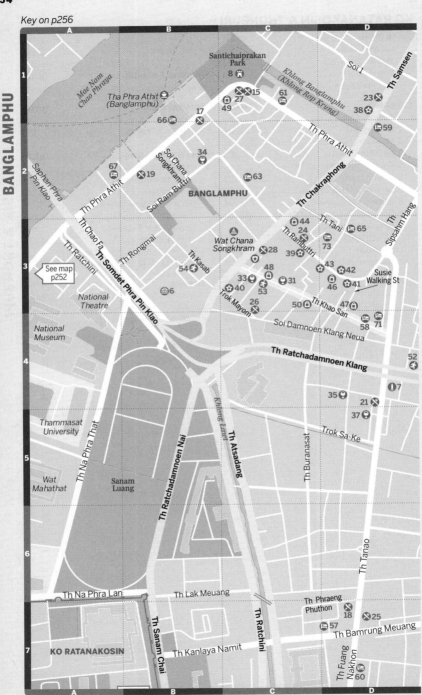

Key on p256

BANGLAMPHU

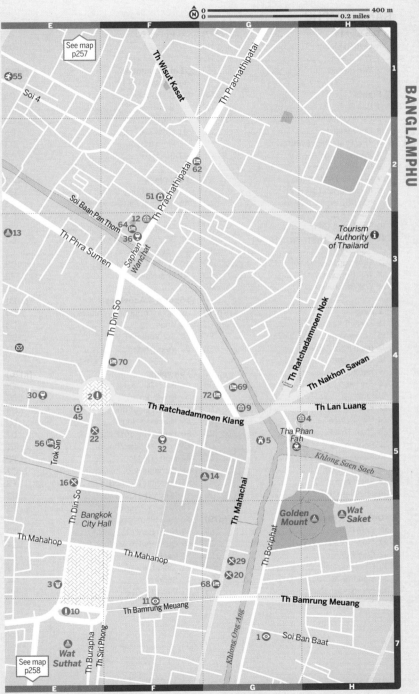

THEWET & DUSIT

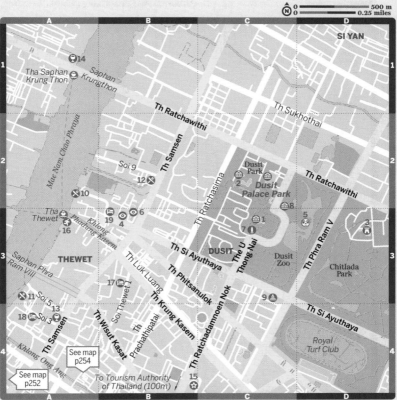

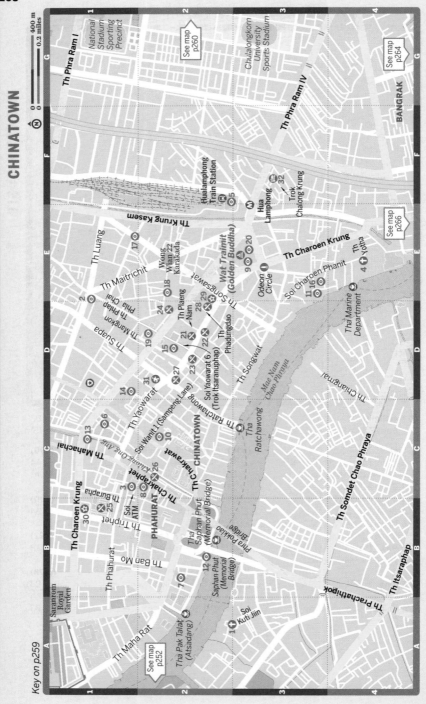

CHINATOWN

Key on p259

400 m
0.2 miles

National Stadium Sporting Precinct

Th Phra Ram I

See map p260

Chulalongkorn University Sports Stadium

Th Phra Ram IV

BANGRAK

See map p264

Hualamphong Train Station

Th Krung Kasem

Hua Lamphong

Trok Chalong Krung

See map p266

Th Charoen Krung

Th Luang

Th Maitrichit

Wong Wian 22 Karakada

Wat Traimit (Golden Buddha)

Th Songsawat

Odeon Circle

Soi Charoen Phanit

Th Yotha

Tha Marine Department

Th Maha Chai

Th Phlap Phla Chai

Th Phadungdao

Th Plaeng Nam

Th Songwat

Mae Nam Chao Phraya

Th Chiangmai

Th Yaowarat

Soi Yaowarat 6 (Trok Itsaranuphap)

Th Ratchawong

Tha Ratchawong

Soi Want 1 (Sampeng Lane)

Trok Itsaranuphap

Khlong Ong Ang

CHINATOWN

Th Chakrawat

Th Maha Chai

Th Charoen Krung

Th Burapha

Th Chakraphet

PHAHURAT

Soi ATM

Th Triphet

Th Ban Mo

Th Phahurat

Saranrom Royal Garden

Th Maha Rat

See map p252

Tha Pak Talat (Atsadang)

Saphan Phut (Memorial Bridge)

Phra Pokklao Bridge

Soi Kuti Jiin

Th Somdet Chao Phraya

Th Prachathipok

Th Itsaraphap

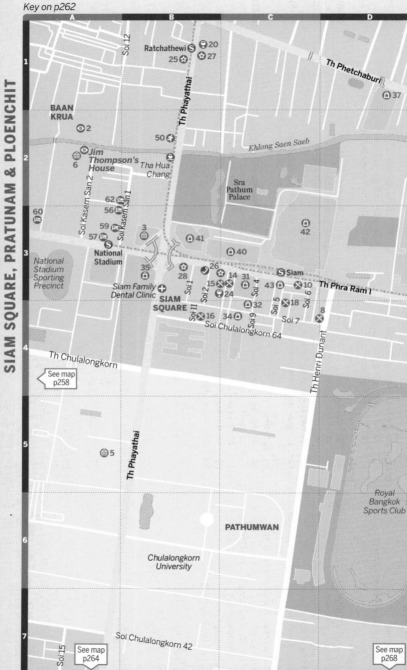

SIAM SQUARE, PRATUNAM & PLOENCHIT

Key on p262

SIAM SQUARE, PRATUNAM & PLOENCHIT *Map on p260*

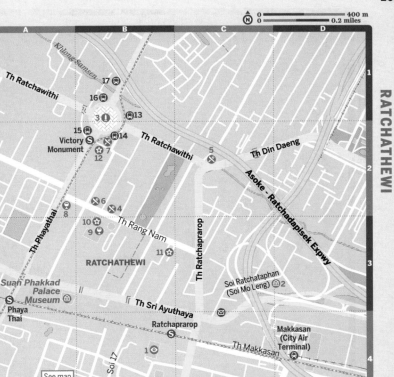

SILOM

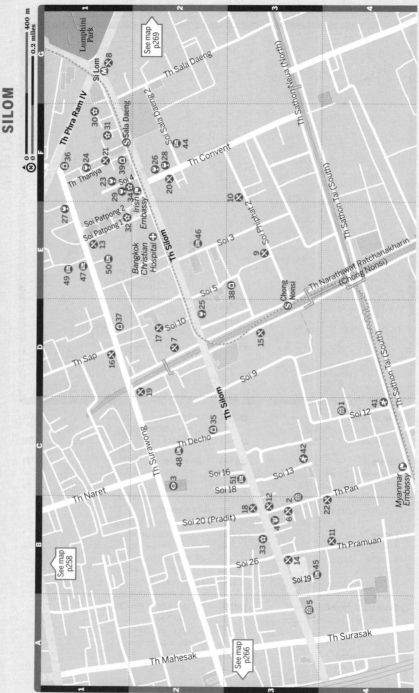

See map p269

See map p258

See map p266

Lumphini Park

Th Phra Ram IV

Th Sala Daeng

Th Sala Daeng 2

Soi Sala Daeng 2

Th Convent

Th Sathon Neua (North)

Th Sathon Tai (South)

Si Lom

Sala Daeng

Th Thaniya

Soi Patpong 2

Soi Patpong 1

Irish Embassy

Bangkok Christian Hospital

Th Silom

Soi Phiphat 2

Soi 3

Th Narathiwat Ratchanakharin (Chong Nonsi)

Chong Nonsi

Soi 5

Soi 9

Soi 10

Th Sap

Th Surawong

Th Silom

Th Decho

Th Naret

Th Sathon Tai (South)

Soi 12

Soi 13

Th Pan

Myanmar Embassy

Soi 16

Soi 18

Soi 20 (Pradit)

Soi 26

Soi 19

Th Pramuan

Th Mahesak

Th Surasak

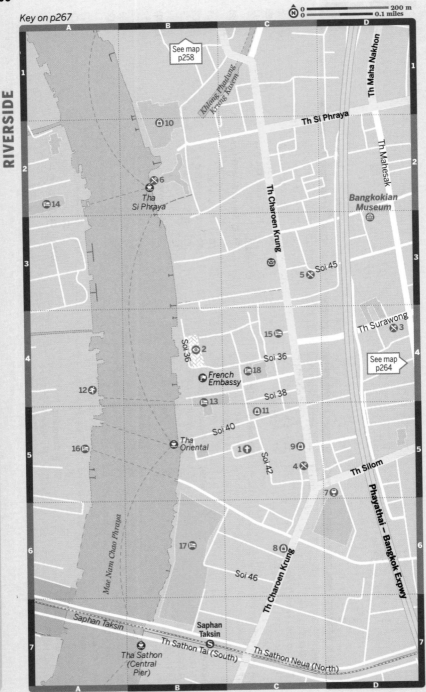

RIVERSIDE

See map p258

Th Maha Nakhon

Th Si Phraya

🔒 10

Th Charoen Krung

Th Mahesak

🔒 6

Tha Si Phraya

📇 14

Bangkokian Museum

😊

5 🍴 Soi 45

Th Surawong

🍴 3

See map p264

Soi 36

15 📇

2 ◎

Soi 36

18 📇

French Embassy

Soi 38

13 📇

11 🔒

12 ⛲

Soi 40

1 ℹ️

9 🔒

4 🍴

16 📇

Tha Oriental

Soi 42

Th Silom

7 🍽️

Phayathai – Bangkok Expwy

8 🔒

Th Charoen Krung

17 📇

Soi 46

Mae Nam Chao Phraya

Saphan Taksin

Saphan Taksin
Ⓢ

Th Sathon Tai (South)

Th Sathon Neua (North)

Tha Sathon (Central Pier)

RIVERSIDE *Map on p266*

RIVERSIDE

LUMPHINI

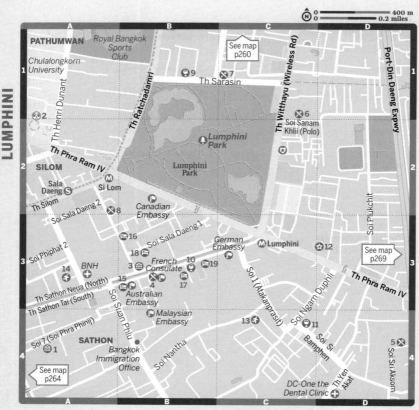

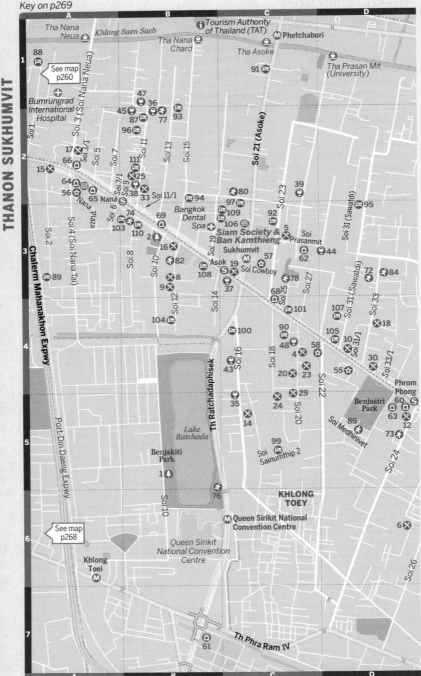

Key on p269

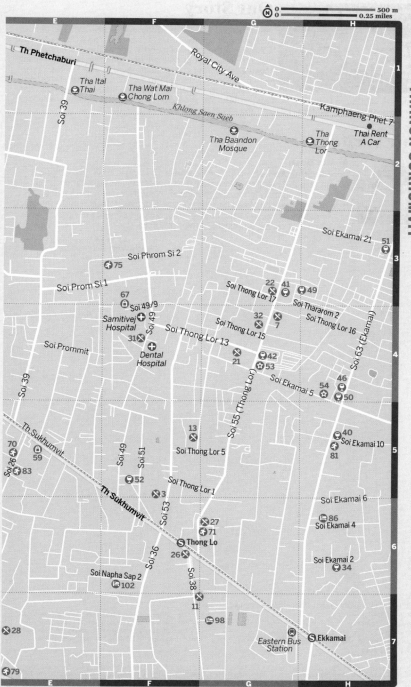

0 500 m
0 0.25 miles

Th Phetchaburi

Royal City Ave

Tha Ital Thai

Tha Wat Mai Chong Lom

Khlong Saen Saeb

Kamphaeng Phet 7

Soi 39

Tha Baandon Mosque

Tha Thong Lor

Thai Rent A Car

Soi Ekamai 21

51

Soi Phrom Si 2

75

Soi Prom Si 1

22
41
49

Soi Thong Lor 17

Soi Thararom 2

67

Soi 49/9

Soi 49

Samitivej Hospital

32
7

Soi Thong Lor 16

Soi Thong Lor 15

Soi Thong Lor 13

Soi 63 (Ekamai)

31

Dental Hospital

21

42
53

54

46
50

Soi Ekamai 5

Soi 55 (Thong Lor)

Soi 39

13

40
81

Soi Ekamai 10

Th Sukhumvit

70
59

Soi 26

83

Soi 49

Soi 51

Soi Thong Lor 5

52

Soi Thong Lor 1

Soi Ekamai 6

3

Soi 53

Th Sukhumvit

86

Soi Ekamai 4

27
71

Thong Lo

26

Soi Ekamai 2

34

Soi 36

Soi Napha Sap 2

102

Soi 38

11

28

98

Eastern Bus Station

Ekkamai

79

Our Story

A beat-up old car, a few dollars in the pocket and a sense of adventure. In 1972 that's all Tony and Maureen Wheeler needed for the trip of a lifetime – across Europe and Asia overland to Australia. It took several months, and at the end – broke but inspired – they sat at their kitchen table writing and stapling together their first travel guide, *Across Asia on the Cheap*. Within a week they'd sold 1500 copies. Lonely Planet was born.

Today, Lonely Planet has offices in Melbourne, London and Oakland, with more than 600 staff and writers. We share Tony's belief that 'a great guidebook should do three things: inform, educate and amuse'.

Our Writers

Austin Bush

Coordinating Author Austin Bush came to Thailand in 1998 on a language scholarship to Chiang Mai University. The lure of city life, employment and spicy food eventually led Austin to Bangkok. City life, employment and spicy food have managed to keep him there since. A native of Oregon and a freelance writer and photographer who often focuses on food, samples of Austin's work can be seen at www.austinbushphotography.com.

Read more about Austin at:
lonelyplanet.com/members/austinbush

Published by Lonely Planet Publications Pty Ltd
ABN 36 005 607 983
10th edition – Sept 2012
ISBN 978 1 74220 019 4
© Lonely Planet 2012   Photographs © as indicated 2012
10 9 8 7 6 5 4 3 2 1
Printed in China

Although the authors and Lonely Planet have taken all reasonable care in preparing this book, we make no warranty about the accuracy or completeness of its content and, to the maximum extent permitted, disclaim all liability arising from its use.